Hearing John's Voice

Hearing John's Voice

Insights for Teaching and Preaching

M. Eugene Boring

William B. Eerdmans Publishing Company
Grand Rapids, Michigan

Wm. B. Eerdmans Publishing Co.
4035 Park East Court SE, Grand Rapids, Michigan 49546
www.eerdmans.com

Published 2019
Printed in the United States of America

25 24 23 22 21 20 19 1 2 3 4 5 6 7

ISBN 978-0-8028-7546-4

Library of Congress Cataloging-in-Publication Data

Names: Boring, M. Eugene, author.
Title: Hearing John's voice : insights for teaching and preaching / M. Eugene Boring.
Description: Grand Rapids : Eerdmans Publishing Co., 2019. | Includes bibliographical references and index.
Identifiers: LCCN 2019021026 | ISBN 9780802875464 (pbk. : alk. paper)
Subjects: LCSH: Bible. John—Criticism, interpretation, etc. | Bible. Epistles of John—Criticism, interpretation, etc. | Bible. Revelation—Criticism, interpretation, etc.
Classification: LCC BS2601 .B67 2019 | DDC 226.5/06—dc23
LC record available at https://lccn.loc.gov/2019021026

שְׁמַע יִשְׂרָאֵל	Hear, O Israel — DEUTERONOMY 6:4
ὁ ἔχων ὦτα ἀκουέτω	Let anyone with ears listen! — MARK 4:9
Μακάριος ὁ ἀναγινώσκων καὶ οἱ ἀκούοντες τοὺς λόγους τῆς προφητείας	Blessed is the one who reads aloud and blessed are those who hear the words of this prophecy. — REVELATION 1:3

Prayers and confessions
of those who interpret the Scriptures
for the people of God

אֲדֹנָי יְהוִֹה נָתַן לִי לְשׁוֹן לִמּוּדִים
לָדַעַת לָעוּת אֶת־יָעֵף דָּבָר
יָעִיר בַּבֹּקֶר בַּבֹּקֶר
יָעִיר לִי אֹזֶן לִשְׁמֹעַ כַּלִּמּוּדִים׃

The Lord God has given me the tongue of a teacher,
that I may know how to sustain the weary with a word.
Morning by morning he wakens—
wakens my ear to listen as those who are taught.

—Isaiah 50:4, an interpreter of the prophet

Πολλοὶ οὖν ἀκούσαντες ἐκ τῶν μαθητῶν αὐτοῦ εἶπαν·
σκληρός ἐστιν ὁ λόγος οὗτος· τίς δύναται αὐτοῦ ἀκούειν;

Many therefore of his disciples,
when they had heard this, said,
This is an hard saying; who can hear it?

—John 6:60 KJV, an interpreter of Jesus

προσευχόμενοι ἅμα καὶ περὶ ἡμῶν,
ἵνα ὁ θεὸς ἀνοίξῃ ἡμῖν θύραν τοῦ λόγου
λαλῆσαι τὸ μυστήριον τοῦ Χριστοῦ . . .
ἵνα φανερώσω αὐτὸ ὡς δεῖ με λαλῆσαι

. . . pray for us also,
that God may open to us a door for the word,
to declare the mystery of Christ . . .
that I may make it clear, as I ought to speak.

—Colossians 4:3–4, an interpreter of the apostle

Contents

Foreword

In a sermon preached many years ago, William Sloane Coffin related how, as a boy, he would often go out after a rainstorm to engage in "puddle-gazing." He marveled, he said, "at how small bodies of water could reflect so much of the sky and earth. Today," he continued, "I still marvel at how so much of the story of heaven and earth can be captured in small, Biblical stories."[1]

M. Eugene Boring's focus in this volume is the Johannine corpus—Revelation, 1–3 John, and the Gospel of John—no mere puddle, of course, but a small bay, perhaps, in the great sea of the New Testament. Even so, when Boring gazes into this literature, he sees the reflection of something even larger, the vastness of the Christian faith. Providence, Christology, the work of the Holy Spirit, eschatology, the church, the rhythms of the Christian life—all of these themes and more can be found in this small collection of late first- and early second-century documents addressed to a cluster of churches in the Roman province of Asia and gathered around the traditions of the Beloved Disciple.

Boring wants to hear the uniqueness of "John's voice" and wants his readers to hear it, too. He desires to discern the distinctive vocabulary and emphases of the Johannine world, but even as he does, he affirms that "John's fundamental worldview is more like than unlike the rest of the New Testament." Even the strangest of the Johannine documents, Revelation, with its bizarre apocalyptic imagery and its insistent dualism, is finally not a departure from the rest of the New Testament but instead an intensification of its core message. "*Revelation*," Boring writes, "*is a whole lot of what all the New Testament is some of.*"

By understanding the Johannine corpus this way, Boring manages to honor its exceptional qualities, its vividness, even its idiosyncrasies and strangeness, while at the same time locking the exits against those who might wish to flee to the seemingly safer regions of Paul and Jesus. Indeed, the apocalyptic demand of John's voice helps us to see anew the apocalyptic themes in the Gospels and Paul and to understand that they are neither ornamental nor dispensable, but essential.

For those readers whose first exposure to New Testament scholarship came from one of the standard New Testament introductory textbooks, there may be a surprise here. Boring builds this book in reverse. Instead of moving from the Gospel of John to the letters of John to Revelation, he travels from Revelation through the letters to the Gospel. He is guided here not by canonical order, or even strictly by chronology, but by theology. The Christian life is lived, by those marching through the middle of things, out of a vision of the end of all things.

Indeed, the book of Revelation is a disclosure, an apocalypse, literally a *revelation*, of the end of all things, of the destination toward which we are traveling. By being a disclosure of what shall surely be, it is also an illumination of how things truly are now. It is this unveiling of the deepest truths, the most profound meanings, and the ultimate destination of human life and history that makes the human journey matter. All human beings are moving toward some dimly perceived *telos*. It is only when we discover, as Paul Ricoeur helped us to do, that this *telos* is actually calling to us, summoning us forward toward the end of all things, that the wandering journey is transformed into a holy pilgrimage.

Boring writes *from* his position as a seasoned, judicious biblical scholar, and he writes *for* churchly teachers and preachers. He writes for teachers by first of all being a marvelous one himself. With a steady hand, he guides the reader through the complex labyrinth of the Johannine worldview, patiently teaching the terms, issues, claims, cultural resources, and doctrines that define this matrix. We who read are enabled to hear "John's voice" and also to understand "John's mind."

Boring writes for preachers in so many ways, and none stronger than his conviction about the power of language. He is convinced, for example, that the best experience of the world of Revelation is not in art or literature but rather in sound, "to hear it read in toto by a good reader in a service of Christian worship." He knows that the sound of "John's voice," spoken so many centuries ago, remains most alive not in commentaries or in ecclesiastical art but in sermonic sound, in the act of preaching faithfully on these texts. For every shaky preacher who has doubted the power of preaching and who has been tempted to forsake the pulpit in favor of a self-help program, a video clip, a leadership gimmick, or something else that might be more effective than a spoken sermon, Boring has a hopeful conviction he acquired from John himself: "*Sometimes a word is worth a thousand pictures.*"

Like the book of Revelation, this book, too, ends with a promise. In this case, it is Boring's welcome promise that the same attention he has turned toward the churches of the Beloved Disciple he will give, in a separate volume, to the churches of Paul. We who are the grateful readers of this volume will undoubtedly respond with words reminiscent of the ending of Revelation itself: Come quickly!

THOMAS G. LONG

Bandy Professor Emeritus of Preaching
Candler School of Theology
Emory University
Atlanta, Georgia

Preface

This book is written for preachers and teachers in the church. The constant goal is to approach within hearing distance of the Bible's own message. The following pages aim to encourage and facilitate *drinking directly from the generative springs from which biblical theology emerges*, wading in them, even submerging and perhaps being overwhelmed by them. These pages do not attempt to survey all biblical theology, not even all Johannine theology or texts, but offer probes and soundings that hopefully both facilitate and illustrate serious, in-depth engagement with the Bible, with ears always open to being taught from the Scriptures, with eyes on communication of its manifold message in Christian proclamation and instruction.

My thanks to the capable Eerdmans editorial staff for encouraging and helping to shape this project, especially to Trevor Thompson and James Ernest, who convinced me that my earlier and larger manuscript should become an informal, open-ended series, of which this is the initial volume.

My deepest gratitude goes to a rather large group of preachers and teachers, most of whom do not know each other, but who have read and responded to various parts and stages of this developing project. The group includes congregational pastors and teachers, college and seminary professors of Bible and homiletics, denominational executives, clergy and laypersons, representing several denominations. They have responded by email and met with me in groups and one-on-one. They sometimes disagree with each other and with me. They have been my students and teachers. All are active members of congregations; virtually all preach and/or teach regularly in congregations. The common denominator is commitment to the church and the desire to be vehicles of the *Verbum Dei* through which the church is called into being and nourished for its witness and mission in the world. I am profoundly grateful to each of them. I especially appreciate the counsel of Thomas G. Long during the formative stages of this project and the foreword he has contributed to this volume. I dedicate this book to this group of colleagues, brothers and sisters in ministry, and to all faithful preachers and teachers who continue to nourish the church in the biblical faith:

> David Artman, Bobby Cook, Miles Cook, Charlotte Coyle, Jerry Coyle, Bryan Feille, Laurie Feille, Jeff Gehle, Kim Hames, Thomas G. Long, Andy Mangum, Roger McMurry, Sammie Maxwell, Lance Pape, Ryan Pfeiffer, Russell Pregeant, Jim L. Robinson, Walter Rogero, Irwin Sentilles, Dawn Weaks, Newell Williams, Raymond B. Williams, Christopher Wilson

M. Eugene Boring
Fort Worth, Texas
July 18, 2019

Prologue

Two travelers walk along the road together, engaged in serious and friendly conversation. It's a familiar road. We know it well. On this road there is no stopping, no turning back. We can remember some of the road behind us, with its joys, sorrows, and things we might do differently now, but there are no do-overs, no "Undo" command. Even if we try to stop, the road itself, an ever-flowing stream, moves relentlessly on. Even if we think we remain the same, our world is different every day, leaving yesterday behind and moving on to who-knows-where. It's a one-way road; we meet no oncoming traffic, no one who has been there and back.

This is just the way the road is, and it does not interfere with the conversation between the two travelers, which is about where the road leads. One believes the road leads nowhere; it either goes on forever or gradually becomes smaller and less distinct and then fizzles out into nothingness. Fade to black.

The other believes the road leads to the City of God.

There are other people on the road. A lot of them. Some are like us; they speak the same language, call the same country their home. Others are different. It is sometimes scary, and we tend to huddle together with those who are like us.

The conversation repeatedly returns to the main question: "Where does the road go?" Some people on the road say, "I don't know where the road is going, don't think anybody knows, haven't thought about it much." Some say, "I know where I *am going. When my body dies, the road may go on and on, but my soul goes to heaven."*

But that's not the question. It's not about me; it's about the road, the world, and all those other people. If we knew where the road and the world itself are headed, we might do some things differently, might even see the bad things that happen along the road in a different light. If the road is actually going someplace, are we all going to the same place, or does it finally divide—some to the right, some to the left? Is there only one road, or are different groups of people on different roads? Are there interchanges, or are we stuck on the road we're on?

All along the road, the two travelers experience the same things, a mixture of good and evil. They have different attitudes, different feelings, about the trip itself. The difference between them is a matter of faith. Not that one has faith and the other does not; each has his or her faith. The one who believes the road leads to the City of God did not figure this out on her own, nor is it a matter of wishful thinking. She believes that the goal and meaning of the road have been revealed. *Not that she has had some personal revelatory experience, but she belongs to a community of pilgrims on the road who believe that the creator has revealed the ultimate goal and meaning of things, including our own little lives.*

Neither, of course, can prove his or her view about the road. But the two can't resolve their differences by agreeing that, after all, it's just the way they feel about it—that each should respect other people's opinions, but no one should claim that his or her view is really true. *Though the world is sufficiently ambiguous to be interpreted theistically or atheistically, at the last turn of the road one of them will turn out to be right about the objective reality, and to have been right all along. Their conversation is not about their feelings but about truth.*[1]

Chapter 1

Beginning at the End

Some of us preachers and teachers in the church might suppose that those who hear us on Sunday mornings, or even we ourselves, don't have conversations about the "meaning of life," "what it's all about," "where it's all going," and all that. And why should we? Why not just live in the now, enjoying the trip? Or is such talk dangerous self-deception?

Human beings seem to be hardwired to ask ultimate questions, aware that we live from the future. We don't need a biblical revelation to know that our life always stretches out ahead of us. Not only biblical prophets and sages but also personal experience, psychologists, and social scientists insist that life as such always resides on the moving line between memory and hope. Whoever has no memory has no identity; whoever has "nothing to look forward to" has no present either. To be given a future is to be given a present. We always live prospectively but interpret retrospectively, seeing the significance of the present only in the later light of the end. But how can anyone know where the road is going?

> God the creator "has made everything suitable for its time; moreover he has put a sense of past and future into their minds, yet they cannot find out what God has done from the beginning to the end."
>
> —Ecclesiastes 3:11 NRSV
>
> "In order to have a sense of who we are, we have to have a notion of how we have become, and of where we are going."
>
> —Charles Taylor, *Sources of the Self: The Making of the Modern Identity* (Cambridge: Cambridge University Press, 1989), 47

One of the embarrassing things about being a human being is that—despite our self-centered desire or claim to be in control—getting a glimpse of "what my life is all about" requires our seeing it in its context on the road we travel with all other human beings, and also requires some idea of where the road is finally going. But only God sees the whole picture, the end from the beginning. God is the one who says,

> I am God, and there is no other;
> I am God, and there is no one like me,
> declaring the end from the beginning
> and from ancient times things not yet done,
> saying, "My purpose shall stand,
> and I will fulfill my intention." (Isa 46:9–10)[1]

Seeing the future requires a revelation from God. We are speaking, of course, not of the particulars of the historical future, as "foretold" by fortune-tellers and "interpreters of biblical prophecy," but of the Ultimate Future. Where is everything going?

The issue turns out to be: Has there been a revelation, or are we on our own?

The Christian faith, as confessed by the church through the centuries and around the world and as documented in the New Testament from its first book to its last, claims that our understanding of who we are, where we are going, the meaning of our fleeting lives, and the meaning of the road itself is not something some of us may have figured out but is something that has been *revealed*. For Christian faith, God's definitive revelation is in Jesus Christ. This is not something we have worked out on our own, as though we observed what Jesus said and did and decided, on the basis of sound common sense, that he must be a revelation from God. Some examples:

- Matthew 16:15–17: "He said to them, 'But who do you say that I am?' Simon Peter answered, 'You are the Messiah, the Son of the living God.' And Jesus answered him, 'Blessed are you, Simon son of Jonah! For flesh and blood has not revealed (*apokalyptō*) this to you, but my Father in heaven.'" Other people, many of them sincere seekers, looked Jesus over, checked him out by their criteria, decided he was a threat to law and order and to sound religion, and took the appropriate action.
- Matthew 11:25–27: "At that time Jesus said, 'I praise you, Father, Lord of heaven and earth, because you have hidden these things from the wise and learned, and revealed (*apokalyptō*) them to little children (NIV; NAB "childlike," CEV "ordinary people"). . . . All things have been committed to me by my Father. No one knows the Son except the Father,

and no one knows the Father except the Son and those to whom the Son chooses to reveal (*apokalyptō*) him.'"

- Romans 16:25–26: "Now to God who is able to strengthen you according to my gospel and the proclamation of Jesus Christ, according to the revelation (*apokalypsis*) of the mystery that was kept secret for long ages but is now disclosed, and through the prophetic writings made known to [us] . . ."
- 1 Corinthians 2:9–10: "But, as it is written, 'What no eye has seen, nor ear heard, / nor the human heart conceived, / what God has prepared for those who love him'—these things God has revealed (*apokalyptō*) to us through the Spirit."
- Galatians 1:11–12: "For I want you to know, brothers and sisters, that the gospel that was proclaimed by me is not of human origin; for I did not receive it from a human source, nor was I taught it, but I received it through a revelation (*apokalypsis*) of Jesus Christ."

Beginning with Revelation

The New Testament book with the most explicit claim to be a revelation from God has the word "revelation" (*apocalypse*) as its first word. Every New Testament book makes this claim implicitly, but it is unavoidable in Revelation, uncomfortably so. We preachers and teachers of the church might thus begin our soundings into biblical theology with the last book of the Christian Bible. This is not necessarily because we will be preaching a lot of sermons from this strange book, nor because we must affirm its apocalyptic worldview as our own. It is because we must understand biblical texts in their own terms—coming within hearing distance—before we interpret them and integrate their message into our own theology. We begin with Revelation because it presents us with a number of crucial issues that face us throughout the New Testament. In other biblical books we may sometimes be unaware of them or able to avoid them, but if we seriously try to understand Revelation (as opposed to merely using the text for our own agenda), we face unavoidable hermeneutical problems. Other New Testament apocalyptic thinkers such as Matthew and Paul are also hard to interpret, but in them we might suppose that we can find texts more congenial to our purposes: in Matthew the Sermon on the Mount, in Paul 1 Corinthians 13 (rarely noticing that both are built on an apocalyptic foundation). It is obvious that to understand Revelation we must understand apocalyptic. This is true of the New Testament as a whole.

In this regard, the difference between Revelation and other New Testament documents is in degree, not in kind. Again, a few examples:

- In Matthew 19:28, Luke 22:30, and 1 Corinthians 6:2, the Jesus of Matthew and Luke—as well as Paul—utilizes the imagery of Christians and their leaders participating in the final judgment involving rebellious humans and angels. Revelation gives expansive elaboration of this imagery that is already found in Paul and the Gospels.
- The powerfully weird imagery of Revelation 12–13, in which the dragon gives the beast from the sea its power (13:2, 4), is only an elaboration of the imagery presupposed in Luke 4:6, where it is Satan who gives the empire its power.
- In Luke 10:18, Jesus sees Satan fall from heaven, and John 12:31–32 pictures the demonic ruler of the world cast out when Jesus is lifted up on the cross.
- In Luke 12:5, Jesus speaks: "But I will warn you whom to fear: fear him who, after he has killed, has authority to cast into hell. Yes, I tell you, fear him!"
- In Galatians 4:26, Paul refers in passing to "the Jerusalem above"; that is, he presupposes and only alludes to what Revelation elaborates.
- Paul describes the church as the fiancée of Christ (2 Cor 11:2), but the bride of Christ in Revelation expands and repeatedly elaborates the image.
- Paul promises that God will shortly crush Satan under the believers' feet (Rom 16:20; cf. 16:25) but does not expand the image; Revelation fills in the picture already present in Romans.
- In 1 Thessalonians 3:13, Jesus returns at the end of history with all his holy ones, a climactic concluding image elaborated in Revelation.
- The imagery and vocabulary of the "wrath (*orgē*) of God," portrayed with frightening or repugnant intensity in Revelation, are common to New Testament theology. The Greek word *orgē* is found thirty-six times in the New Testament, mostly referencing the wrath of God or Jesus (e.g., Matt 3:7; Mark 3:5; Luke 21:23; John 3:36; Rom 1:18; 2:5, 8; 1 Thess 1:10; Heb 3:11).

We cannot escape apocalyptic by fleeing to Jesus or Paul. In the Gospels and Paul's letters, such images can be passed over as incidental (though they are fundamental), but not in Revelation. If our preaching or teaching is based on texts we choose ourselves, in most New Testament books we can simply avoid those that seem too apocalyptic. If we preach from the lectionary, there will usually be something in one of the texts that strikes a responsive chord in our own agenda, something we can handle without getting involved in apocalyptic imagery and worldview. In Revelation, our self-constructed little world comes to an end, and there is no place to hide (Rev 6:12–17). *Revelation is a whole lot of what all the New Testament is some of.* To learn to hear the Christian gospel in its original apocalyptic context is to open up much else in the New Testament to more authentic interpretation. Come clean with Revelation, and we become more honest and capable interpreters of the rest of the New Testament, which will have a better chance of making its own message heard in our preaching and teaching.

Here we mention a few key topics, each explored in the following chapters and subsequent volumes in this series in ways more appropriate to each author's own mode of communicating the faith.

Christology

The Messiah comes at the end. The world is in a mess, always has been, but the world is a story, and the story is not over. Jewish Scriptures and theology looked toward the future, the promise of God to make everything right at the end. The fundamental Christian confession is that the Christ has come, and he is the crucified and risen Jesus of Nazareth. This confession, whether or not dulled by familiarity, is *strange*: it involves the anointing (pouring olive oil on the head) of someone who, it is claimed, is prophet, priest, and king. Prophets do not announce their considered opinions but the Word of God; priests offer sacrifice, atone for sin, intercede for sinners; kings have absolute authority and call for obedience, take responsibility for justice and salvation, and make the laws, which they interpret and enforce. Faith in Jesus as the Messiah is inseparable from eschatology. We democratic moderns don't like any of this. Some thoughtful Jews and Christians regard eschatology, especially its apocalyptic version, as either wishful thinking or nonthinking.

Revelation presents Jesus as the truly human one, who has already lived and died (been killed) on this earth. Hardly anything of the earthly life of Jesus is narrated in Revelation, but Jesus is proclaimed as the one who is united with us in the most human of all acts. He dies. Yet this human one, who stood before the Roman power and was faithful unto death, is not presented merely as a past hero to be remembered, whose ideals are to be followed by those who choose to take up his cause. He is the truly divine One who was present at the creation, who has been exalted to the transcendent world and shares the throne of God, and who continues to speak, to call the church into being through the Word of God, to call for faithfulness even to death. He is the one we will meet at the end of our own lives, and at the end of history. He is the one who not only came to earth; he is the one who is coming again.

Apocalypse

All that Revelation has to say is expressed in the imagery and thought world of apocalyptic (including the messages to the seven churches in chapters 2–3, sometimes thought to be less apocalyptic and more preachable). To understand Revelation, we must understand apocalyptic thought, with its bizarre imagery and the-end-is-coming-soon conviction. The early church, and the New Testament as a whole, grew out of a historical context permeated with apocalyptic thought, which it partially adopted, partially adapted and modified, partially rejected, but could not and did not ignore. This means that not only Revelation but also the New Testament in general will not be understood in its own terms unless heard as responding, in one way or another, to this apocalyptic thought world. In other New Testament books, it is possible to find "preaching values" and "lessons for today" without coming to terms with an apocalyptic worldview so different from our own, and to regard Revelation's apocalypticism as marginal and dispensable. Actually, however, John's fundamental worldview is more like than unlike the rest of the New Testament. Though it remains a disputed point among exegetes and historians, the view that apocalyptic is central to understanding the New Testament is by far the majority view of international New Testament scholarship. Whatever views Jesus himself may have held, whoever wants to understand the New Testament must be familiar with apocalyptic.

Violence, Power, and Judgment

Apocalyptic is a powerful and disturbing literary and theological genre. To read or hear an apocalyptic text such as Revelation all at once, to take its images, sounds, and smells seriously, is to be shaken, perhaps repulsed or even disgusted, by its intense, unrelenting violence. One wonders if this can be the same merciful God of Hosea, the same compassionate Christ of Matthew's Sermon on the Mount. Although Hosea and Matthew have pictures of divine violence (e.g., Hos 5:8–14; Matt 24:37–50), in their books we can find a lot of other material more unproblematically preachable, providing more wiggle room for our personal preferences and homiletical imaginations. Not so in Revelation. But learn to deal honestly with Revelation, and we become more authentic interpreters of Hosea and Matthew.

Ecclesiology, Jews, and Christians

Again, the questions of the relation of the followers of Jesus to Judaism, then and now, are found throughout the New Testament. The church is pictured as the continuation of Israel, sometimes in ways that can be understood as claiming that the church is the new Israel, perhaps even Israel's replacement. Harsh things are sometimes said about the Jews. This issue is intensified in Revelation, where Jews are called the "synagogue of Satan" and Christians are promised that someday Jews will come and grovel at Christian feet (Rev 2:9; 3:9). How should followers of Jesus today, New Testament in hand, understand the church? Can one love Jesus the Jew and disdain the church, which supposedly misunderstood and domesticated him? In Revelation, the church's identity and self-understanding, and its relation to Jesus, Israel, and Judaism, are front and center. Revelation cannot be understood without grasping its ecclesiology. But this is true of the New Testament as a whole. Deal with it here, and countless New Testament texts appear in a new and more authentic light.

Strange New World within the Bible

To read the book of Revelation—better, to hear it read in toto by a good reader in a service of Christian worship—is to enter a new world. This is true of narratives in general, of course, and powerfully true of the Bible narrative as a whole, but it is inescapably, overwhelmingly, even painfully true in reading Revelation. The risen Christ appears, eyes of fiery flame, with trumpet voice like mighty waves crashing against the shore, holding seven stars in his right hand. A throne in the heavenly sky appears, the Almighty seated on the throne, the heavenly court—zoological and humanoid—singing eternal praise. A slaughtered Lamb receives a sealed book, opens it, and great terrors strike not only the earth with its fish, animals, and humans, good and evil alike, but also the solar system, the planets, and the stars.

Seven-headed beasts emerge, who demand the worship that is due only to the Lord God Almighty. Those who resist are beheaded; their death is called their "conquering." A beautifully seductive whore rides one of the beasts, but she is destroyed, as are the beasts and Satan who empowers them. The world is redeemed, the heavenly city New Jerusalem descends to earth, all God's people celebrate the ultimate happy ending.

A summary paragraph in no way can replace the experience of reading or hearing Revelation, but the point is made: here we are confronted with a new world, not just some weird things that intrude into our ordinary world but leave it intact. That, we can handle. Nor is it the fantasy world of J. R. R. Tolkien's Middle Earth or the pungently entertaining science fiction of Douglas Adams's *Hitchhiker's Guide to the Galaxy*. That, too, we can handle. The strange new world within Revelation is not merely a matter of red dragons and fiery pits but turns our everyday world, which we assume to be the real world, upside down (Acts 17:6)—the world of which we are the center, the world in which our values are supreme and the meaning of life is centered in our will being done on earth, with the assumption that heaven agrees and supports our "values."

Revelation claims to reveal how the world, the real world, ultimately *is*—albeit through the medium of bizarre apocalyptic imagery (on which more below). Here is a world created and ruled by the one true God, the Almighty, who rescues his world-gone-astray from the power of evil, and whose almighty power is manifest not in killing his enemies but in the death of his Son at the hands of authorized religious and political leaders. Prior to the final victory of God and the establishment of God's universal rule, God's purpose is carried out in the world by his people, called into being by God's own word, a community of faith called to follow the path of God's Son: loving care for others, which means suffering and even death, confident that God's victorious power will soon be manifest to all. Here is a world centered around God the creator in worship and praise. Our self-centeredness, the pursuit of our individualistic happiness, even our own idealistic efforts to make a better world, here finds its true center.

The strange new world of the Bible is a distant world, in which we should not feel at home too quickly. It is distant not only in time and space but also in language, in culture, and in its basic assumptions about what's what. Perhaps the first task in both pulpit and pew is not to be in too great a hurry to overcome this distance but to acknowledge it, then to respect it. Communication across the gap, if this be the final goal, can't be done unless and until the reality of this gap is acknowledged and respected. Many American tourists have learned not to evaluate other countries and cultures from the perspective of their own assumptions. They are not like us; when we evaluate everything in the world through modern Western eyes, we never see them as they are, we can neither appreciate nor draw back from them as they are, we can say neither an honest yes or an honest no. In the Bible, this respect for the other is called "holiness."

The response that is constantly called for is *repentance* (Greek *metanoia*). As understood by Revelation, repentance is not being-sorry-in-a-religious-mood, not adding on another worthy cause, not trying a little harder to be a little nicer, but a reorientation of the way we think and live, lining up our thought world with reality, God's new creation that is already under way. Repentance is reorientation, getting a new compass, a new understanding of what's what, what's real, and what matters. Such repentance is not a once-for-all act that can be checked off the list. The messages to the seven churches regularly call them to repent (Rev 2:5, 16, 22; 3:3, 19), to renew their awareness of the strange new world revealed to them in the Bible and the good news of the Christian faith, for reality is not what it appears to be through the lens of cultural common sense. It requires a revelation to bring God's world into view. To see the world and ourselves as we really are requires repentance.

This was the life- (and world-) changing reality that grasped the life of a young preacher-theologian of the last century, whose legacy continues to enliven and nourish the church and its ministry. Karl Barth's story is well known in theological circles, but perhaps we have never pondered it from the point of view of the preacher's weekly quest, the burden and joy of authentic preaching.

The young minister was well educated, firmly and pleasantly located as the respected pastor of a county-seat church in a beautiful part of the world. So what's the problem? He discovered that the "Christian principles" he had been taught as the core of the Christian faith did not ring true in the chaos and collapse of idealism of World War I—even though he was at a safe distance in his Swiss mountain-village pastorate. In quest of an authentic word from God, he toiled and struggled with Paul's letter to the Romans, came once again within hearing distance of the Bible's own message, and began to preach in a way that not only renewed his own ministry but also caught the attention of the wider church. In these early days, when he was a congregational pastor who preached every Sunday morning, and later as a professor who preached every Sunday afternoon to the inmates of the Basel prison, Barth was often invited to address groups of ministers about the new dynamism and content of his preaching. These essays were collected. One of his speeches is called "The Strange New World within the Bible."[2] His central point: in-depth study that listens anew for the Word of God that comes through the Scripture doesn't just change the individual (born-again evangelicalism) or transform society (the old liberalism in which he had been educated), but gives a new *world.* The personal and social transformations brought about by God's Word are elements of a cosmic transformation. The same volume includes this memorable first-person account, with which many preachers can identify:

> On Sunday morning when the bell rings to call the congregation and minister to church, there is in the air an expectancy that something great, crucial, and momentous is to happen. How strong this expectancy is in the people who are interested, or even whether there are any people whatever who consciously cherish it, is not our question now. Expectancy is inherent in the whole situation.
>
> . . . Before him lies the Bible, full of mystery: and before him are seated his more or less numerous hearers, also full of mystery—What now? asks the minister.[3]

It was not merely that Barth discovered something new to preach in Romans. A particular biblical text served as the entrance to the strange new world of the Bible as a whole. The world is seen as it truly is—the beloved creation of the one God who has acted and is acting to renew and restore the whole creation. This biblical worldview of the wholeness of history and reality as the beloved creation of the one God who has acted and is acting to reconcile and restore it to himself calls for a reorientation—repentance—that cannot be absorbed piecemeal. It is not a matter of appropriating increments of information, insight, or inspiration that we fit into our old world, the way one brings a few items of new furniture into the same old house. It is a shaking of the foundations, not only of our little self-constructed houses but also of our self-constructed world. Repentance, the transformation of our minds to conform to God's new age and God's new world (Rom 12:1), does not mean making adjustments to new ideas one at a time but is a reorientation of the whole of our thinking, believing, and acting. The sum and center of this new world is expressed in the confession "Jesus is the Christ," "Jesus is Lord," which must be accepted as a whole or not at all. One lives either in one's self-constructed reality or in the world as presented in the Bible, which means accepting its reality. We're not speaking, of course, about the ancient biblical worldview with its three-decker cosmology and demons as the cause of sickness. We speak here of the biblical world of which God is creator, a world God did not abandon when it ignored or rebelled against its maker and Lord, a world in which God has acted definitively, a world God will ultimately restore and redeem. It is not merely a matter of individualistic conversion (born-again evangelicalism) or improving society (old liberalism) but is a matter of a new *world.* It is a matter of which world we believe we actually live in, which world is the real world, not of cosmetic adjustments to the old world. Since the strange new world of the Bible claims to represent ultimate reality, "believing the Bible" or "believing the gospel" cannot mean fitting the kingdom of God and salvation into this-worldly boxes shaped by our view of space-time reality and common sense. This is the nature and claim of *all* God-talk that speaks of and for the biblical God, the claim of every book in the Christian Bible. Elsewhere in the canonical library, biblical authors seem to offer more open space that adjoins our own everyday world, space that gives us more room to retain our own sense of what's what. Revelation provides us much less opportunity for smuggling in our own replacement world. We don't like it, but it can be our door into the strange new world of the Bible.

Revelation Is Prophecy and Theology

The people walking along the road do not and cannot figure out the meaning and destination of the road on their own. John declares that the mystery of God's plan for history has been revealed to God's servants the prophets (Rev 10:7), among whom John numbers himself; he considers what he writes to be prophecy (1:1–3).

In claiming to be a prophet, John does not mean merely that he predicts the future. While there is an element of prediction in biblical prophecy, the forecasting of long-range historical events occurs only minimally, is entirely absent from several prophetic books, and cannot be considered an essential ingredient of biblical prophecy. When biblical prophets do make predictions, these are typically not long-range historical forecasts but the word of God for the short-range future of their hearers, sometimes seen in the framework of God's plan for the ultimate future of the world. The mark of the biblical prophet is neither "It seems to me . . ." nor "Here is some information about what will happen seven hundred years from now" but "Thus says the Lord"—about the meaning of your own life and times. A common definition of a biblical prophet is "one who speaks for God." Better is "One through whom God speaks." John is such a prophet.

To be sure, John is a spokesman for the risen Lord, a prophet who has charismatic visionary and auditory experiences of the reality of God and the transcendent world. He is not a fanatic, not mentally disturbed, does not hallucinate. He is a prophet in the tradition of Amos, Isaiah, Jesus, and Paul. He is also a prophet in the sense that he opposes the power structures of this world in the name of the living God, like Nathan before David, Elijah before Ahab and Jezebel, Jeremiah before Jehoiakim, Jesus before Pilate. Yet, what makes John a prophet is not his courageous resistance to the institutionalized power structures of this world, political and religious. Other audacious nonprophetic types do that as well, speaking truth to power. It is not even his claim to speak by direct revelation from God that makes John a prophet in the biblical sense. John's first-century world abounded in such claims, and they have not ceased in our own time. The prophetic gestalt involves three elements: (1) An event in history in which God is active and in control, which is (2) interpreted by words of a prophet presented as a message of divine revelation and (3) accepted by the community as Word of God.

God's Revelation Happens in Events

Faith in prophetic revelation does not claim that God shouts down information from heaven or reveals mysteries in the hearts of chosen prophets. Nor is revelation merely a matter of ideas, not even the idea that "God is love," not even "God loves you." The biblical faith is not about good ideas but about good news, the mighty acts of God, centered in the climactic act of God in the event of Jesus Christ (e.g., Exod 6:6; Deut 3:24; Ps 145:4; 1 Pet 2:9). The Christian gospel is good news, not good advice. Many interpreters rightly regard John 3:16 as a summary of New Testament theology. This key text is not about an idea or religious theory but about the act of God. Something has *happened* that makes all the difference. The creator and Lord of history brought the world into being and sustains it through the ages, calls a people and delivers them from slavery, sends his Son, renews the people of God in the power of the Spirit that is already generating a new world, and will finally bring history to a worthy conclusion. The Christ event is the defining center of God's mighty (but ambiguous) acts in universal history. The definitive revelation of God is neither an inspiring sunset nor an infallible book, but a person. God is not merely an interested spectator to the drama of history but its producer, director, and leading actor. God acts in history. But how can God's action be discerned?

Biblical Prophets Function as Interpreters of Events

God is active in the events of history, but the act of God is ambiguous. The meaning of particular events and of universal history is the subject matter of prophecy. Decisive events can be interpreted in more than one way.

On the bank of the Red Sea, one might say:

"Lucky for the Israelites the wind came up when it did."	OR	"I will sing to the LORD, for he has triumphed gloriously; horse and rider he has thrown into the sea. The Lord is my strength and my might, and he has become my salvation; this is my God, and I will praise him." (Exod 15:1–2)

In Jerusalem some days after the execution of Jesus, one might say:

"Jesus was a courageous [or deluded] man who resisted imperialism, economic exploitation, and sexual and racial discrimination, but after his death some of his followers continued his cause."	OR	"Therefore let the entire house of Israel know with certainty that God has made him both Lord and Messiah, this Jesus whom you crucified." (Acts 2:36)

In the biblical view, God is active in history, but the meaning is not transparent; God raises up a prophet to speak, to declare the meaning of the history the people are living through, in the context of the meaning of all history.

Biblical prophets proclaim the meaning of the events their hearers are living through in the light of God's plan for history, presented not as the result of their own insight but as the revelation of God. In Revelation 10:7, prophets are those to whom the mystery of God's plan is revealed. In Revelation 17:7, 17, the mystery revealed by the prophetic Word of God is that the demonic aspects of Roman imperial power represent the power of Satan in John's world. As it takes a revelation to discern the presence of the kingdom of God in the "ordinary" events of this world, so it takes a revelation to discern the nature of imperial power. The prophet Moses interprets the strong wind that drives back the Reed Sea so the Israelites can pass through as more than a fortuitous meteorological occurrence, but as the saving act of God (the Egyptians interpreted it differently). The prophet Amos views the threatening rise of Assyrian power not merely in terms of shrewd geopolitical insight but as the coming judgment of God (the royal advisers gave a different interpretation). The prophet Jesus interprets the amazing phenomena of his own ministry as the vanguard of the present-and-coming kingdom of God (some religious teachers saw the same phenomena but had a different interpretation). The prophet John interprets the threats and harassment of the church by the culture and Roman government as the beginning of a great trial that precedes the end, the time of eschatological testing during which the church is called to be faithful. God had acted, definitively and ultimately, in the life, death, and resurrection of Jesus of Nazareth, but the reality of this event was not apparent to spectators. The Christ event was the definitive revelation of God, but perceiving the event as revelation itself required a revelatory act of God in the power of the Holy Spirit (Matt 16:17; 1 Cor 12:3).

To be a prophet is to be *given* a message. Biblical prophets are not typically looking for something to preach. The initiative is with God, who has something to say to the community of faith, and through them, to the world. The people of God, the community of faith—in the New Testament, the church—has prophets within its midst and is itself a prophetic community.

God's Revelation Discerned and Accepted by the Community

As the church faced new situations, it could not simply quote its Bible or the teaching of Jesus but needed the word of Jesus for today and every new today. From the earliest days of the church, prophetic figures arose in worship to interpret the meaning of Jesus's life and death and to proclaim the word of the exalted Lord Jesus to the worshiping congregation. Christian prophets sometimes made conflicting claims. In the Roman province of Asia at the end of the first century CE, John was not the only prophet who claimed to speak the word of the Lord to the present crisis of the churches. The message he communicates competes with the preaching of other prophets John considered false. In the last days in which John believes he is living, false prophets with plausible and attractive messages appear in the churches to mislead the people (Rev 2:20; 16:13; 19:20; 20:10). "Jezebel" and "Balaam" were not, of course, the actual names of John's rivals. By designating them with the names of biblical false prophets, he called on the churches to reject their message—however sincerely delivered—and to accept his own message as "what the Spirit is saying to the churches" (2:7, 11, 17, 29; 3:6, 13, 22). The Holy Spirit not only worked through prophets who claimed to speak on the basis of divine revelation but was also alive and active in the whole church, enabling the Christian community to distinguish authentic revelation from false or misleading claims.

Revelation, Reality, and the Power of Words

Imagine a boat in the Aegean, near the end of the first century CE, en route from Patmos to Ephesus. One passenger's baggage contains a papyrus scroll. The scroll contains words. A messenger will take the scroll from church to church and read the words aloud to the congregation assembled for worship. The potency of Revelation's language is not a matter of paper and ink. Language is not a static reality frozen on the page but an event in which one person speaks to another. The words on the page are only the inert bearers of the living voice, words that come to life only when someone takes them up and reads them aloud (cf. on 2 Tim 3:16–17, discussed in volume 2 of this series). In the ancient world, all reading was reading aloud, a matter of a living voice perceived by the ear. Even private, individual reading was done aloud (Acts 8:30; John 8:8–9), but John's text was specifically intended to be read to the listening congregation (Rev 1:3). To speak to someone meant that one's inner life, one's breath, came forth as words that influenced other persons. In the biblical languages, the same word means "breath" and "spirit" (Hebrew *ruach*; Greek *pneuma*). Speaking is breath, even for God:

> By the word of the Lord the heavens were made,
> and all their host by the breath of his mouth. (Ps 33:6)

To speak to another is to share one's life; to be spoken to is to receive life from another.

John Believes in the Power of Words

All that we have from John's prophetic ministry is contained in the words of the text of Revelation. John believes in the power of these words to change lives, congregations, the world. Every word of Revelation is the word of John, expressed in his language, his thought patterns, reflecting his experience and thoughtful composition. The "words of the prophecy of this book" (Rev 22:18), though spoken by "I, John" (1:9), are also the words of the living Christ who speaks through them, who says, "I, Jesus" (22:16). But he is not merely a mouthpiece or microphone for the heavenly voice. In and through "I, John," "I, Jesus" speaks to the listening congregation. This is a reality of Christian worship, in which the living Christ is present. It is analogous to the priest or minister presenting bread and wine to believers with the words "This is my body," "This is my blood." This is a matter of present address, not historical reporting. The words are not "Jesus said to them that this was his body given for them," but the words speak in the present as the voice of Christ to the worshiping community: ". . . given for you." The sermon is the sacrament of the Word.

John's identity as a Christian minister is that he is part of the revelatory chain that begins with God and comes through Jesus Christ and the Holy Spirit (1:1–3). He is one who "testified to the word of God and to the testimony of Jesus Christ" (1:2). This is the reason he is imprisoned on Patmos (1:2, 9). He is a preacher. Were he not incarcerated, he would be speaking personally to the congregations in Ephesus and elsewhere in Asia. Revelation is not merely a collection of fantastic dreams but *a pastoral letter to congregations he knows* from one who is convinced he speaks on behalf of the risen Christ. Unlike a book or essay, a letter—like a sermon, for which it here substitutes—addresses particular readers in a particular situation.

John's Theology of the Word Is Shaped by His Bible

John did not get this understanding of the power of language from his culture but from his Bible. A few examples:

Genesis 1:1–3

"When God began to create heaven and earth—the earth being unformed and void, with darkness over the surface of the deep and a wind from God sweeping over the water—God *said*, 'Let there be light'; and there was light" (Gen 1:1–3 Jewish Publication Society; cf. NRSV, CEB, NAB, etc.). The first finite verb in the Bible, the primordial act, is that God *speaks*. God speaks, and the universe comes into being.

Genesis 11

In the Genesis 11 story of the tower of Babel, human sin is represented not so much by what people did but by what they said. For who they are and what they do come to expression in their words: "Let us make a name for ourselves." And God's judgment on human presumption is not flood or fire but a touching of humanity at the wellsprings of our being, so that we cannot speak to each other in a way that is understood.

Isaiah 6:1–13

As Isaiah stands in the presence of the holy God, he realizes his own unholiness and declares the woe of his own humanity as "I am a man of unclean lips, and I live among a people of unclean lips." Lips, the organ of speech, represent the whole person, even more than brain, hands, heart, or genitals. "Unclean," of course, does not mean "dirty" but unholy, unfit to stand in the presence of the holiness of God. He becomes aware that he is a sinful human being, in his innermost self, which comes out in his words, his language. His guilt is removed, his sin is blotted out, he is made into a prophet by having the burning coal from God's altar touch his lips, and he is sent forth to *speak*.

Jeremiah 23:29

Jeremiah was a hesitant prophet, inexperienced, unsure of himself (Jer 1:1–10), who faced other prophets who were sure that they proclaimed God's word (5:31; 27:15; 28:1–11). Yet the words of Jeremiah became powerful beyond his own imagining: "Is not my word like fire, says the Lord, and like a hammer that breaks a rock in pieces?" (23:29). A word seems so flimsy, mere breath, fragile as a lightbulb. Jeremiah threw it against the rock, and it was the rock that broke.

Ezekiel 37:3–5

The people of Israel, captive and languishing in exile, are scattered dry bones in the field. But a resurrection can happen, metaphorical but real. How can this be? Nourish the final remnants back to life with pastoral care? There are none to nourish. Plan and execute an emerging new Israel with good committee structure and efficient administration? Dry bones don't respond well. We may be astounded and skeptical, even we preachers may be absolutely stunned, at the command: "He said to me, 'Mortal, can these bones live?' I answered, 'O Lord God, you know.' Then he said to me, 'Prophesy to these bones, and say to them: O dry bones, hear the word of the Lord. Thus says the Lord God to these bones: I will cause breath to enter you, and you shall live.'"

Does Our Culture Believe in the Power of Language?

If we accept our culture's own evaluation of itself—often a dangerous move—we might suppose that we live in a society that usually thinks it devalues the word. In our culture, the view that words are weak and bland might seem to be the generally accepted, commonsense view: "Deeds speak louder than words." "Don't tell me, show me." "I'd rather see a sermon than hear one any day." "Sticks and stones may break my bones, but words will never hurt me"—an old adage taught to children to encourage them not to respond to taunts and name-calling on the playground with physical retaliation, since "it's only words." But "words will never hurt me" was first said by someone who did not believe it, who had been hurt by words, and who wanted to hurt back with words. The word of the sage is more realistic, more in tune with our actual experience:

> The blow of a whip raises a welt,
> but the blow of the tongue crushes the bones. (Sir 28:17)

It takes only a moment to remind ourselves that we do in fact believe in the potency of our words. Like Adam naming the animals (Gen 2:19–20), we too recognize that what one calls something affects its being. "I give you my word" is one of the most personal, deeply meaningful things I can do. I put *myself* on the line. To say "I give you my word" is closer to our real self, in a different category from "I give you my credit card."

Spoken To

A few years ago, on the first Sunday after bombs and missiles had fallen in the Middle East, a lot of us were in church with more than routine seriousness. Karen, my wife, and I sat in our usual place. We greeted, and were greeted by, the people around us. A few minutes before the service began, the preacher came into the sanctuary and spoke informally to us and several others. Though not prescribed in the worship bulletin, Karen and I exchanged a few intimate words during the prelude. The liturgy was worshipful, and God was near. The choir sang James Russell Lowell's hymn written in the 1840s as a protest against the Mexican War, the first American Social Gospel hymn, in the idiom of that day, "Once to every man and nation, comes the moment to decide . . . ," not only singing it as music that stirs the soul but enunciating every word like a judge charging a jury. The sermon spoke of the meaning of prayer in such a time; the text was from John 20, where Jesus comes through sealed doors with the Hebrew greeting *Shalom Lechem*, "Peace be to you." It was not in the sermon, but somehow I thought of the text from Luke 24: "Were not our hearts burning within us while he was talking to us on the road, while he was opening the Scriptures to us?" We went away glad to belong to the church, and that we belonged to a congregation where we were at home.

And yet the next day, as I was expressing to someone else my own warm feelings about a service that had meant a great deal to me, his response was: "I guess that's all good and true, but I was there too, for an hour and a quarter, and not a soul spoke to me."

Think of the times when what you wanted most was a *word*. "I'm sorry." "I love you." "Your application has been accepted." "You are accepted."

Our words are us, our very life and breath, and they make and unmake us. John knew this, and in centering on word he centers on our very life. We preachers must take care not to be seduced by the cultural pressures in which we live, which condition us to think of language in second-rate terms and to devalue both the Bible and our own preaching. Our sermon is the sacrament of God's own word that speaks through it, calling the church into being and nourishing its life.

A Narrative World of Conflicting Imagery

Perhaps we should now just jump into the deep end of the pool, sink or swim, and begin to sound out the message of Revelation. But the better part of valor may be that, before proceeding, we ponder the kinds of language involved in Revelation's address to us. We all know that all language, even all language that communicates truth, is not the same kind. We need to delve into aspects of biblical language.

The language of biblical truth is *fragmentary.*
The language of biblical truth is *verbal-visual.*
The language of biblical truth is *conflicting-dialectical.*
The language of biblical truth is confessional but not *irrational.*
The language of biblical truth is referential but not *objectifying.*
The language of biblical truth projects a *narrative world.*
The language of biblical truth is mythical (that is, verbal-visual *narrative*).

The revealed truth of God is mediated through different genres of language. Although biblical theology fuses these dimensions of revelatory language into a tensive unity, we can deepen our understanding of what happens in biblical language by reflecting on them one at a time.

The Language of Biblical Truth Is Fragmentary

In the courtroom where justice and lives are at stake, witnesses are charged to speak "*the truth, the whole truth, and nothing but the truth, so help me God.*" Could the author of Revelation take this oath? As a matter of fact, John is a witness to the truth of God, as is Jesus, who speaks to him and the followers of Jesus in the churches to which John speaks. Revelation is permeated with the language of witness and testimony (Rev 1:2, 5, 9; 2:13; 3:14; 6:9; 11:3, 7; 12:11; 15:5; 17:6; 19:10; 20:4; 22:16, 18, 20).

But we humans can't really tell the whole truth, neither John nor anyone else. When asked in court if we will speak the truth, the whole truth, and nothing but the truth, we understand the intent of the question and properly respond with a simple "I do." But everyone involved understands that "So far as humanly possible" is necessarily implied in the "*so help me God.*" It's not that we are liars but that we are humans. There is such a thing as absolute truth, the ultimate truth, but it belongs to God, not to humans. For us human beings, apprehension of absolute truth is necessarily filtered and fractured by our finite minds. Human beings have truth, but we have it in fragments. Sometimes the fragments, each of which expresses the truth of God, cannot be put together into a consistent whole.

> "If God were to hold all Truth concealed in his right hand, and in his left only the steady and diligent drive for Truth, albeit with the proviso that I would always and forever err in the process, and to offer me the choice, I would with all humility take the left hand, and say: Father, I will take this one—the pure Truth is for You alone."
>
> —Gotthold Ephraim Lessing (1778)

God has revealed the Truth in his Word, paradigmatically in the Word-become-flesh. "Become flesh" means "in this-worldly terms." The Word is truth (John 17:17), the absolute, but it has entered into the world of flesh, the world of relativity, so that the absolute truth of God appears in our relative world and is truly apprehended, but we mortals receive it in this-worldly, relative terms. Revelation stands in the Pauline tradition, which expresses this as knowing the truth of God indirectly and fragmentarily: "For now we see in a mirror, dimly, but then we will see face to face. Now I know only in part; then I will know fully, even as I have been fully known" (1 Cor 13:12; "in part" is *ek merous*, which might be translated "in fragments"). The context makes clear that the image is not quantitative, as though we now have increments of divine knowledge that will be completed in the world to come. It is not that we have some pieces of the transcendent jigsaw puzzle and will receive the additional pieces at the parousia. Rather, the pieces we have do not fit the other pieces to make a coherent but partial picture. Each piece is a treasured fragment of revealed divine truth for which we give thanks, but they are this-worldly, indirect, and indistinct, with fuzzy edges. They are mirror-like, reflections but not ultimately real, sometimes reversed or distorted. To get the whole picture we need more than additional pieces, we need a *kind* of knowledge only God has now, which we can have only in God's new world to come, when we know as God now knows us.

This is the biblical model of human knowing of divine truth. In regard to God and the things of God, to say simply "I know" is clear, easy, and wrong (also arrogant, consciously or otherwise). To say simply "I don't know" sounds modestly humble, but it is also clear, easy, and risk-free. To say "I know in part" is to claim to have authentic, true knowledge of God, God's plan, and God's new world that is dawning, but to have it only in fragments that cannot now be put together into one whole, coherent picture. If the ultimate truth of God is represented by X (a Greek chi, the symbol for Christ), our apprehensions of God's truth are always $^{a}/X$, $^{b}/X$,

$^{c}/X$, and so on. Claiming that each fragment is true does not mean that the partial truths can be added together such that $^{a\text{-}z}/X$ results in the whole truth, $^{X}/X$. As presented in Revelation, each apprehension of the truth must be held on to, but we fragment-graspers do not and cannot know how to put them together into one united whole. No human has ever beheld the total divine reality, and could not communicate it if he or she had. As Paul struggles to communicate the profound truth of the gospel to the ordinary human beings in the Roman church, he repeatedly makes side comments that express the impossibility of simply declaring God's truth in simple, straightforward language:

- Romans 8:26: "Likewise the Spirit helps us in our weakness; for we do not know how to pray as we ought, but that very Spirit intercedes with sighs too deep for words."
- Romans 3:5: "But if our injustice serves to confirm the justice of God, what should we say? That God is unjust to inflict wrath on us? (I speak in a human way.)"
- Romans 6:19: "I am speaking in human terms because of your natural limitations. For just as you once presented your members as slaves to impurity and to greater and greater iniquity, so now present your members as slaves to righteousness for sanctification."

Paul claims to speak the truth, but he knows his finite mind cannot grasp or declare the wholeness of God's truth, that the truth of the transcendent world cannot be communicated in the language of this world (2 Cor 12:1–5). John stands in this tradition. Like Paul, John does not claim to know it all or to be able to communicate what he knows at some inexpressibly deep level. He hears and sees things in his visions of the heavenly world that he communicates, but some things he cannot and may not share (Rev 10:3–4). Like Paul, John presents us with a series of fragmentary visions, each of which points to God's truth, but they do not fit together. John knows not to claim too much. He has toured the heavenly world and heard the angelic voices. Yet there are things he cannot communicate, and the fragmentary pictures of God's truth he does communicate cannot be fitted together into one superpicture of "the way it really is." This is the nature of biblical truth as such. It is not always obvious in other biblical books. Revelation forces us to confront the nature of biblical revelation.

The Language of Biblical Truth Is Verbal-Visual

Each of John's fragments of God's truth is a visual image, a picture. Everyone knows there can be different pictures of the same reality, whether produced with a camera or paint on canvas, each of which can present a true representation of reality. Mapmakers represent the spherical earth in a variety of two-dimensional projections, none of which represent the earth as it really is, but no one seeing these flat-surface maps and their conflicting representations doubts the reality of the earth or that it is a sphere. In viewing different two-dimensional pictures on the artist's canvas or the computer screen, we have no difficulty picturing in our imaginations what the three-dimensional reality is "really" like, for the world we know by direct experience is a three-dimensional material world of space and time. An old-fashioned stereoscope, or 3D movie viewed through the appropriate glasses, takes two different flat-surface pictures and allows them to be seen in depth. The pictorial language of the Bible is like that. A Johannine letter contemporary with Revelation urges, "We know that the Son of God has come and has given us understanding so that we may know him who is true; and we are in him who is true, in his Son Jesus Christ. He is the true God and eternal life. Little children, keep yourselves from idols" (1 John 5:20–21).

Revelation gives us pictures of divine reality, of God's truth. No one picture can do it. If we had only a single picture, we would tend to see it as objectifying language, claiming to portray how divine reality "really" is; we would tend to make an idol of it. Two or more conflicting pictures not only reveal multiple facets of the one divine truth; they save us from going down dead-end streets.

Sometimes a picture is worth a thousand words. John communicates ultimate reality in the picture language of faith. He has several visionary pictures he wants to communicate to the churches, but he does not send a sheaf of drawings to be placarded on the walls of the house churches of Asia. However well done, graphic art on the flat surface of canvas or monitor can't do the job. Such images, whether on walls, on canvas, or in our minds, can appear to represent the transcendent world as an object in our three-dimensional, space-time world, and thus become idols. Whether metal or mental, graven images are still idols (Exod 20:4). Eyck's *Adoration of the Lamb*, over the altar in Ghent, Belgium, is magnificent art, but by itself it cannot portray the reality to which it points. One who does not know the *words* that go with the picture, the words that generated it in the first place, may stand before it and admire or even be moved at the aesthetic level but will see only quaintly garbed people gathered about a decorated table on which stands a lamb, gushing blood into a cup. Such a viewer can never grasp, or be grasped by, the meaning the picture wants to mediate. There is no way that wordless, visual, two-dimensional images can represent the reality they are trying to communicate. Pictures are not only silent, they are inert (even "moving pictures" are a series of still shots placed together that make a story). Not only is it impossible to portray the word pictures of Revelation on paper, canvas, or computer screen, but they cannot be clearly imagined, boggling the minds that try to reduce them to manageable mental images. Such scenes as Christ with the sharp two-edged sword coming out of his mouth frustrate not only efforts to paint them but also efforts to picture them in our imaginations. John's words point to heavenly gates made of pearl, but should we imagine an enormous heavenly oyster as their source? And how should one draw or imagine the new Jerusalem, clothed as a bride, descending from heaven? Even Revelation's central image of Jesus Christ as the Lamb of God loses its power when reduced to a painting or mental picture. John is not reporting on a bleeding young sheep he has seen in the heavenly world, he is using words to convey the unpicturable and unimaginable truth.

John does not send graphic art, not even well-done and highly symbolic visual artistry. No lasers, video clips, amplifiers, wide screens. He sends a papyrus scroll, also a flat surface, that contains only *words*. When these words become a living voice in the worshiping congregation, they generate mind-boggling imagery in the hearer's imagination, appropriate to the transcendent reality. *Sometimes a word is worth a thousand pictures.*

The Language of Biblical Truth Is Conflicting-Dialectical

What options are available to us serious preacher-theologians when our Bible confronts us with a series of affirmations (or pictures?) that communicate the Word of God but don't fit together, some of which seem to cancel out the others? We may take the variety of pictures of Jesus as the Christ as a key example. In some pictures, the Messiah is portrayed on the divine side of reality, doing what only God can do, walking on the water and forgiving sins, pictures that express the believer's faith in Jesus as the truly divine Son of God. In other pictures, Jesus is the suffering, victimized human being who shares the human lot and dies a truly human death. Related to this fundamental christological paradox are other sets of conflicting claims:

- Christ is present and active in the life of the world and the church // Christ is absent and will come again at the parousia.
- God is truly sovereign, the creator of all, whose will cannot be finally frustrated // humans are truly free and responsible.
- God's love and grace are unconditional and all are accepted // God's acceptance depends on the human response of faith and obedience, so that only obedient believers are saved.

If I take such biblical pictures seriously and want to affirm each side of these tensive pairs, I can choose from a number of possibilities for dealing with conflicting biblical statements. The most common of these are the following:

(1) I can pick the one or ones I like or am comfortable with and eliminate the others as wrong. "If this one is true, the other must be false." If the Bible presents me with pictures of Jesus as truly human and truly divine, then I must take one or the other. Some who think of themselves as "liberal" tend toward "truly human, therefore not truly divine"; some who regard themselves as "conservative" may suppose that if they affirm "truly divine," Jesus was not truly human. Likewise, the Bible's language of universal salvation seems to exclude biblical language of conditional salvation. If God finally saves all, then humans are not truly free and responsible, for salvation depends on God's decision and act. If God finally saves only some, then God's purposes for most of humanity are finally frustrated, and salvation depends on human decisions and actions. In this view, God's truth is clear and simple. I must be clear enough, and courageous enough, to take a stand and make a choice. Some texts can be believed, others must simply be rejected.

(2) I can force the inconvenient truths into the slots made for the convenient ones, trimming and reinterpreting as necessary and achieving a consistent system. "Since they are all true, they must all somehow fit together." Pictures that "seem" to portray Jesus as truly human should be understood in some way combined with his truly divine nature, or pictures of Christ as truly divine "really" reveal his true humanity. Statements that "seem to" imply universal salvation "really" apply only to obedient believers in Jesus Christ, or statements of conditional salvation really mean that God finally accepts everyone.

(3) A third possibility is more in step with the biblical world of thought. It is practiced both by those who have thought it through methodologically and by those who do it without reflecting very much about what they are doing. This approach is often called "dialectical theology," but the designa-

tion does not completely clarify what is intended, since the phrase is defined differently by various advocates. The term is related to "dialogue" and is commonly illustrated by Plato's portrayal of the method used by his teacher Socrates, and by Plato's own composition of dialogues between and among people contending for opposing points of view. Such dialogue is different from debate, in which the goal is to prove one side right and the other wrong. In Plato's dialectic, the back-and-forth discussion is to bring out the inconsistencies in one or both of the opposing claims and thus finally reconcile them. So also in Hegel and Marx, the goal of "dialectic" is the resolution of opposing claims in a single statement of the truth. Either side may have part of the truth; dialectic brings them together.

This version of dialectic values the juxtaposition of opposing statements, for in the dialogue the inconsistency, and thus falsehood, of one side or the other may be seen, or a third way that combines the two may be found. A versus B becomes A but not B, or B but not A, or both A and B. This approach is sometimes valued as "seeing the good in both sides of the argument," as a liberally tolerant both/and rather than a conservatively exclusive either/or. Both A and B are "partly right." There are many situations in which this approach is helpful and valid, and we quite rightly encourage dialogue among advocates of opposed religious and political perspectives. Liberals especially like dialogue rather than what they perceive to be the dogma of conservatives. But conservatives also like dialogue in this sense, looking for the partial biblical truths that can be added together and harmonized to express *the* truth. In some understandings of the significance of mythical thought, myth is valued as a way of reconciling the paradoxical conflicts of actual experience of the world, illustrated by Lévi-Strauss's dictum that "Mythical thought always progresses from the awareness of oppositions toward their resolution."[4]

None of the preceding solutions to the Bible's conflicting imagery does justice to the approach to biblical theology for which I am contending. Rather, "dialectical theology" typically designates that mode of biblical and Jewish thought that affirms and communicates the ultimate truth of God by juxtaposing two or more contrary or logically contradictory statements, each of which communicates God's truth, but *without* claiming to combine or harmonize them. The Bible declines to offer a supermyth in which all conflicting ideas are flattened out. If mythology is so understood, the kind of thought often found in the Bible is in fact the rejection of mythology. Biblical dialectic is "*not* complementary aspects of a single systematic doctrine."[5] Such a harmonizing mode of dialectic remains within the framework of the sovereignty of human logic. The conflicting imagery in the Bible, however, is often *un*settling, and is intended to be so. We like things to be settled, tied up neatly with no loose strings. Biblical language such as apocalyptic offers us unsettling pairs of pictures, refusing to fit the truth of God into the tidiness of our preformed categories. Dialectical theology does not attempt to resolve conflicting statements about God by whittling down or chipping away at the concept of God until it is of manageable size and shape for the slots provided by our finite intellect. This can be done with idols of wood and stone but not with the living God. Jesus's parables did not leave people satisfied; they *un*settled what people supposed was settled.

John's letter to the churches of Asia illustrates this dialectic of biblical apocalyptic theology. A few examples: First, at the last judgment, all people, great and small, stand before the judgment throne (Rev 20:11–15). Books are opened. Some contain the deeds of those being judged, and they are judged according to what they have done. What people do matters, and matters ultimately. Another book is opened, the book of life. The names in this book were inscribed before the foundation of the world, before the people being judged had done anything, good or bad (13:8; 17:8). There are a book of works and a book of grace, a book of human responsibility and the book of God's responsibility. Works and grace are not parceled out such that God is partly just and partly gracious. Responsibility for salvation is not divided into God's part and the believer's part. These stand unharmonized alongside each other. God's judgment and grace are both beyond our grasp. Neither cancels out the other. The Bible's dialectical picture language affirms both, whether or not our human logic can claim to understand it. Second, in some pictures, the kings of the earth, who have been allies of the beast and the great whore, join with the powers of evil against the returning Messiah and are destroyed by him (twice!; cf. 17:2; 18:3; 19:19; 20:9). In other pictures, these same kings are among the redeemed and bring their glory and honor into the new Jerusalem, where the leaves of the trees are for the healing of the nations (21:24; 22:2). Third, sometimes the "coming" of Christ for judgment is conditioned by human repentance—"Repent . . . if not, I will come . . ." (2:5, 16; 3:3)—and sometimes it is unconditional (3:11, 15; 22:7, 12, 20): "Ready or not, here I come." Fourth, John also illustrates the fundamental paradox of New Testament Christology, juxtaposing pictures in which Jesus is the victimized human being who is faithful to God and dies a truly human death (1:5, 18) and pictures in which he is the preexistent cosmic Lord filled with divine power (1:13–20; 3:14; 5:6–14).

Revelation is a good entry point to struggle with this issue, but such dialectical juxtaposition of images is not limited to Revelation. Dialectic is the typical mode of biblical theology. John is himself a truly biblical theologian whose thought is shaped by his Bible. Here are some examples from the rest of the Bible: Genesis 1:1–2:25 contains two conflicting creation stories. Were human beings created first or last? Did the creation start out as watery chaos and proceed to the forming of firm dry ground, or did it start out dry and proceed to the supplying of life-giving water? Distinguishing two creation stories in Genesis 1–2 is sometimes discussed under the rubric of "source analysis," but the point here is that the author combines, without harmonizing, two conflicting stories, each of which mediates God's truth.

Exodus 4–9 sometimes indicates that Pharaoh hardened his own heart (as Exod 8:15), while at other times it says God hardened Pharaoh's heart (4:21). In 9:34–10:1 both affirmations are made together (truly/truly, not partly/partly). Pharaoh is wholly responsible for his actions. God is wholly sovereign, and his purpose will not be frustrated by human decisions.

In 2 Samuel 7:1–17, God promises to David and his descendants that they will always rule over God's people. The promise is unconditional, entirely a matter of God's own grace and faithfulness. It is explicitly said that if the Davidic king sins, he will be chastened and disciplined, but the throne will not be taken away from him; Davidic rule will last forever, for the promise is unconditional (2 Sam 7:14–16). This unconditional promise is repeatedly reaffirmed: 1 Kings 11:36, 15:4, 2 Kings 8:16–19, and 2 Chronicles 21:7. But the editors of the historical books of the Old Testament have included a series of narratives in which the same divine promise is made to David's house, with one qualification: it is entirely dependent upon the obedience of the Davidic kings to God's covenant demands. This conditional version of the promise to David is found in 1 Kings 2:4, 6:12, 8:25, 9:4, and 11:38. The first series of pronouncements expresses God's sovereignty and mercy, which are unqualified. The second series of statements expresses human responsibility, which is also unqualified. The Old Testament authors obviously did not wish to dilute either God's sovereignty or human responsibility, stated both in absolute terms, and were not interested in filtering such pairs of statements through the grid of formal logic. The narrative language of the Old Testament is unself-consciously paradoxical. Since it speaks of the acts of God in history, the Eternal in time, the subject matter emerges in language as paradox and must do so or become an idol.

Jewish teachers, including Jesus of Nazareth, Paul, and other biblical theologians, naturally thought in these terms, which had shaped their understanding of God's truth, how it is appropriated and communicated. Such biblical theology is rooted in the Jewish Scripture, and is at home in Judaism.

> In the days when Rabbis were also judges in religious and legal matters, a member of the community came before him and stated his case persuasively. "You are right, my son," said the Rabbi.
>
> Then his opponent came in and stated his case, with equal persuasion. "You are right, my son," said the Rabbi.
>
> The Rabbi's wife, who had overheard both conversations, came to him and said, "But if the first party is right, the second cannot also be right." The Rabbi responded, "You too are right, my wife."

Such stories show both the dialectical nature of truth and that dialectic or paradox cannot be used as a category to paper over all logical difficulties. Dialectic does not function in the courtroom or at the cash register, where clear, univocal answers are called for. But the rabbis, like their Bible and the Jewish parable-teller Jesus, knew that the ultimate truth of God cannot always be stated directly.

Biblical dialectic is not "doublethink," not "double-talk." In his 1949 novel *1984*, George Orwell described doublethink as "the power to hold simultaneously two opinions . . . knowing them to be contradictory and believing in both of them."[6] Orwell regarded doublethink as a propaganda device used by the authorities to destroy the capacity for critical thinking, in order to control populations and maintain the prevailing power structure. Biblical dialectic is more related to the insights of physicists who, desiring to describe the universe, realize that their language is not equal to the task and cannot be. Physicists do not understand the fundamental nature of light but know that they must think and speak of light as both waves and particles, though there is no way to logically harmonize such statements. The three-dimensional earth can be represented by two-dimensional maps, but it takes two *different* maps to do so.[7]

The Language of Biblical Truth Is Confessional but Not Irrational

We begin by reflecting on a category of biblical confession that is more prevalent in biblical theology than we might suppose, the language of election and predestination. We will discuss understandings of election several times in later soundings in other biblical texts. Here we reflect on the nature of such language as *confessional* language. Revelation designates those who confess faith in Christ as the "called and chosen and faithful" (17:14). Their names have been "written from the foundation of the world in the book of life of the Lamb that was slaughtered" (13:8; cf. 17:8). Such a statement is expressed in confessional language, in the sense that it affirms what it says but does not make claims that fit into a system of logical deduction. In John's view, when Christian believers confess their self-understanding as belonging to God's people who have been elected and called, such we-statements do not permit inferences in the form of you-statements or they-statements. "We are elected" does not mean "you/they are not elected" (though that is its logical implication), but "we/I do not take credit for our salvation, which is entirely a matter of God's initiative and grace." God's grace is not reactive, not a conditional response to human action or nonaction, but inherent in God's essential being and character. Such confessional language is a matter of thanksgiving and praise to God, not a proposition in a syllogism. This does not diminish its truth but identifies it as a particular kind of language. Attempts to better understand the language of faith are not a prescription or instruction about how such language should be used, nor is it suggested that believers who speak in this mode make a conscious decision to use a particular genre of language. What we are attempting to describe is how the confessional language of faith actually works.

So understood, confessional language is not integrated into a larger conceptual system, as one cogwheel in a larger linguistic machine, such that if one wheel turns, all others must turn with it. Confessional language pushes the clutch, disengaging its affirmation from a supposed chain of logical deductions. Confessional language makes affirmations, each of which has its independent fragment of truth, and does not even ask such questions as "How can this be, since if it is true, this statement logically implies other statements that I must regard as false?" Confessional language does not live by the logic that "X cannot be true, because if it is, Y must also be true, and since I know that Y is not true, X cannot be true either." Confessional language affirms what it says, not all that it might imply.

The violent imagery and language of Revelation pose one of the most difficult obstacles to hearing its confession of faith in the God of Jesus Christ. Without claiming to resolve all the difficulties involved in interpreting such language, we can reflect on it as an expression of confessional language and come within hearing distance of what Revelation wants to say (for discussion of specific texts, see below). Disturbing language and images leap from the page. The risen Christ threatens to kill the children of "Jezebel," the false prophet in Thyatira (2:22–23). Those who worship the beast and receive his mark will be tormented with fire and sulfur in the presence of the holy angels and the presence of the Lamb (14:10). Anyone who reads or hears Revelation knows such an image is the tip of a very large iceberg—Revelation abounds in portrayals not only of the thrill of victory but also of the agony of defeat.

But not only Revelation. John's Bible and ours repeatedly celebrates the joys of those whom God saves, but the by-product of such language is misery, death, and worse for the unsaved. Much of John's imagery comes from the exodus, in which God's mighty power overcomes the oppressive pharaoh, sets the captives free, and gives them a land and a future. As the narrator proclaims God's saving acts for Israel, we hear:

> The LORD said to Moses, "Stretch out your hand toward heaven so that hail may fall on the whole land of Egypt, on humans and animals and all the plants of the field in the land of Egypt." Then Moses stretched out his staff toward heaven, and the LORD sent thunder and hail, and fire came down on the earth. And the LORD rained hail on the land of Egypt; there was hail with fire flashing continually in the midst of it, such heavy hail as had never fallen in all the land of Egypt since it became a nation. The hail struck down everything that was in the open field throughout all the land of Egypt, both human and animal; the hail also struck down all the plants of the field, and shattered every tree in the field. Only in the land of Goshen, where the Israelites were, there was no hail. (Exod 9:22–26)

Not only Pharaoh and his elite oppressors are struck, but also innocent peasants, slaves, children, and animals.

> At midnight the LORD struck down all the firstborn in the land of Egypt, from the firstborn of Pharaoh who sat on his throne to the firstborn of the prisoner who was in the dungeon, and all the firstborn of the livestock. Pharaoh arose in the night, he and all his officials and all the Egyptians; and there was a loud cry in Egypt, for there was not a house without someone dead. Then he summoned Moses and Aaron in the night, and said, "Rise up, go away from my people, both you and the Israelites! Go, worship the LORD, as you said." (Exod 12:29–31)

Should Jews and Christians refuse to "Go, worship the LORD" for redemption purchased at such a price? Again, it's the children, the firstborn of prisoners and slaves, and the animals.

Or take the prayers and praises of God's people found in Israel's and the church's hymnal, the book of Psalms—the most-cited book in the New Testament. Psalm 91 is typical of the promises and thanksgivings that echo throughout Israel's worship, prayed in the quiet beauty of temple and synagogue, and at Auschwitz—and in the solemn and joyful liturgy of the church:

> You who live in the shelter of the Most High,
>   who abide in the shadow of the Almighty,
> will say to the LORD, "My refuge and my fortress;
>   my God, in whom I trust."
> For he will deliver you from the snare of the fowler
>   and from the deadly pestilence;
> he will cover you with his pinions,
>   and under his wings you will find refuge;
>   his faithfulness is a shield and buckler.
> You will not fear the terror of the night,
>   or the arrow that flies by day,
> or the pestilence that stalks in darkness,
>   or the destruction that wastes at noonday.
> A thousand may fall at your side,
>   ten thousand at your right hand,
>   but it will not come near you.
> You will only look with your eyes
>   and see the punishment of the wicked. (Ps 91:1–8)

The trusting worshiper is assured of protection—the destruction "will not come near *you*." Does God not care for the thousand at your side, the ten thousand at your right hand? Even if God doesn't care, should not the worshiper care and complain to God (Job!)?

It is not just Revelation or the Old Testament, of course, but the Bible as such, the whole Bible. The violent and hateful language of the last book of the New Testament may remind us of its first book, which we may suppose is easier to preach. Among the opening scenes of the New Testament, if we are not too anesthetized by Christmas hubbub to notice, we see:

> When Herod saw that he had been tricked by the wise men, he was infuriated, and he sent and killed all the children in and around Bethlehem who were two years old or under, according to the time that he had

learned from the wise men. Then was fulfilled what had been spoken through the prophet Jeremiah:

> "A voice was heard in Ramah,
> wailing and loud lamentation,
> Rachel weeping for her children;
> she refused to be consoled, because they are no more."
>
> (Matt 2:16–18)

The children again. Should we not too refuse to be consoled? If we are concerned with our own theological integrity, not to speak of God's, and the congregation's need to be challenged and nurtured by biblical faith, what can we do with such texts? Suppose we retell Matthew's story from another perspective:

"The Other Babies of Bethlehem": A Story

Susanna and Jehoiakim were young parents, both twenty-three years old, just getting started in life together. They had one child, little Davey, who at eighteen months had learned to walk and was getting into everything, was putting sentences together in strange ways, his soft, high-pitched little voice giving a musical lilt even to the Aramaic gutturals. A healthy, happy child, he was the delight of their life. They named him David because they lived in the "city of David," as their village was called, located a few miles south of Jerusalem.

Late one night while everyone was sleeping, the king's soldiers surrounded the village, and at first light they came into town. They ordered all parents with small children into the village square, made a search to ensure that none remained, and without a word killed every boy younger than two years old. "Orders," they said.

After the horror of that day had receded enough for the villagers to take account, they discovered that eleven children had been killed.

It is a cruel world, and such things happen. In our time thousands of babies have been napalmed, gassed, starved, and shot down in the name of "national security" by the order or permission of governments. But human beings are resilient creatures, and after periods of numbness, anger, bitterness, and acceptance, Jehoiakim and Susanna were able to pick up the pieces of their life and go on. Without hostility or condescension, they rejected the "explanations" of the tragedy from well-meaning neighbor-theologians. They themselves had no answer to the question articulated for them in their own Bible-prayer book, "My

God, my God, why?" (Ps 22:1). They even began to find new meaning in synagogue worship.

Until one day when they discovered that on the crucial night before the slaughter of the baby boys an angel had come from God to warn one family to flee. It turns out that God had arranged for Mary, Joseph, and the baby Jesus to escape and that they are now secure in Egypt. The little boy Jesus was alive and well, but not their little Davey.[8]

When told in the above manner, the story raises questions not only of history (Did/could such things actually happen?) but also of ethics (Should such things happen?). If God works in such a way that angels may warn persons of impending danger, is it right that only one family be warned? Which of us, with such information and the ability to save, would share it with one family and withhold it from eleven? Pondering *the nature of such biblical language*, from Genesis 1 through Revelation 22, may help bring us and our congregations within hearing distance of such stories. Matthew's story is his grateful confession of faith that God protected the infant Jesus, despite the threats that could have snuffed out his little life. This was a reality of history, as seen through the eyes of faith, whether or not Herod and his soldiers were involved. Matthew's story focuses on what God did in and through Jesus, and does not bring God's care for the other babies of Bethlehem within its horizon. It was through God's providential care that Jesus Christ lived among us. God saved the newborn Christ child, period. This is said as confession of faith, with praise and thanksgiving. It does not answer the question, or even raise it, of the other babies of Bethlehem, neither in the story world of Matthew's Gospel nor in the space-time world of first-century Palestine. The believers' confession of faith can include and affirm sets of tensive, contrary, paradoxical (not "contradictory") affirmations, each of which is a fragmentary expression of ultimate truth. The difficult language of Revelation, filled with violence though it is, is faith's language of confession.

The Language of Biblical Truth Is Referential but Not Objectifying

One attempt to handle the problems biblical language presents to our logical minds is to limit it to the story world of the Bible and avoid claiming that such language actually refers to anything real. John J. Collins's helpful book, *The Apocalyptic Imagination*, for instance, encourages interpreters to value apocalyptic language but to avoid seeing it as referential, as though it actually refers to realities that exist outside the language itself. He is right, I think, in discouraging "a preoccupation with the referential aspects of language and with the factual information that can be extracted from a text. Such an attitude is especially detrimental to the study of poetic and mythological material, which is expressive language, articulating feelings and attitudes rather than describing reality in an objective way."[9]

None of the above discussion of confessional language should be taken to mean that the biblical authors were merely venting their feelings or expressing their faith, hope, or gratitude, as though their language did not actually refer to anything "out there" in the objectively real world. As delineated above, the kind of confessional language found in the Bible does not claim this sort of objectivization.

This does not mean, however, that the only alternative to such literalism is the expression of one's subjective feelings. To be sure, the language of Genesis 1–2 does not provide objective information about how the universe came into being. But neither are the authors of the Genesis creation stories merely confessing their feelings of dependence on the creator. The stories refer to objective reality, though they make no claim to describe it literally. Once there was no world. Now there is a world. Something happened that brought the world into existence. The creation stories point to something that happened in the real world of time and space that then became the basis for inferring chronological or geographical information about the real world treated by the physical sciences, but such language cannot be used as objectifying statements from which valid inferences can be made.

The same must be said of the resurrection language used both of the eschatological future and of the past event of Jesus's resurrection. The differing stories of Jesus's resurrection show that they cannot all be objectively true in their chronology and how they portray the resurrected body of Jesus, but this does not mean the resurrection occurred only in the disciples' subjectivity or ours. Such stories point to an event, an act of God, prior to and apart from us and what we may feel about it, but the reality to which they point cannot be objectified as a series of literal space-time happenings from which logical inferences can be made.

Each story is true in what it says, but the stories can neither be fitted together into a single objective superstory nor reduced to human feelings and hopes. Even such stories as God's inflicting the plagues on Egypt and delivering Israel at the Red Sea, though each of them may not be literally true in an objectifying sense, are more than Israel's subjectivity ("I'm really glad we got out of Egypt!"). They point to and celebrate something that really happened in history. Those who confess that God delivered them from Egypt, sparing their firstborn while others were killed, drowning the soldiers who were just obeying orders while they came through the waters dry-shod, are neither just expressing their feelings nor celebrating the destruction of other people. In the world of logic, "victory" implies "defeat"; there cannot be winners unless there are losers. Striving for "win-win" solutions in conflictive situations is often the right thing to do, but such language is not *logical.* Confessional language only celebrates the victory of God, without insisting that if *we* are saved, *they* must be lost. Israel's confessional language of the exodus and the plagues celebrates the following reality: Once there was no people of Israel. Something happened, God acted, now there is the elect people of Israel, called by God, to which I belong.

The Language of Biblical Truth Projects a Narrative World

Biblical authors do not deal with the complex issues discussed above by writing essays. Like Jesus, they tell stories. The conflicting verbal-visual pictures presented by New Testament authors are incorporated in a narrative that holds them together and allows them to function theologically.

Suppose one has seven pictures, each of which represents, indirectly and in fragmented form, something of the truth of God, salvation, the meaning of universal history and our brief lives within it. The pictures are conflicting, even contradictory, and must be seen together to function as mediators of God's truth. They can't be harmonized and assembled into one superpicture that communicates the whole truth. They could all be placarded in one large gallery, but we viewers would still have to look at them one at a time, aware of the others but still necessarily looking at them in a particular order. The director of the museum could want them to be seen in a particular order and thus place each in a separate room. The guide could take the viewers from room to room in the specified order, making some comments but allowing the viewers to focus on the pictures themselves. This is what a narrative does; this is what the author John has done with his verbal-visual visions. This is what every book in the New Testament does, but we become more aware of it in reading Revelation.

John writes a letter to the churches of Asia, a letter filled with apocalyptic content. Apocalyptic is itself a narrative form, recounting the visions and heavenly travels of the seer. John incorporates his apocalyptic visionary narratives in a larger narrative framework, a letter. We usually think of biblical narrative in terms of the stories of the patriarchs, the exodus, and the history of Israel, or, in the New Testament, the Gospels and Acts. In addition to these discrete narratives, there is the comprehensive biblical story as a whole, creation to consummation, into which the separate narratives (and nonnarrative materials such as Proverbs and other wisdom texts) are incorporated, to make one biblical-theological metanarrative of which God is the author, producer, director, and behind-the-scenes main character. For Christians, the Bible as such is the self-defining story of God, of which the Christ event is the revelatory center.

Most of the documents of the New Testament are in the form of letters. We seldom reflect on the way letters function, but the letter too is a narrative form. A letter presupposes and projects a story, a narrative that finally includes its readers in its narrative world. This is the way Revelation works. This is the way every document in the New Testament communicates. Early Christianity produced a great volume and variety of literature (stories, songs, prayers, collections of Jesus's sayings, collections of miracle stories, books of church rules and order, histories, commentaries on biblical texts, and other genres). In the Spirit-guided filtering process that resulted in the canonical New Testament, only two genres of literature emerged as normative for the community of faith: gospels and letters. (Acts is the second part of a gospel; Revelation is a letter.) Since gospels and letters are narrative forms, *the New Testament as a whole and each of its books function in the narrative mode.* Narrative corresponds to our own lives, which do not happen synchronically but unfold diachronically. The New Testament documents project the grand narrative, the story of God's saving acts from creation to eschaton, and call us to see the meaning of our individual life stories in the context of this grand narrative. The point here is that narratives (unlike, say, math or logic textbooks) can embrace and communicate conflicting elements. Narratives are not timeless but, like history and our lived experience, are one-thing-at-a-time. Narratives allow the biblical authors to hold up now this picture, now that, arranged in the order they choose, enabling each to speak its own word from God. Narratives hold conflicting truths together without homogenizing or harmonizing them, which would neutralize (= neuter) them.

Narrative is the fundamental biblical genre. Narratives create worlds. Not, of course, in the objective sense—no narrative adds to the number of molecules in the universe nor structures them into objective realities. But this "objective" world is not a world that any human being lives in.[10] Humans, by their language and stories, construct, pass on, and receive from other humans the world(s) we live in. Reading texts, hearing them read in community worship, *is not just informative but is formative*. As the world was initially created by the Word (Gen 1:1–4), so the world we live in is formed by the language in which we live. There is a sense, a real sense, in which we humans create our own lifeworld, the world we perceive as the world in which we live, from this world-potential of atoms, molecules, and time. We humans naturally tend to suppose that this world-of-our-own making, the commonsense world, is simply "the" world, the only world, the real world.

How can the preacher-theologian who wants to tell the truth affirm the conflicting truth claims of different biblical texts? Essays, philosophical reflections, tend to "explain" God and God's acts within the categories of human thought, striving after logical neatness and reducing God to concepts we can handle, even control and manipulate. Such explanations don't finally come to terms with the strange new world of the Bible, the world projected by biblical narrative. In the Bible, conflicting affirmations are held together in vision and narrative, that is, by pictures and stories (which finally turn out to be the same thing). If we work at understanding how the truth claims of Revelation function, this might well open doors to a more biblical understanding of the nature of God's truth as such. We will return to reflections on biblical language when we explore the theology of the Gospel of John.

The Language of Biblical Truth Is Mythical (That Is, Verbal-Visual Narrative)

"Myth" is a biblical word, found in the Bible only in the Pastorals and 2 Peter, only in the negative sense, and only in settings when believers are being warned against the myths of false teachers (1 Tim 1:4; 4:7; 2 Tim 4:4; Titus 1:14) or when the charge that Christian teaching itself was only "cleverly devised myths" is being rejected (2 Pet 1:16). This obscures the fact that myth was not only used in this derogatory sense in the ancient world but was also a term for transcendent truth in narrative form. In the early days of critical biblical study, some scholars such as the old liberal theologians of the nineteenth and early twentieth centuries attempted to preserve an authentic core of truth in the Bible by stripping away its ancient mythological layers in order to get to its "eternally valid principles." Many more recent interpreters have followed the lead of Rudolf Bultmann in seeing the mythological language in which biblical faith is expressed as calling for interpretation, not rejection. Such this-worldly language is the only means available of witnessing to the saving acts of God in history—creation, covenant with Israel, sending the Christ, raising him from the dead, sending the Holy Spirit, guiding the church through history to the eschaton and the return of Christ. Likewise, such images that describe sin as a personal, enslaving power, and God's judgment on sin and justifying sinners taking place in a heavenly law court, are mythological language, referential but not objectifying.

Biblical Theology Is Narrative Theology

"The emphasis on narrative, and the fact that the entire Bible is enclosed in a narrative framework, distinguishes the Bible from a good many other sacred books. The Buddhist sutras employ relatively little narrative, and the Koran consists of revelations gathered up after Mohammed's death and arranged in order of length, with no discernible narrative principle in their sequence. The narrative framework of the Bible is a part of its emphasis on the shape of history and the specific collision with temporal movement that its revelation is assumed to make.

"Literally, the Bible is a gigantic myth, a narrative extending over the whole of time from the creation to the apocalypse."

—Northrop Frye, *The Great Code: The Bible and Literature* (Toronto: University of Toronto Press, 1982), 224

It is unfortunate, but apparently irreparable, that in the popular mind "myth" continues to mean something like "ancient fairy tales" or simply ideas that are popular but untrue ("the idea that rear-engine cars don't get stuck in the snow turned out to be a myth" . . . "the idea that humans don't cause climate change will turn out to be a myth"). False and superficial as these definitions are, we seem to be stuck with the word. We thus need to become more aware of the ways philosophers and theologians have used the word, at least since the time of Plato. Two such ways are particularly important for biblical theology.

"Myth" Is Sometimes Used in the Sense of Thinking and Speaking of the Transcendent World in This-Worldly Concepts and Language

All talk of God is mythological in this sense (Rom 3:5; 6:19; 8:26; 1 Cor 13:12). To speak of God's "love" or of God who "hears" our prayers necessarily uses the thought world and language of the finite human world in order to speak of God. "Love" includes body chemistry, muscles, brain waves, historical interaction in the space-time world. "Hearing" involves ears, sound waves on particular frequencies that travel through air, the formation and perception of words that have originated and have their meaning in a particular language in the historical world of space and time. This is simply what "love" and "hearing" mean to us historical, finite beings, and we cannot think of these words in any other way. We know, of course, that such language does not apply "literally" to God and the transcendent world (no one believes that God the Father has testicles and male hormones), but having said this, thoughtful people must ask, "What/how is such language to be used when speaking of and to God?" Two popular alternatives follow:

Rationalism as Alternative to Myth

A "scientific" view of the world and reality insists, consciously or otherwise, that if God is real, God fits into our space-time view of the "real" world, into our kind of logic. Science and logic have dispensed with myth and superstition. The only reality we can responsibly think and talk about is the reality that can be grasped by human science, often thought of as the only reality there is. If God "exists," God fits, and must fit, into the world of reasonable, scientific thought.

Nonthinking Mysticism as Alternative to Myth

Thoughtful people who become aware that our thinking can never express or be in direct touch with the reality of God can abandon thinking and language. Since thinking about God inevitably distorts God, at worst producing a mental image that is an idol, to truly be in touch with God requires the suppression of thinking, words, and language, such as sitting quietly in a darkened room with incense and rituals and nonlinguistic chants ("*ommm-m-m-m*") that get us beyond ourselves. There are, of course, simplistic as well as sophisticated and venerable ways of doing this.

Biblical theology rejects both of these options. The living God transcends all human thought and language, but this does not mean thought and language must be rejected to experience the reality of God.

"Myth" Is Also Used to Denote the Assumed Framework for All Our Thinking, the World as We Assume It to Be, within Which Our Life and Thought All Take Place

In this sense, we humans cannot live without myths. We function not just by gathering increments of information into our minds; we must always insert them into some kind of framework that is already there. Prior to the fifteenth century CE, the earth was considered the center of the universe. This was a myth not only in the popular sense that it turned out to be untrue but also in the philosophical sense that it was the world-shaping picture of reality assumed in millions of human minds. In this mythological picture, earth is a relatively large planet, around which the sun, moon, other planets, and stars (all relatively small) revolve, once every twenty-four hours. It was a small, cozy universe of which we are the center, in which we are at home. People did not live in this mythical world by choice, did not look over the options and choose this one. It was assumed, unquestioned reality, and whatever was true was fitted into this framework. If it didn't fit, it couldn't be true. When Copernicus gave us a new astronomy—which, of course, did not happen without conflict and mind wrenching—he did not just rearrange the furniture in the world we already live in but gave us a new, alternative world. Its implications are still being worked out. In this sense, the post-Copernican view of the world (and any other such view) is also a myth, the assumed reality in which we live and think.

We might also think of other such myths. The concept of *private property* is simply a given in the capitalistic world in which we live, considered a built-in dimension of reality, just the way the world is, not a socially conditioned way of thinking about the world. Even the suggestion of some alternative myth is met with consternation, hostility, or a gut reaction, in both others and ourselves. The associated myth of *competition* as the framework of our lives shapes the way we think and live. I need not only to do well, I need to do better than others. I need not only to win, but being a winner means others must lose. In this mythical world, the thrill of victory cannot exist without the agony of defeat, and my thrill as a winner is diminished without others feeling the pangs of defeat. The biblical message shakes the foundations, upends and transforms assumptions we didn't even know we had. We thought it was "just the way things are." The Bible challenges us with a new world, not just with add-on features that improve the old world we had constructed for ourselves.

Approaching Revelation, Getting into Apocalyptic

A major dimension of the thought world in which John and (some of) his readers lived is called *apocalyptic.* The designation of this genre of thought is derived from "apocalypse" ("revelation," "uncovering," "removing the veil"), the first word of John's message to the churches. This was John's natural, assumed way of thinking. He did not devise it just for this composition or consciously select apocalyptic as a way of looking at the world. Before he ever became a Christian believer or prophetic spokesman in the church, he simply assumed the apocalyptic framework as representing the reality of the world and history, much as most contemporary Americans assume private property, capitalism, and a Copernican solar system as their worldview *within* which they do their thinking.

What Is an Apocalypse?

"Specifically, an apocalypse is defined as: 'a genre of revelatory literature with a narrative framework, in which a revelation is mediated by an otherworldly being to a human recipient, disclosing a transcendent reality which is both temporal, insofar as it envisages eschatological salvation, and spatial insofar as it involves another, supernatural world.'"

This definition was the considered result of an annual seminar of the Society of Biblical Literature chaired by John J. Collins that for several years researched the whole range of canonical and noncanonical apocalyptic writings. The summary definition was originally published in *Apocalypse: The Morphology of a Genre,* Semeia 14 (Missoula, MT: Scholars Press, 1979). It is repeated in Collins's *The Apocalyptic Imagination,* 2nd ed. (Grand Rapids: Eerdmans, 1989), thoroughly discussed in *The Apocalyptic Imagination,* 3rd ed. (Grand Rapids: Eerdmans, 2016), 5–11, and has been widely accepted in biblical scholarship.

Here, of course, is a fundamental difference between John and his readers, on the one hand, and today's readers, on the other. To understand Revelation, we must consciously attend to this difference in worldviews in a way that the original readers did not have to. This is true of the whole New Testament, of course, but this is not so obvious in reading Matthew or 1 Corinthians.

Christian faith and theology are based on God's self-revelation. But theological information is not revealed from heaven. Theology is the human response to God's revelation, in human language and conceptuality. Already in the prophet's encounter with the divine reality, the appropriation of God's revelation must necessarily occur within the prophet's own linguistic and conceptual world. The truth of John's testimony is not a matter of accurately reporting the details of his visions, as though they were objective realities he observed as a spectator. The truth of John's testimony depends on whether or not it bears authentic witness to the apostolic faith in God's act in the Christ event. The apocalyptic mode of theological thought as the vehicle for communicating the faith is found in many books of the Bible, especially in the New Testament, but is represented especially by Daniel in the Old Testament and Revelation in the New Testament.

The best way for us preachers to acquire our own understanding of the Jewish apocalyptic theology that constituted the matrix of the theology of Jesus, early Christianity, and the New Testament is to read one or more of the noncanonical apocalypses, where our own theology is not directly at stake. Understanding biblical apocalyptic thought is hindered for many readers by the fact that the only such writings they have ever seen are in the Bible, and they lack a category in which to place it. But all understanding is genre-bound. Unless one recognizes the genre, one is bound to misunderstand the text (think of jokes, political cartoons, political convention nomination speeches, historical novels, parables). A good place to start is 4 Ezra (2 Esdras), found in any Bible that has the Apocrypha (it is an appendix in some Roman Catholic editions). Chapters 1–2 and 15–16 are Christian additions, made after the composition of John's Revelation, but 2:1–14:48, the core of the book, is a Jewish apocalypse composed about the same time as Revelation. After reading just one noncanonical apocalyptic book such as 4 Ezra, 1 Enoch, or 2 Baruch, you will never look at the canonical apocalyptic books of Daniel and Revelation the same again.

Though no substitute for thoughtful reading of suggested primary and secondary texts, the following thumbnail sketch has proven to be a helpful framework for getting our minds around apocalyptic thought, summarized from my commentary on Revelation.[11]

Providence, Eschatology, Apocalyptic

Providence: God Is Guiding History

Apocalyptic is a particular kind of *eschatology*, which in turn is a particular understanding of *providence*. *Providence* is the overarching biblical category within which eschatological and apocalyptic thought can best be understood. The English word "providence" is a derivation from two Latin words, *pro-*, which means "before," and *videre*, which means "see." "Providence," therefore, has to do with seeing what is before one, looking out ahead. To believe in the providence of God is to believe that not only our individual lives but history as a whole, the one-way road all of us are traveling, is not rushing blindly along but is under the sovereignty of One who is looking out ahead. Someone is in the driver's seat of history. It is not the case that God is the Great Spectator who can look out ahead—as we humans cannot—and see in advance what is going to happen, as though history were simply a long line of dominoes that, once begun, must fall in a certain pattern that God can see in advance. God is the Lord of history; he guides it, knows where it is going, because he is directing it. The idea is expressed in many ways throughout the Old Testament, with the explicit theological term as a name for God emerging late in Israel's literature. The deuterocanonical Wisdom 14:1–4 offers a typical example:

> Again, one preparing to sail and about to voyage over raging waves
> calls upon a piece of wood more fragile than the ship that carries him.
> For it was desire for gain that planned that vessel,
> and wisdom was the artisan who built it;
> but it is your providence, O Father, that steers its course,
> because you have given it a path in the sea,
> and a safe way through the waves,
> showing that you can save from every danger,
> so that even a person who lacks skill may put to sea.
> (Wis 14:1–4; cf. 17:2; 1 Esd 6:5; 3 Macc 4:21; 5:30; 4 Macc 9:24; 13:19; 17:22)

Eschatology: God Is Guiding History to a Final Goal

Providential thinking has no necessary place for thought about the "end of the world." It is concerned with the process, not the goal, of history. Eschatological thought, on the other hand, is the counterpart to the doctrine of creation: just as the world and history have not always existed but came into being by the act of the creator, so this world and its history are not eternal but will be brought to their goal by the God who declares that he is not only the Alpha but also the Omega of all that is (Rev 1:8; these are the first and last letters of the Greek alphabet). *Eschaton* is simply the Greek word for "end," found often (145 times) in the LXX, both in the ordinary sense (e.g., Gen 33:2; Prov 25:8) and in various theological senses of the "last days" (e.g., Gen 49:1; Num 24:14; Deut 4:30; Isa 2:2; Dan 10:14).

Eschatological thought is not optional in the Christian doctrine of God but is inherent in Christian theology as such. Like the biblical understanding of creation, eschatology is not speculation about the world but is an aspect of the doctrine of God. Only God is eternal. In biblical thought, the world is not eternal, not a given with which God must contend, but is God's creation. It had a beginning. But the present state of the world is not God's will for the creation, and it will have a fulfillment. The world as we know it will have an end, just as it had a beginning. God's bringing history to an end is a fundamental aspect of the biblical doctrine of God, just as is the doctrine of creation. The question addressed by the biblical prophets was not the speculative "will there be an end of the world?" but the existential "Is God faithful?" The canonical prophets and teachers who express their biblical faith in eschatological categories are not principally concerned with a schedule for the end but with the faithfulness and integrity of God.

Biblical eschatology is concerned with the future, but not by discounting the present. If the road on which we all travel has an end, the whole road looks different to us. If there is a destination, the road itself, and everyone on it, receives new meaning. Every day of our lives, not just the last one, is filled with significance. The end already shapes the present, not only psychologically but also ontologically; it shapes not just how we think about the present but the reality of the present itself. For New Testament authors, the end—pictured as the advent of the Messiah, the resurrection, the coming of God's kingdom—is not only something to which we look forward but something that has happened. It not only transforms our thinking about the present, but God's new world breaking in already makes the world itself different.

The issue, of course, is whether we think it happened. If God acted in the event of Jesus Christ, something has in fact happened that makes everything different (not just *look* different). If the coming of the Christ, his death, and his resurrection actually occurred in real history, we cannot choose to live in some other world in which there may be good ideas but no Messiah, no cross and resurrection, no new age breaking in, no kingdom of God already dawning. If it has not happened, does not honesty compel us to lay the Christian faith to rest and try to find some ideals to live by and figure out a rationale for them? For the New Testament authors, the good news is that God has acted, the Messiah has come, the end is already shaping the present. This good news is not our speculative theories in response to the questions of human existence, but the announcement of what God has done—good news, not just good advice. Although "end of the world" thinking is often thought of as gloomy and pessimistic, in the Bible generally and in Revelation in particular, the doctrine of the end of this world is a joyous hope to be celebrated—and that not because of any negative view of this world and its values.

Some are surprised to learn that there is a considerable eschatological element in the Bible. Although there are exceptions in individual books, *most* biblical authors in both the Old and New Testaments operate with the presupposition that God has a plan for the world and history that he will carry to fulfillment. In a vast variety of imagery and forms of thought, many passages in the Old Testament indicate that the present state of the world is not God's final will for it. Rather, God will bring the world into a fulfilled state that actualizes God's own will for his creation. The law and narrative books contain passages that express this eschatological hope, for example, Genesis 12:1–3 (a foundational passage), 49:9–12, and Numbers 24:17–19. Many of the psalms were written to be used in the worship of Israel, which longed for or already celebrated in advance the coming age of salvation, especially as this was linked to the idea that the final age of fulfillment would be brought to realization through the new or coming king God would raise up for this purpose (e.g., Pss 2; 21; 45; 72; 74; 104; 110). The prophets, especially the postexilic ones, frequently portray the eschatological hopes of Israel in terms of both judgment and salvation, for example, Amos 1–2; 5:4, 6, 14, 15, 18–20; 7:4; 8:1–2, 9–10; 9:11–15; Isaiah 2:2–4, 6–20; 4:2–6; 7:1–25; 9:1–7; 11:1–9; 14:24–27; 19:16–25; 35; 40–66; Ezekiel 32–37; 38–39; 40–48; Joel 2–3; Hosea 1:10–11; Jeremiah 31:31–33; Micah 5; Malachi 4:1–6; Zechariah 9–14; and Zephaniah 1:1–18. All these texts are not mere idealistic dreams of what might someday happen but insistent affirmations, in a variety of images, that God's purpose for the world will not finally be frustrated.

Apocalyptic: God Is Guiding History to a Final Goal That God Himself Will Bring About in the Near Future, in a Particular Way That Has Already Been Revealed

Just as eschatology is a certain kind of thinking about God's providence, apocalyptic may be thought of as a certain kind of thinking about eschatology. One can believe in providence and affirm an eschatology without claiming to know how, when, or what one is in fact talking about—God will bring history to a worthy conclusion, and that is all we can know and need to know. Apocalyptic thought claims to go further, to say that there is theological value in thinking about the goal of history in particular ways. Such thought developed late in Israel's history, at times when it seemed impossible that the eschatological hopes expressed by the biblical prophets could ever be fulfilled. Most Old Testament eschatology was "from below"—God would work within this-worldly history and finally empower a deliverer who would bring in the final realm of God's justice and peace. The apocalyptists lived in intolerable situations, when Israel's theological teachers saw no way within this world that God's kingdom could grow out of human actions, even if they were equipped with divine wisdom and power. Mothers saw their babies killed because they had them circumcised in faithfulness to the law (Daniel). Children saw their parents imprisoned or killed because their faithfulness to their confession of Jesus as the only Lord made it impossible for them to yield to the imperial religion (Revelation). In an impossible this-worldly situation, how can one still believe in the faithfulness of God? It was the honor and integrity of God as God that was at stake, not just human selfish longing for golden streets and pearly gates. Faith in the resurrection was first expressed by Israel's apocalyptic thinkers as an affirmation of the faithfulness of God despite the way everything looked through the eyes of "realistic" common sense. Read 1–2 Maccabees, then read Daniel.

The theological problem to which apocalyptic is the response may be generally stated as follows: God has made promises to bless his people (e.g., Deut 28:1–14) and, through his people, the world (e.g., Gen 12:1–3; Isa 42:1–4). When disaster came and the people had been unfaithful by not keeping the law (often the case, especially in the preexilic situation), there was no radical conceptual problem, and the prophets could declare that the disaster was God's judgment on the people because of their sins. This, of course, is the burden of most of the prophets of the Old Testament (cf. Amos; Isa 1–8; Jeremiah). When, however, the people experienced disaster and persecution *because* they were faithful (and it was precisely those who were most faithful to Yahweh and the law who experienced terror and tragedy), what conceptual options were available? In good commonsense logic, it seemed that God was either unwilling or unable to deliver on his promises. Augustine posed the question in terms a thoughtful child could understand:

> God either will not destroy evil, or he cannot.
> If he can but will not, is he good?
> If he will but cannot, is he God?

For the apocalyptists, to believe in a God who was himself somehow victim of circumstances, who wanted to help his suffering people but was unable, was a denial of faith in God as the creator and the Almighty, that is, a denial that God was God. (Note how often the themes of God as the creator and God as the Almighty occur in Revelation!) In the apocalyptic worldview, the reality of present evil is not denied, but it is not the last word. The world is a story of which God is author, director, and main character, and the story is not over. The author will bring it to a worthy conclusion. For the apocalyptists, the evil of the world is too big to be merely of human doing and too big to be overcome by human effort. Apocalyptic is a way of holding on to the faithfulness of God.

Three Key Characteristics of Apocalyptic Thought

We have already noted several features of apocalyptic thought, such as vision reports and the use of bizarre symbolic language. Here we call attention to three further features: the imminence of the coming end, the dualistic language of demons and angels, and the prevalence of violent imagery. None of this was invented by the prophet John or other early Christians. They lived in the symbolic universe provided by their Bible and the Jewish apocalyptic thought world they inherited.

The End Is Coming Soon

There is one God who is ultimately in control and who will bring all evil powers, human and otherwise, to account in the great judgment to come. In the meantime, however, these evil powers who know that their time is limited continue to perpetrate evil in this world. For apocalyptic thought, the intensification of evil experienced in the present world is itself an indication that eschatological salvation is near. For the apocalyptists, the suffering of their own times was not random accident or blind fate but part of the plan of God. Theologians such as John did not begin with abstract questions or curiosity about whether there would be an end of the world but with the concrete reality of unjust suffering, and they placed it in a theological framework that offered hope and encouragement. The apocalyptic perspective allowed them to see the persecutions they experienced as part of the necessary struggles of the end time and revealed that the end was near. Apocalyptists typically did not make speculative predictions of the end of the world at some date centuries hence, which would have been of interest only to futurologists among their contemporaries, but addressed their own generation with the urgency of those who cry out for meaning in their own struggle and suffering. Their conviction that the end must be near was not calendrical calculation but the tenacity of faith, not speculative curiosity but the encouraging word that suffering believers only have to hang on for a little longer. Their question was not "When will the end come?" but "What is the meaning of our suffering?"

In Revelation, and Christian apocalyptic generally, this imminent expectation of the end was intensified and given reality and momentum by the conviction that the Messiah had already come, that his resurrection was the firstfruits of the general resurrection soon to come (1 Cor 15:20), and that harassment by their neighbors and sporadic persecution by the government authorities were the leading edge of history's dramatic conclusion. Thus the expectation that the return of Christ, the general resurrection and judgment, and the final establishment of God's love and justice in the new Jerusalem were near was not incidental to the theology of Revelation but was woven into the whole fabric of its message in a variety of ways (emphasis mine, of course):[12]

1:1	John's revelatory message declares in its opening words that the revelation concerns "what must *soon* take place."
1:3	The introductory blessing and exhortation are based on the conviction that "the time is *near*."
2:16	The risen Jesus warns those in Pergamum to repent, because he is coming *soon*.
2:25	The risen Jesus encourages the faithful at Thyatira to hold fast what they have "until I come." While no interval is specified before this "coming" is to occur, the word loses its function of encouragement to steadfast endurance if a long period is intended, and becomes utterly futile if a span of centuries is what is meant.
3:11	Similarly to the church at Philadelphia, "I am coming *soon*" functions as encouragement to faithfulness.
3:20	"Listen! I am standing at the door, knocking" is not only a spatial image for the church at Laodicea but also a temporal image often found in apocalyptic that reflects the shortness of time before the coming of Christ: *he is already at the door* (cf. Mark 13:29; Luke 12:36; James 5:9).

6:11	When the souls of the martyrs already in heaven cry out for God's eschatological judgment of the world and ask "How long?," they receive the response that they must wait only "a *little longer.*"
10:6	The mighty angel in the vision swears by the creator that there is to be "*no more delay,*" but that the "mystery of God . . . , as he announced to his servants the prophets," that is, the divine plan for the establishment of God's just rule at the end of history, is about to be fulfilled.
11:2–3; 12:6	The longest period mentioned in Revelation is this span of time described variously as forty-two months, or 1,260 days, derived from the period of three and a half years prophesied in Daniel 7:25; 8:14; 9:27; 12:7, 11, 12. This period became a traditional apocalyptic time frame (cf. Luke 4:25 and James 5:17 versus 1 Kings 17:1; 18:1). While there is no reason to think John took the period as a literally exact definition of how much time remained before the end, there is also no reason to interpret it in terms of generations or centuries, as the context in each instance makes clear.
12:12	The evil that John's churches are suffering will intensify, in John's view, because the devil "knows that his time is *short.*"
17:10	There are to be seven "kings" altogether, and John and his hearer-readers live in the time of the sixth. While this passage is difficult to interpret, it is clear that in John's view *only one more "king"* (= emperor) is to reign before the eschatological events begin.
22:6	The angel declares that the preceding visions reveal "what must *soon* take place."
22:7	The risen Christ declares "I am coming *soon.*"
22:10	In contrast to Daniel, which was composed in the literary form of a document written centuries before the events with which it deals were to take place, and then sealed until the appropriate time, Revelation is not to be sealed, "for the time is *near,*" that is, it deals with events of the time in which it is written.
22:12	The risen Christ declares (again!) that he is coming *soon.*
22:20	"Surely I am coming *soon*" are the last words from heaven John hears, forming a frame with the "soon" of 1:1.

This imminent expectation is not peculiar to Revelation but is shared by much of the New Testament (e.g., Mark 9:1; 13:30; 1 Cor 15:51–52; Phil 4:5; 1 Thess 4:13–18; 1 Pet 4:7). When the end did not occur as expected, the various books of the New Testament include a spectrum of responses. Learning to deal with this apocalyptic expectation in Revelation allows us to join the preachers and teachers of the New Testament who dealt with this theological issue in more than one way, and with refreshing honesty.

Angels, Demons, and Penultimate Dualism

Revelation emphasizes that God is the Almighty, the sole ruler of the world. Otherwise he is unworthy of the name "God." Yet the terrible evil that continued unabated in the present world of the apocalyptists' experience meant to them that God could not be directly in control and could not be charged with direct responsibility for the world's evil. Rather, on the basis of ideas already present in the biblical and Jewish traditions, the apocalyptists inferred that God had delegated aspects of the rulership of the world to angelic beings, some of whom misused their power, became demonic, and will themselves be punished in the great judgment to come. This was already a traditional idea generations before New Testament authors began to interpret the Christ event (cf., e.g., 1 En 10:4–5, 11–14; 12:4). Such thinking may seem bizarre to us, but it had long been traditional for the New Testament authors (cf., e.g., 1 Cor 6:3, Jude 6; 2 Pet 2:4). John did not invent these ideas but found them as part of the apocalyptic thought world in which his theology is embedded. They do not represent some sort of fascination with the occult. Such apocalyptic imagery was useful in that it allowed John to accept the reality of radical evil without ascribing it directly to God and without giving up on God as the ultimate power of the universe whose love and justice will finally prevail. In the meantime, we human beings live our lives at the intersection of two conflicting and overlapping force fields. But the story is not over.

Thus apocalyptic thought is "dualistic" in that it typically deals with God and angels on the one hand, and Satan and demons on the other, with human beings living their lives between the "already" of God's act in Christ and the "not yet" of the final coming of God's kingdom. Human experience and responsibility are real, but they are seen in the context of the cosmic struggle between God and the powers of evil.

Such dualism functions with only two categories. Everything is good or evil, truth or lie, black or white, with no shades of gray. Apocalyptic dualism divides all humanity into insiders and outsiders, saved and lost, those destined for the city of God or those destined for the pits of hell. Just as the final exam is entirely yes/no, true/false, with no essay questions, no "undecided," "don't know," "doesn't apply to me," or "none of the above," so the ultimate grade book has only "pass" or "fail."

Apocalyptic dualism is not confined to Revelation. Throughout the New Testament, Christian theology is expressed in alternatives.

- God and Satan: Matthew 4:10; Acts 10:38; 26:18; Romans 16:20; James 4:7; 1 John 3:8, 10
- Saved or Lost: 1 Corinthians 1:18; 5:5; Ephesians 2:5; 2 Thessalonians 2:15; Hebrews 10:39
- Flesh and Spirit: Galatians 3:3; 4:29; 5:17; 6:8; Romans 8:4–13; John 3:6; 6:63; 1 Peter 3:18
- Life and Death: John 5:24; Romans 5:17, 21; 6:4, 23; 8:2; 2 Corinthians 4:12; 1 John 3:14
- Insider and Outsider: Matthew 12:46–50; Mark 3:31–32; 4:11; Luke 13:25–27; 1 Corinthians 5:12–13; 14:16, 23–24
- Above and Below, Heaven and Earth: Matthew 21:25; John 3:31; 8:23; Colossians 3:1–2; James 3:15
- Light and Darkness: Matthew 4:16; 10:27; Luke 1:79; John 1:5; 3:19; 8:12; 12:35, 46; Acts 26:18; Romans 2:19; 13:12; 1 Corinthians 4:5; 2 Corinthians 4:6; 6:14; 1 Thessalonians 5:5; 1 Peter 2:9; 1 John 1:5; 2:8–9
- Faith and Unbelief: Matthew 21:32; Mark 9:24; Romans 11:20; John 3:12, 16–18; 10:37–38

Even when specific dualistic terminology is not used, some of the most beloved and powerful scenes in the New Testament are expressed in bipolar dualistic imagery: in the teaching of Jesus as presented in the Gospels, there are only the two ways, one that leads to destruction and one that leads to life (Matt 7:13–14), and at the last judgment Christ will divide sheep from goats, saved from damned (Matt 25:31–46, which concludes, "And these will go away into eternal punishment, but the righteous into eternal life"). There is no neutral place to stand, where one can survey the options and decide which, if any, to take. *One always already stands someplace*, already is under the power of something. To be human is already to be on one side or the other (see the "either for me or against me" of the synoptic Jesus in Mark 9:40; Matt 12:30; and Luke 9:50 and 11:23). We preachers cannot avoid the dualism inherent in New Testament theology by ignoring Revelation. But from Revelation we can learn how to interpret such dualistic tendencies with authenticity and power, wherever we find them.

This dualism is not ultimate or ontological. Unlike the dualism of Iranian Zoroastrianism, Platonic and Neoplatonic philosophy, and the various streams of Gnosticism, dualism is not inherent in being itself. The forces of good and evil are not locked in an eternal struggle, so that good spiritual people are called to be on the good side. In the faith of Israel and the Bible, there is one God, the creator. The dualistic split in the universe is not between the eternal forces of good and evil. There is only one who is eternal, and biblical dualism is an aspect of the holiness of God, the difference between the creator and all else. In terms of the history of the universe, evil is temporary; its days are numbered. The numbering of the plagues in Exodus and Revelation means they are not endless but limited. Only the eternal life of the dawning new age is endless. Numbering is a sign of hope. Evil has no independent existence, nor is evil a united front against the one God. The beast turns on the whore and devours her (Rev 17:16–17). Rome the great consumer; Rome, which made conspicuous consumption its chief virtue, is finally self-consumed (18:1–24). Evil is selfish, is divided against itself, is finally self-destructive. This does not mean that evil automatically self-destructs. The one God is active in judging and destroying evil. All things are ultimately in one hand, a hand that is gently guiding history toward its omega point in which God will be "all in all" (1 Cor 15:28). The universe is a story, and the story is not over. Believers live in the tension between the already and the not-yet:

NOW: Christians live in two force fields, God/Satan; THEN: Satan destroyed in lake of fire.
NOW: Light and darkness; THEN: no night there.
NOW: Two cities, and the city churches of Asia must decide which is their model; THEN: Babylon destroyed, New Jerusalem descends.
NOW: Two women, the whore and the bride; THEN: Only the bride.

The outcome of the present struggle is not in doubt. The promises have not failed. The vanguard of God's apocalyptic victory has already entered our world of space and time (the Christian gospel is good news about an event, something that happened, not an idea, ideal, or theory). God has already raised up Jesus, and the general resurrection will surely come soon. God will still be faithful. If God's promises cannot be fulfilled in this world, he will bring the world as we know it to an end—not as a punitive gesture of cosmic frustration but as the transitional means of redeeming the whole creation. This is the reason for the apocalyptic emphasis on the future and for what is perceived as the "otherworldliness" of apocalyptic thought. The present situation is so unjust, and the righteous so powerless to correct it, that humanity's ultimate hope cannot be in ourselves but only in the act of God. In the meantime, we can each make a difference by responding to God's call to devote our lives to God's coming kingdom of love and justice, but the ultimate solution is in God's hands. "For from him and through him and to him are all things. To him be the glory forever. Amen" (Rom 11:36).

When the Gospel of John declares "For God so loved the world" (3:16), it is in step with apocalypticism's affirmation of the created world.[13] The apocalyptists are desperately holding on to the faithfulness of God to this world, which is his creation, rather than offering an otherworldly escape hatch—that's what John's "progressive" gnosticizing opponents wanted the church to do! The Gospel of John is very different from Revelation, but both books seem to operate within the same theological network, and on this fundamental point they are in agreement. The apocalyptists are indeed "pessimistic" about this world, but their "pessimism" is not ultimate. God's justice will prevail, even though there is no way in *this* world for it to prevail (except in relative and fragmentary ways that are not to be disdained). This is why apocalyptic thought emphasizes the resurrection and judgment in a transcendent world where the great balancing of books will take place, and why salvation is pictured as breaking into history from the transcendent world rather than arising from immanent good forces or our own efforts in this world. If there is to be redemption for the world, that is, if God is to be considered faithful, then it must come from God himself if it comes at all. The new Jerusalem is not built up from below but comes down out of heaven from God (Rev 21:2). We contemporary Christians who live in situations where we see manifestations of the good rule of God about us and have political and economic power that we can use to change some of the evil in this world can understand Revelation better if we remember that New Testament authors addressed a different situation. Apocalyptic is an expression of the faith of the politically powerless and oppressed in a situation where the empirical evidence of God's goodness was difficult to see. This is one reason why Revelation has continued to speak directly to the church in times and places where Christians with no political or economic power have experienced inhuman cruelty, such as the Nazi era in Europe or the church today in countries governed by oppressive dictatorships. Response to the message of Revelation is an expression of faith in the faithfulness of God in a situation that gives no indication of it in this world; it is faith's "nevertheless" when "therefore" makes no sense.

Apocalyptic is thus not a flight into otherworldliness. The trouble is, liberals and conservatives tend to divide reality between themselves. To oversimplify and overstate: conservatives have taken heaven, hell, and the other world; liberals have taken politics, economics, and the quality of life in this world. Revelation refuses to allow us to make this choice—as does the Bible in general. Revelation, like the Bible as a whole, emphasizes that God is the creator. God's world has been perverted, but God will not give up on the world. The God of Revelation condemns those who corrupt and destroy the world (Rev 11:18!), but he will not give up on this world or simply save a few faithful souls out of it into the "other world." God will renew the creation and will save the world, not just individual souls.

Revelation, like apocalyptic in general (and like the New Testament as a whole), does not call for direct political action to transform the world. The lack of political power in first-century Christianity, and its conviction that the end of history was coming soon, made this unrealistic in their situation. But in our setting, where believers do have political and economic power and no longer share the first century's apocalyptic calendar, the message of Revelation calls for an active stance in resisting oppression in this world, empowered by the sure conviction of God's ultimate victory.

Violence and Power

Apocalyptic is a violent genre. For many modern readers, it is not its first-century eschatology or demonology that makes Revelation difficult to hear as a revelation of God's love and justice, but its intensely violent imagery, mostly perpetrated by God himself, and against the cosmos, not just wicked human beings. This, however, is a problem throughout much of the Bible. But other biblical books have much else that we can accept into our own conceptual value system that allow us preachers to find helpful things to say without dealing with the framework of divine violence in which they are set. Consciously or not, we can overlook or hide from the divine violence there. In Revelation, we must meet the issue head-on.

Christian Adoption and Adaptation of Traditional Apocalyptic

Just as we preachers do not survey the possibilities offered by our situation and consciously decide to express our own views in the language and conceptuality of twenty-first-century American democracy, capitalism, and the post-Newtonian view of the universe, so New Testament writers did not look over the spectrum of theological possibilities and say to themselves something like "I think I will use apocalyptic thought to express our faith in God's act in the Christ event." Apocalyptic was a given element of the thought world in which they lived. While they mostly simply adopted this worldview as the framework, conceptuality, and vocabulary for expressing their faith, they also were selective and made intentional, crucial modifications. Their new faith controlled their inherited apocalypticism, not vice versa. Numerous nuances in the ways New Testament authors are already adapting traditional apocalyptic ways of thinking to their new faith will be explored later in this volume. A crucial conviction, common to them all, meets us in Revelation and calls for consideration up front.

In traditional Jewish apocalyptic thought, the eschatological events were near but still in the future. The earliest Christians believed that the Messiah had already come. What mattered was not that the resurrection of God's people was soon to come but that the one decisive resurrection had already occurred. They not only looked forward to the eschatological harvest but also back in their own immediate past to the resurrection that had already happened, and outward into the church and world where the eschatological realities were already being experienced. *Study of Revelation shows that the clear "someday soon" of traditional apocalyptic became for believers in Jesus as the Christ the tensive dialectic of already/not yet.*

Revelation Is a Church Document

We are all aware that in our times, numbers of sincere and serious people identify themselves as "followers of Jesus" but are hesitant to think of themselves as "church members." It sounds so non-Jesus, so institutional. "Membership" sounds too much like belonging to "organized religion," not enough like being a disciple of Jesus, whose opponents were mostly members of organized religious groups. One result of sustained engagement with the New Testament is that it wants to reshape our inherited, culturally conditioned understandings of what it means to say, "I belong to the church." Revelation, one of the most radical documents of early Christianity, wants to do this.

The first words of Revelation portray the God who speaks through the risen Jesus Christ, whose message to the church is delivered through the angel/Spirit to the prophet, whose message is read aloud to the church assembled in worship. Just as the prophets of Israel pronounced God's judgment on the unfaithfulness and transgressions of the covenant people, so the prophet John is aware of the failings of the church (Rev 2–3!). John is a church prophet, not merely an offbeat individualist. Like the prophets of Israel, he addresses the people of God with a word from God, and he does so from within the community of faith. He does not shout his message from across the street as an outsider. Though he sometimes has a lovers' quarrel with the church, he takes his stance within it and receives his authorization not only from God but also from the community of faith. Likewise, the people he addresses are not a collection of individual admirers or fans of Jesus who have decided, as an optional extra, to join the church. They are the community of Christian faith in continuity with the people of Israel, the church called into being and sustained by the Word of God. In later chapters we will think more comprehensively and deeply on the ecclesiology of Revelation and other New Testament documents, but here we reflect on the fact that Revelation is a document of the church, not merely of the individual John, and on the significance of interpreting Revelation as the composition of one who sees himself as a minister and theologian of the church. "Church" (*ekklēsia*) occurs twenty times in Revelation, more than in any other New Testament book except Acts (twenty-three times) and 1 Corinthians (twenty-two times). In addition, numerous images of the church occur without ecclesial vocabulary, such as "bride," "temple," "city," "Israel," and "saints."

Coming within hearing distance of the Bible will enable its hearers to read it in its context, which is the life of the church. This involves the church's worship, the church's canon, and the church's ongoing hermeneutical task as it listens for a contemporary word from God mediated by a collection of ancient and strange documents.

Revelation, the Church, and the Language of Worship

"Worship God" (Rev 19:10; 22:9). Revelation was composed to be read aloud, in its entirety in one sitting, in Christian worship. Blessing is pronounced on the liturgical reader and the worshiping hearers (1:3). The text is replete with the vocabulary, acts, hymns, prayers, sounds, and smells of worship.

Like our sermons, Revelation is not an objective, analytical theological essay but an address to a worshiping congregation. What is said is expressed in the context and language of worship, spoken *coram Deo*, in the presence of God, as prayer and praise. When Karl Barth declared, "The first and basic act of theological work is prayer,"[14] he did not mean merely that our theological reflections are pondered in a prayerful attitude, but that they are made before God. Preaching is in the personal I-Thou mode addressed *to* God, not the impersonal I-it mode in which God is talked *about*, as an object.

All theology has its living source in the liturgy. The language of worship is a distinctive linguistic genre, which dares to speak to and about God in God's own presence, a language that, without declining into nonthinking sentimentality, knows that the One addressed and in whose presence one speaks transcends all the boundaries of this-worldly commonsense logic. A worshiping community that celebrates the incarnation draws its life from the reality that the Absolute condescends to be spoken to and about in the fragmentary, relative language of this world, in our sermons, teaching, and conversation (see further pp. 200–204 below on John 1:1, 14). Revelation's language of worship opens several doors into biblical theology, three of which we mention here.

The Language of Worship Fuses the Temporal Horizons

Revelation, and biblical theology generally, understands the reality of the present to be the moving point on the line of history between past and future. The mighty acts of God in the past are real: God brought the world into being, God called Israel into being and made a covenant with them, God sent the Messiah, God called the church into being. The line of history moves toward the ultimate future reality, the consummation of God's purpose at the end of history. But for John, one does not merely look back to the past as once-upon-a-time nor forward to the not-yet future. Without dissolving the reality of the past or future, in the language of worship, past and future impinge on the present, and both become real. The prophet John can interchange "I, John" with "I, Jesus" (22:8, 16). The Jesus "back there" in history and the Jesus still to come at history's end speak in the living present. Revelation's language of worship is pervaded with eucharistic imagery (3:20; 22:17), and the book was regularly read (in toto!) during worship services in which the Eucharist was celebrated. Worshipers receiving the eucharistic bread heard the minister speaking in the first person *as* the living Christ, addressing the worshiper directly in the second person: "This is my body given for you."

This collapsing of temporal perspectives is typical of biblical language of worship. In the liturgies for Israel's festivals, a declaration of God's there-and-then act for the ancestors becomes the confession of God's act for the worshiper, as past-tense verb forms modulate into present-tense verbs in the same sentence (Deut 26:1–10). Later generations of Israel, who had not been in Egypt or at Sinai, are specifically enjoined: "The LORD our God made a covenant with *us* at Horeb. Not with our ancestors did the LORD make this covenant, but with *us*, who are *all of us* here alive *today*. . . . I am the LORD your God, who brought *you* out of the land of Egypt" (Deut 5:2–6; cf. also 1:6, 30, 35–40; 4:33; 26:5–9; 29:13–14). To accept Yahweh as one's God is to accept the story of God's people as one's own story, and to have one's present transformed by the past and future of this story.

So also in the Psalms, Israel's worship book. If, for example, one ponders Psalm 104, a hymn of praise that for thirty-four verses celebrates the goodness of God's creation, in this-worldly terms, the world of our everyday experience seems to be replaced by a different world. It is a totally good world in which human life can celebrate and rejoice—and it's good not only for humans. The high mountains, too high for human feet to tread, are for the wild goats, and those rocks high above human habitation are a refuge for the rock badgers (v. 18). Even the great sea monsters frolic in the oceans, and God enjoys watching them (vv. 25–26). There are no rose-colored glasses here. The psalmist looks the real world squarely in the eye, knows the reality of evil, and concludes with a prayer that looks forward to a time when sin, sinners, and wickedness will be destroyed. This implicit eschatology of Israel's worship language celebrates the new world coming, in which not only death but also predatory life will disappear.

> The wolf shall live with the lamb,
>   the leopard shall lie down with the kid. . . .
> They will not hurt or destroy
>   on all my holy mountain;
> for the earth will be full of the knowledge of the LORD
>   as the waters cover the sea.
> (Isa 11:6, 9; cf. Hos 2:18; Isa 35; 65:17–25)

Without hiding from the present evil world, Israel's prophets and psalmists celebrate what is/ought to be/will be as one reality given by God the creator and redeemer. This is what happens in the language of worship.

The Language of Worship Is Symbolic but Not a Code

As biblical interpreters, we preachers and teachers know that all language about the transcendent is metaphorical and symbolic, but in dealing with much of the New Testament, it is too easy to forget this and suppose that the language is simplistic-realistic. Some good preachers speak easily and powerfully about the "love of God" without realizing that this is symbolic language, a metaphor taken from human experience. Thus when faced with other examples of symbolic language such as sacrificial metaphors that interpret the meaning of Jesus's death, ascension imagery for portraying God's act that exalts the figure of Jesus to the transcendent world, or the powerful symbolic language of the "word of God," they may be inclined to ignore or reject it. Revelation keeps the reality of symbolic language constantly before us, allows us to experience the potency of images we had minimized or disdained, and opens doors into biblical theology we had not even noticed were closed.

Sometimes the strange language and imagery of Revelation have been "explained," fitted into our normal thought patterns or dismissed as something written in the language of "code," perhaps devised by John to enable only Christians to "get its meaning" should the document fall into the hands of Romans suspicious of the new Christian movement. This is a well-meaning but misguided approach to understanding the mysterious language of Revelation (and the Bible as a whole). Not only would it take a very dull Roman to miss the import of such statements as Revelation 17:9, 18, "The seven heads are seven mountains on which the woman is seated. . . . The woman you saw is the great city that rules over the kings of the earth," but such an approach misunderstands the nature and power of symbolic language as such. A code is a dispensable tool. A text written in code can be discarded once it has been decoded and the meaning is clearly stated in discursive language. On the other hand, a symbol participates in the reality it communicates and cannot be reduced to straightforward language. The mind-boggling image Revelation uses to describe the throne of God, as flanked by "living creatures, full of eyes in front and behind . . . all around and inside" (4:6–8), is not only more powerful than "clear" statements that those who approach God's throne know themselves to be seen from every direction but also more true than the lamely correct proposition "God is omniscient."

While much of biblical symbolism is transcultural and universally human (light and water as life-giving symbols, darkness and thirst as symbols of deprivation and evil), the Bible is basically oriented to the particularities of human history. The incarnation is the paradigmatic example, bringing the absolute God into the relativities of fleshly human existence (John 1:1, 14). Though all cultures have a symbolism of evil, the particularity of biblical theology is illustrated by the symbol of Satan, prominent in the New Testament as a whole but unavoidable in Revelation. Responsible interpretation calls for interpreting, not ignoring or discarding, such language. Even Rudolf Bultmann, hermeneutical champion of the last century, understood the interpreter's task of demythologizing biblical texts not as rejecting or peeling away their mythological husk to get at some kernel of eternal truth that can still be preached in the modern world, but as affirming and interpreting them in ways that allowed their original intent to challenge the conventions of every time and place. He saw value and meaning in the Satan myth (still expressed in the gendered language of the previous generation): "The conception of Satan as ruler over the world expresses a deep insight, namely the insight that evil is not only to be found here and there in the world, but that all particular evils make up one single power which in the last analysis grows from the very actions of men, which form an atmosphere, a spiritual tradition, which overwhelms every man. The consequences and effects of sins become a power dominating us, and we cannot free ourselves from them. Such language is metaphorical."[15] Symbolic language can function at multiple levels in a way that is frustrating to interpreters who are concerned that truth be communicated in terms of consistent, linear logic. The interpreter cannot simply catalogue the "possible meanings" of Revelation's symbols such as the woman clothed with the sun, with the moon under her feet (12:1); 666 as the number of the beast (13:18); the Lamb and 144,000 followers on Mount Zion (14:1); the twenty-four elders before the heavenly throne with their white garments and golden crowns (4:4); and the sealed scroll that is opened—then eaten by the prophet (5:1–13; 10:1–11). Such symbols must be interpreted, but they cannot mean just anything. They are not Rorschach ink blots that merely reveal the subjectivity of the viewer, but they can mean more than one thing, and all their meanings together cannot be added up and expressed in clear, discursive language.

Such language is not merely a linguistic or conceptual puzzle that can be decoded into our normal language. The symbolic language of the Bible mediates the reality of a new world that is already breaking in. We—preachers and hearers alike—tend to like our present world and to welcome new insights and increments of inspiring information that can be incorporated within its framework. The language of symbol and myth presents a theological and existential challenge that we tend to resist. We naturally want (i.e., our myth calls for) crisp categories, such as insiders and outsiders, who belongs to each, and how one transfers from one group to the other. Biblical pictures mess up our categories, tamper with our conceptual framework, and subvert not merely what we think but how we think. When they hear authentic biblical preaching, outsiders recognize this. Though they may not be able to articulate it, outsiders perceive the threat to their world and respond accordingly. This is not merely a modern phenomenon, "secular humanism's" opposition to religion. Already in the first century, when the Roman historian Tacitus wrote that Christians, who did not worship at the state altar, were "an enemy of the human race," he did not mean merely that he did not like Christians and found them a nuisance, but he rightly perceived that they were a *threat* to decent humanity, the good and wholesome society provided by the general culture and conventional religion.[16] Long before, Plato had decided that poets would have to be banished from the ideal republic. We, too, want things to be neat, sometimes for sincere religious reasons. We may want to know clearly who is in and who is out so we can know where we stand, or so we can be in and our enemies be out, or for academic and intellectual reasons: we want to explain the ancient documents in categories that make sense to us, to show that by our standards their inconsistencies were the result of confused logic or a combination of sources. Either way, our standards remain intact, and we subject the Bible to them. Precisely this is the decision we have to make when confronted by biblical texts, whether a parable of Jesus, a letter of Paul, or a vision of Revelation: Will we use biblical data to serve the mythological worlds we and our congregations have created, or will we let the Bible shake the foundations of our own domain as the new life, structures, and map of the biblical world emerge in and around us?

We preachers and our Sunday morning hearers, church committee members, and counseling conversation partners want the language of faith and the Bible to be orienting, to bring clarity to our fog, and to provide a firm and clear framework to help us sort out the confusing world around and within us. The good news is, there is a sense in which the Christian faith communicated by biblical theology does precisely this. But for God's new world to dawn on and in us, the old world we have constructed—that is, for the most part unconsciously accepted from our culture—must pass away; it's not the real world anyway. *This* is what we resist about the biblical message when we begin to realize that biblical language often *dis*orients us rather than resolves our logical problems. The pictorial, mythical language of the Bible is disorienting not because it presents bizarre scenes and images foreign to our modern rational thought world but because biblical myth presents a challenge to the conventional mythological framework within which we are accustomed to live. This is indeed scary. Revelatory scenes in the Bible often begin with "Fear not . . ." (Rev 1:17; sixty-four times in the Bible, including the announcement of the coming of the Messiah, Luke 1:13, 30). Much of the Bible is amenable to our lust for clarity, and we can fit it into our way of thinking without too much pushing and shoving. This is more difficult to do in Revelation, but entering with fear and trembling into its strange new world can lead us to a more authentic biblical theology. Understanding Revelation the worship book—that is, being grasped by its symbolic language—needs not only the library and the study but also the sanctuary, hymns, and prayer.

The Insider Language Reaches Out

We mainliners are rightly uncomfortable with exclusiveness, celebrate unity-in-diversity, and like to look forward to God's kingdom in which all divisions are overcome. We speak uneasily, or not at all, of fellow Christian believers as "insiders" and others as "outsiders." It sounds exclusive, smug, even arrogant. In Revelation, John challenges—perhaps annoys—us with his dualistic insider/outsider language and imagery (Rev 3:20; 7:1–8; 9:4; 11:12; 13:17; 20:4; 22:15). Yet such language is not peculiar to Revelation. John gets it from his (and our) Bible. It is the language of grace and election, the language of God's gracious choice. It is biblical language, used by Jesus, Paul, and others (Mark 3:31–32; 4:11; 1 Cor 5:12–13; Col 4:5; 1 Thess 4:12; 1 Tim 3:7). The reality of Christian discipleship is that in responding to God's call, by confession and baptism, we have stepped across a line—more biblically, have been moved across a line—that most human beings in the world, who are also God's beloved creatures, have not crossed (not *yet*!). Like it or not, we are insiders in a peculiar community, called to care for outsiders as God does, and that means not withholding our testimony from them.

The language of worship is insider language, as is the language of the New Testament. All the New Testament documents are addressed to insiders, presupposing the Christian confession. Explicit address to outsiders first occurs when the second-century apologists such as Justin begin to address the "cultured despisers" of Christianity in their own terms. In prayer and praise insiders speak to God; they speak to each other in sermon, instruction, and conversation. Outsiders are welcome and overhear the insider language of the worshiping congregation. In the hymns, Scripture, and prayers of worship, everyone, insiders and outsiders, overhears the worship of other congregations, through the centuries and around the world. John's first-century audience hears not only the direct address of the risen Christ to their own congregation but also overhears the whole series of messages intended for the whole church (Rev 2–3). Yet more: they were struck by the mode of communication in which the words of the risen Christ are not spoken directly to the congregation but are spoken to the "angel" of each church. Communication takes place on a transcendent level, and the congregation listens in on a word that is over and beyond them, though intended for them (2:1, 7, 8, 11, 12, 17, 18, 29; 3:1, 6, 7, 13, 14, 22). This, too, John learned from his Bible. In Isaiah 40:1–2, the imperatives that ring forth from the throne of God, "Comfort, O comfort my people, says your God," are plural imperatives, addressing the angelic beings of the heavenly council, "overheard" by the earthly congregation, who could not bear direct, head-on confrontation with the divine Word (cf. also, e.g., Exod 19:7–25; Deut 5:22–33; 1 Kings 22:19–22).

Although the church's worship and confession are directed to God and to insiders, the language of worship has an external, outward orientation as well. Worshiping Christians are not fashioning rational arguments for outsiders about why they should come to church or become Christian believers, nor are we formulating general appeals for ethical living. The basis for such a life is Christian faith that outsiders do not (*yet*!) share. The church does not have a market mentality, asking what prospective buyers want to hear and meeting them on the level of their conscious criteria. In the acts and words of Christian worship, the church confesses its own faith and encourages faithful believers to act on their common faith, but it does not withdraw into isolated cells to celebrate its own spirituality. In worship, the church speaks to God and itself in its own language derived from its Bible, but the church is always aware that it worships and lives in the midst of the world, God's world, and always has the outsider in its peripheral vision, shaping the insider language of its worship, preaching, and teaching in such a way that outsiders overhear both the reality and consequences of such faith.

Revelation, the Church, and the Canon of Holy Scripture

John, and John's church, had a Bible. Revelation is not merely a report of heavenly visions and auditions, it is a claim to communicate the call of God that comes through the church's Bible. After considerable dispute, Revelation, saturated with biblical phrases, allusions, and imagery, was itself finally accepted by what became mainstream Christianity as Holy Scripture. Today we cannot buy a Bible authorized by any church that does not include Revelation, and readings from Revelation are included in every lectionary. We receive the Bible, as we receive ordination, from God, but through the hands of the church.

Beginning our study with Revelation also forces the issue of canonical location. The church placed Revelation at the conclusion of the whole canon. We can hardly imagine Revelation anyplace else, for in no other biblical book do the grand themes of the whole biblical tradition converge so powerfully in the direction of God's eschatological future. In the Bible, understanding is always both retrospective and prospective, a matter of both memory and hope. Beginning with Revelation makes us aware of an important dimension of every New Testament text.

Beginning with Revelation thus inescapably poses the question of the relation of canonical Scripture to our preaching and teaching, as well as issues of whether or to what extent we consider ourselves ministers of the church or independent entrepreneurs of religion. "Do you preach from the Bible?" is of course not a yes-or-no question, but setting out the polar extremes may help us think through our own position, what we see ourselves doing when we preach or teach from a biblical text. On the one hand, we can begin with the Bible as somehow mediating the word of God—the broad range of theories of inspiration and authority is not so important for present considerations—and our task is to facilitate a hearing of this word by the congregation. At the other pole, we can have our own convictions about what is true and right and what it means to be a follower of Jesus, and we can find points of contact and support for our convictions in the text, or from time to time even suppose that we must "preach against the text." We may thus find it easier to preach from, say, the Gospel of Luke than from Revelation. We preachers, from both the right and the left of the theological and political spectrum, can rather handily use Luke as the backboard against which we bounce our own point. With Revelation, not so much. Revelation forces the issue of our "use" of the Bible, rather than listening to it, giving us the opportunity to perceive the array of biblical texts as canon, not cafeteria.

Revelation is itself an example of biblical preaching. The book was written to be understood in continuity with the Scriptures and presupposing them. The author understands himself and his prophetic colleagues in the church as standing in the line of the biblical prophets and presents his book to be read in church alongside them, and with the claim to represent the word of the same God who speaks and is spoken about in Scripture. Revelation is not merely a report of heavenly visions and auditions but is a claim to communicate the meaning of the church's Bible. There was, of course, no New Testament in John's time, but the church has never been without a Bible. John's own mind and heart are saturated with the Scriptures that were repeatedly read in the church's worship. The author's mind is wallpapered with them, floor to ceiling. Expressing his faith in biblical imagery and vocabulary, he writes for people who "know their Bible," that is, who are thoroughly acquainted with the Scriptures of Israel, now also the church's Bible. John had apparently grown up in the synagogue and had heard the Bible read in worship his whole life, but churches in Roman Asia were Greek-speaking, peopled by mostly gentile Christians. These churches had existed for a generation or more, and their members too had heard the Bible read regularly in worship and had internalized its vocabulary and imagery. The language and images of the Bible had become their own; many had grown up hearing this language as their native tongue. John speaks to them in the biblical language of the church. Yet John and his hearers do not live in a Jewish or biblical world but in the Hellenistic world of the Roman Empire. Their heads and hearts are at home in the linguistic world of biblical faith, but their feet are on the ground in the cities of the first-century Roman province of Asia. John writes to Christians in Ephesus and other cities, adopting vocabulary and imagery from their everyday world as well (theater, drama, economics, politics, including imperial worship). His prophetic message confronts his hearers with another, strange world, the world of their Bible. For both preacher and hearers, knowing the Bible was presupposed as necessary for understanding the meaning of Christian faith and life and what it called for in their critical situation. Here I give only three brief illustrations of dozens of possibilities.

In Revelation 15:5, the vision reveals the "temple in heaven." John's Hellenistic readers were already acquainted with temples aplenty, earthly and heavenly. But Revelation immediately identifies this temple with the "tent of witness," that is, the biblical tabernacle of the exodus wanderings, just as the "ark of the covenant" had already been seen in the heavenly temple (11:19). This temple, then, is not one of the typical temples they saw every day. To people who know the Bible, the language evokes the story of Israel. As John writes, tabernacle and temple have been destroyed and the ark of God's covenant with Israel has been lost—in this world, that is.

John's vision reveals the startling reality that the biblical temple and ark that represented and made real God's presence and covenant with his people still exist. This is a powerful expression of hope to those who know the biblical narrative of the covenant people of God and have learned to see their lives as embraced within that story. John doesn't pause to explain what all this means. Those who know the Bible will get it. Others may have some catching up to do. This is analogous to the speeches of Martin Luther King Jr., which included references to key texts in American history as well as many biblical allusions. People were moved by his rhetoric, but for them to grasp the depth of what he said in his "I Have a Dream" speech, its allusions had to reverberate in their souls. When he began with "Five score years ago, a great American . . . ," they had to already know something of Lincoln's Gettysburg Address and the Civil War to recognize the powerful subtlety of what King had done with it. He did not explain, but presupposes it. People either got it or they didn't.

In Revelation 2:14, 20, the prophet warns against the teaching of "Balaam" and "Jezebel" current in the churches, assuming that the warning will have impact among those who know the biblical stories of false prophets and their supporters. In 11:3–10, the two witnesses that represent the prophetic church strike the earth with plagues and call down fire from heaven. The imagery speaks to those who know the stories of Moses and Elijah—true prophets both, though they were rejected—but is lost on those for whom the language of the Bible had not yet become part of their lifeworld.

A particularly telling example is given in John's promise that if the hearers are faithful they will rule their enemies with a rod of iron and shatter them like a potter's vessel (Rev 2:26–27). Such words not only have no appeal but may even be repulsive to those who remember that Jesus taught us to love our enemies. But John writes for those who recognize this as imagery of the Messiah's reign from Psalm 2:9, a reign his followers will share, and who understand that the meaning of "reigning" is now transformed in the faith that the Messiah has come and is the crucified and risen Jesus of Nazareth.

In all this John never once specifically cites a biblical reference. But the text of Revelation is peppered with intertextual allusions to the Scriptures of Israel now adopted as the church's Bible too—about five hundred allusions, an average of ten per page in the current edition of the Greek text. No doubt, much of this simply went over the heads of many listeners in the churches of Asia as John's apocalypse was read forth in the congregation—just as many of

Martin Luther King's listeners didn't get "five score years ago." Neither King nor John dumbs down or flattens out his message in the interest of marketing or "relevance." Both aimed high, challenging people to lift up their heads, and many did and do.

An aside: this means that to understand Revelation (or any New Testament book), we preachers must know the Bible, including the Old Testament, not merely as a reference book but in such a way that its language, images, and cadences have infiltrated the symbolic universe in which we live. This in turn requires that we regard comprehensive Bible study as a major component of our ministry, even when we are not preparing a sermon or lesson—reading the Bible, getting our minds around Deuteronomy as a whole, Isaiah as a whole, *especially* when we are not preparing a particular sermon or lesson. Regular, extensive reading of Matthew as a whole, without a specific immediate purpose, allows the Bible to present its message in terms of its own agenda, allows the reader to live for a while in the biblical world rather than being an occasional tourist. Being a tourist in another country with a different language and culture is not of course bad in itself. It can be both fun and educational. Such tourists may be inspired by the interesting things they see in the foreign land through the windows of the tour bus, listening to the tour guide lecturing in English, but they may tend to (mis)understand them within the framework of their own country. (It goes without saying: sojourning in the biblical world is not an alternative to living in the "real" world of our own time and place but is being a resident alien in the comprehensive world that embraces/encompasses it.) The point here, however, is that we preachers and teachers in the church need to be more than tourists; we are called to be tour guides, which requires getting off the bus and going into the country's own language and culture, that is, within hearing distance of what its voices have to say. Such tour guides will have an effect on tourists, will model the difference between tourists and biblical sojourners aware of the church's message and mission.

This also means that a significant part of the job of preachers and teachers in the church is to develop a biblically literate congregation. This responsibility can't be fulfilled in a Sunday or two, nor in a year or two. It requires an extended ministry with the same congregation and is aided by modeling such biblical understanding in preaching—not by parading one's own knowledge of the Bible or scolding people for not knowing much about it but by preaching on the assumption that the congregation gets the biblical allusions, even though some may have to be briefly explained with an introductory "as you know . . ."

Revelation, the Church, and the Bridge from There-and-Then to Here-and-Now

The church is called to *interpret* the message it hears from its Scripture, first to itself, but always with its mission to outsiders in view. Such listening requires *interpreting in context.* This, of course, is a no-brainer—the littlest child on the premises knows that every text must be interpreted in its context. Yet with most biblical books it is relatively easy to lift a meaty text from its biblical setting, attach some inspirational, nonthreatening thoughts to it, and preach a sermon people like and even find helpful. The content of such sermons may in fact represent valid biblical theology from other parts of the Bible or solid Christian theology from the insights of the church through the centuries. But the sermon may have little to do with what *this* text wants to say. Exhibit A in this regard: in preaching from a gospel text, as far as the sermon is concerned, preachers and teachers sometimes consider it irrelevant *which* gospel the text is from. A healing-the-blind-man story can provide the point of contact for a moving sermon without representing what Matthew, Mark, Luke, or John wanted to say; the parable of the sower can be preached without attention to the theology of Matthew, Mark, or Luke, or how parables work in each gospel. Most New Testament books include a few snappy one-liners that could serve as the launchpad for a sermon. Not so in Revelation, where it is clear that *understanding* any text means grasping and being grasped by the book as a whole. The same is true, of course, of Deuteronomy and Matthew (not to mention *Hamlet* and *Gone with the Wind*), but in those texts we can nonetheless find brief sections useful for our purposes. This is not so easy with Revelation. Like a good movie, and about the same length (1 hour and 20 minutes of reading/hearing time), Revelation's effect is the way it works as a unit. The power of any individual text depends on its mediating the whole. Matthew can be divided atomistically into usable parts, but not Revelation. Having learned to understand a text in Revelation, we can handle Matthew and Deuteronomy more authentically.

A helpful exercise for preacher and congregation: arrange for a group or the congregation as a whole to come together in a worship setting. After a hymn ("Holy, Holy, Holy" [Rev 4:8!] wouldn't be a bad choice) and prayer, listen to the whole of Revelation read by a good reader or readers without dramatics or comments. Not only Revelation, but the Bible as a whole, will never sound the same after that. Snippets will be disdained, and even when short sections are read and talked about, the larger context will hover in the background.

"Interpreting in context" also includes, of course, the contemporary context of preacher and hearers. Everything looks different, depending on where we stand. Both writer and readers of Revelation belonged to a minority group, suspect, often shunned, and sometimes persecuted by both neighbors and local officials. John had been banished to Patmos. He expected others to be jailed and threatened with the death penalty (Rev 2:10). At least one member of the Asian churches had already been killed (2:13). Most of us preachers rightly try to identify with the marginalized, disenfranchised, and oppressed, and in Jesus's name try to help not only as individuals but also as system-changers in a society that sometimes tends to keep them down and out. In our preaching we encourage our hearers to see this as part of what it means to follow Jesus. But we inevitably and necessarily do this, most of us, from a privileged position and have to work at remembering the difference between our own context and the text's, and how to bridge this distance at least partially. John did not have to work at this. Revelation is written from the underside of society, from the outside looking in, and can help us see what the world and life from this perspective look like. Listening to John's prophetic word will make us better interpreters of the New Testament as a whole—all of it emerges from the underside and social outsiders—but Revelation is a good place to start.

It is crucial to remember that Revelation is a letter, as are twenty-one other New Testament books. This means they are not essays addressed to whoever might be interested, but each one addresses a particular group of early Christians that shares a common history with the author. This also means that they were not written to us. Does this mean, as Charlie Brown famously remarked, that when we read the New Testament we are reading someone else's mail? With no double-talk intended, "Yes and no."

Revelation (and each of the other New Testament books) was not written to us. We do not live in Ephesus, Smyrna, Perga, Thyatira, Sardis, Philadelphia, or Laodicea, just as we do not live in Corinth, Thessalonica, or Rome. Understanding Revelation may be difficult (as is understanding Matthew or 1 Thessalonians), but one sure way to misunderstand this, or any other, biblical book is to read it as though it directly addresses us and our situation. Its apocalyptic language and imagery did speak directly to threatened and sometimes persecuted Christian believers near the end of the first century in Roman Asia. They did not need a weekly Thursday night study group on "biblical prophecy" in order to understand it. It was addressed to them, and they understood it. The question was whether they would accept its transforming message and live by it.

Imagine this scene. Five years after the church in Ephesus had received their copy of John's letter, as it is read regularly in their worship, several new members who were not members of the church when the letter was originally received hear it read. The crisis the letter addresses has passed, and the church faces new and different problems. The new members in Ephesus notice that John's letter addresses a lot of other churches in which they have no personal involvement, and they wonder why they should care what the Spirit says to the congregation in Laodicea, for example. The new members may not understand, and are perhaps even repelled by, the letter's apocalyptic language and imagery. "Who is Antipas?" "What's this 'mark of the beast'?" "And how about this business of the world coming to an end? And soon?" Will the older members of the church say something like, "Don't worry about it. Prophet John's letter once spoke an encouraging word to us when we were facing a difficult situation, but that was then and this is now—and John's letter is not addressed to you anyway. You didn't even belong to the church then!" No, of course the church does not say this about Revelation or any other book that has become part of its sacred Scripture, whether the question is raised five or five hundred years later. Even though these books were addressed to various situations in history through which God has led his people, whoever becomes a member of this community of faith is still addressed by these texts. Precisely because we belong to the church, these texts that were not written to us were actually written to us.

Understanding biblical texts is another matter. From the very beginning, the Christian community exercised the responsibility and authority to continually interpret these texts for new members, new times, new situations. It did not enter each new culture and each new generation with a blank slate or a few general principles to be applied, but with a collection of canonical texts in which it had heard and continues to hear the word of God, interpreted by authorized leaders who stand with the whole church in a dynamic tradition. To belong to the church is to participate in an ongoing community of interpretation that facilitates renewed understanding, empowerment, and action.

Having opened the door provided by Revelation as the entrée to biblical theology, we will now devote our efforts to becoming more familiar with the core theology of Revelation itself.

Chapter 2

The Revelation of Jesus Christ and the One True God

Revelation is about God. Those who dip into the Bible for the first time are sometimes surprised that it's not about rules for living, principles of success, finding my center, or inspiring thoughts for daily life. Lamentably, even sincere readers have sometimes plodded through the Bible in bits and pieces without grasping or being grasped by what the Bible is about.

Revelation is about God. The letter is not about politics, sociology, economics, or psychology. It is not even about religion. Neither is it about Christology, ecclesiology, soteriology, or eschatology. It's not about us, not about me. But one cannot come within hearing distance of the God of the Bible without having one's previous ideas of politics, sociology, economics, and psychology shaken up and transformed. And the biblical doctrines of Christ, spirit, salvation, church, and the end of history are not stand-alone topics that can be explored independently. Understandably, theology textbooks mostly treat these as separable topics for pedagogical purposes, but at least since Thomas Aquinas, classical Christian theology has rightly considered them all to be subheadings of theology proper, the Christian understanding of God.

AUTHOR: An otherwise unknown Christian prophet named John—not the apostle John nor the author of the Gospel of John.

DATE: Circa 95 CE.

ADDRESSEES: Churches in the western part of the Roman province of Asia.

PROVENANCE: Patmos, an island in the Aegean about forty miles from the mainland.

LITERARY SOURCES: The only identifiable sources are the Jewish Scriptures. The book includes earlier apocalyptic traditions, Jewish and Christian, interpreted through the author's prophetic experience.

This is immediately apparent in the first sentence of Revelation. The opening phrase of the titular summary presents God → Christ → Spirit → Church → World as one interrelated "chain of command" (1:1–3). As Revelation was read aloud during the worship services of the congregations of Roman Asia, neither John nor the congregations for whom he wrote experienced what was happening as "God told Christ, who told the angel, who told John, who tells us." God is the one and only ultimate source of revelation, yet the revelatory and saving act of God is mediated to the world through Christ, the Spirit, and the church. The One who was, is, and is to come (1:4, 8) always speaks in the living present in which we ourselves live. Diachronic thinking, which proceeds as though each of these terms refers to a separate subject, cannot do justice to the transcendent, synchronic reality to which it refers. God/Christ/Spirit/Church/World are so interwoven in Revelation's language and imagery that to think of any one of them necessarily involves thinking of them all. We may come to good insights by discussing each member as a separate topic using the traditional rubrics of systematic theology—Revelation's doctrine of God, Christology, ecclesiology, etc.—as is done in many valuable New Testament theologies, but Revelation's own theological modus operandi is to present a visionary narrative in which these themes are fused and continually reemerge. The following sections will discuss Revelation's core theological affirmations in this mode, exploring the ways key theological themes are interwoven in the five major sections of the text:

Revelation 1	*Christological Monotheism*
Revelation 2–3	*The Churches and the Church of the Living God*
Revelation 4–5	*The Mission Control of the Universe*
Revelation 6–18	*History's Pageant of Violence, Divine and Human*
Revelation 19–22	*The New World Coming and Already Here*

Revelation 1—Christological Monotheism

Revelation is about God, the one true God, the one and only God. Word statistics do not always tell the theological story, but in this case they are a helpful pointer. What follow are the names, titles, and phrases used for God in Revelation:

- God (*theos*) is found 96 times (versus Christ [*Christos*], 7 times; Jesus [*Iēsous*], 14 times; lamb [*amnos*], 29 times; spirit [*pneuma*] for the Holy Spirit, 23 times).

- Idol (*eidōlon, eidōlolatrēs*) is found 5 times, always with *plural* reference.
- God is the Eternal One "who lives forever and ever" (4:9; 7:12; 10:6; 15:7).
- God is the One "who is and who was and who is to come" (1:4, 8; 4:8, [cf. 11:17], in each case distinguished from Christ and the Spirit/seven spirits of God).
- God is the Alpha and the Omega, who not only creates the universe and brings it to a worthy conclusion but is himself Beginning and End (1:8; 21:6; clearly distinguished from Christ and Spirit).
- God is the Sovereign One "seated on the throne," the sole ruler of the universe (5:1; 7:15; 21:5).
- God is the creator, absolutely distinguished from the creation, not dependent on or conditioned by any other powers (3:14; 4:11; 5:13; 8:9; 10:6).
- God is the Lord God Almighty (1:8; 4:8; 11:17; 15:3; 16:7; 19:6; 21:22), clearly distinguished from Christ and the Spirit.

Revelation does not directly cite any text of Scripture, but it could not be more clear that the author stands in the biblical-Jewish tradition in which the people of God passionately insist on worshiping the one God as expressed in the Shema: "The LORD our God is one LORD" (Deut 6:4). Jewish believers in the one God—men, women, and children—have died rather than compromise this monotheistic, exclusive faith. John is no muddled thinker who might occasionally think of the God of Israel as numbered among the other gods, not even as their superior. Like his Bible and his Jewish tradition, he thinks of the heavenly world as populated by a host of angels and transcendent beings, but he never confuses them with the one true God. John goes out of his way (twice!) to have the revelatory angel clarify precisely this point. Only the one God can be worshiped (Rev 19:10; 22:8–9). The "revelatory chain of command" with which Revelation begins presents the revelation as from and about Jesus Christ, but God is the ultimate source (1:1; "God" is the acting subject, in the nominative case, with "Christ" in the genitive). The risen Christ distinguishes himself from God, speaks of "my God" (3:2; emphatically, four times in 3:12). Revelation is about God. God is one. There is only one God.

And yet. The reader of Revelation is immediately struck by the way this Jewish Christian monotheist talks about (and to!) Jesus Christ.

1:1a The first words of the letter to be read forth in the churches are "the revelation of Jesus Christ." The revelation ultimately comes from God, but

God gives it to the church and the world through Jesus—the human being Jesus of Nazareth. Jesus is a human name, the Greek form of the common biblical name Joshua, the personal name of five different people in the Bible, a name often found in first-century Judaism. The first-century Jewish historian Josephus knows of twenty different individuals named Jesus. The New Testament lists a man named Jesus in the genealogy of Jesus of Nazareth (Luke 3:29), and the early church had a leader named Jesus (Col 4:11). The author of Revelation speaks of the man known as Jesus as the truly human one, who shares a human name and human life with us, who is one of us in the common denominator of our most human experience—he dies a human death. The first words of the risen Jesus include "I died" (Rev 1:18; cf. already 1:5, "firstborn of the dead"). He is the one who was *pierced*, who redeems by his blood (1:5, 7; 5:9; 7:14; 12:11; 19:13; cf. John 19:34–35). In calling for his followers in the churches to be faithful to death (Rev 2:10), he is asking them to follow the path he himself has taken, for the one who speaks to them in Revelation is the one who stood before a Roman governor and offered his testimony not only with his words but also with his life (1:5; 3:14; cf. 2:10, 13; 6:9). It is God's word heard in the voice of Jesus. In speaking and hearing the revelatory word, the one true God and the truly human Jesus merge into one.

1:1b This revelation is "to show his servants what must soon take place." To whom does "his" (*autou*) refer? To ask whether they are servants of "God" or "Jesus Christ" is already to be off on the wrong foot. So also in, for example, John 3:16: "For God so loved the world that he gave his only Son, so that everyone who believes in him may not perish but may have eternal life." To ask whether "believes in him" refers to "God" or "his only Son" is to ask the wrong question, which already leads away from the characteristic modus of New Testament theology, forcing it into our "clear" and "consistent" categories. This undomesticated ambiguity continues throughout Revelation. In the closing words of 22:3–4, the images of God and Christ merge, as in the opening words of 1:1: "The throne of God and of the Lamb will be in it, and *his* servants will worship him; they will see *his* face, and *his* name will be on their foreheads." To ask "Whose servants? whose face? whose name?" is already to fail to grasp the dialectic of biblical theology.

1:2 John "testified to the word of *God* and to the testimony of *Jesus Christ*, even to all that he saw." John's testimony is singular, not divided into two categories. As is clear from John's usage elsewhere (1:9; 6:9; 12:11; 20:4), "word of God" and "testimony of Jesus Christ" here refer to one and the same thing.

1:4, 8 John has referred to the one God in the solemn formulas "who is and who was and who is to come" and "Alpha and Omega," but he does not hesitate to have the risen Jesus Christ use the same formulas to refer to himself (1:17; 22:13, 16).

1:4a The seven spirits of God, the fullness of God's Spirit, are present before the throne. In 3:1 it is the risen *Christ* who has the seven spirits of *God*.

1:4b "The coming one" is identified as God (1:8), and Revelation's theocentric theology never ceases to resonate with the promise that the creator who stands at the beginning of human history is the one that all creation will meet at the end, the one who "makes all things new" (21:5). But "the coming one" is Christ (1:7; 2:5, 16, 25; 3:11; 16:15; 22:7, 12, 20), and the church's prayer is "Come, Lord Jesus" (22:20). The church's final prayer is answered: the coming of Christ at the end is the coming of God. Christian monotheism is Christomorphic, but it is theocentric, not Christocentric.[1]

1:12–20 John describes the epiphany of the risen Christ on Patmos in language and imagery drawn from a variety of biblical texts portraying angels and the transcendent world, including language and imagery used exclusively of God. The dazzling white hair is taken from the "Ancient of Days" in Daniel 7:9. The risen Christ speaks in language appropriate only to the one God of Israel, saying "I am" in a manner that recalls the divine name: "I am the first and the last, and the living one" (Rev 1:17–18; Isa 44:6: "I am the first and I am the last; / besides me there is no god"; 44:8; cf. 45:5, 6; 48:12, 17; Exod 3:13–15; falsely claimed by Babylon/Rome, Isa 47:8; cf. Rev 18:7). In the Ephesus of John's day, Rome/Babylon claimed what only God could claim, "I am, and there is no one besides me," language that is reflected in Revelation and the Gospel of John.

1:17 Most importantly, John is struck down by the majesty of Christ's appearance and falls before him in stunned adoration. Only God may be worshiped. Even transcendent beings from the heavenly world refuse such adoration, with the curt command "Worship *God*," recalling the opening words of the Decalogue (Rev 19:10; 22:8–9). But Christ is worshiped not only by John and earthly beings but also in the heavenly world (5:13). Not only in this opening vision but throughout Revelation, the risen Christ is spoken about in ways that belong only to God. If in the Scripture God is the shepherd and Israel is the sheep, in Revelation Christ is the shepherd. If in the Scripture God is bridegroom and Israel is the bride, Revelation concludes with a grand vision of the marriage supper of the Lamb, and the church is the bride.

Something is wrong here, terribly wrong, unless Christ somehow shares the reality and being of the one God. Revelation gives no explanations of "how" (*pōs*; see p. 264 below) this is legitimate, but in prayer and praise, in mind-stretching, category-shattering verbal imagery, John proclaims the God who has definitively revealed the divine being and character as inseparably bound to the revelation of the truly human Jesus Christ.

Revelation 2–3—the Church of the Living God, Warts and All

The revelation of Jesus Christ carries with it a disclosure of the reality of the church.

The Human Church of God

Without any transition (chapter divisions come much later!), at Revelation 2:1 the author goes directly from the disclosure of God's act in Jesus Christ to messages to and about the church. Humanly speaking, the little Christian communities of Asia are vividly, terribly real to both John and his readers. The congregations are not an optional accessory to these Christians' individual faith, but the encompassing human setting of their fragile and threatened lives. The divine-human reality of the church of the living God is not apparent to human eyes and common sense, whether sympathetic or cynical.

Revelation prevents our idealizing, idolizing, or absolutizing the church of John's day or ours. The congregations John addresses are like the churches we know from our own experience. They include sincere, good, loving people committed to doing the will of God, who remain steadfast to the faith even under duress (2:2, 13, 19; 3:8, 10). Some in the church are poor, experiencing social rejection and hostility, unaware of the abounding riches that are theirs (2:9). Others are wealthy, blissfully unaware of either their true poverty or the threat that looms over them (3:17–18). The church includes preachers and teachers of authentic Christian faith, just as it includes false teachers, false apostles, false prophets, and those who support and listen to them (2:2, 6, 14–15, 20–21). The church we know is a mixed bag of human beings, capable of profound good and abysmal evil. We know the human aspects of the church, especially we who have served as its ministers, teachers, leaders, and there-every-Sunday faithful workers. The church of 96 CE Roman Asia, like the church of every time and place, is a truly human church, addressed lovingly by the warnings and rebukes of the living Christ (3:19), who says in each of the seven messages to the whole church, "I know."

That the church is more than this is another matter. There is a mystery (cf. Eph 1:9; 3:4–6, 9–12; 5:32) to the people of God not available to observation, whether casual or serious, but only by prophetic revelation (Rev 1:12–13, 20; 10:7; 17:5, 7). John's letter to the churches claims to reveal not only the identity of Christ but also the readers' own identity, the true nature of the church to which they belong.

In John's prophetic vision, the risen Christ, who walks in the midst of the churches, holds seven stars in his right hand, which are the seven angels of the seven churches (1:20). Though the message addresses the truly human church and its earthly struggles, the risen Christ directs each message not to the earthly hearers but to a transcendent, heavenly being, the *angel* of each church (2:1, 8, 12, 18; 3:1, 7, 14). Worshipers in the congregations in Asia learn that the church has a counterpart in the heavenly world, that what goes on in Ephesus and Smyrna is talked about in heaven, that each of the little groups of Christian worshipers somehow already participates in the life of God's transcendent world. John here reflects the theology of his Bible. When the prophet of Isaiah 40 speaks the message of hope to despairing exiles in Babylon—the "Comfort ye, comfort ye my people" with which Handel's *Messiah* begins—he portrays God as addressing the heavenly beings. Little Israel, in mighty Babylon, learns that heaven itself resounds with the divine message, "overheard" by the troubled congregations. In Daniel, suffering Israel learns that the people of God have a heavenly counterpart, a kind of guardian angel, who takes their part on the cosmic stage in which struggles of inconceivable proportions are being fought out (Dan 10:13). Some of the congregations to which John's message is directed may be too impressed with the reality of angels, even to the extent of worshiping the heavenly beings (cf. Col 2:18). John rejects such tendencies not by denying the existence of angels but by considering them partners with human ministers in the service of God (cf. Col 2:18; Rev 22:8). John utilizes this prophetic and apocalyptic imagery of the heavenly hosts of angels to communicate the transcendent dimension of the people of God.[2]

When the church gets to see John's vision of the heavenly world, it may be stunned to recognize itself included in the picture. Blended with the praises of the heavenly beings around the throne (4:1–5:14) are the prayers of the saints on earth (5:8). They hear a hymn that includes them, for the risen Christ is praised:

"by your blood you ransomed for God
saints from every tribe and language and people and nation;
you have made them to be a kingdom and priests serving our God,
and they will reign on earth." (5:9–10)

Even more mind-boggling: the Messiah's followers, along with the whole universe, join in worship of the one seated on the throne (5:13; 7:9–17; 14:3), yet this throne is shared not only by Christ but also by *his followers*, who somehow participate in the divine rule, sharing the throne of God and Christ. They already participate in God's coming kingdom, sharing God's throne in the same way as Jesus Christ, by being "faithful witnesses" and by "conquering"—by giving their lives in faithfulness to God (1:5–6; 3:21; 5:1–7). As followers of Jesus, John and his readers are not only destined to participate in the final coming of God's kingdom for which they pray, but they already share "in Jesus" not only his tribulation and patient endurance but also his rule (1:6, 9; 5:10; 20:6; 22:5; cf. the startling imagery in Eph 2:6, in which believers are already enthroned with Christ in the heavenly world). The startling good news of the gospel is that Jesus is already king though crucified. The image of believers sharing the divine throne is not a picture of future reward—"Be a good Christian and you'll get to sit with Jesus in a snazzy big decorated chair in heaven." Jesus's followers in the church already share in the kingdom that is present though hidden, the rule of God manifest in this world in the form of the cross. The Christian life is a tension-filled unity of tribulation and kingdom (Rev 1:9), which will yield at the eschaton to the purified kingdom of God. Within this framework of understanding, the Christian life is marked by "patient endurance," that is, tenaciously holding on to the faith in the glad confidence that Christ's lordship in which Christians participate is real, though at present invisible to empirical observation.[3]

In 6:9–11, the persecuted martyr church is given a vision of the heavenly worship that includes "under the altar the souls of those who had been slaughtered for the word of God and for the testimony they had given." The grim reality is that they were killed in this world—mothers and fathers, wives and husbands, children and parents, leaving behind their loved ones who wonder if it was the right thing to do, if it was worth it. Revelation lets them see that this truly human company of believers already participates in the reality of the divine world. This is not the Platonic idea that the true church is the idea/ideal of the church that exists in the heavenly world, of which the little congregations in Perga, Thyatira, and Tuscaloosa are only imperfect shadows in this material world. In the theology of Revelation, God affirms the material world of flesh and blood. The church's primary existence is in this world, to which the bride and heavenly city shall descend at the end (21:2–5). The church in this world does not go up to join the heavenly church; the communion of saints that already exists is consummated by the heavenly church rejoining the church on earth (as in 1 Thess 3:13; 4:13–18). But this *not yet* is fused with the *already*: the this-worldly church participates in the divine reality, the followers of Jesus share the throne of God. As in Acts 9:4, to persecute the church is to persecute the living Christ. As in Matthew 25:31–46, to act with compassion for the needy people of this world is to serve the living Christ. Paul had pictured the church as the continuing body of Christ on earth. This ecclesiology was being developed in the Pauline tradition of John's time, with the church's body on earth but its head in heaven (Col 1:18; 2:19; Eph 5:23); Ephesus was a center of this theological tradition, with which the author of Revelation was in dialogue. Though John does not use "body of Christ" terminology or conceptuality, he pictures the human church on earth as more than merely human—as the people of God, it participates in the divine reality. We preachers and church folk could never have realized our true identity by looking around the congregations or within our individual selves.

> But, as it is written,
> "What no eye has seen, nor ear heard,
> nor the human heart conceived,
> what God has prepared for those who love him"—
> these things God has revealed to us through the Spirit; for the Spirit searches everything, even the depths of God.
> (1 Cor 2:9–10 [written from Ephesus!])

The Biblical-Jewish People of God and "Synagogue of Satan"

John himself is a Jewish Christian; most of the members of the churches to which he writes are gentile Christians who are more or less aware of the church's Jewish roots. In this they are a microcosm of the church as a whole, through the centuries and around the world. Revelation reaffirms and deepens their identity as members of the ongoing people of God represented in the Bible and historical Judaism.

This is seen first in their name: as Christians (*Christianoi*, Messiah people), they affirm that the hope of the Jewish Messiah has been and is being realized in Jesus of Nazareth, the Jewish Messiah. Though the word "Christian" does not occur in Revelation, it was becoming the name by which Jesus's followers in the church were identified (cf. Acts 11:26; 1 Pet 4:16 [circulated in Asia!]), the name that distinguished them from both Jewish and gentile religious groups. Church members are suffering because they wear this name, the name associated with God's own holy name, because they confess that Jesus is the Christ (Rev 2:3, 13; 3:8; 14:1; 15:4).

Revelation attests the biblical-Jewish identity of the church in the way the Jewish Scriptures are used. The Scripture texts themselves modulate from narrating the mighty acts of God in the past to contemporary address. "They" becomes "you" or "we" (Deut 5:1–5; 26:5–10; Josh 24:2–13). As John's letter was repeatedly read aloud in their worship services, the first hearers realized that they were being addressed with the assumption that they themselves had been incorporated into the story portrayed in the biblical language and imagery projected by the letter. Whether it came as a revelatory shock or a gradual and almost subconscious insight, church members realized that they had accepted the biblical story as their own, that they had been embraced in the story of Israel that began in the Bible and continued into their own world, that they were guests in the house of Israel, adopted into the people of God they read about in the Jewish Bible that had become their spiritual home too. Whether sudden or gradual, this was a genuine conversion of the imagination, as their old world was replaced with the reality of a new symbolic universe. *Biblical narrative is not so much interested in information as in transformation.*

This is not a flight from the "real world" in which readers of the Bible live their everyday lives. Revelation constantly reflects the actuality of the Hellenistic world and Roman imperialism, and those who heard it read in church and had their minds shaped by its imagery recognized the political and economic realities they had to negotiate every day (e.g., Rev 13:1–18; 17:9, 18). The risen Christ says, "I know where you are living, where Satan's throne is" (2:13); the readers daily experienced the reality of this world. But the bulk of John's imagery is drawn from his Bible, so that the church is called to recognize and define itself not merely by the culture, either in accommodation or resistance, but in this biblical story.

The heavenly glory of the throne room scene (chaps. 4–5) is painted with a blend of colors taken from the biblical-Jewish palate: synagogue, Scripture, temple, altar, sacrifice, elders, hymns of praise. A close reading reveals the following parallels:

Revelation 4:2–3 // Pss 11:4; 103:19; 104:2; Ezek 1:26–28
Revelation 4:4–8 // Exod 19:16; 1 Chron 24:7–18; Isa 6:2–3; 24:23; Ezek 1:5, 10, 13, 18, 21–22; 10:12, 14; Amos 3:13 LXX, etc., "the Lord God Almighty"; Zech 4:2; 6:11
Revelation 4:9–11 // 1 Chron 29:11; Dan 4:34; 6:27 (Theodotion); 12:7; Wis 1:14; Sir 18:1
Revelation 5:1–5 // Gen 49:9; Exod 20:4; Deut 5:8; Isa 11:1, 10; 29:11; Jer 32:10–11; Ezek 2:9–10; Dan 12:4, 9
Revelation 5:6–7 // 1 Kings 22:19; 2 Chron 18:18; Ps 47:9; Isa 6:1; 53:7; Jer 11:19; Zech 4:10; Sir 1:8
Revelation 5:8–10 // Exod 19:6, etc.; Pss 141:2; 144:9; Isa 53:7; 61:6
Revelation 5:11–14 // 1 Kings 22:19; Dan 7:10; 1 Chron 22:10–11; Ps 146:6

As John's letter is repeatedly read in worship, the biblical imagery projects a world the worshipers recognize from their Bible, a story in which they are now included, as those redeemed by the blood of the Lamb that "ransomed for God saints from every tribe and language and people and nation" (Rev 5:9). The visionary world of Revelation places the worshiping congregation in continuity with Jerusalem, where their Lord was crucified, on their way to the re-created holy city New Jerusalem (3:12; 11:8; 21:2, 10)—the plot of universal history assumed by Augustine's *City of God*.

The troubles the world is enduring and will endure from the Roman emperor, shared by church and world, are represented as the plagues of the exodus, the righteous and liberating acts of God. The same kind of detailed comparison between the eschatological plagues described in Revelation 6–16 and God's judgment by the plagues on Egypt in Exodus 7–14 pictures the church as the continuing exodus-people of God. Just as Israel celebrated its deliverance in the grateful praise of the Song of Moses on the banks of the Red Sea (Exod 15:1–21), the eschatological people of God addressed in Revelation, ancient and contemporary, sing "the song of Moses, the servant of God, and the song of the Lamb" (NRSV), celebrating the final victory of God over the forces of evil (Rev 15:3). The "and" (*kai*) here is epexegetical, equating the Song of Moses and the song of the Lamb, as translated in the NIV, "the song of Moses the servant of God and the song of the Lamb." One song is sung, not two; the praise of the first-century church and the biblical people of God is one song that joins past and present, heaven and earth.

The numerous occurrences (twenty-eight!) of "twelve" and "twenty-four" explicitly point to the twelve tribes of (restored, eschatological) Israel and the twelve apostles of the apostolic church, the combination indicating that these are one people of God (4:4, 10; 5:8; 7:5–8; 11:16; 12:1; 19:4; 21:12, 14, 22:2). Likewise, the 144,000 redeemed, dwelling securely, surrounded by walls 144 cubits thick, are multiples of twelve. In this vision of the ultimate future, Israel and church are on the road to the city of God to which all history is going, and they will ultimately be united as one eschatological people dwelling with God in the new Jerusalem.

John's vocabulary for the church is drawn from the Bible's declarations about Israel, the people of God. "Church" (*ekklēsia*) is used twenty times in Revelation, which number is exceeded in the New Testament only by Acts (twenty-three times) and 1 Corinthians (twenty-two times). Etymologically, *ekklēsia* means those "called out" to be a separate community. As is the case with his other imagery for the church, John fills in the content of the word *ekklēsia* from his Bible, where the word often refers to Israel, those delivered from Egyptian oppression and constituted the holy people of God (100 times in the LXX, always representing the Hebrew *qahal*, e.g., Deut 4:10; 31:30; Ezra 10:8; 2 Chron 6:3). The LXX also uses *synagōgē* (synagogue) in this sense, but John never uses this term for the church. In his time and place, the "parting of the ways" between Judaism and the church was under way or had already occurred; believers in Jesus as the Messiah were no longer a group within the synagogue, but John's address to them as *ekklēsia* encourages them to see their identity as the continuation of the people of God they read about in their Bible.

Ekklēsia is also a hermeneutical bridge word with deep roots in gentile culture. It was used in classical Greek tradition and Hellenistic culture for the assembly of full citizens of the city-state, where decisions were made that shaped the political and economic life of the city. In Roman times, such assemblies still functioned but were supervised by and responsible to the provincial authorities responsible to Rome (cf. Acts 19:21–41, esp. vv. 39, 41, where *ekklēsia* refers to the local assembly in Ephesus that could act only with Rome looking over its shoulder). Such assemblies did not include everyone, but only full citizens with property and voting rights. John, in using *ekklēsia*, is of course aware of the political connotations of the term, to which it poses an alternative. Most of John's audience had presumably never been accepted as members of the local political assembly, but now all of them (men and women, free and slave, Jews and gentiles of all peoples and languages) belonged to an alternative assembly representing the true Ruler of the universe (Rev 4:1–5:14). In claiming their biblical identity, members of the church were the called-out ones, the holy ones, the saints set apart from society in general, business as usual.

This separateness is also represented in John's other favorite word for the church, "the saints," *hagioi* ("holy ones," "saints"), used fourteen times in Revelation, always in the plural when referring to the church (e.g., 5:8; 8:3; 13:10; 14:12; 18:20, 24; 22:21). "Holy," of course, does not connote "sanctimonious," but separate, different, other. As the Holy One, God is the wholly other, the creator, *different* from every created being. As with *ekklēsia*, so with *hagioi*, John is in the tradition of Paul and the early church in identifying the communities of Christian believers by a key biblical term that had been used of Israel (Exod 22:31 ["people consecrated to me"]; Lev 11:44; 19:2; 20:24–26 ["You shall be holy to me; for I the LORD am holy, and I have separated you from the other peoples to be mine"]; Num 16:3; Pss 16:3; 34:9; 68:35 [LXX 67:36, "Admirable is God among his saints; the God of Israel, he will give power and strength to his people"]; Isa 4:3; Dan 7:18, 21–22, 25; 8:24). The use of the word in Daniel, written to a persecuted community, found particular resonance in John and his churches.

John portrays the church as the holy community with a particular vocation: it is a *priestly* community. Every member is a priest (explicitly so designated in Rev 1:6; 5:10; 20:6). Although biblical Israel had priests who served the community in a special way, every Israelite was a priest. All Israel was called to be a holy, priestly community in the world, representing God to the world and the world to God. In the text to which John alludes, God declares to Israel: "Now therefore, if you obey my voice and keep my covenant, you shall be my treasured possession out of all the peoples. Indeed, the whole earth is mine, but you shall be for me a priestly kingdom and a holy nation" (Exod 19:5–6). God's concern for the *world* is built into the biblical understanding of Israel and church as a priestly community. The "priesthood of all believers" does not mean "I don't need a priest, I'm my own priest." We do need other members of the community to pray for us, and we are to serve as priests for others and for the world. The "priesthood of all believers" means "I belong to the whole community of priests, who, like biblical Israel, are intercessors before God who offer sacrifice on behalf of the world." The sacrifice they offer is themselves (Rev 6:9; Rom 12:1–3). All the world, and everyone in it, is already God's world and God's people. But within the whole human community, all of whom are beloved creatures of the one God, the creator has called forth a holy people to be God's witnesses in this world, even to suffer on its behalf (Servant Israel in Isa 53!). To belong to the church now means to enter into this vocation of Israel. Christians are not the only ones saved; they are the priestly community that prays for the world, offers sacrifice on behalf of the world, representing and mediating God's salvation to the world. They are not those who sacrifice to the emperor but are those who sacrifice themselves on the transcendent altar (Rev 6:9). The death of martyrs such as Antipas (2:13)—in John's vision, the first of many to come—is not a meaningless or futile act of resistance but a priestly sacrifice. Cross-like, the earthly executioner's block is the heavenly altar (6:9–11). Israel's priests were a special class who had to consider their calling more important than even family ties (Deut 33:8–11). This was not fanaticism; it was part of their identity as priests. Identifying all Israel as a priestly community acknowledged that confession of faith in the one true God took priority over all other commitments, and many faithful Israelites had given their lives for this confession. John addresses his readers as belonging to the priestly people of God, eschatologically renewed Israel (cf. Mark 3:31–35; John 12:25; Luke 14:26–27; 1 Pet 2:5, 9). In John's vision, church members in Asia (and Berlin, Bangkok, and Baton Rouge) see themselves as participants in a transcendent liturgy, purified and clothed in the holy garments of priests that allow them to be in God's presence (Rev 3:4–5, 18; 6:11; 7:9, 13–14) and to mediate God's salvation to the world.

True to form, John does not "explain" all this in a theological essay but presents verbal-visual pictures in which the church is incorporated into the ongoing biblical-Jewish people of God. The most dramatic of these is the drama that unfolds in the hearer's imagination as 12:1–13:18 is read forth in the church's worship. Before reading further in this book, we contemporary readers might well pause and thoughtfully read or listen to these words, letting the scene detonate and ricochet across the stage of our own imaginations.

A woman appears in the sky, clothed with the sun, with the moon under her feet, wearing a crown of twelve stars. John calls this a *sign* (12:1). It is not an allegory, but its features conjure up images already deeply embedded in the psyche of the hearer. The astrological and mythological imagery is familiar to everyone in the Hellenistic world (who are familiar with Zeus, Leto, Python, Apollo, etc.), but for those whose imaginations have been reshaped by their Bible, the woman is Jerusalem/Zion/Israel, the people of God, the bride/wife of Yahweh. Later rabbis, perhaps already in John's time, regarded Israel as a transcendent reality created before the sun and the moon. The woman of John's vision is an earthly reality, delivered from Egypt and made into the historical people of God, the Israel who has endured the ups and downs of a tumultuous this-worldly history. The earthly people of God have a heavenly counterpart; they participate in God's transcendent reality. The woman wears the crown that symbolizes the twelve tribes of restored, eschatological Israel, already experiencing the promised eschatological sovereignty. The pregnant queen is in the final stages of labor; the promised Messiah is about to appear (12:2). The Messiah comes from Israel—salvation is of the Jews (Rom 9:4–5; John 4:22)—he comes from the heavenly world *and* comes from the people of Israel. Cosmic evil is threatened, on the way out, and awaits this final challenge. Intensified for the ultimate struggle in these eschatological times, the present world-ruler—a.k.a. the Dragon, the devil, Satan, the primeval snake, the accuser—also wears crowns (Rev 12:3, 9). As the woman labors to bring forth, the personified power of evil awaits to confront and destroy the one who challenges his dominion, the one who will restore God's sovereignty to the creation. His weapon is death. Christian readers then and now think of Herod and Bethlehem, of Pilate and Jerusalem, and of believers through the ages who have been faithful witnesses at the cost of their lives. Even though the unthinkable happens—the promised Messiah is killed—he is not destroyed but is taken up by God to God's throne.

Satan's last-ditch effort to hold on to his control did not succeed. He killed Jesus, but Jesus-the-faithful-witness is vindicated, raised, and installed as ruler not only of planet earth but of the cosmos. Thwarted in his efforts to destroy the Messiah, already defeated on the cosmic stage (12:7–10), the devil does not give up. If the Messiah cannot be destroyed, the woman, now pictured in this world, can still become the victim of Satan's power of death. She flees to the wilderness, like Israel fleeing from the pharaoh. The earth, God's good creation, is not neutral in this conflict and comes to the aid of the woman (12:14–15). But the woman has other children; the Messiah has brothers and sisters who remain in this world though the Messiah now reigns in heaven. These saints include the faithful Jewish people, their martyrs, and the followers of Jesus who remain faithful to God, as he did (12:17). As a contemporary of John wrote, Christian people should not be surprised at the fiery ordeal they are facing, for they have been incorporated into the holy people of God, and this is their calling (1 Pet 4:12). The churches of Asia receive a revelation of their identity that John claims is valid for all time: to confess Jesus as the Messiah is to belong with him to that biblical-Jewish people of God called into being to be God's witnesses in this world, which means to take one's place in that grand company, already participating in the reality of God's world, that resists all other claims to ultimate sovereignty. "Salvation is from the Jews" (John 4:22).

Once we have become aware of the New Testament's insistence that the identity of the church is imbedded in the biblical-Israel-Jewish people of God, sensitive Christian readers may be startled to find the following in Revelation, cited as the words of the risen Christ:

> "I know your affliction and your poverty, even though you are rich. I know the slander on the part of those who say that they are Jews and are not, but are a synagogue of Satan." (Rev 2:9)
>
> "I will make those of the synagogue of Satan who say that they are Jews and are not, but are lying—I will make them come and bow down before your feet, and they will learn that I have loved you." (3:9)

Such harsh language must not be glossed over, but neither should it be too quickly accepted nor explained away. In later sections of this book and subsequent volumes in this series, we will ponder such texts more carefully in reflecting on 1 Thessalonians 2:14–16 and statements about "the Jews" in Matthew and John. Here, historical considerations enable us to hear such language in its context.

In the first century, such invective was characteristic of religious debates, including inner-Jewish polemic.[4] Jews took the claim to belong to the people of God very seriously. Some Jews who regarded other Jews as having no right to make that claim were reviled as traitors, children of the devil, and the like. Without compromising their convictions, later generations have (sometimes) learned to express them in ways that do not vilify or demonize others.

Jews in Revelation's time, as in New Testament times generally, lived a precarious existence in a hostile world. Two centuries before, in Maccabean times, they had shed their martyr's blood in resisting imperial powers trying to destroy the Jewish faith. While anti-Jewish prejudice remained, most Jewish communities had convinced the Roman authorities that they were a loyal and stable element in society, not attempting to overthrow the government. Yet in John's time, the Zealot movement in Palestine had rebelled and been crushed by the Roman army, generating fresh suspicions against local Jewish communities (70 CE). The Arch of Titus that memorialized the Roman defeat of the Jewish rebels can still be seen, on the Via Sacra just outside the Roman Forum. As John writes about twenty-five years later, the aftermath of the war understandably produced severe problems for local synagogues that included Jews who believed the Messiah had come, the crucified and risen Jesus, and who spoke of the kingship of Jesus and the coming kingdom of God. The problem became even more critical when these "messianic Jews" admitted gentiles to the holy community without requiring them to become Jews. Such tensions eventually resulted in the separation of synagogue and church. So long as Christians remained within the synagogue, they enjoyed the same kind of toleration from the government as did the Jews. When Christian groups separated or were expelled—generalizations should be avoided on this historical point—it became important for synagogue leaders to point out that "they're not us, they're not Jews." Christians, on the other hand, both gentiles and ethnic Jews, saw themselves as in reality belonging to the continuing biblical-Jewish people of God, sometimes claiming *they* were the "true Israelites." This was by no means only to remain under the umbrella provided by their presumed status as Jews but was the identity instilled in them by the Christian message, their baptism, and their understanding of the Scriptures of Judaism now adopted and reread from their new perspective. Such a self-understanding reversed the Jewish charge against them. "Jew" continues as a good and valued title for the people of God, but, in the ugly polemical language of the day, they charged their accusers who rejected their testimony to Jesus as the Messiah as not really being Jews. Since, in the apocalyptic dualism often inherent in such language, one either belongs to God or the devil, such synagogues are "synagogues of Satan." Such polemical language, used by some Jews against other Jews, was not anti-Semitic or anti-Jewish. It expressed a deep theological conviction. It gave rise to later tragic events. While historical study makes it understandable in its own context, no use of such language by contemporary interpreters can be justified or excused. "Salvation is from the Jews" (John 4:22).

Little Churches, the Big Church, and Church Growth

The congregations to which Revelation is addressed were little churches. We don't know how many Christians were in the world at the end of the first century CE, but a typical estimate is that, in an empire of perhaps seventy million, there were about forty thousand Christians. If the average population of the cities addressed by John's letter was about seventy thousand, this would mean those cities might have forty Christians each—two house churches of about twenty members each. In Ephesus, a city of about two hundred thousand in John's day, there may have been eighty or ninety followers of Jesus in three or four different house churches in which his letter was read. It is difficult to imagine belonging to such a tiny group, so insignificant in such a large, bustling city. In first-century Ephesus, we would leave the eucharistic service celebrated in the living room of someone's home in the evening of a day not a public holiday and walk out into the busy street, past the soaring temples to Caesar and the traditional Greek and Roman gods—including the Temple of Artemis (Diana), one of the Seven Wonders of the World—mingle in the crowds on our way to the magnificent theater that seats twenty-four thousand, with its splendid view of the harbor, and think of our little congregation. Small potatoes.

We saw in the preceding chapter that the church participates vertically in the transcendent world of God and horizontally in the history of Israel, the people of God. We now can see that these little congregations also participate laterally in the worldwide and future church. It's a big church, destined to be bigger, and finally to be all-encompassing. This, too, is not apparent to casual observation but requires a revelation. We might now pause and read Revelation 7, not resisting the incredible vista it presents to our imagination, challenging and enabling church members to see the church as it really is from the God's-eye view, in the worship mode of is/ought/will be.

Four angels stand on the four corners of the earth. While no one today takes this literally, the vision portrays a worldwide event. God's servants are *sealed* (7:2), which the Roman church a little later understood as baptism (Shepherd of Hermas, Vision 3.7.3; cf. 2 Clem 7:6; 8:6), and which was probably already so understood in the Pauline tradition current in the churches of Revelation (cf. 2 Cor 1:21–22). In the tense situation of threatened persecution, followers of Jesus in Asia were tempted to keep a low profile, have their own personal "spirituality," and not publicly identify themselves with the emerging "institutional religion" visible in the churches. Baptism was a public event that identified Jesus's followers with a visible social reality. John's vision pictures them as sealed by a heavenly act.

Here, the important point is that those sealed belong to a worldwide community, and there are a *lot* of them. To modern ears, the number 144,000 may not sound so huge, but it tells the little congregation of eighteen members in Perga that they belong to an enormous multitude. The 144 is of course the square of 12, twelve tribes and twelve apostles (cf. Rev 21:12–14, the new Jerusalem incorporates the foundational figures of Israel and church). This is multiplied by 1,000, the largest number available in Greek—there were no designations for "million," "trillion," etc., which were expressed by multiples of 1,000. John looks to see the 144,000, already a huge number of believers, and what he sees is an innumerable congregation without borders or limits. The already-vast 144,000 Israel-Jewish-church turns out to be "a great multitude that no one could count, from every nation, from all tribes and peoples and languages, standing before the throne and before the Lamb" (7:9). They wear the priestly stoles of the people of God, purified, in God's temple, waving the palm branches as those who celebrate the festivals of God's saving acts (Lev 23:40; Jub 16:31; cf. John 12:13). They already and always do what the whole universe is destined to do. Their work is over. They have suffered, died, and have been purified not by their own good deeds but by the blood of the Lamb. The Lamb is now their Shepherd, who leads them to springs of living water (Rev 7:17). God wipes away all tears, and it turns out that what they belong to and suffer for is not a local Jesus club but the people of God through the centuries and around the world, an innumerable, multicolored, international host of brothers and sisters. No small potatoes.

The Church: Testing and Being Tested

The risen Christ, speaking in Revelation, addresses churches that are being put to the test:

> "Do not fear what you are about to suffer. Beware, the devil is about to throw some of you into prison so that you may be tested." (2:10)
>
> "Because you have kept my word of patient endurance, I will keep you from the hour of trial that is coming on the whole world to test the inhabitants of the earth." (3:10)

The churches are also commended for testing others: "I know your works, your toil and your patient endurance. I know that you cannot tolerate evildoers; you have tested those who claim to be apostles but are not, and have found them to be false" (2:2). The church is always in a situation of being tested and is called to endure. The church is always in a situation of testing itself and others. These are related, two sides of the same coin.

The Church Is Always Being Tested

"Test" in these words of warning and encouragement translates the verb *peirazō* ("test"; *peirasmos*, cognate noun "testing"), found in a prayer of the church already common in Revelation's time, traditionally translated "lead us not into temptation" (Matt 6:13). In this prayer, "temptation" does not refer to moral temptations small or great (having another drink or dessert, a liaison with the secretary or manager, padding one's expense account). Many worshipers have wondered why we ask God not to lead us into temptation, as though God tempts us to do such things. But the petition in the Lord's Prayer means "don't let us come into a situation where we are tested, where the pressure put on us to deny our faith might be more than we can handle, where we are unfaithful" (cf. NRSV, REB, NAB, NJB, TEV). John warns his readers of this danger, that the time of testing was coming, and the followers of Jesus might fail the test. Consider the scene in Matthew 26:31–41, on the last night of Jesus's life, as Jesus warns his disciples, "Stay awake and pray that you may not come into the time of trial" (v. 41; *peirasmos*, the same word as in Rev 3:10). Both John in Revelation and Jesus in Matthew speak within the framework of the apocalyptic idea that just before the consummation of history, Satan makes one last gasp to retain control of the world, intensifying pressure on God's people to deny their faith.

John's visionary warning does not mean they were all aware of the threat, all of them good and faithful Christians facing the possibility or actuality of persecution, wringing their hands in perplexity and wondering what to do. Some were (2:10). Others were complacent, unaware of their threatening situation, or had taken the advice of "Jezebel" and "Balaam" and adjusted quite well to what they supposed were the realities of the world. Some were lukewarm (Laodicea, 3:15–16), some were virtually dead, though they had the reputation for being a lively congregation (Sardis, 3:1; bouncy music, parking lot full). But all the messages were directed to and heard by all the churches, as indicated by the closing line of each of the messages: "Let anyone who has an ear listen to what the Spirit is saying to the churches" (2:7, 11, 17, 29; 3:6, 13, 22). There was no one-size-fits-all. Some heard comforting and encouraging words spoken into a situation that seemed hopeless. Others did not know what the question was until they were confronted by John's answer. John addresses a threatened church that faces triple perils: (1) the anxiety in the face of actual or potential persecution; (2) the indifference of those who are blissfully unaware of their actual situation as God's people caught in the conflicting force fields of a threatening world; (3) charismatic speakers who, believing they are empowered by the Spirit of God, promulgate false remedies for the church's response to the threat. John considers such would-be church leaders to be false prophets and apostles, part of the problem rather than the solution. The church is commended for testing apostolic claims and rejecting those that are false (2:2).

The Church Tests Apostolic Claims

"Those who claim to be apostles but are not" (2:2) does not of course refer to individuals traveling among the congregations purporting to be Peter or Paul, or any of the first-generation followers of Jesus. Nor does John claim that status for himself; his rejection of false apostles is not a matter of personal status but of theological integrity. The church of John's generation and later generations, which could not choose to follow Jesus of Nazareth personally in the way his pre-Easter disciples are pictured doing in the Gospels, has always necessarily followed some interpretation or group of interpretations of the meaning(s) of God's act in Jesus. A variety of interpretations had been handed on in the diverse traditions preserved and propagated by various individuals and groups claiming to represent Jesus. John is one such person active among the churches of Asia near the end of the first century. While he does not claim to be an apostle himself, he makes the prophetic claim that, inspired and guided by the Holy Spirit, he speaks for the risen Christ and thus represents authentic apostolic faith. He is not the only one who makes this claim. The churches have other charismatic leaders whose teaching and preaching call the church to a different kind of life in response to the pressures it is currently facing. ("Charismatic" does not refer here to the dynamic personalities of church teachers but to their claim to function by the gift [*charisma*] of the Spirit; cf. 1 Corinthians 12–14.) They did not see themselves as false prophets who misled the people of God. They were sincere teachers who wanted to help the church adjust to changing times. John casts these prophetic teachers in the biblical role of the false prophets and teachers that appeared in Israel, typified by Jezebel's advocacy of accommodation to Canaanite culture, including worship of Baal (1 Kings 16–2 Kings 9, especially 1 Kings 18–19, Jezebel versus Elijah), and Balaam, prophet-for-hire against Israel (Num 23–24). Both "Jezebel" and "Balaam" represented preachers and teachers in the church speaking in the name of the risen Jesus, encouraging Christian believers to accommodate their faith to the popular wave of patriotic cultural religion promoting the emperor cult. Their biblical prototypes had claimed economic, political, and divine support for adjusting Israel's faith to the current cultural and political scene. John sees them represented by the false prophet in league with the imperial beast, "progressive" leaders encouraging Christians to express their faith in terms popular in contemporary culture (Rev 13:11–18; 16:13; 19:20; 20:10). In the tradition of the biblical prophets, John's term "eating meat sacrificed to idols" represents these adjustments to the realities of modern life as not merely a matter of diet but one of betrayal of the church's Lord, the unfaithfulness of the bride to her husband, as "adultery" (2:22; cf., e.g., Hos 1–5).

From the first generation onward, the community of Jesus's followers that was to become aware of itself as the one holy catholic apostolic church has found it necessary to distinguish true from false apostles. The church's testing of apostolic claims is not a separate dimension of the church's life from the church itself being tested by persecution and indifference, as though some in the church are interested in having good theology, sound doctrine, while others want to live faithful lives. For John, apostolicity and endurance are inseparably related. The church threatened by persecution and indifference needs to survive, but to survive as *church*. The content of the faith for which the church is called to give its life matters. When John, in the name of the risen Christ, charges the churches to "be faithful until death, and I will give you the crown of life" (Rev 2:10), he is charging them to hold fast to Jesus's name, to be baptized, and to go public with their confession. But it is more than that as well. The church's mission of bearing witness to the gospel to the whole world calls for some clarity in the content of this confession: What is worth dying for, what is the faith to be believed, both by the martyr church and by those to whom it is called to preach? Part of the church's endurance in the face of both external persecution and internal indifference is to clarify the substance of its own faith. The church not only believes, but it believes something. John sees the identification of this content of the faith as integral to the church's life and mission. This means that adequate and appropriate ways of expressing authentic faith and distinguishing it from inadequate and inappropriate ways are vital for the church's life and work. Designating some ways of expressing the faith as those of "false apostles" and "false prophets" is not merely intolerance or lack of taste but necessary for the church to be true to itself and its Lord.

This is the point of John's prescriptions, charged with heavenly authority, to "remember then what you received and heard" (3:3) and "hold fast to what you have" (2:25; 3:11; cf. 1 Thess 2:4; 5:21; 2 Tim 1:14; 1 John 1:1–3). Such determined retention of a firm grasp on the faith they have been taught is not a matter of bigoted or ossified traditionalism. In John's situation, it is a matter of confessing or denying Christ, a matter of life and death, and he lets us see that this is the situation of the church through the centuries and around the world. The church in the critical situation of John's time was already learning that this cannot mean simply repeating the past, encrusted with its own cultural assumptions on such issues as economics, nationalism, divorce, slavery, segregation, and gay rights (whether these be liberal or conservative). It must mean interpreting the tradition for a new situation. This in turn means the church must know its own tradition, must *have* and *hold on to* the tradition before it can interpret it and be true to it. Eating idol meat was a crucial issue for John's time; it is not crucial for ours, but the basic issue is the same: What is the tradition and how are the followers of Jesus to be true to it in new and different situations? What this means in particular circumstances on particular issues was already receiving a spectrum of answers in John's time, more than one of which became canonical for the church of all time—including John's own epistolary Revelation.

In practice, how does the church find the right path among the variety of theologies advocated by sincere and capable would-be leaders? In John's time, not only is the historical Jesus a figure of the past, but the original apostles likewise belong to the past. They are the foundation, but whose claim to build on it is to be accepted (Rev 21:14; cf. 1 Cor 3:10–15; Eph 2:20)? There is no indication in Revelation that the churches he addresses have ordained leadership, already emerging among his network of Asian churches (cf. 1–3 John, Eph 4:7–16), nothing like the later authorized clergy that will guide the church in sorting out authentic from heretical theology (Pastorals, 1 Clement, Ignatius). John's own claim to authority is entirely charismatic, given by the risen Christ, expressed by the Spirit. But other leaders, advocating theologies John considers to betray the faith, also claim such direct, Spirit-given authority.

The church addressed in Revelation is a charismatic church in which the Spirit is alive, a church that has prophetic figures such as John who speak the word of the risen Lord directly, by divine inspiration. In later times, including our own, "charismatic" and "traditional" would often be seen as alternatives. People either quoted the Bible and tradition to validate their belief and practice (an appeal to the past) or they appealed to direct inspiration by the Spirit, who speaks in the living present. Surprisingly to us, the charismatic churches of Asia are encouraged to hold on to their *tradition* and that from their *charismatic* leader. The seemingly lively church at Sardis is in fact dead or at the point of dying, not because it lacks spirituality but because it has forgotten the tradition it has received (Rev 3:3). The faithful churches in Thyatira and Philadelphia are encouraged to hold fast what they have (2:25–28; 3:11). Other answers besides John's are already being given, and the writings of later church teachers will give different answers, which are also included in the church's limited spectrum of options that became the New Testament. But Revelation will finally be included in that canon, too, and will continue not only to focus the issue in an inescapable way but also to provide *one* answer to it.

Revelation 4–5—the Triune God: Mission Control of the Universe

John's vision report begins with the transcendent Christ (chap. 1), which morphs into a revelation of the true nature and identity of the church (chaps. 2–3). John is on earth, and the revelation comes to him on Patmos. The real fulcrum and center of gravity of Revelation, however, appear when John is called into the heavenly world to behold the throne room imagery of chapters 4–5. This scene then expands into the series of judgments and the final victory of God that constitute the rest of the book. While it is a unitary vision that must be experienced as a whole, it has been carefully structured—not as a series of topics but as a grand visionary narrative:

Revelation 4–5	The Triune God: Mission Control of the Universe
Revelation 6–18	God the Righteous Judge: Violence, Human and Divine
Revelation 19–22	God the Creator: The New World Coming and Already Here

There is widespread agreement that chapters 4–5 are "the theological center of the apocalypse,"[5] on which everything else is based. This means not only that the book must be understood as a whole but also that nothing in Revelation can be understood unless it is seen as embraced within the grandeur and theological depth of this paradigmatic scene. It is totally awesome, in the original sense of "awful" = "full of awe"; this is a God-awful vision. Before proceeding, these two chapters need to be read and pondered as a unit.

The vision pushes every envelope of our minds beyond what we can imagine. John's revelatory experience is no in-my-heart individualistic spirituality; its panorama embraces all that is. Although such concepts and terminology would not be used until generations later, it is a revelation of the triune God. Through John's earthly eyes, the readers too find themselves in the transcendent Mission Control of the universe. Our little lives are not bits of flotsam in a vast cosmic sea, not random combinations of atoms in the black infinity of space, but they are integrated into a creation thought out and intended by the creator. Each of our lives is a creation. We are neither accidents nor self-made.

God the Father: Maker of Heaven and Earth

There is one God, the Eternal One, the creator of all that is, subatomic to pan-galactic, transcending all space and time, "who was, and is, and who is to come, . . . who lives forever and ever." Our planet, and all its life—everything that crawls, swims, walks, or flies, including all human beings—are the creatures of this one God, and human voices, insiders and outsiders, join with all life in worshiping the creator of all that is, *ta panta* (4:8–10). The creation was no accident, compromise, or result of some sort of cosmic compulsion, but was intended, *willed* by the creator. The whole creation, whether inanimate or teeming with life, does not therefore just passively accept its dependent status but *praises* the God who was not satisfied to dwell in the untroubled splendor of eternal solitude (4:11b). God wanted to have a creation, and we are here because God wanted us, and God was powerful enough to pull it off. Revelation has much to say about power. The creator is the Lord God *Almighty*.

There is much talk of thrones: one central throne, and it is not vacant. There is one who sits on the throne. The universe is not a huge, mindless, random affair but has a governing center. The one who sits on the throne is neither computer program nor oblong blur, but a person, the Father of our Lord Jesus Christ. He holds a book that contains the mystery of where the universe is headed, what it's all about. There is meaning in the universe and in our individual lives. Someone is in charge. Not only so, but twenty-four other figures surround the throne—the reader of Revelation is already familiar with them, the heavenly counterparts of the tribal-Israel/apostolic-church people of God—who also are seated on thrones.

We are rightly distrustful of this concentration of power in the hands of one person or a select few. Though mainline churches are often unaware of it, this is because we still preserve at least a dim understanding of the biblical theology of systemic evil, original sin. Human beings are born into a world that inevitably conditions us to be sinful and selfish; this us/them mentality molds us into creatures whose primal reflex is to look out for ourselves and our group, whether family, state, nation, race, or religion. Power corrupts even more; absolute power corrupts absolutely. Thus our constitutions divide up power and spread it out with a system of checks and balances. But already Aristotle, in the cradle of Western democracy, after he and his students had examined scores of constitutions of the free city-states, declared that the best kind of human government was *monarchy*—if there were a king good enough, wise enough, and strong enough to govern. Alas, bitter experience has taught us that there is no such king; we are suspicious of thrones and throne imagery and devise democratic checks and balances against concentrations of too much power.

And yet, Israel knew the weakness and evil of even the best human kings, regarded the Lord God Almighty as the one true King, and prayed, "Thy kingdom come," as did Israel's greatest son (not "Thy representative committee come," "Thy democracy come"). Revelation portrays the true kingdom as already existing in the transcendent world (chaps. 4–5) and finally to come in this world (chaps. 20–22), in which the will of God is done on earth as it is in heaven. Revelation expresses the conviction that this will happen, that we are involved in something that is already happening, that the prayer "Thy kingdom come" will finally be answered in ways beyond our imagination, because the almighty God wills it and has the power to make it happen. Phony realism, idealistically and moralistically, encourages us to abandon utopian wishful thinking and settle for "If we work hard, we can make some things a little better." Biblical realism is radical and universal: "*Everything* is going to be *all* right." This is so certain that it can already be celebrated in worship and acted on in the way we live, vote, and manage our portfolios and credit cards.

God the Son: The Lamb of God Who Takes Away the Sin of the World

The revelation of the creator's power in chapter 4 is not complete until the character of absolute power is revealed in chapter 5 (again: there were no chapters or chapter divisions in the unitary letter read and heard as a whole!). In the real world projected by the biblical narrative, God had promised that the world's present evil would be overcome by God's own power. God would send a mighty deliverer, a David-like figure, the Lion of Judah, who in righteous indignation and violence would slay all the Goliaths of injustice (Gen 49:9–10; Num 24:3–9; Isa 11:1–10). The author of the Ezra apocalypse, a contemporary of Revelation, is explicit:

> "And as for *the lion* whom you saw rousing up out of the forest and roaring and speaking to the eagle and reproving him for his unrighteousness, and as for all his words that you have heard, *this is the Messiah* whom the Most High has kept until the end of days, who will *arise from the offspring of David*, and will come and speak with them. He will denounce them for their ungodliness and for their wickedness, and will display before them their contemptuous dealings. For first he will bring them alive

> before his judgment seat, and when he has reproved them, then he will destroy them. But in mercy he will set free the remnant of my people, those who have been saved throughout my borders, and he will make them joyful until the end comes, the day of judgment, of which I spoke to you at the beginning." (4 Ezra 12:31–34)

Israel often prayed to the Shepherd God of Israel who had made promises but seemed to have abandoned his sheep to the slaughter. Israel found itself as lambs at the mercy of the lion-like empires that had often surrounded it (Ps 44!). But just wait: the promise of God is sure, and we will not always be the powerless lambs bullied and devoured by others. What goes around comes around—the Lion will come. It seems so right.

Revelation does not abandon this hope, and the proclamation reverberates through the throne room of the universe that the Great Lion of God will come—in fact *has* come.

> All turn to greet and praise the fulfillment of the hopes and fears of all the years,
> and there, in the *Lion*-slot of traditional theology
> stands the slaughtered *Lamb*,
> the one whose sacrificial blood
> redeems people from every tribe, language, and nation.

The promised Messiah has come, and he is the crucified Jesus of Nazareth, the one "crucified in weakness" (2 Cor 13:4). Such weakness is not an alternative to the power of the Lord God Almighty, but its ultimate expression. The crucified Lamb is represented in this vision as having and exercising God's power. His seven horns (Rev 5:6) represent all-inclusive power. He takes the sealed book from the hand of the creator, opens it, and not only reveals its contents but holds them in his hand. He's got the whole world in his hand. The "weak" Lamb who actually came does not replace the "strong" Lion who was promised but continues to identify himself as "the root and descendant of David" (22:16)—the Lamb *is* the Lion.

Christological Redefinition of Winning

The power of the Lamb is repeatedly expressed in the verb *nikaō* (to conquer), corresponding to the noun *nikē*, "victory," familiar the world over as a sports brand name for "winning." God in Christ overcomes all resistance and wins the ultimate victory. There is no renunciation of power or winning here, but a mind-wrenching christological redefinition of what it means to have power and win. The ultimate victory belongs to God. It is a victory in which there will be no losers. The power that brings about this victory is the self-giving love manifest in the cross of Christ. The hard thing about accepting the message of Revelation is not its weird imagery but its claim that at the heart of the universe is the almighty power of God; that this power is made known and effective in Jesus as the crucified and risen one, the one who gives himself for all; and that this power, already at work in the world and in our lives, will ultimately prevail.

In the vision, the Lamb is a separate figure from the creator, the Son is a separate figure from the Father. Yet the verbal-visual imagery that communicates this ultimate good news is fluid. Static, consistent pictures and propositions cannot encapsulate the ultimate truth of God. The Lamb not only takes the sealed book from the right hand of the creator who sits on the throne of the universe, but also sits on this throne himself. There is one throne and one God, the creator, the Almighty. All things are ultimately in one hand. And yet, this almighty power is exercised by the Lamb, who shares the throne of God (the Lamb is "in the midst of the throne," 5:6 [KJV's properly literal translation of *en mesō tou thronou*, followed by, e.g., NAB, NJB, NIV, TNIV, TEV, NKJV). This image is not incidental but recurs, for example, in 7:15–17, where there is "one who is seated on the throne," but "the Lamb [is] at the center of the throne"—the *Lamb* who is also the Good *Shepherd* of Psalm 23, who will guide his people to springs of living water and wipe away all tears. It so happens that the image of two sovereigns sharing one throne was familiar in the Hellenistic world. The image on a 13 BCE coin shows Augustus and his designated heir, Agrippa, sharing the same throne.[6] While such imagery may have provided a point of contact with Revelation's original readers, it cannot be considered the key to John's theological point, which resists reduction to flat-surface, this-worldly reality. It is clear from other aspects of John's vision that somehow picturing "God *and* Christ" as corulers of the creation does not grasp the reality communicated by John's tensive imagery. The Christ/Lamb is both a separate figure who can approach the throne as the one who has suffered and died for others, and the one who occupies the throne. We see two persons in some verbal-visual images, one God in other such images, all in the same scene (see pp. 186–87 below on John 1:1–2).

Mainstream Christian preachers have become hesitant about the atonement language of the New Testament—rightly so in regard to some of its simplistic and popular forms. John's dialectical, verbal-visual expression of this scene and its action allows him to portray the atoning act of God-in-Christ without scapegoating. The heavenly representatives of God's people praise the Lamb in the words of a "new song," corresponding to the new covenant and the new creation:

> "You are worthy to take the scroll and to open its seals,
> for you were slaughtered and by your blood you ransomed for God
> saints from every tribe and language and people and nation."
> (Rev 5:9b)

The saving power of God is manifest and made real not by top-down coercion but by the one who came down, shared our life, and gave his own life for us. This one who redeems by his blood is not a third party, different from both the one true God and sinful humanity, as though *Christ* offered his life so that somehow *God* could accept sinful humanity without violating God's own holiness that insisted that "*somebody* has to die for this." John's imagery, like some other streams of New Testament theology, identifies God and Christ. God does not inflict the sins of humanity on a third party. Christ shares God's rule, God's throne, God's being (later: *homoousios*, "of one substance with the Father"). In Christ, God does not punish someone else for the sins of the world but takes them into God's own being.

The vision reveals the one God, the creator, the Almighty, whose almightiness is the power of self-giving, loving care for others. The verbal-visual imagery presents God the almighty Father and Christ the Lamb, "one God in two persons." The reader may anticipate where the vision is leading, but it is not yet complete.

God the Holy Spirit: Present and Active in the World and the Church

The initial greeting of John to the seven churches pronounced grace and peace not only from the eternal God and Jesus Christ but also from "the seven spirits who are before his throne" (Rev 1:4). The sixty references to the number seven in Revelation often symbolize fullness, completeness, as in the seven churches, stars, seals, trumpets, and plagues. "Seven spirits of God" points to the fullness of God's Spirit, not seven from among a greater number but the Spirit per se, that is, the Holy Spirit. Seven spirits also have a particular biblical tradition that became christological: the Spirit of the Lord that will empower the coming king would be filled with the seven spirits of God, that is, the fullness of the Spirit of God (Isa 11:2 LXX). When John is taken up into the transcendent world of God, amidst the lightning, rumblings, and peals of thunder, in front of the throne he sees the seven flaming lamps (NRSV "torches"), which are the seven spirits of God (Rev 4:5). The spirits/Spirit of God is distinct from God, before the throne, not on it, envisioned as a separate multiflame reality. Likewise, the Spirit can speak with a voice distinct from God and Christ, even joining with the voice of the church in calling on the Christ to "come" (22:17). Yet, in the same vision, these seven spirits are identified christologically—the seven *eyes* of the *Lamb* are the seven *spirits* of *God* sent out into all the earth (5:6). In addressing the church in Sardis, the risen Christ had already claimed, "These are the words of him who has the seven spirits of God" (3:1). Each of the messages to the churches, presented as the words of the risen *Christ*, concludes with "Let anyone who has an ear listen to what the *Spirit* is saying to the churches" (2:7, 11, 17, 29: 3:6, 13, 22). As with images of Father and Son, so John's visionary mind's eye perceives God's Spirit in multiple pictures that are impossible to neatly conceptualize or express in logically consistent discursive language. John does not picture the Spirit as sharing the throne with the Father and the Son, but he nonetheless portrays the Spirit as both a separate "person" and integral to the being of both Father and Son. For John, as for other New Testament writers, the Holy Spirit is not an impersonal force but a "person" of the triune God, identified with the Father and the Son. This is very like Paul's theology, in which "Spirit" is virtually interchangeable with "God" and "Christ" (e.g., Rom 8:9–11), and which can even refer almost in passing to "the Lord, who is the Spirit" (2 Cor 3:18 NIV). John is acquainted with theological currents in Ephesus, where Paul had worked and composed his letters to the Corinthians and others, and where Pauline traditions were still vital in John's time near the end of the century. In Revelation we have aspects of Pauline theology writ large, in expanded verbal-visual images. It is not the encoded language of allegory in which each element can be deciphered into what it "really means," but language that stimulates deeper reflection, pointing and provoking in parabolic picture-language.

As in Jesus's kingdom parables, John's images teasingly shatter previous conventional imagery, saying the unsayable and unpicturable in ways that rattle one's conceptual cage but resist being decoded into flat, manageable statements. Thus none of what is written here is intended to "explain" Revelation, much less "explain" the church's later Trinitarian thinking, but it is written to help us come within hearing distance of John's potent verbal-visual communication that will disclose its own message to those who not only think hard and deep but also pray for open hearts, eyes that see, ears that hear (Deut 29:4; Ezek 12:2; Matt 13:16; Mark 8:18; Rom 11:8). Even then, we will not be able to express it in clear language or concepts and will be unable even to imagine it. But we can sing it: "Holy, Holy, Holy . . . Lord God Almighty . . . God in three persons, blessed Trinity."

Having come this far, John's vision takes us even further. His way of speaking of the Spirit not only involves identifying Spirit with God and Christ but also integrally relates the Spirit to the people of God, especially to their prophetic ministry and to prophetic figures such as John himself. As a Spirit-inspired prophet in the church, John receives and delivers his message "in the Spirit" (Rev 1:10) and is taken "in the Spirit" to see visions of the transcendent world (4:2; 17:3; 21:10) and hear the Spirit speaking (14:13; 22:17). The Spirit that inspires prophecy is not a vague spiritual ecstasy but the Jesus testimony, both from and about Jesus (i.e., God's act in Jesus), in continuity with Jesus's own testimony to which he was faithful as he stood before the Roman governor (19:10). The prophet's message is revealed from heaven but also mediated by a book. The preacher is commanded to eat the book, to devour it—to read, mark, learn, and inwardly digest its message (10:8–9), which sweetens the mouth, bitters the stomach.

Not only prophets but every person who struggles to hear, teach, and preach the word of God that comes from the Spirit through this book knows this bittersweet experience, this taste, this satisfaction, and this sickness in the stomach. Prophets are not the only ones who stand before such Roman governors and must decide whether to be faithful to the Jesus testimony, and prophets are not the only ones empowered by the Spirit. All followers of Jesus belong to the prophetic church, empowered by the Holy Spirit, sharing the mission and destiny of the biblical prophets (11:3–13). In the final scene of Revelation, the bride-church joins the Spirit in the communal prayer, "Come, Lord Jesus" (22:17). The inspired prophet John shares the tribulation, kingdom, and patient endurance with all others who are "in Jesus," those who are incorporated into the body of Christ that lives by the very breath of God, the Spirit (1:9). Thus not only Christ but also Christ's people, the people of God, share the throne of God (3:21; cf. 4:4; 11:16; 20:4).

> "Blessed Lord, who caused all holy Scriptures to be written for our learning: Grant us so to hear them, read, mark, learn, and inwardly digest them, that we may embrace and ever hold fast the blessed hope of everlasting life, which you have given us in our Savior Jesus Christ; who lives and reigns with you and the Holy Spirit, one God, for ever and ever. Amen."
>
> —Book of Common Prayer ("The Collect for Proper" 28)

Even more: John's vision emerges from the biblical tradition in which the Spirit of God is not only given to God's people but also extends to the whole creation. Just as God the Father is creator of all and God the Son is ruler of all ("with" the Father), so God the Spirit permeates and is present to all things and all people. The first paragraph of the Bible portrays the creative, life-giving spirit of God bringing order out of chaos (Gen 1:1–2). God the creator breathes life into Adam/humanity. Long before there was a called and chosen covenant people, God was present to and among humanity in general (see pp. 188–200 below on John 1:5–13). Here we perhaps need to remind ourselves that both the Hebrew (*ruach*) and Greek (*pneuma*) have the triple meaning "wind," "breath," and "spirit." Thus, the question whether Genesis 1:2 is translated "wind" or "breath" is a false alternative: it is the powerful wind/breath/Spirit of God that gives shape to the world and sustains it in being (cf., e.g., 2 Sam 22:16; Ps 33:6; Isa 42:5). The lifeless soil from which Adam is made first becomes a living being when God breathes life into it (Gen 2:7; cf. Job 12:10; 27:3; 32:8; 33:4; 34:14–15; Eccles 12:7). The breath/Spirit of God breathes life into the dead (Ezek 37:5–10; Rom 8:11; Rev 11:11). This Spirit/breath/life of God by which God is always present to every atom of the created universe not only sustains it but is also a constant threat. Nothing is independent of God, and nothing can comport itself as though it were autonomous, responsible only to itself. If God were to withdraw the divine breath, to inhale rather than exhale, the created order would collapse into the nothingness from which it came (Ps 104:27–30; Job 34:14–15). If the creation acts as though it were the sovereign creator ("self-made man" versus Ps 100:3!), or if creatures worship the creation rather than the creator (Rom 1:25), the breath of God becomes a destructive wind that fans the flames of judgment (Isa 30:33; 40:7; Job 4:9).

The point here is that this all-powerful Spirit that is the very being of God is present and active not only in the people of God but also in humanity and throughout the whole world. It does not depend on the presence of preachers or the "institutional church." The sevenfold fullness of God's Spirit not only gazes through the eyes of the Lamb on the insiders, the called and chosen people of God, but also "is sent out into all the *earth*" (Rev 5:6). Through the Spirit, the gospel of the one God who has definitively acted in the one true human being Jesus Christ is universalized. The whole creation does not yet know it or believe it. Nonetheless, the universe is already embraced through the life-giving and life-threatening Spirit by its creator. God has sent the Messiah not only for Israel but for the world. The world, in church and out, is for the most part still unaware of this good news, but the continuing people of God, Israel and the church, knows it and has a mission to testify to its truth to the whole world.

The church, called and empowered by God, is presently engaged in this mission. Not everyone believes its message; most remain outsiders to its confession, its sacraments, its life that claims to be a foretaste of life in God's kingdom yet to come, its understanding of what things are all about, the destination of the road we are all on. At present the world appears to be divided into insiders and outsiders, those who believe the good news of God's saving act in Christ and are incorporated into the people of God, and those who haven't heard or don't believe. At present, being an insider to the people of God depends not only on the call of God communicated by preaching the gospel but also on the obedient response of faith to that call, that gospel. The gospel proclaimed by the church is inclusive in the sense that it invites people from every tribe and language and people and nation, but the creator has blessed all human beings with wonderful and fearful response-ability; some of them respond, but at present far from all do (5:9–10). Those who respond in faith are cast in the role of Israel, the people of God, called out from among the nations to be a special community, a royal priesthood to all the earth. This line between already-insider and still-outsider continues in the fearful imagery that follows throughout John's vision—the faithful believers who presently bear the seal of the living God are, thank God, already an immense community of faith, but they are still only a fraction of "those who dwell on the earth," some of whom not only reject the gospel but also persecute those who accept it (3:10; 6:10; 8:13; 11:10; 13:8, 12, 14; 14:6; 17:2, 8).

The scene in Revelation 4–5 does not climax with a celebration of the insiders, the called and chosen who have remained faithful. Here we have dialectical theology, in which salvation is affirmed as conditional and partial *and* as unconditional and universal. The throne room is reminiscent of the sacral images of Roman authority, which claimed to unite all peoples under one benevolent rule. What Rome promises, the one true God will deliver, and is already celebrated and lived out. The myriads in heaven and on earth, already from every tribe and tongue and people and nation (5:9), are joined by

> every creature in heaven and on earth and under the earth and in the sea, and all that is in them, singing,
> "To the one seated on the throne and to the Lamb
> be blessing and honor and glory and might
> forever and ever!" (5:13)

The scene that began with the enthroned creator of *all* (4:2, 11, *ta panta*, "all that is") concludes with the redemption of *all* (5:13, *ta panta*, "all that is"). This God is praised by the whole creation as the Lord God Almighty. This God could not conceivably end up saying, "I created the whole world, but most of it rebelled and, much as I wanted to save them all, I only managed to win back and save some of them." Such a God whose power to say yes to us is finally stronger than our power to say no to God, without ever violating our freedom and responsibility, cannot be imagined throwing up his hands and finally saying, "All right, have it your way." This nondialectical, nonparadoxical way of thinking, though managing to fit into our minds cramped by human logic and limited imagination, can never do justice to the unimaginable reality of the almighty One in whose kingdom his redeemed creatures participate as kings, without compromising their own responsibility and freedom. It is important that the New Testament's proto-Trinitarian imagery is concentrated in this one scene. It is no accident that reverberations from this scene echo in the English-speaking church's favorite Trinitarian hymn, Reginald Heber's 1827 "Holy, Holy, Holy," which celebrates the triune God as "merciful *and* mighty." This scene must be present to the mind's eye, and this song must continue to resound in the church's worship, as it turns the page to see and hear God's judgment on the violent history of the world in the visions that follow.

Revelation 6–18—God the Righteous Judge: Violence, Divine and Human

We see it. There, in the hand of the one true God, is a sealed scroll that reveals and makes effective the destiny of the world, the troubles of the last days the beloved creation must endure on the way to the final kingdom of

God. This scroll is now in the hands of the Lamb who gave himself in sacrificial love for the sins of the world. Torture and death could not deter him. He is in control. Death and Hades still rampage through the streets of history (6:7–8), but the Messiah holds the keys to Death and Hades (1:18) and will finally cast them—the transcendent abstract powers, not their human victims—into the lake of fire (20:14). The Lamb/Messiah breaks the first seal. One of the living creatures, representing all created life, speaks, and the word "Come" resounds through the creation. John's readers have heard this resounding, one-word prayer/command/plea before, and may have uttered it themselves. From the earliest days, this is the prayer of the church gathered about the eucharistic table, the prayer that the church, inspired by the Spirit, continues to pray as it joins the heavenly worship (22:17; cf. 1 Cor 11:26, "until he comes"; 16:22, "Marana tha, O Lord, come!"). The promised Messiah is the *Coming* One, as is the God who sent him. The heart and core of early Christian faith is that the promised Messiah had finally come. But suffering and injustice continued. Believers did not give up their hope that the promised Redeemer had come (contrast the sad words of Luke 24:21). God raised up Jesus, hope was reborn, he was made known to them in the breaking of bread, they believed that God's promise would be fulfilled, they prayed, "Come, Lord Jesus," and fulfill your messianic mission. Here, the prayers of the church on earth resound in heaven, joining with the heavenly worship. The whole creation prays: "Come" (Rom 8:18–21).

And the prayer is answered. A conqueror comes forth, riding on a white horse and wearing a crown. Surely this is the Messiah, returning in power and glory. Hope has not been in vain. *Now* evil will be destroyed. At the end of John's revelation, the Messiah does indeed return, riding a white horse, the one called Faithful and True. He destroys evil and fulfills God's promise (Rev 19:11). But between the visions of 6:1 and 19:11—the major part of the book—are violent scenes of destruction and suffering. The first rider on the white horse goes forth to conquer, but instead of conquering evil he increases human suffering by continuing the kind of military conquest that victors have celebrated and victims have endured throughout human history. It seems to be an ironic reversal of the preceding scene in which God's ultimate power is that of suffering love. The conqueror of chapter 6 seems to be a reversion to this-worldly violence.[7]

The church's prayer continues to reverberate throughout the cosmos: "Come!" But it only gets worse. Conquest is followed by civil war—our own generation has seen this aplenty—with repeated prayers followed only by plague, hunger, sickness, ferocious animals, and death. The Messiah has come, but violence only increases (6:1–8). People are killed because of their faithfulness to God, and they cry out for justice (6:9–11). Sun, moon, and stars are struck, mountains and islands are displaced, as everyone from king to slave tries to escape the approaching wrath (6:12–17). The earth is struck with hail and fire mixed with blood (8:7), and sea and rivers turn to blood (8:8–11; 16:3–4). Demonic locust-like creatures stream out of the abyss to torment humanity, and people cry out for death but continue to suffer (9:1–11). A *Twilight Zone* supernatural horde of cavalry 200-million-strong pours across the Euphrates from the east (9:13–19). Those who worship the beast are tormented with sulfurous fire in the presence of the holy angels and the Lamb (14:10–11). Horses wade for two hundred miles in bridle-deep blood (14:20). The kings of the earth mount a final battle against God and his Messiah, and vultures are gorged with the flesh of both the lowly foot soldiers who fight the world's battles and their high and mighty commanders (16:14–16; 19:17–18). Humans continue not only to perpetrate violence but also to suffer the wrath of the violent God. The world itself trembles, the cosmos comes unglued, as sun and moon are darkened and stars fall. One whose eyes and ears are assaulted by the pageant of historical and cosmic suffering that intensifies for fourteen long chapters, afflicting humans, animal life, and the created universe, comes away exhausted and repelled. The church's prayer "Come" only makes matters worse. Does any Christian believer want to pray "Thy kingdom come" if it means invoking horrific divine wrath on evildoers and the cosmos as the price of final justice?

The theological problem is compounded by the fact that the source of violence is God and the Lamb. The Deliverer has become the Perpetrator, whose violence is sometimes invoked with cries for "vengeance," that is, justice. This whole range of imagery has posed a severe problem for interpreting Revelation as a Christian book, particularly when compared with the pictures of Jesus in the Gospels.

We cannot respond to this problem by minimizing it; it must be allowed to emerge in all its ferocity and ugliness. None of the following suggestions, nor all of them together, removes this gigantic boulder in the path of Christian faith, theology, and life. It is hoped that the paragraphs below will make us more able not only to live with but also to hear and see these visionary depictions of the awfulness of violence—human and divine—as inherent in biblical theology and to understand them in the context of biblical revelation as a whole, in which the central image is a scene of unspeakable violence: the death by torture of the best man we have ever known.

The Givenness of Revelation's Situation of Suffering

John's thought began not with visions about future suffering but with the fact of suffering in his own present. The sociological and psychological realities of such a situation must be taken into account. John has experienced personal suffering as the price of faithfulness to the gospel and writes to churches who know people who have been arrested and killed for their faith. They may have suffered loss of property or status or have felt the pain of ruptured relationships and being relegated to the margins of society; they are people who, with various degrees of awareness, lived in the actuality or threat of mob or government-sanctioned violence. His letter is no abstract "theology of suffering" but a cry from the depths. John and his readers, then and now, are sincere Christian believers dedicated to following in the footsteps of Jesus, people convinced that the meaning of human history and their own lives has been revealed in the love of God made real in Christ. They and we are also human beings who, despite the presence of God's Spirit in our lives, remain subject to human feelings of retaliation, vindictive justice, and revenge. Paul Minear refers to John's own humanity and suffering, which generated deep feelings not free from thoughts of retaliation and revenge: "Some readers have felt that the writer of the book of The Revelation of John succumbed to such temptations and thus proved himself to be a false prophet. It is not necessary for later friends to maintain the blamelessness of the prisoner John. After all, his faith was subjected to greater strain than that of most of his critics."[8] As illustrated by Israel's imprecatory psalms (Pss 35; 55; 69; 109; 137), a community that feels itself pushed to the edge of society and the edges of its own endurance will, in its worship, give vent to the human feelings of resentment, even revenge, as it anticipates the eschatological turning of the tables. Even then, cries for "revenge" are not personal but are a plea for the justice of God to be manifest publicly. Interpreters should be wary of using the vocabulary of "revenge," "vindictive," and "vengeance" in reference to Revelation and other New Testament books. In this regard, I have not been careful enough in my previous writings on Revelation. While it is true that even faithful Christians under duress were not free from vengeful human feelings, there is remarkably little of this in the texts themselves. Such terminology occurs in Revelation only at 6:10 ("avenge") and 19:2 ("avenged"), in each case translating *ekdikeō*, whose primary meaning is "procure justice for someone."[9] God does not wreak vengeance. God establishes justice.

Revelation's Theological Framework and Modus Operandi

Image, Word, and Reality

Here the relation of language and reality emphasized above is crucial, especially the discussions of dialectical thought and confessional language above. Precisely because John thinks dialectically, presenting the righteous judgment of God in these images does not mean the dilution or compromise of John's images of absolute and universal grace. None of the violence in the scenes of chapters 6–18 is a description of literal, objective violence against the real world, but is violence in a visionary scene of the future, expressed in metaphorical language (9:7!). The bloody hail and fire launched from heaven against the earth (8:7) are pictures of something, and something terribly real. Though not "just" pictures, they are still pictures. The sword and fire by which the evil of the earth is judged (and even "tormented") are not a literal sword and fire, but metaphors for the cutting, searing Word (1:16; 11:5). In the first-century Mediterranean world of the readers, there are no beasts arising from the sea, no violence erupting from heaven. Though John hears the martyrs already in heaven calling out for God to "avenge" their blood, John himself issues no calls for the readers to engage in violence. Christians are not called to participate in the eschatological battle, just as they are not to engage in violence against the Romans they face every day. John is in the tradition of Paul, who quotes the Scripture of Israel and the church: "Beloved, never avenge yourselves, but leave room for the wrath of God; for it is written, 'Vengeance is mine, I will repay, says the Lord.' No, 'if your enemies are hungry, feed them; if they are thirsty, give them something to drink.' . . . Do not be overcome by evil, but overcome evil with good" (Rom 12:19–21, citing Prov 25:21–22). John does not explicitly call for turning the other cheek or praying for enemies, but his casting the church in the role of priests for the world includes praying for and sacrificing on behalf of all the world's people. When God's violent judgment comes, there is no gloating, but lamentation (Rev 18:1–24). John sees the visionary destruction of the evil city represented by Babylon, but John does not dance on the grave of Rome.

The Apocalyptic Scheme of History in Which John Thinks

The traditional mode of apocalyptic thought in which John thinks includes much violent imagery. Such theological modes give experienced suffering a meaning by placing it in a cosmic context, functioning as hermeneutics of the present, not speculation about future violence to be inflicted on one's enemies. Apocalyptic thought generally begins in the readers' present with the reality of violence already experienced. The predestined apocalyptic scheme typically understands present distress as the vanguard of the last throes of the world's struggle, the time when the suprapersonal power of evil intensifies the world's suffering in a last-ditch effort just before its final defeat. It is this period that is so vividly portrayed in the series of sevenfold visions of violent judgment in Revelation 6–18. The violence of this period is temporary, penultimate. There is no "abandon hope, all ye who enter here." Rather, John calls his readers to live by *hope*; evil and violence are not ultimate—their present existence fuels the eschatological hope. This period is short, in Revelation a maximum of three and a half years. The days of judgment and violence are numbered, and the number is small.

The repeated emphasis on the "shortness of the time" also applies to the time it takes to read the document aloud in worship. Again, remember that this verbal-visual text so full of violence was intended to be read aloud as a whole in the church's worship. One might think of watching a violent movie with a happy ending. The shortness of the time filled with violent scenes is good news. If one reads a small section of Revelation at a time, followed by days or weeks of nonreading, it takes a long time to get through the whole, and one forgets that the whole text is read in less than an hour and a half, and the violent spasms just before the end pass quickly on the way to the final coming of the kingdom of God, which endures "forever and ever."

The "messianic woes." A specific dimension of the thought world of apocalyptic is helpful in putting this feature of its apocalyptic imagery in perspective—the scheme of the "messianic woes," the messianic "labor pains." Jewish apocalyptic had developed a widespread pattern that interpreted the present troubles of the faithful community as the world's labor pains, the onset of the period of suffering that must come just before the final victory, just as labor pains precede birth. In 2 (Syriac) Baruch 26:1–30:5, for instance, twelve disasters are announced as preliminary to the coming of the Messiah, resurrection, and judgment. For a couple longing for a child, the onset of labor, painful as it is for the mother, is greeted with joyful hope. Suffering and pain are placed within a meaningful context. John's theology was worked out within the framework of traditional apocalyptic thought, which included the "messianic woes" as an integral part of the plot. He takes over this language, including its macabre details. For instance, the image of horses wading up to their bridles in blood (Rev 14:19–20) was not originated by John but was already a proverbial picture of the woes of the last days (1 En 100:3; cf. 4 Ezra 15:35–36). The world heaves and groans in labor pains as it brings forth the Messiah and the new age. The terrible period of suffering is not the last word, but the harbinger of good news. It is in this sense that the announcement of the coming violence of God's judgment can be called "good news" in Revelation 14:6–7.

John's Appropriation and Interpretation of Scripture and Tradition

It is not as though when John sat down to compose Revelation he began with a blank page at square one and devised this violent language and imagery from scratch. In both form and content, most of it was adopted and adapted by him from his tradition. We continue with some important elements of this tradition.

The Language of Scripture

Virtually everything in the violent pictures of the seals, trumpets, and bowls of chapters 6–19 is drawn from biblical imagery and is expressed in biblical language. The language and imagery of the exodus naturally become John's means of proclaiming the eschatological deliverance from the contemporary (Roman) "pharaoh." By labeling the eschatological disasters "plagues" (Rev 9:18; 15:6; and often; cf. Exod 7–12), which God will visit on the arrogance of the contemporary "pharaoh"/"Egypt" before the evil empire will "let my people go," he interprets the present Roman pressures and their anticipated intensification as an extension of the biblical story into his churches' own experience.

The Ancient Near Eastern Combat Myth

Lurking in the background of much of the religious imagery that pervaded John's world was the mythical story of creation in which the chaos monster (the Sea, Tiamat, Lotan [= Leviathan], etc.) was subdued and held at bay at creation, not destroyed but still there at the edges of the secure created world, still threatening and disrupting the ordered creation. The evil of the present world is understood as the remnants of chaos, the uncreated still resisting the creator. The present world thus has a built-in tension. There will be a final abolition of the chaos monster, and a new creation will emerge.

But just before the final victory of the creator, the forces of chaos will make one last push, a final reassertion of their threat, causing great havoc to the creation before chaos is finally defeated forever. The final victory includes pictures of violence. Virtually every people of the Greco-Roman world had its own version or versions of the combat myth. John does not invent these violent scenes, nor does he merely dutifully record what he sees in the heavenly visions. He writes within and for a context in which such images were generally presupposed as a part of everyone's mental furniture.

God's Wrath

The terminology of God's "wrath" (6:16–17; 11:18; 14:10; 16:19; 19:15) is not John's creation but a dimension of a deep stream of biblical theology (here is only a sampling, including the great prophets of Israel, the Gospels, and Paul: Exod 22:21–24; Deut 9:7–8; Pss 2:5; 78:21–22; 90:7–9; Isa 1:24; 9:19; 13:9, 13; 51:17, 22; Jer 4:4; 10:10, 25; 25:15; Ezek 7:8, 12; 13:13; 20:8, 13; Hos 5:10; 13:11; Mic 5:15; Matt 3:7; John 3:36; Rom 1:18[!]; 2:5; 5:9; 9:22; 12:19; 1 Thess 1:10; 2:16; 5:9). The stream of biblical theology represented by these texts pictures not a petty deity overcome by emotional outbursts but the relentless, inexorable punishment of sin by a God of justice. "Wrath" is basically a judicial term, expressing the condemnation of those found guilty and sentenced in God's courtroom (Rev 11:18; cf. Rom 5:1, 9; 8:1; etc.; the punitive justice of human courts is called "wrath" in Rom 13:4–5).

The biblical prophets' woes against Babylon as the enemy of God's people are transmuted into the eschatological woes against the "Babylon" of John's time (e.g., Isa 13; Jer 51:1–19). The source of John's language is not merely his bitterness against his oppressors but his Bible. Again, imagery from the imprecatory psalms is used in portraying God's wrath against the contemporary embodiment of evil (Ps 69:24/Rev 16:1).

Some of John's imagery, such as earthquakes, storms, and hail, does not primarily refer to the punishment of humanity but is the awesome glory accompanying the appearance of God. It is not punishment language but theophany language: the earth reels because it cannot *stand* in the presence of God (cf. such scenes as 8:7 and 11:19, and cf. Exod 9:23–25; 19:18–19; Judg 5:4–5; 1 Kings 19:11–13; Pss 18:7–15; 29:3–9; Ezek 38:22; Joel 3:16).

The other side of this is to show that the basic elements on which human life depends, such as fertility of the fields, water, sun, moon, and bodily health, are not finally under human control. As human beings, we live in Somebody Else's world, and this truth is eschatologically demonstrated, that is, pictured for us. In the portrayals of the terrors of earthquake, plague, and other catastrophes that afflict the cosmos just before the final victory, the community confesses its faith that it does not control the universe and its destiny, but acknowledges that that destiny is in the hands of an indescribably awesome power over which we have no control. As in Exodus and the Psalter, this, and not the fate of those portrayed as suffering the final woes and its justice or injustice, is the "point" of such imagery.

Revelation's Core Theological Content

God Is the Righteous and Powerful Judge

John's dialectical theology sets him free to present the judgment of God in all its awful power. He need pull no punches, as though presenting God as partly just and partly merciful; both the justice and the mercy of God surpass the grasp of human logic and imagination. Each can be presented in its full force without compromising the other. From Revelation 6:1 on, when the Lamb begins to open the sealed book, John's vision is pervaded by the language of judgment (6:10; 11:18; 14:7; 15:4; 16:5, 7; 17:1; 18:8, 10, 20; 19:2, 11; 20:4, 12, 13).

For John's readers, courtroom scenes and the language of judgment are not abstract or hypothetical. The church people to whom he writes are threatened with judgment in actual courtrooms; some have already experienced it and been condemned. Jesus had stood before a Roman judge, had remained a faithful witness, was condemned in a Roman court, but was vindicated by the supreme court in which God is the judge, beyond which there is no appeal. John himself had probably been convicted in a human court; he certainly had personal experience of such trials. All John's judgment imagery and vocabulary should be seen in the framework of this reality. It is not just personal vindictiveness. It is not to be dispensed with; it is related to the justice of God. Nor should the judgment language of Revelation be contrasted with the teaching and example of Jesus in the Gospels. To be sure, the Jesus pictured as teaching in Galilee and Judea forbade his disciples to usurp the place of God-the-judge and take judgment into their own hands, but Jesus's teaching too is replete with images of God the final judge, with himself as the Son of Man exercising God's judgment (e.g., Matt 10:15; 11:22–24; 12:36, 41; 25:31–46; Luke 11:31; 18:1–6; 22:28–30; John 3:19; 5:22–27; 8:16, 50; 9:39; 12:48).

In the biblical tradition, the judge is not only the authorized officer who decides who or what is right but is also the powerful savior figure who acts to establish justice, uniting judicial and executive powers. The savior figures of early Israel, the series of leaders in the book of Judges, were mostly warriors. They did not merely sit behind the judicial bench and decide cases but were active in delivering God's people from their oppressors by power that comes from God. The operative word here is "power."

John insists that we must derive our understanding of power not from the powers of this age we know by experience and can observe just by looking around. John's theology, like that of New Testament authors in general, operates in terms of the traditional apocalyptic framework of the two ages—the present, old age dominated by sin, that is, self-assertive rebellion against the creator, and the age to come in which the creator will restore the original goodness of creation. The words translated "age" or "world" (Hebrew *ōlam* and Greek *aiōn*) have both temporal and spatial dimensions, but in theological contexts in the New Testament they do not refer to a specific historical period, even a very long one, but to the space-time continuum as a totality. The contrast between the space-time world as presently experienced by humans and the transcendent world of divine reality can be metaphorically expressed as this age/world in contrast to the age/world to come. John does not use the specific terminology of "this age" in contrast to "the age to come," but he often uses *aiōn* and "new" to refer to God's new world coming and already here.

In this world, all governments and all societies operate by power. Human efforts to establish justice, that is, to put justice into practice rather than hold it up as an ideal, involve power—violence or the threat of violence. Human efforts to establish justice are always hampered by imperfect discernment of what justice is and inadequate power to enforce justice, even when it is rightly discerned. In God's kingdom the discernment of justice is not hampered by faulty perception, neither is it thwarted by lack of power. We may assume we already know what *power* essentially is. But God's revelatory act in Jesus Christ calls our assumptions into question. God's justice can only be established by God's power, but as Richard Bauckham has stated, "It would subvert the whole purpose of John's prophecy if his depiction of the divine sovereignty appeared to be a projection into heaven of the absolute power claimed by human rulers on earth. . . . No writer of Scripture shows himself more aware of this difference than John."[10] The basic Christian confession, "The Christ is Jesus," already declares this. This confession does not abandon the believers' prayer that God's almighty power will finally make things right, but redefines it. It clings to the biblical imagery, in which a new world emerges by the power of God's anointed king of the new world coming and already here. This imagery involves awesome violence such as that read in Christian worship every Advent (Isa 11:1–9). These images are both affirmed and reinterpreted in the light of the Christ event.

Ponder the image of the "grapes of wrath":

> So the angel swung his sickle over the earth and gathered the vintage of the earth, and he threw it into the great wine press of the wrath of God. And the wine press was trodden outside the city, and blood flowed from the wine press, as high as a horse's bridle, for a distance of about two hundred miles. (Rev 14:19–20)

> From his mouth comes a sharp sword with which to strike down the nations, and he will rule them with a rod of iron; he will tread the wine press of the fury of the wrath of God the Almighty. (19:15)

John does not devise these images himself but adopts and adapts them from his Bible. The wine press, a familiar element in the grape culture of the Mediterranean world, frequently became an image of prosperity and God's blessing, including the blessing brought by the eschatological king—wine will be so plentiful people can wash their clothes in it (Num 18:27; Deut 15:14; 16:13; cf. Gen 49:10–12). Such lavish abundance of the fulfillment of God's purpose cannot have been meant literally, but it already represents the mind-stretching effort of language to express God's ultimate salvation. This image of the final blessing can encompass a powerful image of judgment (Lam 1:15; Joel 3:13). The promised and coming victory of God is graphically portrayed by the prophet who writes the latter part of Isaiah, which is already combining prophecy and apocalyptic, representing a dialogue between the prophet and Yahweh the divine Warrior:

> "Who is this that comes from Edom,
> from Bozrah in garments stained crimson?
> Who is this so splendidly robed,
> marching in his great might?"
> "It is I, announcing vindication,
> mighty to save."
> "Why are your robes red,
> and your garments like theirs who tread the wine press?"

> "I have trodden the wine press alone,
> and from the peoples no one was with me;
> I trod them in my anger
> and trampled them in my wrath;
> their juice spattered on my garments,
> and stained all my robes." (Isa 63:1–3)

John takes up this image of the God who treads "the wine press of the wrath of God." That he adds the detail "outside the city" may not be trivial. The early Christians remembered that Jesus's blood was shed outside the city (Mark 15:20–21; Luke 23:26; John 19:20). The author of Hebrews combines this memory with his insistence that Jesus did not offer the blood of others but "his own blood," and calls for Christian believers to join him "outside the city gate" (Heb 13:12–13). It is still the blood-drenched divine Warrior, but it is no longer the blood of his enemies that stains his clothes, and he makes war by the divine Word that he speaks and is, the sword of his mouth (Rev 1:16; 19:13, 21).

During the American Civil War, this image was again reinterpreted, this time with its original representation of actual violence. In the early days of the conflict, a battle song evolved among the Union troops celebrating John Brown, who had been killed in an attempt to free slaves at Harpers Ferry. The song's lyrics, though sung with gusto, were deemed irreverent, and scholar and author Julia Ward Howe, during a visit with Abraham Lincoln, accepted the suggestion of Unitarian minister and Harvard professor James Freeman Clarke that she write new words for the popular song. The "Battle Hymn of the Republic" became an expression of American patriotism and freedom:

> Mine eyes have seen the glory of the coming of the Lord:
> He is trampling out the vintage where the grapes of wrath are stored.

John Steinbeck's 1939 novel gave the phrase "grapes of wrath" yet another new dimension, this time moving back in the biblical direction. Though the story was fraught with the suffering of Depression-era poor being driven off their land, it also contained images of self-giving love, climaxed in the final scene in which Rose of Sharon feeds a starving man with her own breast milk.

The last public speech of Martin Luther King Jr. included words from the "Battle Hymn of the Republic." This champion of nonviolence as the means of establishing the justice of God's rule did not hesitate to use images of war, including the divine Warrior who will finally establish the kingdom of God.

The "grapes of wrath" were already being trampled out in the struggles of the civil rights movement; the "glory of the coming of the Lord" was not only the eschatological victory still to come but was already being realized in the victories for freedom and justice. Martin Luther King, like Rose of Sharon, and like Jesus, gave his own body and blood; he sang Revelation's song about those who conquer (the "overcomers," in King James English). He did not shun images of violence and war but preached from within the context of the powerful christological interpretation found in Revelation and the New Testament. The Lord tramples out the vintage of the grapes of wrath, but it is the wrath of the Lamb.

The Wrath of the Lamb: Christological Transformation of Traditional Imagery

Like other images in Revelation, "the wrath of the Lamb" can be trivialized or cartooned—a lamb portrayed as a small woolly creature in the pasture that is really, really mad. Just as Abraham and Sarah laughed when confronted with the incredible divine promise (Gen 17:17; 18:12–15), such laughter can express the experience of those who find themselves in the presence of the ultimately serious and ultimately personal and attempt to shrug it off with a joke. John, however, means it seriously. The "wrath of God," occurring five times in Revelation, is a common image throughout the Bible, including in the teaching of Jesus in the Gospels, the Jesus who was baptized by the one who proclaimed the coming wrath of God (Matt 3:7; 5:22; 18:34; Mark 3:5; Luke 14:21; 21:23; John 3:36). The traditional imagery of apocalyptic terror is adopted and used by John, but like everything else in his revelation, it is transformed within his christological perspective. The imagery of the lion is still used, but the Lion-Messiah turns out to be the slain Lamb. As in mathematics, when one changes the valence of the sign outside the parentheses, the formulae within the parentheses are retained, but all their values are reversed. In Revelation and the New Testament, the same imagery is used, but every minus is marked out and transformed into a plus. *Crossed* out.

John's Theology of Sin, Repentance, Judgment

John does not picture innocent or self-righteous Christians suffering at the hands of sinful Romans, but sinful humans, Christians included, reeling under the judgment of the holy God. The violent imagery repeatedly expresses John's conviction of universal human sinfulness. It is not only arrogant Babylon who sins (Rev 18:4–5) but also those who confess Jesus as the Christ (1:5), fulsomely illustrated in the messages to the seven churches (2:1–3:22). As in the plagues of the exodus story, events intended by God to call people to repentance (cf. 11:13) only serve to reveal how hardened are their hearts (9:20). The catastrophes are not simply terrible, tragic events—they are repeatedly placed in the category of God's judgments (6:10; 11:18; 14:7; 16:5, 7; 17:1; 18:8, 10, 20; 19:2, 11; 20:12, 13). The eschatological terrors are therefore an expression of John's sense of justice. Considering the situation, this is done in a remarkably nonsmug manner. The us/them mentality, while present, is not absolute: *we* are also judged as sinners; *they* are not excluded from salvation.

The increasingly intense judgments are not mere punishments for human sinfulness but are intended to call people to repentance. When they only harden human hearts and increase human rebellion, this is not an indication of divine frustration, as though God tried violence and it didn't work, as though God must either abandon most of the world to damnation or try a different approach. Rather, the depictions of divine violence are to *show the reader* that punitive judgment does not work, that it does not represent God's ultimate plan and never did. The love of God revealed in Jesus Christ was not a rethinking of divine strategy when violence failed to work; the book of life of the slaughtered Lamb has been there "from the foundation of the world" (13:8; 17:8). This love is already experienced both by believers who know its source and by those who do not yet know how to name it and respond to it. This love will finally prevail and will include everything and everyone. "Only when we acknowledge that Revelation hopes for the conversion of the nations . . . will we be able to see that it does not advocate a 'theology of resentment' but a theology of justice."[11] These considerations lead to more explicit and vivid pictures of where the road is finally going. These pictures interpret not only the destination but also the trip.

Revelation 19–22—in the End, God: The New World Coming and Already Here

At the last turn of the road, the city of God comes into view. It turns out that there is only one road, and it does not go on forever but has a final destination. The road through tragedy, suffering, and history is accompanied throughout by the presence of God in judgment and grace, and it will reach its goal. As we have come to expect, human minds and imaginations are not adequate to picture the ultimate act of God in one tableau. As hallelujah choruses reverberate in the heavenly worship (19:1–10), the new Jerusalem appears as the grand finale of God's eternal purpose, the climax of seven overlapping scenes: Jesus Christ returns as the divine Conqueror (19:11–16); the last battle is fought and won (19:17–21); Satan is captured, bound, and imprisoned (20:1–3); the martyred saints are raised and reign with Christ on earth for a thousand years (20:4–6); Satan is released, deceives the nations, and is destroyed (20:7–10); all the dead are raised and face the last judgment (20:11–15); the old creation passes away, and the new heaven and new earth are the setting for the fulfillment of history in the new Jerusalem (21:1–22:5).

The City of God

Readers may have noticed the repeated allusion to Augustine's great work of the fifth century, *De civitate Dei*, written in response to the population's worries about the decline of the Roman Empire. The sack of the self-proclaimed "Eternal City" by the Visigoths in 410 sent shock waves throughout the empire. Augustine's *City of God* contrasted the city of Rome with the city of God, within an exposition of the final chapters of Revelation. Virgil's first-century optimism celebrating Rome as the city that would last as long as the world was challenged by Revelation long before the decline of the Roman Empire that altered the mood of late antiquity.

Like Revelation's other mind-wrenching visions, these poetic scenes cannot be summarized or reduced to prosaic "meanings"—the message is inseparable from the medium. Some observations on John's literary-theological strategy help us to perceive some of the themes interwoven in his transcendent tapestry.

The Destination and the Trip

The world in which we live will in fact come to an end. It's not merely that our brief lives will come to an end and we will disappear from the road—the road itself will end. We now know that the universe is not eternal, and we know that not only from biblical revelation. Just as it is not only believers who talk about the beginning of the universe, so with its end: astrophysicists not only speak confidently of ultimate beginnings (big bang or whatever), but they also know that the universe will have an end (big crunch or whatever). For Christian faith, the road of history neither suddenly runs off a cliff of some cosmic catastrophe nor dwindles down to nothingness, neither bang nor whimper, but at the last turn of the road arrives at its destination, the city of God. The revelation of the end of the road discloses not only the ultimate future, but every turn of the road we travel now looks different. We not only look forward to the ultimate goal but the trip itself takes on new meaning, bigger than our little lives, and, whether or not our fellow sojourners share our faith, we look at them and ourselves with new eyes.

Multiple Images, Dynamic

If we ask John to tell us, in the light of Christian faith, what the end is like, he does not respond with an essay. By the time we reach chapter 19, we are not surprised that he holds before us a picture, and that it is not a single, static, unified picture. No one scene can communicate the purpose of God, the goal of the aeons of cosmic and human history. While the seven scenes cannot be presented or viewed all at once, their presentation as a series of separate images is not intended as a chronology. Each picture is held before the reader with its own discrete message of the ultimate triumph of God. The pictures overlap and fuse into each other without presenting an eschatological program.

The Final Battle

Evil doesn't last forever. There are two basic biblical pictures of what finally happens to evil:

> It is destroyed, overcome in a final battle, thrown into the lake of fire.
> It is redeemed and transformed, and shares in God's new world, no longer as evil but as belonging to God's beloved creation.

These two pictures cannot be blended into one superpicture. John, and the New Testament as a whole, has both. Neither can be eliminated without damaging the other. To live with this paradoxical pair of visions is realism, coming to terms with the way the world really is.

Proto-Trinitarian Verbal-Visual Images

John's theology continues to be expressed in the theological mode he has utilized throughout, in roles portraying God, Christ, and Spirit. The goal of history is for the whole creation to rejoice in the presence of the one God, the creator. The one God, the maker of all things, who stood at the beginning, declares, "I am the Alpha and the Omega"; he is the one "who is and who was and who is to come" (1:8). This same God stands at the end as creator who declares, "I am making all things new. . . . It is done! I am the Alpha and the Omega, the beginning and the end" (21:5–6). It is the flaming power of God from heaven that destroys the final spasm of evil (20:7–10), celebrated with the proclamation from the throne, "God himself will be with them" (21:3). Alongside such theocentric images in which Christ plays no role as a discrete figure, we see pictures that portray the end as the second coming of Christ, who destroys the powers of evil in the final battle (19:11–21), reigns with the resurrected saints for a thousand years (20:4–6), presides at the last judgment (20:11–15), and is the bridegroom at the ultimate wedding feast. To ask whether it is "God" *or* "Christ" who is met at the end of history, or to arrange them in a series, fails to engage John's mode of theology.

The specific image of the "second coming of Christ" in fact occupies only minimal space in the text of Revelation—this is surprising to those who get their impressions of the book from the culture of pop eschatology. John devotes fewer words to the second coming than he does to, for instance, the description of the city wall of the new Jerusalem. Nonetheless, mainliners who have downplayed talk of the second coming might note that the image is crucial to Revelation's theology because it is the second coming of *Jesus*, the *second* coming of the Messiah who has been here before. We know what he is like. At the end of history, we do not meet a newcomer, or a different person from the man of Nazareth who gave himself for others. It is a perversion of John's theology, and of the New Testament as a whole, to claim that when Jesus appeared in the first century he represented the love of God, but the Jesus who returns at the end represents God's wrath, as though God and Jesus "tried" love during the ministry of Jesus and through the centuries, but that at the eschaton we meet a Christ different from the one God revealed in *Jesus*. For John and the New Testament generally, the revelatory and salvific act of God is Jesus as the Word of God (19:16), God's ultimate and last word. There is no plan B.

John compresses a wealth of theological depth into this dazzling array of eschatological images. We will have occasion to explore several of them in later volumes in this series, as we take soundings in the theology of other biblical authors. Here we will only examine some of the facets of his final and most developed image, the bejeweled city of God.

In the End, Beauty

Even at best, there is plenty of ugliness in our world. Beautiful lives sometimes end with ugly sights, voices, sounds, smells. Ugliness does not have the last word; ugliness is not "just a part of life" to which we must finally, eternally, adjust. The city of God is a beautiful city. Each of its twelve gates is made from a single pearl, its streets are pure gold, transparent as glass. The foundations of its wall are precious stones of enormous size. This is not overdone gaudiness, not "then we'll all be rich" eschatological fulfillment of individualistic selfishness. It hardly needs to be said that there can be no literalism here—who will ask about the cosmic oyster that is the source of such pearls, or how pure gold can be transparent? It is John's effort to portray ultimate beauty. Think of the best music you have ever heard, the most breathtakingly beautiful scene you have ever beheld, and multiply it by infinity. That's where the universe is headed.

Surprise! It's a City

We might have supposed that John would have pictured the goal to which God is leading the universe more romantically, as a rural scene replete with natural beauty, far from the evil city (think of the Edenic images in the art of Thomas Cole and Albert Bierstadt). John could have read his Bible in a way that encouraged this. God originally placed humanity in a garden paradise. But alas, our first ancestors rebelled against the creator and were thrown out of the garden. Their son, the first murderer, built the first city, and ever since, civilization (= the citification of the natural world) has been built on violence, the murder of brothers by brothers. The Bible is thus filled with prophetic judgments of God against the procession of big, powerful, evil cities built on the backs of slaves and oppressed workers: the Egyptian cities Pithom and Rameses; the Philistine cities Gaza, Gath, Ashdod, Ashkelon, and Ekron; the imperial city Nineveh of the Assyrians; Babylon the Great, the Macedonian and Greek cities of Alexander and his successors, and now the greatest of them all, Rome. John has himself pronounced God's judgment on Rome, the great whore. Even many of Rome's wealthy citizens disdained living in the ugly and dangerous violence of the city and retired to their country estates.

Big Road, Little Lives

"My days are swifter than a weaver's shuttle" (Job 7:6). "What is your life? For you are a mist that appears for a little while and then vanishes" (James 4:14). Job and James express the lament of all humanity on the brevity of human life. The road we earthlings are traveling stretches out behind us for at least twelve billion years.

Our solar system is relatively young, but at least 4.5 billion years old. The sun will not burn its fuel supply for millions of years in the future. No one knows how long the road ahead of us may be.

Imagine the life of planet earth from its origin until today as one year:

1 January—Formation of the earth
1 May—Primitive marine organisms, like algae
25 October—Many-celled life-forms in the seas
20 November—Primitive fish
30 November—First amphibians
7 December—Reptiles dominant, age of dinosaurs
15 December—First mammals
31 December—First hominoids
31 December, 11 p.m.—Homo sapiens
31 December, 11:59, 59.2 seconds—birth of Jesus
31 December, 11:59, 59.9 seconds—World War II

In cosmic time, a video of the history of the earth would not even flicker on the screen. The horrors of Auschwitz, the joy and sorrow of an individual human life, are utterly beyond notice. Who remembers the tribespeople of Mongolia, 1800 BCE, and the struggles of parents and children who lived then, now vanished without a trace? Does it matter who they were and what they did? If my life of seventy or eighty years (Ps 90!) will not matter to anyone four thousand years from now, does it matter who I am and what I do in the here and now? What gives them the significance the author of Psalm 90 wonders about and Psalm 8 sings about? "How Great Thou Art" was first sung by one who recognized that the One without whose knowledge not a sparrow falls, who created us, numbers the hairs of our heads, knows us by name, is the creator who has a plan that embraces our little lives.

Wrong! John portrays the end of the road of universal history as a great city. What is a city? City life means living together, in mutual dependence. The traditional stereotype of preindustrial country life glorifies the independent individual. There, people raise their own crops, build their own houses, rule their own individualistic lives, and resent the incursion of city people with their laws, telling them what they must do. John pictures the purpose of God in universal history as preparing people to live together, all kinds of different people, all members of the one family of God. The church is already the prototype of such a community.

A Universal, Particular City

The city of God is inclusive, but it is not generic, not homogenized; it is a harmonious, colorful combination of names. It belongs to the new age as the capital city of the new creation, but it bears the name and character of a particular historical city of the old age. Jerusalem had been a Canaanite city, then it was conquered by David and became the capital of the united kingdom of the people of God. It lived through many ups and downs, was destroyed and rebuilt more than once. The church that extends to the end of the earth began in a particular city, Jerusalem (Acts 1:8). History is a matter of particulars, as are our little lives. The road that leads through history finds its fulfillment not in Anytown or Universalville but in the new Jerusalem. Its gates are named after the twelve tribes of Israel, its foundations bear the names of the twelve apostles of Jesus Christ. This means that the agony-and-ecstasy story of human history, with its struggles to build a city in which truly human life could flourish, is not abolished; the slate is not wiped clean and the story begun afresh with a new city from heaven.

The new Jerusalem does indeed come down from heaven—it can never be constructed by even the most idealistic human efforts—but when it comes, it does not nullify all human efforts throughout history to build a decent city. Neither does it revert to some prehistory, pre-Fall golden age before this-worldly history went wrong. Ultimate salvation is not going back to the garden, but bringing the primal created goodness of the garden into the eschatological city of God. The tree of life is transplanted in the new Jerusalem (Rev 22:2). The city of God is not a final escape from the troubles of historical existence along the road of life, a final retreat into the castle where the door is locked from the inside; it is a fulfillment in which the road traveled, the splendid variety of human culture developed in the toil of history, is not neutralized but redeemed and glorified. God "will dwell with them; / they will be his peoples" (21:3). As the one redeemed people of God, they retain their particular historical character, including their languages.

The new Jerusalem is multicultural and international; it will not go back to a pre–Tower of Babel uniformity but will celebrate the colorful variety of historical human life. The past centuries of human struggle are not nullified and replaced but redeemed. The city of God is a conversion project, not a replacement project. The new Jerusalem is built from the stones not only of the old Jerusalem but also of Babylon, Athens, and Rome, as well as Tokyo, Cairo, Walla Walla, and Beulah Valley. This applies not only to social realities but also to our individual lives. The fragmented moments that make up a human life are not left behind but gathered up and presented whole in the eternal city. Not only will we "know each other in heaven," we will, for the first time, know ourselves and our little historical lives, transformed and made whole (see further on John 1:1–14). At the end, God does not make all new things, but makes all things new (Rev 21:5).

Will We Know Each Other in Heaven?

I'm not here claiming to explain the details of eternal life in the transcendent world of God beyond history and biology. Of course, I intend such phrases metaphorically, attempting to express that the details that make up our individual lives are not lost in a great cosmic blender but are preserved in ways we cannot imagine. To claim otherwise betrays that we "know neither the scriptures nor the power of God" (Mark 12:24).

A Big City

In cities such as Ephesus and Pergamum, the little Christian congregations were dwarfed by pagan culture and pagan temples. The theater in Ephesus could seat all the Christians in Asia, and then some; four such theaters could seat all the Christian believers in the world. The natural human inclination would be to think, "We are just the faithful few, but we are the ones who will finally be saved, a tiny town at last free from the sinful masses. We're the little group of outsiders now, but just wait, we'll see who's on the inside and who's on the outside." We have already seen that Revelation presents mind-stretching visions of the size and cosmic proportions of the people of God. John's vision of the new Jerusalem presents an enormous city—1,500 miles *cubed*—with room for all. The insider/outsider distinction, apparently so important now, is blurred. There is no temple (21:22), and no need for one. There is no distinction between the holy and the profane, not because what has been considered holiness is unimportant but because the special area and dimension of reality once called "holy" in distinction from "unholy" have now been universalized. God is the Holy One (Isa 1:4; 6:3; Rev 4:8; and dozens of times), God is all in all (1 Cor 15:28), and all is finally holy.

A Walled City with Eternally Open Gates

City walls are for defense, for security. Those who dwell within them are finally, ultimately secure; will no longer live by the compulsions of their own insecurities, personal or national; and will no longer have anything to prove, to themselves or others. Yet there are no longer any enemies to be feared, no reason to have a *walled* city at all, no reason to ever again invoke "national security" as a political argument. Walls have always had a deeply symbolic meaning that is often more important than their practical military value. Walls distinguish insiders from outsiders, us from them; they give us a sense of identity and community. To finally belong, to be accepted as an insider, is worth something. Everyone in the new Jerusalem knows what it means to be accepted; everyone is an insider, safely within the walls. Yet the walls have gates that are always open. The new Jerusalem will never close the door in anyone's face. What sort of walls are these that cancel out their very reason for existing? Here again, John's imagery struggles to represent the tensive, dialectic truth of God.

On the one hand, John specifically states that "nothing unclean will enter [the city], nor anyone who practices abomination or falsehood, but only those who are written in the Lamb's book of life" (Rev 21:27). "Outside are the dogs and sorcerers and fornicators and murderers and idolaters, and everyone who loves and practices falsehood" (22:15). The kings of the earth have usurped God's authority and persecuted his people, but they are destroyed (twice over, 19:21; 20:9!). The final picture still has people who are outside the walls of the new Jerusalem, "the cowardly, the faithless, the polluted, the murderers, the fornicators, the sorcerers, the idolaters, and all liars," whose place will be in the lake that burns with fire and sulfur (21:8). Even if we have come to appreciate and affirm the terrifying pictures of God's judgment in chapters 6–18 and are now ready to see such scenes as a temporary phase of judgment on the way to an ultimate acceptance of everyone, John's dialectic is not so neat and mentally satisfying. We might note that those still outside are not excluded because they have not become Christians. Nothing is said of their theological confession; it's all about their conduct, the kind of people they are. This is John's way of avoiding the false conclusion posed by those who object to universal grace, universal salvation: "If everyone is going to finally be saved, then it doesn't matter what we do, right?" Like Jesus, Paul, and the other New Testament writers, this line of thought, logical and consistent as it may be, is rejected. What we do matters, matters in a way that cannot be expressed or exaggerated. John's pictures of the exclusion of certain ways of living one's life are also John's way of portraying the quality of life of the final city of God. The sinful life that has characterized all humanity will not be continued within the walls of the new Jerusalem. So long as people continue their sinful practices, so long will they remain outsiders (see further in volume 2 of this series, on the "broken wall" in Ephesians).

On the other hand, the new Jerusalem is the ultimately inclusive city with room for everyone who has ever lived, the hometown of all humanity. The kings of the earth, the arrogant rulers who had usurped God's rule, bring their honor and glory into the city (21:24). Here John presents one of his numerous christological reinterpretations of biblical imagery. Ezekiel's vision of the eschatologically restored Jerusalem included trees that bore their fruit every month, whose leaves were for healing—no hunger there, no sickness there. In John's vision, the leaves are for the healing *of the nations.* The gentile, outsider nations, with their false religions and their suspicions and hostilities that have divided humanity into warring camps, will not finally be destroyed (as in the eschatological pictures of some biblical prophecies) but will be healed. God will dwell with them as their God; "they will be his peoples" (21:3, note plural!). It might seem to us champions of logical consistency that John, and the New Testament generally, should have had the theological courage and clarity to come down on one side or the other of the clear alternative: either opt for conditional salvation, including those who meet the conditions of faith and/or works, or opt for unconditional salvation that includes everyone. We do not know whether John would have agreed with Ralph Waldo Emerson's "A foolish consistency is the hobgoblin of little minds." We do know that he has a big mind that will not relax its grip on either human responsibility or divine sovereignty, and that he continues to his last page to affirm that the distinctions that our little minds must perhaps continue to make "are to be consumed in the fire of Him whose judgment and love are both beyond our comprehension."[12]

Chapter 3

Tensions and Conflicts in the Beloved Community: The Johannine Letters

Revelation was a letter that functioned as one of several teaching documents that circulated within the network of Johannine churches in the Roman province of Asia in the 90s of the first century CE. What we now know as 2 and 3 John were letters addressed to the same cluster of congregations, closely resembling the conventional form of Hellenistic letters. First John was a letter-like tract, a teaching document composed to be read and studied in the churches. The Gospel of John was the crowning work of this Johannine circle of teachers, presenting the unifying theology of the Johannine school in the gospel form that retells the Jesus Christ story and mediates the voice of the risen Christ to the contemporary church—theirs and ours.

We have begun with Revelation, in order to remind ourselves of the strangeness of the biblical world and to restrain our tendency to read our own way of thinking, with its priorities and agendas, into the biblical text. Before proceeding to the other biblical texts from Revelation's own time and place, we might remind ourselves that these writings, different as they are from our customary mind-set, also represent a world that is very much *like* our own. We live in a world of cultural and religious pluralism, as a divided church struggling to be true to our origins in a history carrying us further and further from our historical beginnings. The church from which the letters and Gospel of John come would say exactly the same.

The elder's brief letters mostly let us listen in on the questions and problems of this early generation of our ancestors in the faith, and let us perceive something of the context into which the Gospel of John was directed as a comprehensive corrective and normative statement of Christian faith. The letters themselves, however, not only pose and illustrate the questions that trouble the church but also offer provisional answers. Not only questions and issues but all the basic themes of Johannine theology are already present in 1–3 John.

JOHANNINE CORPUS: Revelation, 1–3 John, and the Gospel of John form a loose unity, sharing the same general geographical and historical setting, with overlapping vocabularies and theological conceptions, that is, they are all associated with the Johannine community.

AUTHORS: The Gospel and 1–3 John were composed by a group of authors in the Johannine school tradition, with which Revelation was less directly associated. The letters 2 John and 3 John were written by an unnamed elder; 1 John and the Gospel are anonymous. The final edition of the Gospel was attributed to the Beloved Disciple, a leading member and probable founder of the Johannine school tradition. The Johannine school regarded the risen Christ as the church's continuing teacher, acting and speaking through the Holy Spirit at work in the church's teachers and in the community as a whole.

DATE: 2–3 John were written in the 90s of the first century CE, 1 John a little later. Begun circa 80 CE, the Gospel had an evolving compositional history within the Johannine community. The final edition that became canonical appeared early in the second century CE, after 1–3 John.

ADDRESSEES: The network of churches in the stream of tradition associated with the Beloved Disciple, in the Roman province of Asia.

PROVENANCE: A central location of the Johannine stream of tradition in Asia, most probably Ephesus.

LITERARY SOURCES: The Fourth Gospel utilized the Jewish Scriptures and appears to have been influenced by one or more of the Synoptic Gospels. The substance of its narrative is based on the oral traditions from and about Jesus that were handed on "from the beginning" in the Johannine community. The author(s) probably knew and were influenced by other Christian writings circulating in Asia at the turn of the century, including Pauline letters. None of these were directly used as sources in the same way that Matthew and Luke used Mark.

The *theo*logical danger the elder sees threatening the churches is explicitly *christo*logical: false teachers are promoting the view that Christ did not truly come "in the flesh" (2 John 7; cf. 1 John 4:2). While Christology is indeed a core issue of all Christian theology, and it is a false christological understanding that is most upsetting to the elder, our own understanding of what is at stake here is better facilitated by beginning with ecclesiology, his understanding of church-in-the-world. This is in step with the Jewish Scriptures and theology inherited by the Johannine Christians. The Johannine community in Asia had apparently been begun by Jewish Christians and was later influenced by Jewish Christians migrating from Palestine, fleeing the devastation of the 66–70 war. In the intervening decades, their thinking had been affected by the more Hellenistic thought world of Roman Asia and by an influx of gentile believers. While some members of the community relaxed their grip on Jewish tradition and Scriptures, the church's basic DNA continued to include the core conviction that the saving act of God involved the *calling of a chosen people* through whom God's purpose for the world would be effected. The first words of the elder's earliest extant letter address the congregation in words and images he need not explain to his readers—they are the elect people of God (2 John 1). In the Jewish consciousness shaped by the Scripture, God's initial and fundamental response to the world's sin, not remedied by the judgment of the flood (Gen 3–11), was not to promise that a Messiah would come for the world's salvation but, astoundingly, to *call a people within this world*, a covenant community, as the means and guarantee of God's saving purpose (Gen 12:1–3). The concept and imagery of the people of God as the fundamental, comprehensive theological framework for biblical theology are not explicated in the Johannine letters—there is no focus on ecclesiology per se, as there is on Christology—but ecclesiology is implicit in every paragraph. In attempting to draw within hearing distance of what these letters have to say, we do well to begin with ecclesiology. Then as now, believers did not consciously occupy themselves with christological issues that seemed more theoretical and remote, but with the concrete life of the believing communities to which they belonged. Then as now, the church lived in a pluralistic world.

Pluralistic World

We twenty-first-century believers have become increasingly aware of the size and diversity of our world. Whether we live on a farm or in a metropolitan high-rise, we are daily confronted with TV and Internet that instantly bring the whole world to our dens, living rooms, and cell phones. In the nineteenth-century village or the persistent village mentality that sometimes continues to dog both preacher and congregation today, we deal only or mainly with people like ourselves and are tempted to shape our faith to fit our little world. We (preacher and congregation) may even long for a return to the "simple world of the Bible," away from "the complexity of the modern world." It may be a welcome insight that the New Testament writings

Jesus's Call to Decision Implied an Ecclesiology

When I was in seminary in the 1960s, Christology was a focal point. Many students, ministers, and churchpeople were bothered by the apparent reality that the "historical Jesus" had not made explicit christological claims; these were to be attributed to the later church. Should Christians believe things about Jesus he did not believe about himself? Is it legitimate to use the New Testament's exalted language for Jesus to confess my faith—not only "Christ" and "Son of God" but even including "my Lord and my God" (John 20:28)—if Jesus did not speak this way about himself?

Many of my contemporaries found Rudolf Bultmann, *Theology of the New Testament*, trans. Kendrick Grobel, 2 vols. (New York: Scribner's Sons, 1951), to offer a helpful perspective. He argued for the legitimacy of the church's later christological affirmations, summing up his approach by asserting that "Jesus' call to decision implied a Christology" (1:43), so that the New Testament's use of christological titles is rightly to be seen as drawing out the implications of Jesus's own claim.

This was indeed a helpful move. Faith expressed in the confessional christological language of the New Testament was legitimate theology and the foundation for a life of discipleship to Jesus, even though Jesus had not used that language about himself. We hardly noticed, however, that the critical point had now shifted from Christology to ecclesiology. Some streams of pop theology have since welcomed reconstructions of the "real Jesus," whose life and message had supposedly been domesticated and obscured by the church and its New Testament. Their solution: "Follow Jesus" but minimize or reject the church and its Bible. The challenge now is not so much christological as ecclesiological. The Johannine school understood that authentic discipleship to Jesus involves not only thinking through the meaning of Christology, but that this is inseparable from a doctrine of the church. God not only sent Jesus but raised him from the dead, and through the word of the risen Christ called into being a renewed people of God, the church.

emerged from a pluralistic world in which Christians were a tiny minority, often unwelcome and suspect. Our New Testament texts come from early Christian teachers who formulated—and reformulated—their theology within the big world that embraces all God's creation, in all its entrancing and threatening complexity. We may be just discovering the multicultural complexities of our own world, but the gospel was born in a multicultural world. We may be just catching up with our Bible. It can help us.

Christians in Ephesus were of course aware of the particulars of their own world and heard their Christian texts within this context, for they were reminded at every turn that their lives were interwoven with the religions, cultures, and politics of the wider world. For them, this meant the Mediterranean, from Spain to Syria and Egypt, from the Sahara to the Alps. Ephesus was a port city, center of a metropolitan population of about two hundred thousand diverse inhabitants, the proud capital of a province. The city was visited by vessels from all over the world and was an international showcase, home of one of the Seven Wonders—the temple of Artemis/Diana, four times the size of the Parthenon. This dazzling architectural achievement, treasured and celebrated as a focus of patriotic and religious life, also served as an international bank that stabilized the economy not only of Asia but also of the world of its far-flung depositors and investors. The Celsus Library, built around the same time the Gospel of John was composed, ranked third in the world. Statesmen, scholars, tourists, pilgrims, and merchants from distant lands rubbed elbows in Ephesus's crowded streets. Many languages were heard in its marble plazas, but Hellenistic Greek was universally understood by urban citizens across the empire, and the Roman Empire itself provided a sense of political and economic stability and belonging to the wider world. Townsfolk of outlying villages could still live in their traditional, small-scale world, but residents of Ephesus were *cosmo*politan and lived their lives with an awareness of the *cosmos*—a key word in Johannine theology (occurring 105 times in Johannine writings and only 16 times in Matthew, Mark, Luke, and Acts).

This world included, front and center, a pluralistic spectrum of religions. Sincere, searching human beings, looking for a larger framework of meaning, looking for ways to come to terms with the mystery in which we live our little lives, had inherited and developed a variety of religious faiths. Some of these we might regard as only the magic and superstition of prescientific minds. Looking more closely and deeply, we might find that some of these were profound and beautiful, expressing the universal longing of the human heart for something or someone worthy of worship, to whom to give thanks, to call out to for help, hoping and praying that we are not alone and on our own in the cold vastness of a silent and uncaring universe. The preachers and teachers in the Johannine school addressed Christian believers who sought to find their own way, the way revealed by God's act in Christ, in the midst of a dazzling array of religious faiths.

In this regard, we are now to some extent catching up with the early Christians of Ephesus. The Christian missionaries who planted churches in the first-century Roman province of Asia did not bring religion to a nonreligious world but proclaimed the Christian gospel as one item on an imposing menu of inviting religious faiths. Diversity was the order of the day. Alongside the superstitions of local folk religion, fortune-telling, and astrology that exist in all societies, including our own, the world to which the Christian faith was proclaimed boasted an impressive breadth and depth of religions.

In that world the classical Greek and Roman religions were by no means dead. They continued to flourish, generating fervent support, as illustrated by the pilgrims that thronged the temple of Artemis (cf. Acts 19:23–41). Philosophical universalism offered an intellectually sophisticated spirituality that saw all religions as expressions of one universal divine principle. Stoicism, as illustrated in the writings of the slave Epictetus and the emperor Marcus Aurelius, was among the philosophical approaches to life that was not only popular among intellectuals but also found a broad response among the populace. Human beings found that the reason (*logos*) that separated them from unreasoning animals and the material world joined them to the supreme principle of an orderly universe. By the time the New Testament was written, Cleanthes's "Hymn to Zeus" had long proclaimed a faith that saw all the gods as manifestations of Zeus: "Many are thy names. . . . How great thou art, King above all forever."

The Mystery Cults

The mystery cults, ancient and international, inserted a profoundly moving experience of personal initiation into the story of savior gods who delivered from death and united believers in a community that transcended national and racial differences. (A reminder: the term "cult" in studies of the history of religion does not have the negative connotations it has often accumulated in contemporary discourse, but refers to the structured worship of a religious community or institution.)

The Emperor Cult

The emperor cult, in which the Caesar was praised as "Son of God" and "Savior of the World," was not merely an ego-trip, top-down initiative promoted by the rulers in Rome and provincial capitals. Worship of the emperor was mainly a grassroots movement that saw Rome and the emperor as a symbol of international stability, bringing peace and prosperity to the world. Cities such as Ephesus, which built a magnificent temple to the emperor, competed with other cities for permission from Rome for the privilege, just as modern cities compete for the opportunity to host the Super Bowl or the Olympics.

Judaism

Judaism had long been present in most of the urban centers evangelized by early Christian missionaries and formed a significant element in the religious context of the church even after it became predominately gentile. The church had begun, of course, as a movement within Judaism. When it became increasingly apparent, over the course of two or three generations, that Jews who confessed Jesus to be the Messiah could not continue to participate in the synagogue, the painful process of the "parting of the ways" left many live wounds and slow-to-heal scars on both sides. The church(es) in Ephesus began from Jewish Christian roots. Local Jews would have an ambivalent response to the new Christian movement, and vice versa. The church's neighbors, and sometimes Christians themselves, had difficulty sorting out differences between Jews and Christians (cf. Acts 19:34!). For Revelation and the Gospel of John, the church's intense but ambiguous relation to Judaism lies near the surface. This is not so explicit in 1–3 John, but any community that confesses the Jewish Messiah as Lord, regularly reads the Jewish Scriptures in its worship, and thinks of itself as the biblical people of God must be seen in terms of its relation to Judaism. We Christian preachers and teachers who want to come within hearing distance of these texts need an informed grasp of first-century Judaism.

Gnosticism

Along with Judaism, Gnosticism is the most important stream of ancient religious thought for understanding the Johannine writings. Gnosticism only became an identifiable movement in post–New Testament times, but the mood and elements of what was later considered the gnostic heresy were already present in the first century. This proto-Gnosticism was not an obscurantist cult, but in the popular mind it represented the progressive scientific and philosophical knowledge of the day.

Proto-Gnosticism can be no more adequately summarized in a sentence than can the versions of Christianity that came to be accepted as orthodox. Christian teachers who wanted to fit the church's faith into the gnosticizing mold called for serious, long-term study to grasp the real meaning of the Christian faith in respectable scientific and philosophical terms, in contrast to the "simple faith" of ordinary believers. An admittedly inadequate thumbnail sketch of the belief system would include the following elements:

1. *One God*, the Ultimate, Unthinkable, Unknowable One, dwells in the transcendent world far beyond what the human mind can conceive.
2. *The material world* came into being through a long, complex process not intended by the one God. Creation was some kind of cosmic mistake by a lesser divine being.
3. *Human beings* (*or some of them*), in their inner spirit, belong to the world of the one true God, but their spirits have somehow been trapped in this material world. Although they do not now know it, in their inner spirit they are united with God and with each other.

Preaching the Gospel at Old First Gnostic

"Old First Gnostic Church stands in a prominent place in town—actually in every town. Among its members are the 'best and the brightest'—attorneys, physicians, teachers, thoughtful and open-minded people of every stripe. Old First Gnostic is Presbyterian, or perhaps it's Methodist or Baptist or Lutheran or U.C.C. or Disciples. Stewardship at Old First Gnostic is always a challenge, especially in these economic times, but the money seems to come in eventually, and, of course, there is always the endowment. Parents at Old First Gnostic hope their children will grow up to make wise choices about their religion, but the main desire is for their children to be happy in life and to be good people. Old First Gnostic has a handsome and historic building and is holding its own in terms of membership, but worship attendance is a constant concern. The church has a professional (and expensive) music program and a fine choir, which provides inspiring and quality music in the Sunday services. The leadership of Old First Gnostic is well aware of the wildfire growth of the so-called 'mega churches' in town, the ones with the energetic, digital-fueled worship services and sermons on topics like 'Tweeting Jesus,' but their heads are not turned. In fact, Old First Gnostic sniffs at pop Christianity and understands itself as the alternative to such flashy and superficial churches. At Old First Gnostic, there are challenging adult forums on 'ecology,' 'understanding Islam,' and 'What does the Bible really say about sex?' Old First Gnostic is progressive, inclusive, committed to education, and the pews are populated by smart, probing, intellectually honest people who prize thought-provoking and spiritually challenging sermons. It is the kind of church many astute clergy yearn to serve."

—Thomas G. Long, "Preaching Easter at Old First Gnostic,"
Journal for Preachers, 2011

What is the message of the Gospel of John for the good, sincere people of Old First Gnostic?

Salvation comes by knowledge of one's true origin, one's true spiritual identity, a spiritual core encased in a this-worldly body. The *gnōsis* of Gnosticism is the Greek word for "knowledge." This knowledge is salvation, for it allows one to make sense of and endure life in this stinking world (cf. John 11:39!) and finally to escape this world and return to our true home. The sparks of divine light trapped in the flesh-and-blood bodies of this world cannot attain such knowledge on their own, for they have been numbed or lulled to sleep and have forgotten their divine origin. The way to salvation must be revealed and has in fact been provided by a Teacher, or series of teachers, sent from the divine spiritual world. Such knowledge is complex and not easily learned; the "knowers" are superior not only to unbelievers but also to simplistic believers.

The church of the first century, and still today, struggles with whether and how to appropriate gnosticizing spirituality, which it does sometimes consciously, sometimes without awareness of what is going on—interpreting the Christian faith in terms that were opposed in the New Testament and branded as heretical in mainstream ancient Christianity. Numerous sermons and church newsletters speak of our "spiritual core," or a "part of God" that is embedded in us, which resonates with God and the "part of God" found in other people. Gnosticism is alive and well in American culture, secular and religious. Many Christians, "mainline" and otherwise, resonate with William Wordsworth's "Intimations of Immortality," supposing it reflects Christian spirituality.

> "Our birth is but a sleep and a forgetting:
> The Soul that rises with us, our life's Star,
> Hath had elsewhere its setting,
> And cometh from afar:
> Not in entire forgetfulness,
> And not in utter nakedness,
> But trailing clouds of glory do we come
> From God, who is our home."
>
> —from William Wordsworth, "Ode: Intimations of Immortality"

Echoes of the gnostic perspective are still found in songs popular in some Christian religious traditions ("This world is not my home . . ."). In Gnosticism, the gospel is not about God's act in the incarnation, life, death, and resurrection of Jesus, but is the revelation of something about ourselves, our own true being as sparks of the divine Light. In this view, Jesus was the great teacher of divine truths, telling or reminding us of our true spiritual selves.

All these religious communities, movements, and perspectives existed prior to the beginnings of the church. They continued to exist alongside the new churches in Ephesus, interacting with emerging Christian understandings. Some of these could offer helpful insights for our understanding of the faith. Others might betray essential elements of the very faith they were trying to bring up to date. But which was which, who gets to say, and on what basis? In Ephesus, as elsewhere, this necessary and vital interaction produced a variety of theologies and communities, relating to each other in various combinations of respect and suspicion. The church with a mission within a pluralistic world is itself a fragmented church.

Fragmented Church

We might here remind ourselves that when we speak of "the church," "the Christian community," or "the followers of Jesus" in Ephesus and environs in the province of Asia, we are using shorthand terms for quite a wide-ranging assortment of religious groups. By the end of the first century CE, Ephesus was home to at least the following clusters of people and traditions, sometimes overlapping, all claiming loyalty to Jesus Christ.

1. *The Palestinian connection*: The Palestinian prophet John the Baptist still had his admirers and followers in Ephesus, sixty years after his martyrdom (Acts 18:24–26; 19:1–6). The claims of this group were still problematic for Johannine Christians in Ephesus (cf. John 1:6–8, 15, 19–34; 3:26–4:1; 5:33; 10:40–42).
2. *Jews from Asia* were among those converted on the first Pentecost, according to Acts 2:9. If this verse includes historical information, such Jewish Christians, upon their return to their home cities, would have already in 30 CE established one or more congregations in Roman Asia, presumably like the earliest church in Jerusalem.
3. *Jewish Christians with Pontus, Roman, Corinthian, and Pauline connections*: Priscilla and Aquila, originally from Pontus, were Jewish Christians who came to Corinth in 49 CE because the emperor had expelled all Jews from Rome. We do not know how or when they became Christians, nor the origins of the Roman church of which they had been members, but they presumably reflected the Jewish roots of the Roman church. They worked closely with Paul for a year and a half, establishing the church in Corinth, then went with him to Ephesus,

where they seem to have been the first Christians in town. Paul himself, after a brief discussion with some Jews that did not result in founding a church, left for Jerusalem, leaving Aquila and Priscilla in Ephesus. During his absence, they began a Christian congregation in their home, presumably reflecting the traditions of Jewish converts like themselves, now in a gentile context (Acts 18:1–23).

4. *Apollos and early Alexandrian Christianity*: During Paul's absence, an outstanding Christian preacher and teacher from Alexandria came to Ephesus. In the judgment of Priscilla and Aquila, he had a faulty understanding of baptism and the Holy Spirit but received further instruction from them and was accepted by the congregation they had begun. After some time, he departed for Corinth with a letter of recommendation from the congregation in Ephesus (Acts 18:24–19:7).
5. *Gentile Christians of the Pauline type*: The letters and Gospel of John were written over a period of some years or decades in a setting in which the authors were in dialogue with a vigorous stream of Pauline Christianity. The church in Ephesus had not been founded by Paul, nor had he been active in its formative period, but upon his reestablishing contact with his colleagues there, he spent more than two years in mission work in Ephesus (Acts 19:8–20), working alongside Priscilla and Aquila. He sent greetings from them to the Corinthian church (1 Cor 16:19) and later greeted them after they had returned to Rome (Rom 16:3). Paul considered Priscilla, Aquila, and Apollos to be valued colleagues and coworkers, but they were not his subordinates, nor did the congregations they established and led affirm the strictly Pauline version of the Christian faith (cf. 1 Cor 1:12; 3:4–6, 22; 4:6; 16:12). Ephesus became a center of the Pauline mission. Paul never wrote a letter *to* the Ephesian Christians (the canonical letter to the Ephesians is by a Pauline disciple some decades later), but at the time the Johannine letters were being written at the end of the century, Ephesus had apparently become the center of the "Pauline school," an informal network of teachers who collected, edited, interpreted, and circulated Paul's letters to the wider church. These Pauline teachers also composed new works in the name of their revered teacher, interpreting the Pauline version of the gospel for new situations (Colossians, Ephesians, 2 Thessalonians, the Pastorals).
6. *Anti-Pauline Christians and those suspicious of Paul*: When Paul wrote Philippians from an Ephesian prison circa 52, most local church members lamented his imprisonment, but some were glad to have him out of

the way (Phil 1:12–18). Some of these may have been the stricter or more cautious members of Ephesian congregations in the Jewish Christian stream.

7. *Petrine Christians with Roman connections*: The circular letter of 1 Peter, written about the same time as 1–3 John, included Roman Asia in its list of addressees (1 Pet 1:1). This indicates that there must have been some resonance among the Christians of Asia for the emerging role of the Roman church in leading the wider church through a period of theological conflict and political unease, coming from a "fellow elder" (1 Pet 5:1; cf. 5:5). The letter was written in Peter's name but was heavily influenced by Pauline theology and represented the confluence and combination of Pauline and Petrine Christianity in Rome near the end of the first century CE—under the name of *Peter*.
8. *John the prophet of Revelation*: John was an itinerant prophet familiar to the network of Johannine congregations in Asia. Claiming direct authority from the risen Lord, John portrays elders enthroned in heaven but ignores or seems unaware of any "elders" with authority in the earthly congregations. He takes hard-line stances on disputed issues of eating sacrificial meat offered to idols, a part of his opposition to the accommodation to the religious claims of the emperor advocated by the "progressives" (Rev 1–3).
9. *Other outspoken Christian prophets* influenced the theology and churches in Ephesus at the close of the first century. The rivals of John, "Jezebel" and "Balaam," were influential in the same churches in which he preached, proclaiming opposing views on theology, ethics, and politics. In the view of the author of 1 John, it is not only the Holy Spirit who is inspiring prophets among the churches; evil spirits, indeed the antichrist himself, are sending false prophets, and the church needs ways to discern which is which (1 John 4:1–3).
10. *Ignatius, bishop of Antioch*, was arrested, condemned, and sent to Rome for execution. As a prisoner en route to Rome, he passed through Asia about 110 CE and met with some church leaders, including Onesimus, the bishop of Ephesus. Ignatius warned the Asian churches he addressed against heretical christological teaching that undermines the faith and urged the congregations to support and obey their bishops. While some of Ignatius's directions may represent the way he would like the church to be rather than the reality of his time, on both theology and church polity his letters present a different picture of the church than other testimonies from the same time and place.

11. *Proto-gnostic interpretations of the Christian faith*: Elements of the gnostic mood and perspective were present in the culture and religions surrounding the new churches and were sometimes adopted, consciously or unconsciously, as ways of expressing the Christian faith. Just as thoughtful preachers, teachers, and church members had to think through how best to appropriate their Jewish heritage, so too did they have to think through the validity of interpreting the meaning of God's saving act in Christ in the "gnostic" (translate "scientific" or "philosophical") categories of their times.
12. *Teachers of the sayings and stories of Jesus*: Teachers were active among the Asian churches by the end of the first century CE. None of the types of Christians discussed above confessed their faith by rehearsing the teaching of Jesus or telling stories about him. They all proclaimed the act of God in the Christ event as a whole, but neither Paul and the tradition descended from him nor any of the other preachers and teachers documented above made the teaching of the 30 CE Jesus and the stories from his ministry in Galilee and Judea the vehicle of Christian proclamation and teaching. Alongside the epistolary form of Christian instruction appeared the gospel mode of preaching and teaching. Some Christian teachers collected, interpreted, edited, and composed collections of Jesus's sayings and stories about him, which they used in preaching and teaching the gospel. The Gospel of Mark had been composed circa 70 CE. Though there is no direct evidence, such texts were surely known among the churches of Asia by the end of the first century. The Johannine letters make no reference to any saying of Jesus or story about him (!). There is one brief, indirect indication that some members of the Johannine community were using materials from the "life of Jesus" as models for the Christian life ("whoever says, 'I abide in him,' ought to walk just as he walked," 1 John 2:6). By the time the Gospel of John was written, we may confidently assume the following were available to Christian teachers in Asia:
    a. A variety of oral traditions portraying the words and deeds of the pre-Easter Jesus, including perhaps some written collections of Jesus's sayings such as Q and collections of his deeds such as the "Signs Source" postulated by some scholars.
    b. Preliminary forms of what became the Gospel of John. Such were probably circulating among the churches of Asia at the time the letters were composed, but the acceptance and use of the gospel form as such were still disputed at this time.

c. The Gospels of Mark and Matthew. Mark was written prior to both the letters and the Gospel of John. Matthew, and possibly Luke, were also available to the author of the canonical form of the gospel. Also, a number of similarities between Luke and John suggest that the author of John shared traditions that appear elsewhere only in Luke.

The Johannine community itself had split, with many or most of its members having left the network of congregations addressed by the elder and the Gospel (1 John 2:19; John 6:60–71).

The Johannine teachers address a fragmented community in a pluralistic world, a community struggling with a variety of understandings of the church's identity. We may now note some particular features of the way the church is described in 1–3 John.

God's Church in God's World

The teachers in the Johannine school who composed 1–3 John did not write systematic essays on "the meaning of church membership" and the like, but two letters and a brief letter-like teaching document addressing particular issues in the life of their church. As we overhear these passionate communications, we become aware once again that we have entered the strange new world of the Bible.

In the letters and Gospel of John, the term "church" (*ekklēsia*) occurs only in 3 John 6, 9, 10, in each case referring to the local congregation or cluster of house churches in a particular location. We know, however, from Revelation, where *ekklēsia* occurs twenty times, that the term was a common designation for the Christian community among some Johannine believers, and that they thought of their faith in terms of life together in the church. It is not difficult to assemble a list of a dozen or more words, phrases, and images pointing to the church. The following inventory is my own, not the elder's. He does not compile a list of "ways we think about the church." This makes his references all the more important, since these descriptions and characterizations shine through almost incidentally as he teaches about life together in the Christian community. As we reflect on these, we preachers and teachers might reflect on the list that would emerge from our own conversation about the church. We might ponder what the result might be if we polled our congregations, asking, "How would you identify the church you belong to?" How should we best relate the resulting list to the lists drawn from the New Testament?

Those Who Confess Christ, the Son of God, to Be Jesus (1 John 5:1, 5)

This sounds familiar enough, for from earliest times it is this fundamental and widespread confession that identifies the church and makes it distinct from "the world." Yet the community struggles with the question of whether all who make this confession belong to "us," or whether it must be understood in a particular way to be valid. Can the confession mean just anything? If so, has it become meaningless? If not, what are acceptable understandings of the confession? Who gets to decide, on what basis, and how is this restrictive interpretation enforced? Do those who make the confession but understand it in ways not acceptable to "us" still belong to the Christian community, or have they returned to the world to which they always belonged? Do questions of ecclesiology always involve Christology, and vice versa?

The Elect People of God

The first words of the oldest extant text from the Johannine community address the readers as "the elect" (2 John 1, 13), the biblical designation for God's chosen people Israel (see on 1 Thess 1:4 in volume 2 of this series). The Johannine churches in Asia probably began among refugees from Palestine in the wake of the 66–70 war, groups of Christian believers who understood themselves as belonging to the ongoing history of the chosen people Israel, with nonbelievers as "gentiles" (cf. *ethnikoi*, 3 John 7). This would have resonated with the earliest Christian group in Ephesus, founded not by Paul but by the Jewish Christians Priscilla and Aquila (Acts 18:18–25). Some of the readers addressed by the elder may have been only vaguely aware of the Jewish roots of their church, many of them being gentile converts for whom the thought of themselves as "elect" who belong to the "chosen people" would have been unfamiliar, perhaps even unpalatable—a situation faced by many preachers and teachers in the church of the twenty-first century.

Those who are born of God (1 John 2:29; 3:9; 4:7; 5:1, 4, 18) are *children of God* (*tekna*, "children," nine times; the diminutives "little children," *teknia*, six times, and *paidia*, three times) and *brothers and sisters to each other* (*adelphos*, eighteen times, mostly of all church members, sometimes apparently in a special sense of traveling missionaries [3 John 3, 5, 10]). The phrase "born/begotten by God the Father" refers not to a special class of Christians but to every believer: "Everyone who believes that Jesus is the Christ has been born of God, and everyone who loves the parent loves the child" (1 John 5:1; cf. 2:29; 3:9; 4:7; 5:4, 18 = to love God is to love God's people, here identified as confessing Christian believers). Just as children have no choice, play no role, in their own conception and birth, which is 100 percent gift, an act of love and grace, so too believers offer thanks to God for the act of love and grace that gave them life. The house church (2 John 10) refers not to the building where the churches meet but to the household in which God is Father and church is Mother with family and ecclesiological connotations, not simply personal hospitality. Being born/begotten by God is a very personal experience but is not merely individualistic; the new birth is a deeply ecclesiological image, in which church membership is not optional or secondary. Those who have been born again/from above (1:12–13; 3:3–5) do not then decide whether to go looking for a church to join. They have been born into a family, the household of faith, which not only has a Father in heaven but also has a large number of sisters and brothers. This is similar to Luke's idiom and conceptuality, in which believers do not "join" but are "added to" the church (Acts 2:47; 5:14).

Church as "Lady" and Her Children (2 John 1, 5)

Confessing the church as "Lady" is the counterpart of confessing Jesus as "Lord." "Lady" (*kyria*) is the feminine counterpart of "Lord" (*kyrios*), as in the Roman Curia, the designation for the comprehensive administrative apparatus for the Roman Catholic Church. Modern secularized Christians, especially non-Catholics, might find the phraseology a bit strange and might think of Lord Macbeth/Lady Macbeth; Prince Charles/Lady Diana; Prince Harry/Lady Meghan. Just as we don't normally use the language of lords and ladies in ordinary conversation, so also, many modern Christians, especially Protestants, do not think of the church as the bride of Christ, her Lord and Bridegroom, despite the prominence of this imagery in classical hymns that reflect biblical and historical imagery for the church (e.g., "The Church's One Foundation"). This was common imagery used in the Scripture and Jewish tradition for Yahweh and Israel (Isa 50:1; 54:5–8; 61:10; 62:5; Jer 2:20–25; 3:1–14; Ezek 16; Hos 1–3), adopted by early Christians, including the Johannine community, as language for Christ and the church (e.g., John 3:29; Rev 12:17 [followers of Jesus are the children of the transcendent Lady enthroned in heaven and present and protected by God on earth]; 19:7; 21:2, 9; 22:17; cf. Mark 2:19–20; 2 Cor 11:2: Eph 5:25–32). The elder addresses church members not as merely individual followers of Jesus but as children of Mother Church, who has borne and nurtured them, with God as Father (sixteen times of God), who has *begotten* them, members of the household of faith.

> "From heaven he came and sought her
> To be his holy bride.
> With his own blood he bought her,
> And for her life he died."
>
> —from "The Church's One Foundation"

We/Us/Our

The letters presuppose that writer(s) and hearer-readers share an extraordinary community consciousness. The Greek text of these three short letters contains 170 (!) instances of verbs or pronouns in the first-person plural ("we," "us," "our"), an average of 13 times per page of Greek text. This use of "we" and "our" is three or four times the average of other New Testament letters and contrasts even more with ancient letters in general. These data document the intense community sense of the network of Johannine churches, at the opposite pole from individualistic "following Jesus" or "personal salvation." Most of the "we" statements are inclusive, embracing both author and readers as "us" in contrast to "them," that is, "church" in contrast to "world" or "Johannine Christians" in contrast to everyone else. The great majority of "we" texts include the whole church, distinguishing the church from "the world." Belonging to the church means learning to say "we." This corporate mind-set for the perception of discipleship reflects Jesus's own teaching. Even when alone with God in the inner room, Jesus taught his followers pray to "*our* Father" (Matt 6:6).

1 John 1:1: "We declare to you what was from the beginning, what we have heard, what we have seen with our eyes, what we have looked at and touched with our hands, concerning the word of life."

This "we" is not a claim that the author was an eyewitness to the earthly ministry of Jesus but a claim that the church includes and goes back to such eyewitnesses. In the late second century, Irenaeus could still declare, "We would not be able to know, unless we had seen our master and heard his voice with our own ears" (*Against Heresies* 5.1.1; see also Justin, *First Apology* 30). This is a churchly claim, valid for every Christian generation, in line with the biblical understanding of the community of the saints that extends through history (cf. Deut 4:9, 33–34; 5:1–5; 6:22; Josh 24:17).

"We" who live in the twenty-first century also belong to a church that has seen, heard, and touched its origins. Traditional Christian faith is never a secondhand matter of hearsay. We have heard for ourselves.

Those Who Have Seen/Know/Have God/the Father/the Son/the Spirit (2 John 9; 3 John 11; 1 John 2:3, 20, 27)

The Johannine school advocates a transcendent ecclesiology, sometimes called "mystical," that is, a participatory understanding of the reality of the church in which its members participate in a transcendent reality. Church membership is not a matter of names on a list, or of belonging to an institution I can support and join if I believe in its cause, but a deep personal reality in which believers are truly united with God, Christ, the Holy Spirit, and each other. The Spirit is given to the church as a whole, and all believers participate in the life of the Spirit, the very life of God. This is not necessarily a matter of emotional experience, of "feeling God in my heart," though of course it does not rule that out. The point is that membership in the people of God is a matter not of subjective feelings but of objective reality. The elder of 1 John wants to be clear that the "anointing" of every member by the Spirit means that the church is not dependent on a special class of teachers who alone have the true teaching given by the Spirit (1 John 2:20, 27). The Spirit belongs to the community as a whole and all its members; authentic teachers emerge from this Spirit-led, Spirit-empowered community, not vice versa.

"In Him," "in God"

The church is "in God," "in the Father" (1 John 4:15, 16) or "in the Son" (2:24; 5:20). Although never using the specific Pauline phrase "in Christ," current among other Christian groups in Asia in his time, the elder speaks thirteen times of the believer being "in him," with the antecedent unclear—though 1 John 5:20 has "we are in him who is true, in his Son Jesus Christ." Does "in him" refer to God or Christ? We will see that this is an un-Johannine question that cannot receive a satisfactory biblical answer. As in Paul, believers have a "mystical" relationship to God; the sphere of their life is in Christ, not in the world. In such language, the reality of God, Christ, and Spirit merges into each other, in a proto-Trinitarian language the author does not attempt to clarify. Language about the church and the believer's place in it morphs inevitably into christological language, and vice versa. This line of thought will be developed in the culminating work of the Johannine school, the Gospel of John.

All Those Who Know the Truth (2 John 1)

To walk in the light means not to be blind but to know the truth. "True" and "truth" occur twenty-eight times in these brief letters, by far the highest density in the New Testament. It is not clear whether the elder understands such terms as applying only to Johannine Christians or to all believers in Jesus as the Christ. The same could be said of other descriptive phrases for the Christian or Johannine community, such as those who receive "grace, mercy, and peace" from God and Christ (2 John 3) and those who have received (the love commandment, the teaching of Christ) "from the beginning" (2 John 5, 9–10). The Johannine church represented by 1–3 John appeared to be going through a sectarian phase that it was in the process of outgrowing, whose more mature perspective will appear in the Gospel of John (see, e.g., Eph 4:13, written to churches in Asia contemporary with the Johannine letters).

Those Who "Walk in the Light" (1 John 1:5–7; 2:8–11)

Since God is the light in whom there is no darkness, those who are "in God" are "in the light." This is a matter not merely of status or theology but of ethics, of how one lives ("walks").

Those Who Keep the Command(s) (1 John 2:3) and the Word (1 John 2:5), Who Do Good (3 John 11) and Right (1 John 2:29), and Who Act in Love (1 John 2:5)

The elder is insistent that being a member of the believing community is not only a matter of knowing and believing the truth but also a matter of living out this faith in action: "Little children, let us love, not in word or speech, but in truth and action" (1 John 3:18). Some form of *agapē/agapaō* occurs sixty-two times in these letters, the highest density of the word in the New Testament. Believers are "the beloved" (by God, not only by each other, six times in 1 John, four times in 3 John). The love command is not a fluffy moralism or general humanitarianism but a response to the love of God. As in Paul, it is God's love that becomes effective in their lives in their love for other people (Rom 5:5). Not, as in the KJV, continued by the NKJV, "We love *him* . . . ," but as in virtually all modern translations, "We love because he first loved us" (1 John 4:19).

Friends (3 John 15)

We know from John's Gospel that "friends" was not only a social term but also an ecclesiological one, a reinterpretation of "slaves" (*doulos* means "slave," often translated "servant"), which was a common term for Christians in some churches in the Johannine tradition (Rev 2:20; 7:3; 19:2).

Those Who Believe in the Name of the Son of God (1 John 3:23; 5:13)

We have seen in listening to Revelation that in the biblical understanding, "name" is more than merely a label, but stands for the essence, the essential being, of the person named (see Gen 2:19–20 on Adam naming the animals). To believe in the name of God's Son is the same as believing in God's Son—personal faith in his being, in who he *is*, not merely believing something about him, for instance, that he is God's Son. In the Johannine community, Jesus comes in God's name (John 5:43; 10:25). This does not mean that Jesus identifies himself as Yahweh, the biblical name of God, nor do the "I am" statements of the Johannine Jesus represent a claim to be Yahweh. Such language is a claim to participate in the authority and very being of God.

The name of God revealed in Exodus 3:13–15 is both a revelation and the announcement of a mystery: "I will be who I will be." The Son of God shares this mysterious reality; he bears a name that no one else knows (Rev 19:12). To "believe in his name" also has a public, confessional aspect. The Gospel of John will later emphasize that being identified by the name of Christ was important in the Johannine community, where some wanted to "believe" but not be publicly identified as Christians (John 12:42–43). The Christian community is not a collection of individuals who practice their own private spirituality. It believes in his name, is baptized in his name, bears his name, which is the very name of God.

Missing from the above list are ecclesiological terms common in non-Johannine churches. We do not find "slave" (*doulos*), "saints," "holy ones" (*hagios*, only 1 John 2:20, of God/Christ); "people" or "people of God" (*laos, laos theou*); "Israel"; "sons of God" (*huios*, "Son," is used only of Jesus Christ), "disciple" (*mathētēs*, though seventy-eight times in John's Gospel) and the corresponding verb "follow" (*akoloutheō*). We should not assume that 1–3 John includes the whole ecclesiological vocabulary of the Johannine community. If it were not for 3 John 6, 9, 10 and the connection with Revelation, which uses *ekklēsia* often, we might mistakenly suppose that the Johannine community avoided the word "church" entirely. The later Gospel of John will adjust some of the above terminology to what was becoming "mainstream" Christianity.

Penultimate Dualism: The World and the People of God

Several of the above terms reflect a dualistic tendency in Johannine theology. The elder and the Johannine teachers share the primal biblical view that the one God, the creator, did not abandon the rebellious creation but chose a people to be the saved people distinct from the world (2 John 1, the church as the "elect"). Author and readers identify themselves with this elect people of God, in contrast to the outsiders, the "gentiles" (*ethnikoi*; 2 John 1; 3 John 7; cf. Matt 5:47; 6:7). This insider-outsider mentality presupposed by the Johannine authors had hardened into a dualistic model of reality somewhat characteristic of Jewish apocalypticism, tinged and radicalized by the emerging proto-gnostic thought patterns with which they are engaged. The dramatically abrupt conclusion of the teaching document 1 John starkly contrasts "us," God's children who are born of God, with "the whole world [that] lies under the power of the evil one." Readers are "in his Son Jesus Christ.

He is the true God and eternal life." All else is idolatry (1 John 5:19–21). Christology and ecclesiology are inseparable.

Following are the polarities of this dualistic perspective:

True God /	Idols	1 John 5:20–21
God /	Devil	1 John 3:8, 10
God /	World	1 John 4:4–5; 5:19
Christ /	Antichrist	1 John 2:18, 22; 4:3; [2 John 7]
Spirit of God /	Spirit of antichrist	1 John 4:2
Spirit of truth /	Spirit of error	1 John 4:6
Church /	World	1 John 2:2; 3:1, 13; 4:1; 5:19
In you /	In the world	1 John 4:4
Speaking, hearing from God /	Speaking, hearing from the world	1 John 4:4–5
Abel, good works /	Cain, bad works	1 John 3:12
Elect /	Gentiles	2 John 1; 3 John 7
We who are "of God" /	They who are "not of God"	1 John 4:6
Children of God /	Children of the devil	1 John 3:1, 10; 5:19
Born of God /	Born of the devil	1 John 3:9; 4:7; 5:1, 4, 18
Life /	Death	1 John 3:14
Light /	Darkness	1 John 1:5, 6; 2:9, 10
Sin not to death /	Sin to death	1 John 5:16, 17
Truth /	Lie	1 John 1:6; 2:21
Love /	Hate	1 John 2:11; 3:13; 4:20
Righteousness /	Sin	1 John 2:29; 3:12

Many modern readers of the Bible are uneasy about such dualistic language. Our initial, knee-jerk theological response is sometimes well grounded: life cannot be negotiated simply in black/white terms, for much of it is sorting out and acting on various shades of gray. But even in our own experience, there are places where we live by either/or and do not and cannot have it any other way. At graduation time, one either graduates or does not. In the wedding ceremony, one either says "I do" or does not. We tend to think we prefer discussion questions for all of life's exams, or at least multiple-choice questions. But life has its share of true/false.

The elder's understanding of sin is cast in this framework of eschatological dualism—thus "sin" occurs on both sides of this ledger. Thoughtful believers today might thus decide this dualistic line not only separates church from world but also cuts through the church, even through each individual member. Sin is not merely a moral failing; it is a belonging to the realm of sin. The troublesome claim that believers are "not able to sin" (1 John 3:7–10) is made within this dualistic framework, in which all human beings are divided into the two categories of children of God / children of the devil, sinners / not sinners. Jesus Christ was not a sinner (1 John 2:1; 3:5; cf. John 8:46). Believers are "in him," and in this sense cannot and do not sin (1 John 3:8–9; 5:18). Just as Jesus's "sinlessness" cannot be understood as a *criterion* by which he may be judged, and either vindicated or condemned, so too the "sinlessness" of the community of faith cannot be judged by empirical observation but must be understood christologically.[1] Of course, believers too, like all human beings, commit individual sins (1 John 1:8), but they are already delivered from the realm of sin, from its dominating power that determines my life even if I am unaware, even if I reject the whole idea of sin—*especially* then (see on Rom 6 in volume 2 of this series). This dualistic understanding is also the context in which the elder places the distinction between "mortal sins" and those that are "not mortal" (1 John 5:16–19). The meaning of this text continues to be disputed and may reflect a historical context no longer clear to us. It is clear that, for the elder, sin is not merely a matter of individual personal acts but is a matter of where one stands, one's location within this dualistic worldview. Those guilty of mortal sin are not merely personally guilty of doing wrong; they have denied or refused to accept the saving act of God and (re)joined the other side, the "whole world [that] lies under the power of the evil one," the world of death (1 John 3:14; 5:19). *This* is what believers are saved from. *We* may or may not be persuaded by this way of thinking, but if we want to understand our Bible—which is necessary before we can say an honest yes, no, or maybe—we must get within hearing distance of what it says, within the world in which it thinks.

Within this assumed thought world, the Johannine teachers struggled to think through the meaning of the Christ event, in the process both affirming and fundamentally modifying its basic dualism. As with us, the basic insights and core convictions of the Christian faith pushed the envelope and sometimes broke through the categories in which they habitually thought. While "church" and "world" are elemental polarities, so that believers do not belong to the world and are exhorted, "Do not love the world" (1 John 2:15), already in 1 John 4:14 it is declared that "the Father has sent his Son as the Savior of the world"—not only Savior of believers, and salvation is not only "out of" this world and into heaven. To anticipate: the final form of Johannine theology explicated in the Gospel of John will (re)appropriate biblical and Jewish traditions that had characterized its origins, will critically engage Mosaic and Abrahamic traditions, will ponder more deeply the biblical understanding of God as creator, and will declare that "God so loved the world that he gave his only Son . . ." (John 3:16). As the Johannine community struggles with identifying what can count as authentic Christian faith and what cannot, they will outgrow the view that to belong to the church means not to love the world (1 John 2:15) and will find authentic ways to overcome a too-simple dualism. Nonetheless, they do not simply discard their earlier understanding, for it too has a certain validity. The emerging New Testament canon thus preserves both 1 John and the Gospel of John.

Wind/Breath/Spirit/Word of God: An Experiential Theology of the Holy Spirit

The Johannine community knows it is called into being, nourished, and empowered by God—the Word/Spirit of God, the Son of God, the risen Christ (see pp. 105–6). Their Christian faith and life are not only a matter of tradition handed on from the beginning (1 John 1:1; 2:7, 14, 24; 3:11; 2 John 5, 6) but also a matter of present experience. Jesus Christ, one with the Father (1 John 1:3; 2:22; 5:20; 2 John 9), not only came to this world in visible, audible, touchable flesh and blood (1 John 1:1–3; 4:2; 5:6; 2 John 7) but continues to be present and active in the church through the Spirit (1 John 3:24; 4:13; 5:6). Jesus is not only "back there" in history but also "up there" in the heavenly world, and present, active, and audible in and beyond the community of faith, in the here and now of this world.

But other spirits are also at work in the world and the church, and the

> "It is the spirit that gives life; the flesh is useless. The words that I have spoken to you are spirit and life" (John 6:63). Recall that *pneuma* not only means "wind," "breath," and "spirit" but also "word." Since "word" is literally an expression of one's breath and life, the virtual identity of "word" and "spirit" is vital in Johannine theology (John 3:34; 6:63; Rev 22:6).

followers of Jesus cannot believe every spirit that comes along (see 1 John 4:1–3). In the long history of Israel and from the earliest days of the church, various tests had been devised for distinguishing the authentic voice of God or the risen Christ from the persuasive voices of false prophets:

1. Miraculous validation (1 Kings 17–19; John 6:14). But false prophets also work miracles (Deut 13:1–3; Matt 7:21–23; 24:24; Rev 13:11–18 [cf. 16:13]; 19:20).
2. Accurate predictions (Deut 18:18–22; 1 Kings 22:28; Isa 30:8). But, apart from the fact that the bulk of what claims to be prophecy is not predictive anyway, the hearers must typically decide whether the speaker mediates the word of God to the church before it can be determined whether or not the predictions are accurate.
3. Manner of reception. True prophets receive their messages in visions or are caught up into the presence of God to hear the words to be delivered, while the message of false prophets comes through dreams (Jer 23:16–18, 25–28). Yet dreams are also evaluated positively by those who affirm prophetic revelation, and the Bible pictures God's message coming to people in dreams (Num 12:6–8; Dan 2; 4; 7:1; Matt 1–2).
4. The character of the prophet. True prophets will be unselfish and sincere, with deep convictions, willing to suffer for the faith. Though false prophets are often considered liars who know that their prophecy is false and intend to deceive the people (e.g., Jer 14:14), Israel also knew of prophets who had themselves been deceived, sincerely supposing that their message was a revelation from God (1 Kings 22:22–23). The prophets in the churches of Asia identified by John as "Jezebel" and "Balaam" thought of themselves as authentic proclaimers of the message of the risen Christ. Here the criteria may be clear enough, but their application will always be ambiguous.
5. Community benefit. True prophets do and speak that which builds up the community (1 Thess 5:21–22; 1 Cor 14:40 [cf. 7:35]). Yet what constitutes "building up the community" and "good order" is itself a matter of interpretation.
6. Focus on God's judgment. The true prophet proclaims doom, the false prophet salvation (Jer 23:17; 28:8; 1 Kings 22; Ezek 13:10). But some prophets (e.g., Second Isaiah) are entirely positive, and most prophecies contain a combination of judgment and salvation.
7. Creedal or traditional orthodoxy. True prophets are loyal to the covenant, tradition, or creed and cannot contradict what has become the

normative guiding tradition of the people of God (Deut 13:1–3; Matt 7:15–20; Rom 12:6; 1 Cor 12:3; 1 John 4:1–3; cf. Did 11.1, 8, 10). But what constitutes such fidelity is often a matter of interpretation. Who gets to interpret, and on what basis? Strictly and consistently applied, this criterion means the community always already knows the truth and the will of God, and nothing *new* can ever be revealed.

Through the centuries of its history, the believing community has found value in each of these criteria. But no one of them, nor all of them together, form an objective grid through which purported revelations may be sifted, nor do the teachers of the Johannine community expect that it is or can be so. Like Paul a generation earlier (e.g., 1 Thess 5:21), they believe that the Spirit of God dwells among and within the community of believers (1 John 2:27), and that they are fully qualified, risky though it may be, to accept some prophetic messages as authentic divine word to the particular situation and reject others as contrary or irrelevant to the will of God. The churches of Roman Asia from 90 to 130 CE were being forced to decide what constitutes authorized ministers, canonical Scriptures, and reliable tradition to guide them through the dangers that threatened their mission (see on the ecclesiology of Ephesians and the Pastorals in volume 2 of this series).

Ethics: Living the Truth in Love

Authentic faith and proclamation are identified simply as "the truth," a word that occurs twenty times in these brief letters, the highest density in the New Testament. Yet the truth is not a matter of abstract theological ideas; truth and love determine how the believer lives. Believers are those who "walk in the truth" (3 John 3, 4; 2 John 4), equivalent to walking in the commandment (2 John 4, 6), "walk[ing] in the light" (1 John 1:7), walking "just as he walked" (1 John 2:6). The one-word summary of this ethic is "love," a word used sixty-two times in the letters, related to the whole of the believer's life and actions and to the very being of God. Love is not thought of as merely a quality of God, alongside, for example, righteousness and holiness. God is not merely "loving," but God *is* love (1 John 4:8, 16). Christian love is not a moral quality they might select and practice, a virtue they might try a little harder to cultivate, but the reflex of God's love for us (1 John 4:19).

The Christian ethic begins not with ideas but with *tangible experience*. The addressees live in a church that has heard, seen, and touched the realities on which their faith is based (1 John 1:1–3). Their life together and in the world must be expressed in tangible reality. The Christian ethic has an essential worldly *social dimension*: the needy must be helped. In 1 John 3:17–18, love is not in *logos*, or words, but in *ergon* and *alētheia* (work/action and truth/faithfulness); it is not a matter of ideas but of faithfulness. The Christian ethic has an essential *community dimension*: believers belong to a church in which there are particular people who have suffered and been deprived because of their faith. These are to be helped. Church members are to know that they belong to such a community of faith. John's Gospel will explicate the meaning of the love ethic in the narrative of Jesus and his disciples.

Disputed Christology

Then as now, the believers' understanding of the Christian life and mission of the church rests on a christological foundation, so that what one means by the confession "Jesus is the Christ, the Son of the living God" is crucial to how believers understand themselves and the church to which they belong. Everyone who denies the true teaching about Christ (*hē didachē tou Christou*, 2 John 9) "does not have God." Here, the "teaching of Christ" is an objective genitive, what the church teaches about the Christ event, not a subjective genitive, what Christ taught/teaches, although the Johannine school does not rigidly distinguish these: what the church, guided by the Holy Spirit, teaches about Christ *is* the teaching of Christ. The risen Christ is alive and at work in the church, interpreting the meaning of the once-for-all Christ event. Alongside the traditional categories of "Jesus's understanding of himself" and "the church's later understanding of the Christ event" there emerges a third category, "Christ's self-interpretation in the life of the church." This is the elder's view, which will be expanded and nuanced in the later Gospel of John.

"Gnostic" Perspectives?

We do not know if the gnosticizing teachers opposed by the letters and Gospel of John wrote documents that circulated in Asia about 100 CE. If there were such, none were included in the New Testament canon. We do have texts from later generations that advocate the kind of gnosticizing Christology that the elder opposed. We can get some idea of their understanding of the Christ event and Christian faith from them, without claiming that these specific views or texts were already available in the elder's time. We will illustrate with two examples.

The Acts of John: Jesus Could (and Did!) Come Down from the Cross

It is no accident that this book, probably written in the late second century, was attributed to the same apostle John who, according to later tradition, wrote Revelation, 1–3 John, and the Gospel of John, for it stands in the same stream of early Christian tradition in which docetism was a strong contender for how the Christ event was to be understood. The author considered himself a faithful teacher of the true faith and intended only to glorify Jesus and the splendor of the Christian life, which he expressed in a docetic perspective. In this document Jesus appears to John as "bald-headed but with a thick and flowing beard," but at the same time to James as "a youth whose beard was just starting" (Acts of John 89). Sometimes he felt soft to the touch, at other times "hard, like stone," and sometimes could not be felt at all (Acts of John 89, 93).[2]

Once John pretended to be asleep and, in a twilight-zone scene, beheld the supposedly physical body of Jesus conversing with its spiritual double lying beside it (Acts of John 92). John records, "I, because he loved me, went to him quietly as though he should not see, and stood looking upon his back. And I saw that he was not dressed in garments, but was seen by us as naked and not at all like a man" (Acts of John 90). This curious passage is reminiscent of Moses being permitted to view only "the hind parts" of God (Exod 33:23) and also probably intends to settle the question (negatively!) of whether the divine Jesus was equipped with human sexual and excretory apparatus. Here, as elsewhere in the Acts of John, Jesus is truly divine but in no way human. Jesus complains to his spiritual double that his disciples do not sufficiently believe in him.

The author does not hesitate to carry through the logical consequences of this view of Jesus into the crucifixion scene.

> Even I, when I saw him suffer, did not abide at this passion but fled to the Mount of Olives, weeping over what had taken place. And when he was hung upon the cross on Friday, at the sixth hour of the day, there came

> darkness over all the earth. And my Lord stood in the middle of the cave and lit it up, and said, "John, to the multitude down below in Jerusalem I am being crucified, and pierced with lances and reeds, and gall and vinegar is given me to drink. But to you I am speaking, and pay attention to what I say. I put it into your mind to come up to this mountain, so that you might hear matters needful for a disciple to learn from his teacher, and for a man to learn from his God [Jesus]." (Acts of John 97)[3]

Here the divine Son of God does come down from the cross, responding to the challenge of Mark 15:30–32. He only appears to be suffering and dying. He reveals a glorified cross of light to John, the true "spiritual" cross, and explains: "But this is not the cross of wood which you will see when you go down here: neither am I he who is upon the cross. . . . I was reckoned to be what I am not, not being what I was to many others: but they will call me something else, which is vile and not worthy of me. . . . Therefore I have suffered none of the things which they will say of me" (Acts of John 99–101).[4] The "something" that is "vile and not worthy of" Jesus that will be said about him by less-enlightened Christians (in the author's view) is that Jesus truly suffered and died as a human being on the cross. But the author of the Acts of John knows that if Jesus was truly the Son of God, he could not have been impaled on the cross as a weak human being but could have come down, and in fact did so. This author operates within the same logic as the chief priests in Mark's account of the crucifixion, affirms the premises they deny, and extends this logic to its ultimate conclusion. John goes back to the crucifixion scene and laughs at the ignorance of those who suppose that Jesus really suffered (Acts of John 102).

The Gospel of Thomas: The Samaritan Was Bad (or at Least Ignorant)

This second-century collection of 114 sayings, each of which is introduced with "The Living Jesus says," has no narrative framework. There are no stories of his birth, life, and ministry, no crucifixion, no resurrection. The "Living Jesus" speaks to each believer in the present. While several of the sayings resemble or are virtually identical with the sayings of Jesus preserved in the Synoptic Gospels, they are all to be understood as the teaching of Jesus, the heavenly messenger of divine Wisdom, sent to enlighten those who will listen about the meaning of their own life.

For example, saying 42 is: "Jesus said: 'Become passers-by.'"[5] This brief maxim, understood from the proto-gnostic perspective on being a follower of Jesus, encourages disengagement from the world. Truly spiritual people, who know their own origin in the heavenly world, disdain this world and its problems. The precise meaning the author of the Gospel of Thomas intended is disputed. All agree that he thinks true followers of Jesus will withdraw from the world, for they do not belong to it, and will be saved out of it. For the emerging "mainline" Christians who know the sayings of Jesus in the Synoptic Gospels, there is a clear allusion to Jesus's parable of the Good Samaritan. In the Gospel of Thomas, the true believer is the one who understands that people who have been beaten up and thrown into the ditch are "not my problem" and are encouraged to "pass by" on the other side ("This world is not my home, I'm just a-passin' through, and I can't feel at home in this world anymore"; see also "In the World but Not of It?" sidebar, p. 297 below).

Truly Human/Truly Divine

The task of responding to these false views generated increased clarity in understanding the content of authentic Christian confession. The focal point is the paradoxical, dialectical confession of Christ as truly divine and truly human. Of course, the elder does not express himself in the categories of the later Chalcedonian Creed (451 CE), but his summary affirmations are already going in that direction.

The Johannine Community Confesses Christ as Truly Human

As the elder writes, affirmation that "Jesus Christ has come in the flesh" was the combustion point of Christian confession in the Johannine community (2 John 7; 1 John 4:2). The letters insist that Jesus was no ghost, no docetic phantasm, but a tangible, truly human being of flesh and blood, who truly suffered and died. The teaching document 1 John begins abruptly with this affirmation (1 John 1:1), making (the shedding of) his blood crucial to his mission (1 John 1:7; 5:6, 8). Giving his life for us, dying a truly human death, was indispensable to the saving event (1 John 3:16; 4:10). "Jesus" is the name of a human being; not merely confession of the Christ, but that the Christ is *Jesus*, is at the heart of Christian faith.

The Johannine Community Confesses Christ as Truly Divine

Christ is the Son of God in a unique sense. In distinction from other New Testament authors, the writers of the Johannine school use "Son" (*huios*) only of Jesus (twenty-four times in 1–3 John). Believers, too, are children of God (*tekna*, used eight times in 1–3 John), begotten/born of God (nine times in 1–3 John), but not in the same sense as the unique Son (*monogenēs*, 1 John 4:9, only of Jesus). The Son preexisted with the Father and was sent into this world (1 John 2:13, 14; 4:9, 10, 14). The elder does not of course use the later creedal language, but the unity of Father and Son is fundamental to his theology (1 John 1:3; 2:22, 24; 4:14; 2 John 3, 9). In his culminating final statement, the elder does not hesitate to use God language of Christ, the unique Son who has been begotten by the Father, the Son who is truly God. All else is a human construct, that is, idolatry (1 John 5:18–20).

Stories and Sayings of the Jesus "Back There"

During the time when the letters were written, some Christian teachers and preachers were relating stories and sayings of Jesus within the pre-Easter framework as a means of communicating and nourishing Christian faith. Oral and written collections of the mighty deeds of the pre-Easter Jesus—the Gospel of Mark, perhaps Matthew, an early version or versions of what became the canonical Gospel of John—were in circulation in the Johannine churches, along with numerous other versions of the "life and teachings of Jesus" (John 20:30–31; 21:25!). The elder seems to have been aware of such narratives but uninterested or suspicious of them. He never narrates a story or quotes a saying of the pre-Easter Jesus and refers only ambiguously to the life of Jesus as a model for the Christian life (1 John 2:6). He remains strictly in the epistolary mode of *kenosis* Christology, in which the preexistent Son divested himself of divine power when he came to earth. He has no interest in combining this with epiphany Christology, which pictures the life of the earthly Jesus as filled with the power of God (cf. Phil 2:5b–11, a hymn circulating among the Asian churches as the elder writes). The letters are passionately committed to affirming the faith based on the reality of the incarnational Christ event, the Jesus "back there" in history, but it is the "thatness" of the event, *that* God was incarnate in the human Jesus, that he truly suffered and died, that is crucial for Christian faith, not the particular events that formed the content of the "life and teaching of

Jesus." Like Revelation, the Johannine letters never cite a particular saying of the pre-Easter Jesus.

The Jesus Who Spoke and Who Still Speaks

The elder insists that authentic faith rests on the tangible reality of the life of Jesus (1 John 1:1–3). Does that definitive word spoken at the *archē* mean that the faith of all later generations must be secondhand (or thirdhand, or fiftiethhand)? Or does Christ still speak to post-Easter believers of later generations and centuries? Does faith in the risen Christ carry with it the reality that Christ continues to speak, that we later believers too are called to discipleship by the continuing voice of Jesus, by the Word of God? How should we understand this claim? Does the risen Christ, somehow or other, continue to speak in Scripture? In our hearts? In Christian teaching and sermons? Directly from heaven through chosen inspired prophets who speak in his name? Or should we understand that the historical Jesus once spoke the truth of God and that his teaching, what Jesus once said to "them," is now handed on and applied to "us" by preachers, teachers, or our own best judgment? We preachers and teachers may not have thought much about these questions, but they were a driving force that generated the theology of the letters and Gospel of John. The final response of the Johannine school to these issues appears in the Gospel of John, which we will engage in the next chapter.

Centering and Decentering

A good bit of pop spirituality seems to be focused on "finding my own center."

When we are born, we are in fact at the center of our own world, and the space-time universe revolves around each of us. We carry this egocentric world around with us. If I'm in Iceland, I look out through my eyes, and Canada is to *my* west, England to my east. In England, Iceland is to the west and France to the east. I remain the center, the point of orientation. I am likewise the center of time. The past is what happened before *I* got here, the future is what lies ahead of *me*.

Society tries to socialize us so that the community and the nation are our center—but it's still my community, my country.

In Bonhoeffer's incisive phrase, Jesus the Messiah was "the man for others." Conversion is decentering, making God the center. The church, the people of God, is an eccentric group, a peculiar people.

Atoning Death

The reality of Jesus's human life and death is crucial because the saving act of God is the atoning death of the Son, who cleanses us from all sins through his blood (1 John 1:7; 2:2; 3:5, 16; 4:10; see pp. 99–100 above on Rev 5). As in Revelation (cf. pp. 77, 118 above on Rev 12:11; 19:13), the focus on the blood of Jesus emphasizes his true humanity and the reality of his death (1 John 5:6). The language of soteriology (*sōzō*, "save"; *sōtēria*, "salvation"; *sōtēr*, "savior") is not prominent in the letters (only in 1 John 4:14, "And we have seen and do testify that the Father has sent his Son as the Savior of the world"), although it is more frequent in John's Gospel (eight times) and Revelation (three times). In the letters, the soteriological dimension of the Christ event is conveyed by describing the human plight from which God's act in Jesus saved us. The writer designates this problem as "darkness" (seven times), "death" (1 John 3:14), the "devil" or "evil one" (nine times), all summed up in the word "sin" (twenty-seven times). The teaching document 1 John begins and concludes with its doctrine of human sin (1 John 1:5–2:2; 5:16–19). When the elder's opponents contend that "we have not sinned" (1 John 1:10), they are not claiming that they never do anything amiss, or that, judged by human standards, they are relatively good, as though they were merely acknowledging that "Nobody's perfect; I'm not all that bad." Rather, their view of the world and life simply does not include "sin," so that there is no need for atonement and forgiveness. Likewise, when the elder pictures them as "those who do not love" (1 John 3:10), he does not mean that they never do anything nice but that they live in the self-centered realm that reduces care for others to a strategy or an obligation, just as it blinds one to one's own need of forgiveness. The believer's life is not self-centered navel-gazing but essentially *ec*centric (off center); it does not see itself as the center of the universe. Believers look outside (*ek*-) themselves for the organizing center of their existence (see Rom 5).

Eschatology: The Present Christ Who Is to Come

John the prophet of Revelation had adopted the apocalyptic scheme that projected an evil power that would emerge just before the end, through which he interpreted the idolatrous claims of the Roman emperors and the final persecution of God's faithful people that he saw already beginning. Revelation never used the term "antichrist," but it portrayed the ultimate evil to appear at the end time as an ungodly "trinity": the dragon, the beast, and the false prophet. The prophet John did not begin with an apocalyptic text and ask, "Who is the beast?," but he began with the reality of his own situation, asking, "What is Rome?" His prophetic answer: Rome is not the world-uniting beneficent power it claims to be but society organized around itself as the center, the final opponent of the one true God.

Likewise, the elder, a teacher in the Johannine school tradition, does not ask, "Who is the antichrist?," a current image he assumes as understood, but asks, "What does it mean that destructive false teaching about the meaning of the Christ event is being promulgated in the churches?" His answer: *this* is the antichrist, a sign of the end.

In each case, a church leader and teacher interpreted the present in terms of apocalyptic theology. John identified the beast with the political events of his time, which he saw in an ultimately religious sense, and urged the followers of Jesus to be faithful, even to death (Rev 2:10). The elder identified the expected antichrist with the false teachers he saw corrupting the church of his own time. In the apocalyptic drama, they were to appear just before the end. The elder saw them as already on the horizon and urged the believers to hold on to the true faith. Revelation on the one hand, and 1–3 John on the other, illustrate the different interpretations of current events within the same apocalyptic framework that disturbed the Johannine churches of Asia in the 90s. Just as the prophet John of Revelation believed the antichrist was already present and the end was near, so the elder saw the theological crisis signaled by the appearance of "many antichrists" as proof that it was already "the last hour" (1 John 2:18, 22; 2 John 7) and lived in renewed hope of the parousia (1 John 2:28–3:3; 4:3, 17).

As history moved on, neither the political threat John saw already emerging nor the theological corruption perceived by the elder turned out to be a sign that the end was near. How, then, should the church understand its eschatological hopes? This is not a trivial question. The Messiah is the savior promised by God who comes at the end to bring the creation into the kingdom of God. If the Messiah is Jesus, what does it mean that the Messiah has come but history continues business as usual?

Core Convictions and Provisional Theologies

Core Convictions

One's deepest convictions can be expressed as explicit declarations with an intentional focus. If we could ask the elder, he would probably name one main item under this heading: Christology, the saving act of God in the truly human Jesus. But one's theology, especially one's core convictions, is often represented not so much by what one consciously articulates as by what one presupposes, the substructures inherent in all one thinks, says, writes, and does, the assumptions on which one habitually acts. This is the case with the elder.

Provisional Theologies

There is, of course, a sense in which every theological statement of a historical faith is provisional—we now know in part, when our fragmentary, provisional insights are only en route to the full knowledge of the transcendent world to which God is leading us (1 Cor 13:12). The written texts of Scripture always require the continuing interpretation of the community (2 Pet 1:20). Theology as such is always incomplete and provisional. Here we are pondering the theology expressed in the letters, addressing a specific situation in the Asian churches circa 100 CE. The elder considers his written statements in 2–3 John as provisional, to be supplemented by his personal visits (2 John 12; 3 John 13–14). Even the teaching doc-

Storms and Storm Windows

Langdon Gilkey compares the work of the theologian, that is, the task of anyone who both believes and thinks, to the situation of one inside a house during a bad storm. "It is like having six storm windows to cover eight dilapidated windows—wherever you put the six, leaks will appear behind you. Thus the theologian rushes continually about trying to plug up the openings that old formulations have created, only to find new leaks appearing at his rear."

—Langdon Gilkey, *Naming the Whirlwind: The Renewal of God-Language* (Indianapolis: Bobbs-Merrill, 1969), 147

ument 1 John, more firmly fixed for a particular situation, is still a work in progress. The extant Johannine letters leave important options still on the table, to find a more comprehensive and definitive expression in the Gospel of John.

Christology

How should the church think and talk about the truly human Jesus as "also" truly divine? Are we living in the last days? Is he "coming back" at all? (It's been a long time already.)

Church and Ecumenism

How far does the "we" extend? How about those other believers in Jesus who are not in the Johannine community? Can we contend against false Christian teachers without lapsing into we're-the-only-ones-who-have-the-truth sectarianism?

The Church and Other Religions

Is there salvation outside the church? How should believers in Jesus Christ understand and relate to people of other religions? Is God at work there too?

Charisma and Church Office

What about this emerging presbytery? What about the emerging monarchial episcopacy? Is it a threat to Christian freedom or the protection against heresy? How do particular congregations relate to the emerging power structure?

Letter and Gospel

Following in the tradition of Paul that had become widespread by the end of the first century CE, the Johannine community expressed and communicated its faith in normative teaching documents in the form of letters. But it is aware of other ways of expressing the faith that focus on the words and deeds of Jesus of Nazareth prior to his death and resurrection. Can faith of God's act in Christ that culminated in atoning death and vindicating resurrection be represented in stories and sayings from the pre-Easter life of Jesus? We have had letters as normative statements of our faith since the early days of Paul. What are we to make of this new genre of Christian confession, the "gospel," that tells stories about the earthly life of Jesus?

All these issues are still troubling the churches as the Johannine school retells the story of Jesus in the Gospel of John.

Chapter 4

Retelling the Jesus Christ Story: Soundings in the Theology of the Gospel of John

A Brief Theological Introduction to the Gospel of John

John's own introduction is his prologue (1:1–18), which we will explore below.

John's Options

Revelation and 1–3 John present us with a fragmented church with a mission in and to a multicultural world. Let us picture ourselves as belonging to a small group of teachers and preachers within this network of churches in Roman Asia about 100 CE. We believe we have been charged and empowered by the Spirit of God to develop a comprehensive teaching document to guide the community (not just our own house church) forward into a better understanding of its faith and mission. The document cannot be imposed by ecclesiastical authority; it must be somewhat normative but not dogmatic, must leave room for local congregations and individuals to formulate their own theological response to their particular situations. What sort of document would we produce? Or if I were a layperson who wanted further instruction on how to better understand my faith, what sort of text would be most helpful to guide my congregation, my family, my own life?

- We could write more letters, on the model of the Pauline letters circulating in Roman Asia or the letters already circulating in the Johannine community: Revelation, 1–3 John.
- We could write a book of church order like the Didache or the Qumran Rule of the Community.

- We could collect and organize a collection of Jesus's sayings, as the "Q Community" had done in Palestine, or collections of Jesus's miracle stories that were already circulating among Christians in Roman Asia.
- We could compose a clear, concise statement of our core beliefs, or a collection of such creedal statements. Brief fixed formulas, normative creedal affirmations summarizing the Christian gospel and defining its boundaries, had been used from the earliest days of the church and were circulating among the network of Johannine churches (e.g., Rom 10:9; 1 Cor 8:6; 15:3–5). Such a summary could serve as the church's guide for continuing interpretation of the Scripture and the varieties of Christian tradition.
- We could assemble a worship book with hymns, prayers, and liturgies. Such a collection was made in ancient Israel, which could be amplified with Christian hymns and prayers, including those already circulating in the Johannine community (cf. the hymnic texts of Rev 4:8, 11; 5:9–10, 12, 13; 7:12, 14–17; 11:15, 16–18; 12:10–12; 13:9–10; 15:3–4; 16:5–6, 7; 19:2, 3, 4, 5, 6–8; 21:3–4, as well as hymns from the Pauline churches such as Phil 2:6–11). What people sing and pray in worship is formative for their faith and life.
- We could compose an outline of the basic principles of the Christian faith or an essay on the meaning of the gospel of Christ. Such a document is represented, for example, in the Gospel of Truth, apparently composed by a gnosticizing teacher in the Roman church a generation or so after the Gospel of John.
- We could compose a gospel to communicate a normative teaching document expressing the theological understanding that undergirds our community. About a generation before the teachers in the Johannine school tradition became active, a Christian teacher had transformed the Hellenistic biography into a new literary form appropriate to communicating the Christian faith—the Gospel of Mark. Unlike the letter form, this new narrative genre, already adopted and adapted by Matthew and Luke, was able to express the gospel as a narrative of the life of Jesus. It was relatively new, risky, and open to misinterpretation, but the Johannine teachers chose to formulate its normative teaching about the meaning of the Christian faith as a narrative of the life and work of Jesus of Nazareth.

John's Narrative Theology

The teachers of the Johannine school decide that the way forward for their community is to undergird its understanding of the faith by retelling the story of Jesus in a way that fuses it with the ancient stream of narrative theology of their Bible. The Jewish Scriptures express theology as a grand narrative. The Torah ("Law") contained laws and instructions, but they were incorporated into the narrative of God's saving acts.

Jesus, of course, belonged to the Jewish tradition and was himself something of a narrative theologian who had not always given clear, straight answers to legal questions. He told parables. After Jesus's death, his disciples not only continued to tell his stories but they also told stories about him, stories in which he was the key figure in God's saving act. The letters and gospels that had already been written by early Christian teachers were tensive narratives that preserved the story forms appropriate to expressing and communicating the dialectic truth of the faith. The Johannine teachers are aware of these texts; they affirm and appropriate various elements from them; and they decide to express their definitive statement of the Christian faith, their teaching document for the churches, in the form of a gospel. John's Gospel contains no parables. John's Gospel is a parable. The parable is the literary form that corresponds to the incarnation.[1]

The gospel has certain similarities to the Hellenistic biography (*bios*), the literary genre for telling the story of great figures in human history such as Socrates and the Caesars. But the gospel is not a "biography of Jesus," not merely a Christian adaption of this conventional form. Awareness of six distinctive hallmarks of the gospel genre will help us come within hearing distance of this literary-theological means of communicating the Christian faith: (1) *deity*, (2) *humanity*, (3) *paradox*, (4) *secrecy*, (5) *denouement*, and (6) *contemporaneity*.

Deity: The Epiphany Christology Incorporated in the Gospel Genre Presents Jesus as the Truly Divine One, the Manifestation of the Glory of God within This World of Time and Space

At the beginning of the Fourth Gospel, the narrator declares that the Word was with God before creation and became incarnate in Jesus of Nazareth, and that this Word "was God" (1:1, 14). In the narrative itself, Jesus is portrayed as doing what only God can do. He changes water to wine and manifests the divine glory (2:1–11). He multiplies the loaves and fish and feeds the multitudes (6:1–15). He walks on the water (6:16–21), heals the sick (4:46–54; 5:1–9), and gives sight to a man born blind (9:1–12). He raises the dead (5:21; 6:40, 54; 11:1–44). He has life in himself (5:26), the divine life that he gives to the world (6:33). As deity, the Johannine Jesus needs no one to tell him about other people, for he knows what is in the heart of every human being (2:24–25). Jesus typically does not ask informational questions. When he does ask, it is only to test other people, not because he doesn't already know (6:6). He knows the historical and ultimate future (6:64; 13:11), just as he knows of his own preexistence with God (13:1, 3; 17:5). At the conclusion of the story, the disciple Thomas confesses that the risen Jesus is "my Lord and my God!" (20:28).

In all this, Christ is not identified as some sort of angel, heavenly being, or superhero with exceptional powers, but as the one who was present with God, as God, before the creation, the one through whom all things were made (1:3). He speaks as God, using divine predicates of himself (e.g., "I am the good shepherd," 10:11, 14), and speaks the divine "I am" with overtones of deity (Exod 3:13–15). The Jews misunderstand him when they charge him with making himself God (John 10:33), equal with God (5:18), though he is only a human being. He does not "make himself" anything, but he does claim that he and the Father are one (10:30) and declares that those who have seen him have seen the Father (12:45; 14:9). He contrasts himself with his this-worldly opponents: "You are from below, I am from above; you are of this world, I am not of this world" (8:23). This-worldly human beings are sinners, but he challenges his opponents, "Which of you convicts me of sin?" (8:46). If we had only this collection of texts, we could hardly dispute the conclusion of those who consider John to represent a "naïve docetism," that the Fourth Gospel portrays Jesus as "God going about on the earth."[2] Even so, readers who want to come within hearing distance of John's Gospel must understand that the central figure of this narrative is God, that to deal with Jesus is to deal with God.

Humanity: The *Kenōsis* Christology Incorporated in the Gospel Genre Presents Jesus as the Truly Human One, the Manifestation of Authentic Humanity

Juxtaposed and interwoven with the texts and images cited above is another series of texts in which Jesus is presented as one of us, a truly human being who shares our life, who knows what it is (not just "what it is like") to be human. He became flesh and lived among us, sharing our flesh and blood (1:14). He was born of two human parents (1:45; 6:42; 18:37). He has brothers (who did not believe in him, 2:12; 7:3, 5). He was a Jew (4:9). He has the limitations of space and time and must travel to get from one place to another (1:43; 4:4). He gets tired, hungry, and thirsty (4:1–34). He has friends whom he loves, and he weeps at the tomb of one who dies (11:1–3, 35). He groans and suffers in spirit (11:38; 13:21). He prays (11:41; 17:1–26). He suffers and bleeds (19:34). He shares with us the ultimate act that unites all us human beings: he dies (19:31–34).

Mary

The mother of Jesus (John 2:1–5, 12; 6:42; 19:26–27) is never named in the Fourth Gospel. Jesus was known as the son of Joseph (1:45; 6:42), with no suggestion that Joseph was not his biological father. John makes no reference to a miraculous conception. Given the date of composition and the author's awareness of other Christian traditions and texts, John surely knew the stories of the virginal conception but is not interested in attempting to combine this tradition with his own theology of preexistence. John knows the idea of divine begetting but applies it to believers, not to Jesus (1:12–13). "Son of God" does not mean for John "not son of Joseph," just as "coming from heaven" is not an alternative to "coming from Nazareth." The paradox is that Jesus is Son of God and son of Joseph, from God and from Nazareth.

The Johannine school was aware of earlier clashes between teachers such as Paul who preached the gospel of Jesus who "died for our sins" (1 Cor 15:3), who was "crucified in weakness" (2 Cor 13:4), and those who preached a "different gospel" about "another Jesus" (2 Cor 11:4). We do not have their writings, but presumably the Jesus portrayed in the Christology of Paul's opponents was the powerful Son of God who overcame all of life's enemies by his divine power. John sees the value, indeed the necessity, of confessing the faith in more than one way. Each Christology has irreplaceable insights. The *kenosis Christology* allows God's saving act in Jesus to be presented as the life and death of a truly human being, a vulnerable, victimized man whose love cost him everything, who willingly suffered and died as one of us. Yet this way of telling the Jesus story could not tell of God's saving act in the Christ event by narrating stories of miracles Jesus performed during his preresurrection life. Such a Jesus could not really die. For Paul and his followers, holding on to the centrality and reality of the crucifixion meant ignoring or rejecting such stories. It also meant abandoning the effort to proclaim the gospel by telling stories from Jesus's life. If we only had Paul and the New Testament epistles, we could speak of Christ's divine glory in his transcendent existence prebirth and postresurrection but could tell no stories of the power of God at work in the human Jesus as he interacts with other human beings in Galilee and Jerusalem. Without these stories, the Christian faith would be immeasurably the poorer, and the Christian confession would have nothing to say between "born of the Virgin Mary" and "suffered under Pontius Pilate." On the other hand, the *epiphany Christology* could preach the saving act of God in Christ by telling of his mighty deeds that freed us from all the enemies of life—sickness, hunger, alienation, sin, blindness, death—but at the risk of portraying a Jesus who only masqueraded as human, a Jesus who could come down from the cross and laugh at the human folly of those who suppose they could actually kill a divine being. This kind of Christology was tending in the direction of Gnosticism. We can understand that Christian teachers who expressed their faith as advocates of epiphany Christology considered teachers who pictured Jesus as truly human enemies of the faith, and vice versa.

Paradox: Narrative Holds Together Conflicting Affirmations

When taken by themselves, each of these theologies—truly divine epiphany Christology and truly human *kenosis* Christology—would later be considered heretical, a betrayal of the faith it was trying to confess. But how can thoughtful Christians who affirm that the one true God acted in the truly human Jesus for the salvation of the world proclaim the faith in a way that holds on to the values of each Christology? Three options were advanced in the early church. All were sincere, commonsense approaches. All were reasonable and logical. All were rejected.

Jesus Was Truly Divine, and So Could Not Be Truly Human

The divine Son of God could not and did not live as a human being and die a human death, but only pretended to be human. This was the interpretation of docetism.

Jesus Was Truly Human, and So Could Not Be Truly Divine

Like the great prophets of the Bible, the human being Jesus of Nazareth was inspired by God's Spirit to do greater deeds than other human beings. The human being Jesus was adopted by God, but a monotheistic faith cannot speak of him in language only appropriate to the one true God. This was the interpretation of Ebionism.

Jesus Was a Hybrid Being, Partly Divine but with Human Features, Like an Angel

Neither true God nor true man, Jesus was more divine than other humans but less divine than the one true God. "Angel" seemed to some Christians to offer a category into which Jesus could fit. "Truly God, truly man" of the later creeds is preempted by "sort of divine, sort of human." The letter to the Hebrews seems to oppose such a Christology (Heb 1–2).

These first three ventures fit christological language into the framework of ordinary human logic, which remains unshaken in speaking of God. Each of them was advocated by sincere and thoughtful Christian teachers of the early church. No documents advocating any of these options were included in the New Testament. All three views were later considered heretical by what came to be mainline Christianity. All three views, in a variety of forms, are still with us.

Here are three narrative approaches, all of which were included in the New Testament:

First, the truly human Jesus lived an exemplary life obedient to God and was raised from the dead and exalted to heaven to become the truly divine Son of God. This two-stage "Christology from below" handles the conceptual problem chronologically: Jesus was first truly *human*, then became truly divine. Some New Testament witnesses, such as the creed cited by Paul in Romans 1:3–4, express their faith in these terms, though this is not Paul's own view. The Gospel of Mark has sometimes been understood to represent this "adoptionist" Christology, but this is a misunderstanding.

Second, the divine Son of God became human, lived a human life and died a human death, and was then exalted by God to his former transcendent state. In this three-stage "Christology from above," the story of the Son of God begins in the heavenly world, the divine Son is incarnate as the truly human Jesus, then is exalted to his present status as heavenly Lord at the resurrection. This Christology is represented by the letters of the apostle Paul and the prophet-author of Revelation and their followers, who adopted the epistolary genre of theological instruction. They were able to hold together Christ's divinity and humanity by projecting a cosmic narrative in which the truly divine Christ became truly human for a "little while" (e.g., Phil 2:5–9; Heb 2:5–9). It is a diachronic pattern presenting the Jesus story in a U-shaped drama in three acts: divine to human to divine. In the Johannine community, this Christology is represented by Revelation and 1–3 John.

Third, the divine Son of God became human, and during his human life the divine glory shone through his human life (though it was perceived only by believers, and only in the light of the cross and resurrection). This is represented in the paradoxical literary form of the gospel. It is crucial to recognize that this literary-theological move does not claim to explain, in philosophical ontological terms, how a *being* could be both truly divine and truly human. Such "explanations" either compromise what they are trying to explain or reduce the mystery of the incarnation to manageable proportions that can be handled by human logic that operates within the confines of the space-time world, the only world we can clearly imagine. What Mark and his followers did was to find a responsible theological form to confess Christian faith in a way that combines two contrary ways of thinking and speaking about God's saving act in Jesus. The gospel genre is a narrative form that includes both categories of language about the Christ event without compromise. It deals with the world of *language* about Jesus, not the metaphysical world of the *being* of the person of Jesus. Christians cannot imagine or explain in either philosophical or commonsense terms how a *being* could be both fully human and fully divine at the same time, but some early Christian teachers knew that to be true to their confession of God's act in Jesus, they had to use both kinds of language to express their faith. This is true not only of theological language but also of all human language that attempts to speak of ultimacy. Physicists must speak of light as both waves and particles, though these ways of *speaking* cannot be harmonized into what light really *is*. Early Christian confession of Jesus was not a matter of ontology but linguistics. This does not mean that the Christian gospel deals only with the story world of words, as though the Jesus portrayed in the Gospels only lived and died in a story. All the Gospels insist, and John is especially insistent, that something really happened in the space-time world of the "flesh" (*sarx*, John 1:14). But when the story of God's saving act in the Christ event is told in the form of the life of Jesus, *what* happened can only be communicated by portraying Jesus as truly the divine Son of God *and* as the truly human Jesus of Nazareth. *How?*

Secrecy: The Literary Strategy of the "Messianic Secret" Facilitates Juxtaposing the Two Christologies in One Narrative. The Saving Power of the One True God and the True Humanity of the Human Jesus Are Both Fully Represented by the New Literary-Theological Genre, the Gospel

About a generation before the flourishing of the Johannine community in Roman Asia, the author of the Gospel of Mark devised a genre of narrative Christology for juxtaposing epiphany Christology and *kenosis* Christology. This narrative genre included ways of confessing Christian faith not only as a cosmic narrative but also within the story line of the life of Jesus. But how could both views of Jesus be presented in one story? The Christian teacher known as Mark, developing elements already present in the tradition, was the first to devise the "messianic secret" as the literary means of holding the two Christologies together, resulting in the new literary genre *gospel.* Mark's narrative framework of the "secret messiahship" tells the story of God's mighty acts in the person of Jesus in such a way that God's saving power is already manifest during the life of Jesus (as in the epiphany Christology) but no human being in the story perceives the identity of Jesus and the meaning of his life until the story is over (as in the *kenosis* Christology). Mark's solution was still basically diachronic. The stories of God's mighty power at work in Jesus dominated the first half of his story, Mark 1:1–8:26; the story of Jesus's suffering and death controlled the story from Mark 8:26 to the end. The reality of God's saving act in Jesus, and the identity of Jesus as Son of God, could not be recognized until the event of the cross-resurrection, after the story was over. The postresurrection reader knows all along, but the mystery of what is happening is concealed from the characters in the story. Not only unbelievers and enemies but also Jesus's family and disciples misunderstand throughout. The first human being to recognize Jesus as Son of God is the centurion in charge of the crucifixion detail: "Truly this *man* was *God's* Son" (15:39). The disciples do not understand until they receive the good news of the cross and resurrection.

The Johannine teachers adopt the gospel form and the messianic secret inherent in it, but they interpret each element in their own way. They intensify both the divine and the human perspectives. Preexistence and ascension are made explicit. God language is explicitly used of Jesus, and miracles are made more majestic (the healed man had been sick *thirty-eight* years [John 5:5], the sightless man was *born* blind [9:1], Lazarus had been dead *four days* [11:17]). More graphically than in the Synoptics, Jesus is explicitly human (only in John does Jesus bleed, with a spear thrust to guarantee his death

[19:34]). As John's Gospel begins and ends with God language of the Messiah ("God" in 1:1; 20:28), so "Behold the *man*" occurs in a dramatic, climactic scene (19:5). To tell such a story, John necessarily adopts the secrecy motif, the narrative strategy inherent in the genre "gospel." However, rather than Mark's diachronic pattern in which the characters in the story do not perceive Jesus's identity until the end, John reconceives the messianic secret as a synchronic, simultaneous paradox. Throughout the story, from the first page onward, Jesus clearly declares who he is, his identity is recognized at some level by both believers and opponents, and christological titles are freely used (e.g., 1:29–51; 2:11; 4:26, 42; 5:19–46; the several "I am" sayings [4:26; 6:35, 41; 8:12; 10:7, 9, 11, 14, 25; 14:6; 15:1, 5; cf. 8:28, 58; 13:19; 18:5, 6]). In obvious contrast to Mark, Jesus declares that he has taught nothing in secret (18:19–20). Yet no one understands, nor can understand, until the story is over and the Holy Spirit comes to teach them the understanding of both Scripture and the events of Jesus's life they themselves have lived through (2:22; 12:16; 16:12; 20:9). The Markan Jesus had spoken in parables so that those who heard him during his lifetime *could not* understand (Mark 4:10–12). The Johannine Jesus does not speak in parables but says everything plainly (John 10:6, 25, 29), speaking not only to the characters in the story but also to the post-Easter reader (see below). Coming within hearing distance of John's message calls for a grasp of the nature of the gospel narrative and the messianic secret inherent in the gospel form.

Denouement: The Story of Jesus Is Narrated as the Definitive Segment of Universal History, the Individual Life That Reveals and Defines the Meaning of All History

As in the earliest gospel the good news from and about Jesus is the "gospel of *God*" (Mark 1:14), so the gospel genre devised by Mark narrates the life, death, and resurrection of Jesus as the definitive segment of the creation-to-consummation metanarrative of the saving acts of God. In Greek drama, at least from Aristotle on, the key scene that revealed the meaning of the whole, typically near the end of the story, was called the *denouement* (*lysis*), the unraveling of the tangled plot, the revelation and clarification of the meaning of the whole story, the resolution of its problems. The *denouement* is the "aha" scene in which the meaning of the whole is seen. This revelatory, defining segment of the whole story does not change previous or subsequent facts but lets them be seen in a new light, in their ultimate context.

For Judaism and its Scripture, God is the creator, the Lord of the world and universal history. The world has somehow become perverted and rebellious against its Maker, and the meaning and purpose of life and history have become obscure and uncertain. In the Jewish hope nurtured by God's covenant and promises of a future, the tragedies of human history are redeemed in the grand denouement to come, when God asserts his own royal power and establishes justice and the blessedness of God's ultimate kingdom. When the city of God comes into view at the last turn of the road of universal and personal history, the meaning of the whole road, creation to eschaton, past, present, and future, is revealed. God has not abandoned the world but has promised to guide history to its consummation in the kingdom of God. In those visions of the future that featured a Messiah, the final king empowered by God comes at the *end* of history. One cannot ask, "But what happened *after* 'They lived happily ever after'?"

The New Testament authors never integrate Jesus into an open-ended series of God's revelatory events. To confess that the Christ has come, that he is Jesus of Nazareth, crucified and risen, projects a narrative world that includes all history and gives it its meaning. But if God's Messiah is the crucified and risen Jesus of Nazareth, the meaning of kingship and messiahship must be reconfigured in the light of who Jesus actually was and is, and what it means for God to save the world by sending his Son the Messiah. In John's adaptation of the gospel genre, the Christ was with God at the creation, was present in the world and in the covenant history of Israel, was incarnate in Jesus, accompanies his church in the power of the Holy Spirit through its historical journey, and will appear to all at the end of history as its goal and judge. To tell the story of the Messiah is to narrate the definitive segment of all history, the self-defining story of God. To come within hearing distance of the gospel is to read it not merely as "stories about Jesus" but as the meaning of our lives—with "our" finally including all human beings and the whole creation.

Contemporaneity: The Story Is Told in Such a Way That the Jesus within the Narrative Is Transparent to the Reader as the Contemporary Heavenly Lord, Who Speaks through and beyond the Narrative into the Reader's Own World

The main character is presented as both a real person of past history who once spoke to his there-and-then contemporaries *and* the present Lord who *still* speaks. Already in the earliest gospel, Mark presented Jesus as speaking both to his first disciples and over their heads to Mark's hearer-readers. In Mark 13, Jesus takes the first four disciples aside and concludes his last and longest discourse with direct address to the readers: "And what I say to you I say to all" (Mark 13:37). This is one meaning of the resurrection: Jesus's teaching recorded on the pages of the gospel is not the heritage of a wise sage of the past that can then be "applied" to the readers' own day. In the gospel form, time is compressed, the wall between then and now is collapsed, and the risen Christ speaks through the gospel to every generation. "Then" and "now" are not only linked in a diachronic chain but are interwoven in a synchronic tapestry. The separate threads can be critically distinguished, examined, and commented on, as in a commentary, but they function together in the gospel, as the "then" of Jesus and the "now" of the risen Christ and the readers' present are fused in the reality of the continuing Christ event. It is the narrative mode of theology that makes this possible. A story (like a sermon or church-school lesson) can only be told diachronically, one word following another. But it can be told in such a way as to weave together and create a word picture in the imagination that can't be done on the page or computer screen. Various temporal strands can come together in the same word picture. This can be clearly seen in John's portrayal of the Last Supper, where Jesus speaks from the post-Easter perspective. The "now" of the 30 CE Jesus never becomes merely an objective past that can be looked *back* on.

This collapsing of temporal boundaries also means that Christology and ecclesiology cannot be separated. John's readers recognize their own history in the Gospel's story of Christ. The story is for insiders, who get its double meaning in scene after scene. Though outsiders can "overhear," they do not and cannot comprehend the constant dual references to the mission before and after Easter. A long list of texts documents John's view that the disciples share Jesus's being and mission.[3] This requires sharing the gospel's own faith in Jesus as the risen One. The mission of Jesus is continued in the church, not as a separate epoch (as in Luke-Acts) but as the continuing work and presence of Christ himself. This is the Johannine version of Paul's understanding of the church as the body of Christ (see, e.g., 1 Cor 12; Rom 12).

All these dimensions of John's narrative theology become real not in these abstract prefatory discussions but in engagement with the text of the Fourth Gospel itself, to which we now turn. After a brief reflection on John's distinctive portrait of Jesus and a survey of the structure and story line of the Gospel as a whole, we will engage in a close reading of selected texts in which central themes of John's theology emerge.

John's Distinctive Picture of Jesus[4]

There is ultimately a deep unity between the theology of John and that of Paul, the Synoptics, and the other New Testament writers. But prior to any too-easy harmonizing talk of unity, the distinctiveness of each must be seen.

- The Fourth Gospel presents Jesus as from God, the Son of God, the Preexistent One who has come down from heaven, but he is also from Nazareth, born the son of Mary and Joseph. This simultaneous paradox is not explained in terms of a miraculous birth.
- In the Synoptics, Jesus is tested by Satan at the beginning of his ministry, is transfigured before his disciples in a central scene, and agonizes in Gethsemane at the end. None of these scenes is present in the Fourth Gospel—90 percent of John's narrative, in fact, has no parallel in the other gospels.
- Jesus's teaching is not about the kingdom of God, as in the Synoptics, but about himself, that is, his identity as the Son of God sent from heaven. During his ministry the Johannine Jesus refers to the kingdom of God only once, in the private nighttime meeting with Nicodemus (John 3:3, 5). Jesus's public teaching is about his relation to God and his role as God's revealer. Jesus does not dispute with Jewish teachers about interpretation of the Torah but about his equality with God. He publicly calls for faith in himself as Messiah and Son of God. People disbelieve and misunderstand, but Jesus's claims to be Messiah and Son of God are clear and public. There is no messianic secret in the Markan sense.
- Other words and concepts common in the Synoptics are missing from John, such as "mercy" (*eleos*, verb *eleeō*, "to have mercy"), "preach" (*kērussō*), "proclaim the good news" (*euangelizō*), and "gospel, good news" (*euangelion*).
- There is no citation of the Great Commandment from the Bible; instead, Jesus gives his own "new commandment" (13:34).
- In the Synoptics, Davidic imagery is important for interpreting the meaning of Jesus's messiahship, in comparison and contrast. In the Johannine community, this perspective is represented only by Revelation (Rev 3:7; 5:5; 22:16). David is mentioned thirty-seven times in the Synoptics but only once in the Fourth Gospel, and there as an example of "the Jews'" misunderstanding of both their Scripture and the messianic hope (John 7:42). In John, not David the king but Moses the revealer is the primary biblical model for the Messiah, with whom Jesus is both

compared and contrasted: at Sinai, Moses first ascends and then descends, relays what he has heard from God, but—in contrast to Jesus, who first descends and then ascends—Moses never saw God (1:17–18).

- There are no parables. In the Synoptics Jesus tells brief provocative secular stories about other people—the prodigal son, the good Samaritan, the woman who lost and found the coin, the rich man and Lazarus—as a way of talking about the kingdom of God. In the Fourth Gospel Jesus tells no stories; the subject of his lengthy discourses is not the kingdom of God but himself. The series of "I am" sayings has no parallel in the Synoptics. Whereas the kingdom of God in the Synoptics is like yeast (Matt 13:33 par.), in John Jesus himself is the bread of life (John 6:35). Whereas the Synoptic Jesus speaks of the shepherd and lost sheep (Matt 18:12; Luke 15:4–6), in John, Jesus himself is the Good Shepherd (John 10:11). Whereas the Synoptic Jesus tells a parable in which the kingdom is like a vineyard that will be handed over to others (Mark 12:1–11 par.), the Johannine Jesus is himself the vine (John 15:1–5).
- There are no exorcisms. As in the Bible generally, evil is more than the misdeeds of individual humans; it is a power to which all human beings are subject. John conceives God's defeat of Satan in the Christ event in cosmic terms (12:31), not as casting demons out of individuals.
- There are no scenes or sayings in which Jesus is champion and friend of the lower classes and oppressed. In the Fourth Gospel, there are no poor people, no wicked rich, no publicans, no sinners (7:53–8:11 is a later addition), no shepherds, no fishermen (except in the final edition of John's Gospel that includes chapter 21), no widows, no children, no women fellow travelers, no unclean demoniacs, no repentance or forgiveness of sins, no lepers, no prostitutes, no "other criminals" crucified with Jesus. In general, the Johannine Jesus is portrayed as somewhat aloof, without the warm compassion characteristic of the synoptic Jesus. In 2:1–10 Jesus declines his mother's request to help the bride and groom out of an embarrassing situation, then acts on his own initiative "to reveal his glory." In chapters 5 and 9, he takes the initiative to heal a man lame for thirty-eight years and a man born blind, without either of them asking for his help. Even though he has shown that he has power to heal from a distance (4:46–54), he coolly delays going to Bethany in order to make the miracle of Lazarus's restoration to life the more dramatic (11:1–44; cf. vv. 3, 14). In human terms, this calculated response seems to represent an unattractive remoteness, but in the Fourth Gospel this is the theological expression of the holiness of God. God's compassion for the

world is manifest in the Christ event itself (3:16!), not in the individual stories in which this ultimate act of God is symbolically portrayed. This literary-theological modus operandi somewhat moderates the problem of picturing Jesus as healing only those fortunate enough to have been born in his geographical and temporal vicinity. Both the synoptic portrayals and the Johannine representation of Jesus have their theological validity, which should not be lost or compromised by homogenization.

- Jesus's ministry in the Synoptics includes only one Jewish festival, the Passover at which he is killed. His public ministry, baptism to crucifixion, lasted less than a year. In John, Jesus attends the Passover twice (a third is mentioned in 6:4), as well as the festival of booths (tabernacles), dedication (Hanukkah), and the unnamed feast of 5:1. In the Synoptics, the cleansing of the temple occurs at the conclusion of a ministry that lasts several months but less than a year; in John, it occurs at the beginning of a ministry that lasts more than two years.
- In the Synoptics, Jesus does not begin his ministry until John the Baptist is arrested and off the scene (Mark 1:14–15). In the Fourth Gospel, John the Baptist and Jesus have overlapping, parallel, even competitive ministries (John 3:22–23; 4:1–3).
- In the Synoptics, Jesus disputes with Pharisees, Sadducees, Herodians, and scribes. The Johannine narrative contains many Pharisees and speaks often of "the Jews," but it has no scribes, Sadducees, or Herodians.
- In both the Synoptics and John, Jesus celebrates a last meal with his disciples on Thursday evening and is crucified the next day. In the Synoptics, this Last Supper is a Passover meal; in John, the final events of Jesus's life occur one day earlier. The Last Supper is not a Passover, but Jesus the Lamb of God dies as the Passover lambs are being slain.
- In Mark and Matthew, resurrection appearances occur only in Galilee. In Luke and John 20, the risen Jesus appears only in Jerusalem. The final edition of the Fourth Gospel that includes chapter 21 then includes a Galilean appearance, affirming both the Mark-Matthew and the Lukan perspectives.

Structure as Theology

John's distinctive picture of God is seen not only in its content but also in its structure.

In creating the gospel genre, Mark structured the narrative as a two-part story, beginning in Galilee (chaps. 1–9), followed by the journey and final week in Jerusalem (chaps. 10–16). John also configures the narrative in two parts, but with a different structure expressing his own theology. In the Fourth Gospel, the story begins in Judea or southern Transjordan, the primary arena of Jesus's work. Twice he ventures briefly into Galilee (Cana, chaps. 2 and 4; around the Sea of Galilee, chap. 6). Although Jesus is "from Nazareth," the Fourth Gospel never narrates any scene located there, and the center of gravity of the story is not Galilee and Capernaum but Judea and Jerusalem.

Following the Markan pattern, the synoptic Jesus instructs his disciples throughout the Galilean ministry, but in John Jesus never teaches his disciples until the last evening before the crucifixion. After the prologue and introductory call scenes of chapter 1, in chapters 2–12 the disciples only overhear his dialogues and discourses in confrontation with the world. Then in chapters 13–17, Jesus compresses all his instruction to "his own" into the Farewell Discourse of the Last Supper. John narrates two and a half years in the first twelve chapters, then takes five chapters for the last evening of Jesus's life. There is no "last week," as in the Synoptics, but only a "last night." One-third of the book is devoted to the last twenty-four hours.

Victim or Victor?

The four canonical Gospels are structured along two contrasting story lines, classically designating Jesus Christ as victim or victor.[5] In the Synoptics, following Mark's basic structure, the first part of the story is filled with success and huge response to the powerful Son of God from the crowds in Galilee. Then Jesus makes the trip to Jerusalem, where there are no salvific miracles, and he meets only opposition and death. Jesus is abandoned by all and cries out in despair in Gethsemane the night before the trial and crucifixion. The story line "descends" from Galilean success to Judean rejection. The resurrection is the great reversal of this downward trend. God vindicates Jesus the victim of human political and religious rejection, summarized in Luke's portrayal of the first Christian sermon: "God has made this same Jesus, whom you crucified, both Lord and Messiah" (Acts 2:36 REB).

The Fourth Gospel, too, has the narrative shape of the redemptive U-shaped event. In his final instruction to his disciples, the Johannine Jesus is insistently clear on this fundamental structure of the Christian message: "I came from the Father and have come into the world; again, I am leaving the world and am going to the Father." His disciples said, "Yes, now you are speaking plainly, not in any figure of speech!" (John 16:28–29). Looking back on his ministry, he then declares, "In the world you face persecution. But take courage; I have conquered the world!" (16:33). In John, the glory of God is manifest throughout Jesus's ministry; there is no one-way descent from Galilee to Jerusalem; and the passion story is the triumphal march of Jesus the victor back to his heavenly glory. The triumphal entry does not wait until Jesus rides into Jerusalem at the end of his ministry but occurs with Jesus's coming into the world, already a triumph and manifestation of his glory. For the Johannine teachers, the cross is not the low point of the story of Jesus, not the ultimate humiliation of the Son of God that is then reversed at the resurrection, but is itself already the triumphal exit, as the Son of God is "lifted up" and returns to the Father (3:14; 8:28; 12:32–34), having finished the work he had been sent to do (19:28–30). This is why Jesus's characteristic term for God, "the One who sent me," is basic to both Johannine Christology and the Johannine understanding of the church. Jesus's identity is essentially the one sent by the Father, the Son who comes obediently and willingly, and who himself sends the disciples as the continuation of God's mission in the world (17:18; 20:21). It is thus no exaggeration to designate the bipartite structure of John's Gospel as the drama of the triumph of God in two acts presenting the mission of the Son God sent into the world:

I. Triumphal Entry: Christ confronts and conquers the world in a series of life-giving signs (chaps. 1–12)
II. Triumphal Exit: Christ is "lifted up" on the cross and returns to the Father (chaps. 13–21)[6]

Throughout John's Gospel, Jesus Christ represents the triumph of God. As is the case with kingship, messiahship, victory, and other vocabulary of Christian confession, the language of God's triumph need not be avoided or toned down as too triumphalistic to express the biblical doctrine of salvation. The New Testament's christological redefinition of winning is inherent in the confession that the Christ is Jesus, the crucified man of Nazareth. *How* the all-conquering power of God redeems the world is explicated in the individual stories of the Gospel itself.

John's Introduction: Prologue and Testimony

Hymnic Prologue: The Transcendent Context of the Jesus Story (1:1–18)

John prefaces his story of Jesus with a prologue to help his hearer-readers come within hearing distance of the selection of stories and discourses he intends to tell. The following considerations are intended to help today's preachers and teachers hear the prologue itself in accord with its intended purpose.

The Prologue Is a Hymn That Sets the Whole Story within the Context of Christian Worship

The author begins with a hymn, insider language drawn from church tradition, presumably sung, chanted, or recited in worship as a familiar element of the church's confession. This community knows itself to be sent into the world, that it has a mission in continuity with God's sending of the Son into the world (17:18; 20:21), but it doesn't begin with the question, "What does the world want and need?" The story will get there soon enough (see on 1:38, "What are you looking for?," pp. 222–23 herein). Mission and evangelism are not matters of market research. As the community engages in its mission to the world, it must broaden and deepen its understanding of its own faith. Such theological reflection is inherent in the church's mission. The Fourth Gospel is not a missionary tract addressed to outsiders but a teaching document to further equip insiders for mission.

The Johannine teachers are creative and groundbreaking as they reformulate Christian theology for a new situation, but they also call the church to hold on to its familiar tradition (cf. 1 John 1:1–3). It is the nature of the church as a living organism never to be simply a static, fixed reality that can be replicated generation after generation. The church has always been the "emerging church" and must continually be reunderstanding itself and its mission in an ever-changing world. But the church does not begin every new day with a blank page. It is of the essence of the church to reflect on its Scripture and tradition handed on and celebrated in worship, guided by its reason and experience imbued by the Holy Spirit. Like Israel, the church does not explain its faith before the bar of reason; in worship, it confesses and sings its faith before God.

The Prologue Provides the Whole Story as the Context for Each of the Little Stories

We now begin soundings in particular Johannine texts, with the reminder that John's Gospel is a seamless whole (cf. John 19:23!), which must be understood holistically. Each scene presupposes that the reader knows the whole narrative. Each little story in the Gospel presupposes that the reader knows the big story in which it is embedded. Post-Easter readers know this comprehensive, cosmic framework for the Jesus story, though the characters in the story do not. This is an aspect of John's version of the "messianic secret" that is inherent in the gospel genre. Likewise, the prologue presupposes that its "readers" (who hear the text sung, chanted, or recited in worship) know the stories and discourses from the life of Jesus that constitute the Gospel. The Gospel not only has flashbacks (e.g., 7:21; 15:20) but also flash-forwards, prequels in which the scene being narrated refers to scenes that have not yet occurred in the story line as plotted (e.g., 2:22; 12:16; 11:2 refers to Mary's act of anointing that will not occur until the next chapter; the beginning of the narrative already presupposes the cross and resurrection stories). No text or story in the Gospel can be understood without entering the story world projected by the narrative as a whole. Before proceeding, it is well worth the time to pause and read through the Gospel nonstop (it will take about an hour and a half), getting the *Johannine* story in mind. The holistic narrative undermines the tendency to quote key verses in isolation, such as John 3:16, as though such proof texts severed from the message of the story as a whole could solve any of the difficult problems presented by the New Testament to all serious readers. Like Jesus's parables, the story as a whole undermines simplistic attempts at superficial clarity.

The hymn celebrates the mighty acts of God. The Gospel begins in worship, with a song. The vocabulary is mostly from the Hellenistic world, expressed in the straightforward contemporary language of the authors' and readers' situation, understandable by newcomers and there-every-Sunday traditional churchgoers alike. But it is essentially a Jewish hymn celebrating the mighty acts of God. Like some of Israel's psalms (e.g., 78; 105; 106; 135; 136), the hymn is a narrative drama of the saving acts of God. In Revelation and elsewhere, we have already seen the Christian adoption and adaptation of basic structure of *Jewish* theology: creation/covenant/consummation. The Johannine version of this drama of universal history is portrayed in three acts.

Grammar Illuminates Theology

Two grammatical points are helpful:

(1) Like other Hellenistic authors such as Philo, John in this text uses the anarthrous *theos* for the Logos as God, to be identified as the Son, reserving the articular *ho theos* for Yahweh, the Self-Existent One, to be identified as the Father.

(2) To grasp the powerful two-level subtlety present throughout the prologue, English readers must here be aware of the difference in the way English and Greek use pronouns. English uses masculine or feminine for personal antecedents, neuter for impersonal. Greek choice of pronouns is determined by the grammatical gender of the antecedent. In Greek, God (*theos*) and Word (*logos*) are both masculine. In English, God is personal and must be "he" or "she," while Word is impersonal and is normally an "it," unless personified as a personal name. So also, "Life" (*zōē*, feminine), "Light" (*phōs*, neuter), and "Wisdom" (*sophia*, feminine) are impersonal; unless personified, each will be rendered as "it" in English, regardless of the gender of the nouns in Greek. In some grammatical cases in the Greek text, the neuter pronoun for "Light" and the masculine pronoun for "Word" have the identical form as the masculine pronoun for God, Jesus, and Christ. This allows John to express a theologically profound ambiguity, using the same pronoun (*autou*, *autō*) that can point to the universal Light and Life, the preexistent Word, and the truly human Jesus Christ in whom this Word became incarnate. In English, Word is "it" and Jesus is "he"; for Greek, both are "he." Syntactically, the pronouns of John 1:3–4 refer to the universal Light, Life, and Word that pervades all creation, in each case an "it." But John is already thinking of the incarnate Jesus Christ, which English would render as "him." The Greek does not have to decide in each case whether the pronoun means "it" or "him," but the English translator does. Thus 1:3–4: "Through it/him all things were made . . . in it/him was life, and that life was the light of all people" (translation mine; cf. TNIV).

I. God-the-Word in Creation (1:1–4)
II. God-the-Word Revealed in History: Universal and Particular (1:5[6–8]–13)
III. God-the-Word Incarnate in Jesus Christ (1:14–18)

Act 1: The Hymn Celebrates the One God, the Creator (1:1–4)

As in the Bible itself, the story begins with creation. In contrast to the proto-Gnosticism John opposes, there is no precreation mythology that claims to explain the perplexities of this world by telling what happened before creation. There is one God, the creator of all that is, *ta panta*, everything and everyone that exists. All people are God's people. All life comes from God; all life is sustained by God (John 1:1–3; cf. Gen 1–2; Ps 104; etc.). Every human being is given life from God; every human being is illuminated by God's eternal light (1:4, 9), nourished by God's creative word that was not only spoken at creation but continues to address the world. God not only stood at the beginning but is continually and universally present.

The subject throughout the hymn is the Logos, but this is only another way of saying that the hymn throughout is about God. The first sentence of the hymn makes three affirmations about this Logos: it/he was in the beginning with God, it/he was with God, it/he was God. Then, without retracting the declaration that the Word *was* God, the hymn repeats the second declaration: the Word was *with* God. This tensive "was"/"was-with" is the hymn writer's way of affirming that the Word of God was God himself, but neither in a way that equates the Word with God nor in a way that makes the Word a separate being from God. Taken by itself, "the-Word-was-God" says too much, too simply, and is in danger of misunderstanding. Taken by itself, "the-Word-was-with-God" says too little, too simply, and is in danger of misunderstanding. Both must be said together in trying to express what cannot be expressed in the this-worldly grammar of space-time reality.

The prologue provides the framework for what will be illustrated in the narrative. Jesus will pray to the One who is "the only true God" (17:3). He will declare, "The Father and I are *one*" (10:30, where "one" is the neuter *hen*, "one reality," not the masculine *hena*, "one person"). He will also clearly insist that he and the Father are *two* distinct persons, and that "it is not I alone who judge, but I and the Father who sent me. In your law it is written that the testimony of two witnesses is valid. I testify on my own behalf, and the Father who sent me testifies on my behalf" (8:16–18). The hymn thus presupposes that the God Christians worship cannot be thought of or talked about without speaking of Christ, and that Jesus Christ cannot be thought of or spoken about without speaking of God.

In accord with New Testament theology and Christian faith in general, the hymn does not suppose that one can begin with *God*, then, having gotten clear about the doctrine of God, go on to *Christ* and the *church*, as though these were separate topics. If this were the case, Christology (and Christ!) would be dispensable, an optional extra accepted by Christians but rejected by other monotheists such as Jews and Muslims. The God Christians talk about is the God revealed in Christ. The Christ Christians talk about is the One alive and active in the mission of the church. The creeds are necessarily somewhat misleading in this regard, if they encourage the view that we can begin with God as the first article, then go on to Christ and the Spirit in articles 2 and 3. For Christians, confession of faith in Jesus Christ is built into the first article of faith. "I believe in God . . ." is all and enough, if faith is confessed in the Christian God revealed in Christ, whose presence is continued in this world as the Holy Spirit at work in the world and the church.

Act 2: The Hymn Celebrates the Revelation of the One God in History: Universal and Particular (1:5[6–8]–13)

God's Word, as the very life and light of God, encounters the world through all history, in every place and time. "It/he was in the world" (1:10) depicts universal history, creation to Jesus Christ. Those who respond to God's revelation receive life from God, are born from above, become children of God (Wis 9:7, of Israel). Contra the pop stoicism of Max Ehrmann's 1926 poem "Desiderata," I am not a self-proclaimed "child of the universe" who "has a right to be here," but am a child of the one God, the creator. I receive my life from God, as part of the world God made and loves, and can know this from God's revelation in the creation itself.

In acts 1 and 2, the hymnic drama praises God in universal and secular language. God encounters "all people" (1:4), "all" (1:7), "everyone" (1:9), "the world" (1:9, 10), and "his own" (world, people), whom he had created (1:11), and refers objectively to "all who received him" as those in the epoch between creation and the coming of Christ (1:12). Prior to act 3, which introduces Moses, the Torah, and Jesus Christ, the whole hymn can be sung and understood by anyone, without prior knowledge of the Bible or Judaism or without prior religious commitments. Everyone can join in the first two verses of this song, at their own level of understanding, and celebrate the God who created the world, gives to all life and light, and welcomes all who receive him, accepting them as children of God.

Just as John rejects the gnosticizing view that creation was a cosmic mistake from which spiritual beings entangled in this fallen world must be saved, he rejects the gnosticizing view that the true God's saving action first appeared in Jesus Christ. Nor does John elaborate a picture of the Fall, rejecting gnosticizing explanations of how the world for which the one God is ultimately responsible came to be overrun with evil. John insists that the world between creation and Christ, including the world outside the stream of Israel's history, had not been abandoned by God.

John adopts the pattern of the Jewish wisdom myth to affirm the continuing and universal revelation of the creator God. The Jewish Scriptures have numerous places in which God's general revelation in the world, nature, and history is affirmed (e.g., Ps 104), many texts that declare God's special revelation to Israel (Amos 3:2), and even some texts explicitly combining the two, such as Psalm 19—the first half declares the revelation that bespeaks the glory of God in the world of nature without words, the second half the particular gift of the Torah to Israel. So also Psalm 103, which declares that the God who "rules over all" is the God who "made known his ways to Moses, his acts to the people of Israel."

This general perspective of Israel's prophets, and teachers, and sages was focused in the wisdom tradition.

- Wisdom was identified with the creative Logos of God through whom the world was made (e.g., Wis 9:1) and with the Spirit of God that pervades all God's creation (Wis 9:17; 12:1). She was active in the world from Adam to Moses (Wis 10:1–14). She sought, and still seeks, a dwelling place among human beings, preaching and teaching divine truth, but her seeking was in vain, for her revelation was mostly rejected, and continues to be. She came to what was her own (for she had participated in its creation), but her own did not accept her (Prov 1:20–32; 9:5–6; Sir 6:23; 24:6, Bar 3:12; 1 En 4:1–3; 42:1–3; 84:3).
- Wisdom's mission in the world found a response in Israel, Moses, and the prophets, and Wisdom's message came to be focused in the "book of the covenant of the Most High God, / the law that Moses commanded us" (Sir 24:23; cf. 24:19–34; Bar 3:29–4:1), which is not for Israel alone but "for all who seek wisdom" (Sir 24:34).
- Such revelation happened among the gentile peoples. Thus, for example, Job and his three friends are not Israelites and know nothing of the Torah and the covenant with Israel, but they encounter and respond to God in the world and their own experience.
- In the meantime, Wisdom's witness to the world continues, centered in Israel's testimony but not confined to the Torah and God's covenant with Israel.

John has adopted and adapted the Jewish wisdom myth, but the subject throughout is the Word (*Logos*), not Wisdom (*Sophia*). *Sophia* and *Logos* were generally synonymous in religious and philosophical contexts in the Hellenistic world, yet John uses the *Sophia* pattern to communicate his *Logos* theology. One might legitimately wonder why this is so, since there is a strong Sophia Christology in other New Testament texts (cf., e.g., Matt 11:19, 28–30; Luke 7:35; 11:49 [Luke's "Wisdom of God" = the Matthean Jesus's "I," Matt 23:34]; 1 Cor 1:17–30; 2:7; Col 2:3). Exegetical reflection reveals four reasons:

1. *John's preference for* Logos *over* Sophia *is a matter of grammatical and theological subtlety*. Since *sophia* is a feminine noun, the pronouns for it/her would be distinguishable from pronouns for God. The pronoun used for God would be *autos*, "he"; the corresponding pronoun for *Sophia* would be *autē*, "she." John needed to use a noun with the same grammatical gender as the noun for God (we remember that such gender references are functions of grammar, not indicators of sex). *Logos* is a masculine noun, so that the same pronoun (the various forms of *autos*) could refer to God and the *Logos* simultaneously. This linguistic strategy, which works in Greek but not in English, facilitates the use of pronouns that can refer to both God and Word.
2. *Wisdom can be thought of as a part of creation, as God's first creature, who then assisted in the rest of creation.*

   > The LORD created me at the beginning of his work,
   > the first of his acts of long ago. (Prov 8:22)

   "Wisdom was created before all other things" (Sir 1:4). This conceptuality was in fact employed by some Christian teachers in the early church to interpret the significance of Christ. The profound hymn of Colossians 1:15–20 has many similarities to the Johannine prologue. Its two stanzas present Christ as the "firstborn" of both creation (1:15–17) and the dead. The interpretation of the Colossian hymn continues to be disputed, but the structure and vocabulary leave the way open to (mis)understanding Jesus Christ as the first of God's creatures in both the original creation and the new creation that began at Christ's resurrection. This is indeed a "high" Christology, but it leaves the door open to an understanding of Christ who, though preexistent, remains a creature, a part of creation though its preeminent figure. John, and the hymn with which he begins his Gospel, wanted to close this door. By reproducing the first words of his Bible as the first words of his Gospel, he presents the Word of God as already present when the creation begins and insists that "all things came into being through him, and without him not one thing came into being" (John 1:3). The Johannine Logos was not a creature, not even the first and best. "And the Word was *God*."

3. *The choice of* Logos *as the key term also provided a hermeneutical bridge to popular philosophy of the day.* Especially in Stoicism, but elsewhere in popular religious thought of the day, *logos* was the term for universal reason. Up to verse 14, the hymn made contact and resonated with many serious first-century religious people who celebrated the presence of universal reason in an orderly world and recognized their own ability to reason as kinship with the supreme principle of the universe. They could hear the Christian gospel as proclaiming that this universal reason had become incarnate in Jesus Christ.
4. *A final reason is that while* sophia, *"wisdom," tends to be thought of as static, internal, and reflective, the* logos, *"word," is outward-directed, dialogical, and implies a speaker and hearers. Logos* is relational in a way that *sophia* is not. In the Greek framework of understanding, *logos* and *sophia* could be virtual synonyms, so that revelation as *logos* can be understood as static, impersonal rationality. In Hebrew-Jewish tradition, revelation is personal address, a matter of speaking/hearing. In Hebrew thought, when I speak, I communicate not just ideas but myself, my own life, by taking in breath, taking the initiative to speak, expelling my breath—my very life—as word/*logos. Logos,* "speaking," involves words, relationship. In John's theology, relationship precedes even the creation of the universe. John has not yet made the final step that would be taken at Nicaea, where it was insisted that the Son is "begotten, not made," but he never envisions a time when God was a lonely, self-satisfied Being content to meditate in the solitary mood of philosophical wisdom. Not reason, but dialogue-speech-relationship characterizes the biblical God. "In the beginning was the Word."

The pattern developed by Israel's sages combined universalism and particularism. God's wisdom was available throughout the world but was mostly rejected. God's wisdom was revealed in a particular way to the covenant people of Israel, where, as in the world in general, it was sometimes accepted, sometimes rejected. Israel's theologians who confessed their faith in response to God's distinctive revelation in the history of the elect people did not generally make inferences as to the meaning of this for the rest of the world, the gentile nations, who are also God's people (on such confessional language see pp. 31–36 above). To the extent that the teachers of Israel did reflect on the destiny of the nations prior to and outside the revelatory *Heilsgeschichte* of Israel, their thinking tended toward an eschatological future resolution, thought of in basically two ways.

First, the idolatrous nations are destroyed, only Israel remains (Isa 24:21–23; 45:14–17). *In the final act of world history, the elect people of God constitute all the world's people.*

Second, the worshipers of false gods are finally converted. This may be pictured as incorporation within Israel (e.g., Ps 87:4–6; Isa 56:3–8; Jer 12:14–16; Zeph 3:9); as subordination to Israel, worshiping Yahweh and looking to Israel for instruction (e.g., Pss 22:27–28; 86:9; Isa 2:2–4; 25:6–10; Mic 4:1–3); or as continuing their national existence alongside Israel, now acknowledging the God of Israel and being acknowledged by God as his people Israel (e.g., Isa 19:19–25; Jer 3:15–18; 16:19–21; Ezek 16:52–63; Zech 2:11).

However it is pictured, *all the world's people finally become the people of God.* The distinction between insiders and outsiders will ultimately be eliminated. The God the gentiles have been worshiping under other names is the only true God, the God who has revealed his character and purpose to Israel. Israel's God is in truth the God of the whole world and all peoples. They do not know this now, but they shall finally come to know this. Such a theology can be seen as a kind of religious imperialism ("*Our* God will finally become everybody's God"), but it need not be. It is the theological result of two convictions: there is only one God, and this God has revealed his identity and purpose for the whole creation in the history of Israel. Likewise, when early Christian teachers adopt this pattern, proclaiming that all the kingdoms of the world will become the kingdom of the one God and his Christ (Rev 11:15), that the Christian community—itself the continuity and fulfillment of God's purpose manifest in Israel—is the foretaste and pledge on the destiny of all humanity (e.g., Eph 1:3–10), this need not be seen as the Christian version of religious imperialism. This New Testament pattern was adopted from the Scripture and tradition of Judaism. As in retrospect the teachers of Israel came to see that the light of God that already shines universally was all along the light of the one God of Israel, so the teachers of the church came to see that the God already dimly made known among the nations, the one in whom we trust without knowing what or who it is we trust, is the one true God definitively made known in Jesus Christ (John 17:3). Those who received it/him (the Logos, the Light), who believed in his name, to whom "he gave power to become children of God" and were "born of God," do indeed include believers in Jesus as the Christ, but the reference is not exclusively to them (John 1:12–13). The universal Light and Word that pervades the whole world and all history generated faith in all who responded, giving them the right/power (*exousia*) to become children of God.

Faith

> "When we walk to the edge of the light we have
> and take the first step into the darkness of the unknown,
> we must believe one of two things will happen:
> There will be something solid for us to stand on.
> or, we will be taught to fly."
>
> —Patrick Overton, *Rebuilding the Front Porch of America: Essays on the Art of Community Making* (Hayden, ID: Bitterroot Mountain Publishing, 1997, 2017), 163

As the hymn on which the prologue is based was circulated and sung in the Johannine churches, it was subject to a gnosticizing misinterpretation. The "children of God" seem to have been understood in the gnosticizing sense of those who by birth belonged to the spiritual realm. Their choice and decision were not involved. Salvation came as the knowledge of their true being when the heavenly redeemer appeared with the revelation that they belonged to the heavenly world. This gnosticizing reading, which understands the hymnic narrative to jump over all history between the fallen creation and the advent of Christ, might seem to be supported by two features of the text: (1) John the Baptist appears already in 1:6, suggesting that the narrative immediately following refers to the time of Jesus and the church, and (2) the phrase "those who believe *in his name*," who are born from God, might be understood as referring exclusively to Christian "born-again" believers. The phrase is exclusive to the Johannine writings (1 John 3:23; 5:13; John 1:12; 2:23; 3:18), where it elsewhere refers to Christian believers. It is understandable that many readers then and now could interpret the text this way, but three considerations argue for the reading here adopted:

1. All the verbs are in the past tense ("received," "believed," "gave," "believed," "born") and third person, looking back on events prior to the readers' time. From 1:14 on, verbs in the first person appear ("we beheld," "we received"), looking back on the Christ event and the believers' reception of it in faith.
2. The word "name" (*onoma*) in biblical theology often designates a label, but it also points to the being of the person named. The world before and apart from the advent of Christ that had never heard the *name* of Abra-

ham, Moses, Isaiah, or Jesus was confronted by the universal revelation of God's life and light, the reality of God's *being*. To be grasped by this *reality* is to "believe in his *name*." They may have called this Reality by another name—Baal, Marduk, Zeus, Jupiter, Reason, Nature, Universal Spirit. Some non-Jewish, non-Christian monotheists of John's own time prayed to and praised God as "O Zeus of many names."

3. The Logos theology of the Johannine authors collapses space and time. Those who responded in faith to God's universal revelation were responding to the Logos, the one revealed more fully in the revelation to Israel and definitively in Jesus Christ, the Word-become-flesh. They were responding to the one true God and became God's children before and apart from a specific confession of faith in Yahweh or Jesus. This is John's version of the theology expressed in Matthew 25:31–46, where those who had loved and served their fellow human beings are joyfully surprised to learn they had been serving the God revealed in Jesus Christ, the Son of Man.

"It Was You All Along"

C. S. Lewis once imagined that when we get to heaven, we will say to God, "So, it was you all along. Everyone I ever loved, it was you. Everything decent or fine that ever happened to me, everything that made me reach out and try to be better, it was you all along."

—Cited in Thomas G. Long,
Testimony: Talking Ourselves into Being Christian
(San Francisco: Jossey-Bass, 2004), 126

We may now ponder why it was important for the author to interrupt the poetic flow of the traditional hymn with claims about John the Baptist, protestations that at first seem intrusive. Couldn't the author have waited until the song is over, for the scene that begins in John 1:19 with John the Baptist on the stage? Why disturb the rhythm and course of the hymnic narrative with these anachronistic insertions? We may discern three reasons:

1. There was in early Christianity a strong tradition that the proclamation of the gospel of Jesus Christ begins with John the Baptist. Each of the Gospels begins with the story of John the Baptist before introducing Jesus. In the first line of the earliest gospel, Mark 1:1, the beginning (*archē*,

same as John 1:1) is John the Baptist, whose preaching and baptizing precede the introduction of Jesus into the narrative in 1:2–11. Both Matthew (3:1–12) and Luke (3:1–22) follow this pattern, with Luke prefacing an extensive birth story of John the Baptist before narrating the birth of Jesus (Luke 1–2). The preachers of Acts proclaim John the Baptist as the beginning of the gospel of Jesus (Acts 1:22; 10:37). The Johannine school is intensely concerned with beginnings (*archē* in 1 John 1:1; John 1:1). To speak of the *archē*, one must speak of John the Baptist. The Johannine teachers are being faithful to this tradition by presenting John the Baptist and his message in 1:6–8 before announcing the advent of Jesus in 1:14.

2. The Johannine community carried on its mission in a context in which followers of John the Baptist were active, and to some extent competitors. The introduction of John the Baptist in the context of the universal Light of God called for the disclaimer that John the Baptist was not the Light itself (as elaborated in the Gospel, 5:31–35).
3. John the Baptist was not only the forerunner of *Jesus* but also a witness to the *Light*, the pre- and para-Jesus universal light of God. To bear witness to Jesus is not only to proclaim the act of God in the man of Nazareth but also to witness to the divine Light that illuminates every human being and the whole world. John the Baptist thus takes his place with Abraham, who "rejoiced that he would see my day," said by the Christ who claims, "Very truly, I tell you, before Abraham was, I am" (8:52–58). John the Baptist takes his place with Isaiah, who, like Jesus's first-century disciples, "saw his glory and spoke about him" (12:38–41). In Johannine theology, such references do not mean that the prophets of Israel looked ahead through the centuries and saw what would happen later in the ministry of Jesus, but that in their own time, in the events of the pre-Christian history they experienced, they saw the glory of the preexistent Christ, the Logos of God who transcends all time and space. Thus in John 1:6–8, John the Baptist is not (only) witnessing to the earthly ministry of the first-century Jesus; he is witnessing to the Light that enlightens every human being. Accordingly, John 1:7 might be translated, "He came as a witness to testify to the light, so that all might believe through *it*" (i.e., the Light). So also, those who respond to the Light and are born of God in 1:10–13 are not limited to Christian believers of the first and following centuries, but they are all those throughout the world and its history who have responded to the Light of God, the Logos, the only true God (17:3). It is important to go carefully into these

details, in order to see that the hymn celebrates the presence of God in the world, from creation to its consummation in Christ.

How should we understand what the world was like in act 2 of the divine drama of universal history, the epochs between creation and Christ? The God definitively revealed in Jesus Christ is the creator, who was and is universally present throughout the creation. Darkness and death are also present. Darkness is not merely the absence of light but is itself an active power. The light shines in the darkness, and the darkness *pushes back*. As darkness is not merely the absence of light, so death is not merely the absence of life. Both darkness and death are this-worldly powers that resist the creative power of God. The teacher in the Johannine community who composed this hymn is aware of the transcendent power of evil, the devil, and Satan, who is "ruler of this world" and inspires its evil (8:44; 12:31; 13:2, 27; cf. 1 John 2:18, 22; 3:8, 10; 4:3; 2 John 7, and the powerful imagery of Rev 2:9–10, 13, 24; 3:9; 12:1–13:18; 20:2, 7, 10). All is from God, but when the world first appears in the song, it is not the paradise of Eden but the world of our own experience, the world as it first appears to us, who are born into a world permeated by the powers of evil, darkness, and death. The hymn writer does not speculate, picture, or try to explain how this came to be. There is no separate story of the "fall." Unlike the Genesis creation story, there is no two-stage drama in which the good world is created by God, then rebels against God. In contrast to emerging gnosticizing ideas attractive to many in the Johannine community, neither is there a multistaged, complex explanation of how an evil world came into being from the hands of a supremely good God. The world is God's creation, but it is not only passively unaware of the source of its life, it is actively aggressive against One who gives it life and light. But the creator does not abandon the rebellious creation or put it on hold until the coming of the Messiah. The Light and Life of God's creative Word continually shines into the darkness. The one true God (17:3) is encountered in the world of nature, in human history and experience. This is a revelation from God, always present in the world. "Discovering God in nature," "finding God in my own experience," is not a matter of human inference ("The world runs by natural laws, like a clock; a clock infers a Clockmaker"). God can be universally encountered in nature, human history, and experience not because human beings are clever enough to infer the existence of a "Supreme Being" from the evidence of nature and history, but because the Light of God shines forth in the world, the Word of God speaks in the creation and human history and experience.

Jesus = "Son" or "Child" or God?

Unlike other New Testament writers such as Matthew and Paul, who use "son" generically and refer to all believers as "sons" of God (e.g., Matt 5:9, 45; Rom 8:14, 19), John speaks of believers as "children of God" (*tekna theou*) but reserves "son" (*huios*) for Jesus. In the language of Johannine theology, the father has many children, male and female, but there is only one Son, as there is only one Father.

The creator speaks not only universally to all but in particular to Israel. The God of creation is the God of the covenant, the God revealed in Israel's history. The God encountered in the history and experience of all peoples is the God of Israel. They do not know this, but Israel knows, and is called to be a light to the nations (Isa 42:6; 49:6; 60:3; Tob 13:11). The Word of the one God is proclaimed by the creation and by the Torah, the revelation through Moses (Ps 19; etc.). Israel claimed that the God known in their own history is the God universally known in nature, history, and experience. Those who respond to that revelation become children of God. Who are these people?

1. The believers of the Johannine churches rightfully recognize themselves in these words. "Born of God," "child of God," characterize those who have come to faith in Jesus Christ; it is the language of the church about itself—those born into the family of God by their response to God's word (John 3:1–21, which elaborates 1:10–13 as the experience of Christian believers). The prologue, which sets the tone and parameters for interpreting the stories and dialogues in the Gospel, speaks of being born of God but not of being "born *again*." The Gospel considers *this* language for conversion and Christian experience as a misunderstanding. The issue is not "how many times" but "from where" one is born (John 3:1–13).
2. It is certainly true and right for Christian believers to see a mirror of their own experience in 1:10–13 and to think of themselves as born of God, but in the hymn, these words primarily describe those who responded to God in the ages before the coming of Christ. Christian believers are not to think of themselves as the first human beings on the planet to become children of God, for followers of Jesus join—are joined to—the people of Israel, who are themselves a special, chosen, holy segment of the larger family of God. The concluding words of the hymn refer to God's gift of the law through Moses (1:17). The passive "was given" is a

divine passive and means "God gave." The law (Torah, instruction) is here considered a gift but not the ultimate gift, which came through Christ. Just as the Jewish Scriptures often picture the covenant people of Israel as God's children, called into being by the Word of God (cf., e.g., Exod 4:22; Deut 14:1; 32:5, 20; Ps 82:6; Isa 1:2; 30:1; Jer 3:14; Hos 1:10; Wis 5:5; 16:26), when this phrase is used as a designation for Christian believers, it applies to the church an honored title for Israel, God's people. In the view of the Johannine teachers, it is false to suppose that in the Roman province of Asia there were no children of God, born from God, until Christian missionaries arrived there, preaching the gospel of Jesus Christ, baptizing those who believed, organizing churches to extend God's mission to the world in the name of Jesus Christ. The story of Jesus presented in the Gospel of John is set within the history outlined in the prologue, in which believers in Jesus are joined to the stream of saving history represented by God's people Israel. The hymn pictures one God and one creation, but a rebellious creation ruled by darkness and death. God's Word mediates God's gift of life and light to the whole world and finds a response in Israel, God's covenant people, which comes to include believers in the Messiah, Jew and gentile.

Torah = "Law"?

The Greek term in John 1:17 is *nomos*, the standard LXX translation of the Hebrew Bible's Torah. In Greek, *nomos* usually means "law," but John understands it in its Hebrew-biblical sense of teaching, direction, instruction for living, and includes this instruction within the narration of the mighty acts of God, creation to eschaton, in the covenant history of Israel.

3. But what about the vast majority of humanity, who lived and died in the world before or outside the stream of history that included Moses, Israel, Jesus, and the church? These are deep questions, raised both by church insiders and by those to whom they preached in first-century Ephesus, questions that still weigh heavily on thoughtful church people. We will explore this more carefully below; here we note only that the Johannine teachers preface their retelling the story of Jesus with a picture of the Word of God at work in the whole creation and all history. From creation onward, in the whole world, the Logos, that is, God himself, gives life and light to the whole world. Those who respond to the uni-

versal gift of life and light become children of God. The teachers of the Johannine community understood that, prior to Jesus and the church, and apart from the stream of history represented by the covenant people of Israel, there were authentic believers in the one true God—born-from-God people who became children of God, generated by God's Word. This seems to mean that people of all religions and none might still respond to God's revelation, receiving life from God according to the light they have. Is Jesus Christ then only one of many ways to the one true God? Do not the Johannine teachers themselves present Jesus as the unique Son of God who not only says, "I am the light of the *world*," but says plainly, "I am the way, and the truth, and the life. No one comes to the Father except through *me*" (John 14:6)? In the multicultural and secularized world in which we all live, this is a deeply significant issue for all Christian believers who take their faith seriously.

Many Christian believers of all theological persuasions may be attracted to a theology that gives biblical warrant for the hope that the vast majority of humanity that have lived and died outside the perimeter of the Judeo-Christian faith may have become believers and are accepted by God without a personal confession of Jesus Christ. Nonetheless, we may overhear sincere Christian believers muttering in the back row, or even in the depths of our own always-fragmentary understanding, "If people already can know God and be born from above as God's children apart from explicit faith in Christ, why should the church preach the Christian gospel to them?" Indeed, many Christians are hesitant to engage in or support evangelistic proclamation of the Christian message to adherents of other religions. The options sometimes seem to be to claim explicit Christian faith as the absolute and exclusive way to salvation or to relativize the Christian message as "the way it seems to us," "*one* of the roads that leads to the city of God," and "our religion which we should not impose on others." While such questions sometimes represent a shallow "tolerance" without clear Christian convictions, the issue is mostly raised by thoughtful, sincere believers informed by the Bible they rightfully hear as normative for their faith.

Does John 14:6 mean that "Only those who confess Jesus as Lord before they die are saved"? No. Not for John. The "I am . . ." of this and other christological Johannine texts is not restricted to the historical Jesus but points to the universal Light and Life of the Word of God.

Does the Logos theology of John 1:1–18 mean that Jesus Christ is only one of the ways to God? No. Not for John. Those who respond in faith to the

Light and Word they have, prior to and apart from the revelation of God in the 30 CE Christ event, are responding to the one true God. This God is the One who has acted in Jesus Christ for the salvation of the world.

Does John's Logos theology mean it is not necessary, even wrong, to preach the gospel of God's act in Jesus Christ to those to whom the universal Light is already available in other ways, before and apart from Christ? No. Not for John. As the One sent by God, the incarnate Word has a mission to the world; the Sent One sends his disciples, incorporating them into the divine mission (17:18; 20:21).

I do not presume to claim a completely satisfactory answer, but I do believe that John's theology, which has struggled with how to authentically proclaim the Christian faith in a multicultured world, offers a helpful biblical approach. Before pursuing it further, we must reflect more carefully on the third act of the cosmic drama, the time in which we all live.

Act 3: The Climax of the Hymn Is the Celebration of the Incarnation of the One God in Jesus Christ (1:14–18)

The climax of the story is not the manifestation of the Word/Wisdom of God in Israel, Moses, and the Torah, but the incarnation of the Word/Wisdom of God in Jesus Christ. God's special revelation in Israel and the Scripture is affirmed but is now incorporated into the universal drama of God's saving revelation. The ultimate, definitive revelatory act is not a holy people or a holy book but a person (6:69). God had spoken in nature, history, human experience, and in a distinctive way in Israel and Scripture, but God's definitive Word is now the fulfillment of all these in the incarnation of the personal God in the person Jesus of Nazareth.

> "Jesus Christ,
> as he is testified to us in the Holy Scripture,
> is the one Word of God,
> whom we are to trust and obey in life and in death."
>
> —Barmen Declaration, Germany, 1933,
> the Confessing Church versus the Nazi regime and the
> German Christians who compromised with the fascist government

The Word Has Become Flesh and Lived among Us

The climax of the long history of the encounter is this startling declaration: the creative, universal Word that shares God's own being became incarnate in the space-time, material world of flesh as a human being. At 1:14, for the first time the scene shifts from "then" and "them" to "now" and "us," the readers' present, and the confessional language of "we" and "us" enters the picture, as those who respond to the incarnate Word. Not until 1:17 is this Word given a human name: Jesus Christ, who stands in the narrow stream of covenantal history in which God gave the law through Moses.

The Climactic Act of the Divine Drama Proclaims That the Transcendent Is Preexistent

The Word communicates that God's universal grace and truth has come among us as a human being, as the definitive climax of that stream of history in which God's law had been given to the covenant people through Moses, that he is the Messiah named Jesus. The "doctrine" of preexistence is thus not just a dispensable, somewhat bizarre curiosity of Johannine theology, but a presupposition for the faith that the universal Light is the one definitively revealed in Jesus Christ, that Jesus Christ, the light of the world, is the revelation of the same Light that has shone into the world's darkness since creation. We now briefly explore some key features of John's incarnational theology of 1:14–18.

The Word Is Absolute

John is insistent that the gospel's story of Jesus he is about to tell is the story of God. "The Word was God" (1:1). The word "God" frames the prologue (1:1, 18), as it frames the Gospel as a whole. The one declared to be "God" in 1:1, 18 is then confessed to be "Lord and God" by his disciples in the closing scene of the story (20:28). The council at Nicaea affirmed that Jesus Christ is not the incarnation of a lesser divine being downscale from God, the revelation of a relative being that might later be superseded, and insisted that Christ shares the very being of God. The Johannine school is not yet at Nicaea but already points in that direction. "The Word became flesh" confesses and celebrates the truth and absolute claim about Christ.

The Logos: "Word" Doesn't Mean "Word"

Not in the sense of an individual vocabulary item. The standard Greek lexicon gives as its initial, summarizing definition for *logos*: "communication whereby the mind finds expression." This is followed by three large, double-column pages of fine print, elaborating the way *logos* was used in the ancient world, with dozens of references to ancient literature, biblical and nonbiblical. This term never means simply "word" in the sense of a single term listed as the head word of a dictionary entry, which is typically expressed by *rhēma.*

The major categories:

1. a. oral utterance, including word, a speech, a statement, a declaration. *Logos* can be translated "word" in the sense of "I would like to have a word with you" or "The word from headquarters is . . ."
   b. literary or oratorical productions, such as the separate books of a set, treatise; in Acts 1:1, *logos* refers to a single volume of a two-volume work.
2. computation, reckoning, including the reason or cause for something, a case made for something. The opposite, *alogos,* is used for that which is contrary to reason, and of animals who lack reasoning capacity. *Logos* is the linguistic root behind the English "logic" and all our "-ology" words, such as "psychology," "sociology," etc. *Logizomai* and its combinations mean to think, reason, discourse, dialogue.
3. the independent personified expression of God, the Logos. The Logos was already used this way by theists such as Hellenistic Jew Philo, and by non-theistic Stoics for the Reason inherent in the world and the human mind.

—Frederick W. Danker, Walter Bauer,
William F. Arndt, and F. Wilbur Gingrich,
A Greek-English Lexicon of the New Testament and Other Early Christian Literature, 3rd ed.
(Chicago: University of Chicago Press, 2000), 599–601

This Logos theology sheds light on the question raised above, why Christians should preach Christ if people of other religions can come to know God, be accepted, and become God's children apart from explicit personal confession of faith in Jesus Christ. The Johannine teachers did not consider the revelation in Jesus Christ as relative and incremental, merely supplementing previous revelation. Apart from Christ, religious people do not know the true character and demand of God and God's mission in the world, which means they do not know themselves. There is a kind of "progressive revelation" in Johannine theology: the Light and Life of God is universally revealed throughout the world, but God's character and God's purpose for the world and history are more fully revealed in the particular revelation in the history of Israel. Even within Israel's history, there is a progressive revelation. As only one example, the theology of Deuteronomy has a clearer grasp of God's character and will than do Exodus and the earlier traditions on which Deuteronomy is based (e.g., compare instructions on the treatment of slaves in Deut 5:6, 14–15, 21; 6:12, 21; 7:8; 8:14; 12:12, 18; 13:5, 10; 15:13–17; 16:11–14; 21:14; 23:15; 24:18, 22; 28:68 with their earlier counterparts). However, God's revelation in the Christ event is not a further step in this relative progression but a quantum leap. The revelation in Jesus does not fit into a series of insights in which his life teaching is the "best so far." As the Messiah, he not only comes at the end of a historical series of revelatory events but transcends the whole series. John makes this specific. While the Spirit of God is active in the world in various degrees prior to and apart from Christ (Elisha receives a "double portion" of the Spirit that empowered his teacher Elijah, 2 Kings 2:9, 15; Sir 48:12), Jesus has and gives the Spirit "without measure" (John 3:34; cf. 1:16). The world of nature, the prophets of Israel, and even John the Baptist bear witness to the Light of God. In this sense, the Matthean Jesus could say to his disciples, "You are the light of the world," that is, they bear witness to the truth of God revealed in nature, history, Scripture, and Jesus Christ. The Johannine Jesus says, "I am the light of the world" (John 8:12). He not only says, like John the Baptist and Jesus's own disciples who will receive the Holy Spirit, "I bear witness to the truth" (5:33; 15:26; 18:37), but "I am the truth" (14:6). The Word-made-flesh, the revelation in Jesus Christ, is the definitive revelation of the absolute God. While, in historical terms, there can be a "before Christ," there can be no "after Christ." Here, we are confronted with the Absolute, the one true God (17:3).

But *we* are not absolute; we belong to the space-time material world of relativity, the world of flesh.

Incarnation and the Love of God

"The incarnation is the ultimate act of love of the Creator who brought the world into being as his counterpart, especially his dearest creature, the human being created in his own image, without whom God does not want to be God."

—Reinhard Feldmeier and Hermann Spieckermann, *Menschwerdung*, Topoi Biblischer Theologie (Tübingen: Mohr Siebeck, 2018), 329 (translation mine)

The Flesh Is Relative

The confession not only declares something about the Word but also makes an astounding claim about "the flesh." The incarnation portrays not only the descent of *God* into the world but also the descent of God into the *world*, the nitty-gritty, space-time world of our own little lives. *This* world is the creation of God, this relative world in which we live, filled with ambiguity and lack of certainty; this world where our knowledge is always fragmentary and relative is affirmed by God as the arena of God's revelation. The absolute God did not remain aloof, waiting for us to attain acceptability, but sought us out (4:23) in this world. The original Word of God repeated at creation as the heartthrob that pulses through the universe and our little planet still rings true: God saw this world, this life, and declared it to be good. In the creator's evaluation of his own work, the grades range from "good" to "very good" (Gen 1:4, 10, 12, 18, 21, 25, 31). Our brief lives within God's creation are not lived out in a waiting room or proving ground before we go someplace else. God disdains neither the world nor our lives in it, but came among us as one of us, sharing our life. Strangely enough, this is in contrast to the Fourth Gospel's picture of John the Baptist, who is a witness to the Light and to Jesus as the Messiah, but he is never pictured as participating in the life of the world, its culture and politics, its parties and its problems. John the Baptist stands apart, but Jesus goes to wedding parties, visits friends, savors the ordinary joys of human life, weeps at Lazarus's tomb. Johannine theology is not "otherworldly," neither in its more apocalyptic form in Revelation and the letters nor in its final form represented by the Gospel. John affirms this world, this human life we live, as the locus of God's grace and salvation. In the light of this faith, "After all, I'm only human" cannot be apology or excuse for our faults but is a celebration of the lives we have been given as the gift of God the creator and Savior. The world in its present shape still bears the odor of death, but it is precisely in this stinking world that the power of the resurrection is let loose (John 11:39).

"Only Begotten" or "Unique"?

For John, confession of faith in Jesus as the Son of God belongs to the core of Christian faith (1:18, 34, 49; 3:16–18, 35; 5:19–26; 6:40, 42; 11:4, 27; 14:13; 17:1; 19:7; 20:31). John does not, however, confess the church's faith in Jesus as the Son of God by telling stories of the virginal conception. Disciples who confess him to be Son of God regard Joseph as his father (1:45), and it is only those with false or inadequate faith who regard "this Jesus, the son of Joseph, whose father and mother we know" as incompatible with the confession that he is the Son of God who "came down from heaven" (6:41–42). The paradox of divine revelation is that the Jesus who is "from Nazareth" is also "from heaven," that the "son of Joseph" is the unique Son of God (cf. 1:45–46).

The Johannine community does indeed know the concept of divine parentage, of being begotten/born from above, but this image is applied to human believers in general, who are called "children of God" (1 John 2:29; 3:1–2, 9–10; 4:7; 5:1–2, 4, 18; John 1:12–13; 3:3–8). When Jesus is called *monogenēs* (1 John 4:9; John 1:14, 18; 3:16, 18), the Greek word means "one of a kind," as can be seen even from the English cognates of its elements (*mono* = only; *gen-* = kind, as in "*gen*eric"). The word does not mean he is a "begotten Son" by means of a virginal conception, but that he is uniquely the Son of God, a singularity, a category of one. Revelation 21:7 indicates that some members of the Johannine community used "son of God" language of Christian believers. The Fourth Gospel is distinctive in New Testament theology for using "son of God" terminology only in the singular and of Jesus, and "children of God" in the plural for believers (contrast, e.g., Matt 5:9, where Jesus declares that peacemakers will be called "sons of God" [as translated in the RSV, ESV, NKJV; obscured by other modern translations in the interest of gender-inclusive language]; so also Luke 20:36; Rom 8:14, 19; 9:26; Gal 3:26; 4:6–7; Heb 12:7).

"We Have Seen His Glory"

In John 1:14, for the first time in the prologue, the verbs shift to the first person, the hearer-readers' own present. This "we" is the "ecclesial we," the first-person confessional "we" of the believing community. This "we" is not restricted to eyewitnesses of the first generation; John 1:14 is not a claim to apostolic authorship (see pp. 146–47 above). This text is a claim that the "we" of the believing community is not founded on a great idea or ideal but on a tangible event, that "we" belong to a community in which some members have actually seen, heard, and touched the Word-become-flesh. John will conclude his Easter narrative with the story of the disciple Thomas, who insists on seeing and touching (20:19–31). We later believers who belong to this same community should not berate "doubting Thomas." In line with the interpretation of the hymn already reflected in 1 John 1:1–3, the Fourth Gospel presents Thomas as rightly insisting on the reality of the risen body of Christ; in the story, this reality is portrayed as a visible and touchable body.

The Thomas story is a Johannine sign. The story of 20:24–29 is seamlessly followed by verse 30, "Now Jesus did many other signs . . . ," of 20:30–31. Like the other Johannine sign stories, this sign points to the Christ event as such, a sign story in which the risen Christ manifests himself to believers who can then witness to the this-worldly reality of the incarnation. It really happened, in this world of space and time, and we later believers belong to a community that offers this testimony.

In John's first-century Roman world, "glory" (*doxa*) typically referred to the high status of a person or a person's vanity and conceit. John uses it primarily in its biblical and Jewish sense to refer to the presence of God. The phrase "the glory of the LORD" appears thirty-six times in the Old Testament, pointing, for example, to God's appearance on Sinai or in the tabernacle (e.g., Exod 24:16–18; 40:34–35). John's Greek word for "dwelt [among us]" is *eskēnōsen*, which shares the same consonants as the Hebrew word for "tabernacle." For John, "We have seen his glory" does not mean that those who looked at the historical Jesus could see objectively visible demonstrations of God's splendor—he didn't glow in the dark—but that the believers' post-Easter eyes of faith saw the definitive manifestation of the presence of God in the Christ event. The reality of God's presence with Israel, symbolized by God's tent pitched among the Israelite tents, has now become real to Christian believers who have seen the presence of God incarnate in Jesus of Nazareth, who "tabernacled" (= tented) among us, taking his place among us human beings as one of us.

Jesus's "glory" shares and reflects the glory of the one true God (John 11:4, 40; 13:31). This glory is not the praise and exalted status attributed to him by human beings (5:41–44) but the glory of the preexistent Christ (17:5, 24), the transcendent glory perceived by Israel's prophets (12:41), the hidden glory already present during Jesus's ministry but recognized by his disciples only after the resurrection (2:11; 7:39; 12:16, 23), the glory to which he returns by being "lifted up" in the crucifixion, resurrection, and ascension, thought of as one event (12:23, 32; 17:1). Johannine theology does not contrast a "theology of glory" with a "theology of the cross," as though these were alternative perspectives for interpreting the Jesus Christ story, but fuses them into one event. Humiliation, exaltation, and glorification are all combined in Isaiah's image of the Servant of Yahweh. It is widely accepted that the idea of being glorified by being lifted up on the cross is influenced by Isaiah 52:13: "See, my Servant shall have true insight and succeed, and he shall be lifted up [*hypsōthēsetai*, as in John 3:14; 8:28; 12:32, 34] and glorified exceedingly" (LXX, my English translation).

Moses and Jesus, Law and Grace

Just as "glory" signifies continuity with the theology of John's Bible, identifying Jesus as the presence of God in the world, so the reference to Moses joins the definitive revelation of God in Jesus Christ to the story of God's revelation in Israel and Israel's Scripture. In Johannine theology, Moses and the law are not contrasted with Christ and grace, as though the Jewish Scriptures only proclaimed the harsh and punitive law as the false way of salvation, to be replaced by the grace of God finally revealed in Jesus Christ. John is not thinking of a presumed clash between the "works righteousness" of the Old Testament and "salvation by grace" in the New Testament. Paul is subject to this (mis)understanding, but John specifically avoids making this contrast. There is no "but" in the Greek text, as in the KJV and some other English translations. John simply has two affirmative statements, without any conjunction, as in the NRSV and most modern translations: "The law indeed was given through Moses; grace and truth came through Jesus Christ." Continuity, not contrast, is John's emphasis. John 1:16 concludes the prologue's panorama of God's three-act revelatory history with the declaration that the coming of Christ was "fullness . . . grace upon grace" (not "grace replacing law"). Moses, the mediator of God's grace and truth in the time of Israel, is followed by the full revelation of God in Christ, who brings (the fullness of) grace upon grace (already revealed in Moses and the Torah).

There is, however, a contrast between Jesus and Moses, a contrast important in John's situation that affects the way he tells the story of Jesus Christ in his Gospel. Some of the Johannine Christians have left or been expelled from the synagogue. Synagogue leaders claimed to be followers of Moses, who had ascended (Mount Sinai) and "seen God," and they "set their hope" on him (5:45). They branded the new Christian group as followers of the newcomer upstart Jesus. They revered the ancient and authenticated revelation given through Moses, "but as for this man, we do not know where he comes from" (9:28–29). John declines to accept this categorization, never says anything like "You can have Moses and we'll take Jesus." Rather, he claims that faithfulness to Moses and the Jewish Scriptures is inherent in Christian faith. Moses in the law wrote about the Messiah Jesus, as did the prophets (1:45). God's saving acts through Moses in the wilderness prefigure God's saving act in Christ in "lifting up" the Son of Man (3:14). To believe in Moses's writings is to believe in Christ, and conversely, to believe in Christ is to believe the Word of God that comes through Moses and the prophets (5:46). But, contrary to the Jewish claim and their interpretation of the Scripture, *Moses never saw God.* All such human claims to see God filter the revelation through human perceptions of the space-time material world of flesh. No one has "seen God" in the real sense except the one who was with God before the world was made, the one who is himself God. "It is God the only Son, who is close to the Father's heart, who has made him known" (1:18). The prologue is followed by the carefully composed and edited collection of sign stories that make up the Gospel, in which John will spell out what he means by "God the only Son," "made him known," and "we have seen his glory."

Testimony: Christology and Discipleship (1:19–50)

The Incarnation as the Judgment and Salvation of the World

The Fourth Evangelist narrates the presence of the incarnate Christ in this world as a judgment scene. The narrative curtain opens on a trial in progress. The language of judgment pervades the whole narrative and evokes a variety of images for John's readers.

- In the last judgment, the destiny of every human being will be decided as he or she stands before God. The evangelist portrays this as already happening as Jesus confronts the world during his ministry (3:18–19; 5:25–27; 8:16; 9:39; 12:31, 48; 16:8–11).
- In the extensive passion story of each of the Synoptic Gospels, Jesus himself is put on trial, condemned, and executed by the world's religious and political authorities. The evangelist narrates the whole Gospel as a trial in which, despite all this-worldly appearances, Jesus himself is the Son of Man who has authority to judge, and it is the world that stands before God's judgment.
- The Jesus of the Synoptic Gospels warns his disciples that after his death and resurrection they will stand before human courts (Mark 13:9; Matt 10:17–18; Luke 21:12–18). John's readers look back on a history in which Jesus had been tried, convicted, and executed and members of the Johannine community had been called before Jewish and Roman courts. They had given their testimony (or failed to do so), and some had been condemned. The prophet-author of Revelation addresses a church in which members have been tried, convicted, and executed (Rev 2:13). In

the Fourth Gospel, the trial does not occur only at the end of the narrative, and it is not Jesus who is on trial, but the world. Thus the language of witness and testimony plays a major role.

- The evangelist casts his whole narrative as a judgment scene in which a series of witnesses is called: Jesus himself, his works, the Father, John the Baptist, Moses, the Scripture (cf. John 5:31–47). As the curtain opens on the first scene of the Gospel of the Logos-become-flesh, the action is already under way. It is a courtroom scene, a trial is in progress, and a witness is on the stand. The first witness is John the Baptist, whose testimony the evangelist has already injected into the prologue. John the Baptist represents continuity. Not only is he one of the witnesses to the universal Light but he also stands in the line of Israel and the biblical prophets, identifying himself as the voice predicted by Isaiah. He has disciples who have already accepted his testimony, some of whom had become Jesus's disciples. This reflects not only the evangelist's view of the role of John the Baptist in salvation history but also the historical reality of their own situation, in which a group of John the Baptist's followers continued alongside those who believed Jesus was the Messiah. Thus John the Baptist's first words are insistent (he confesses, does not deny, but confesses), "I am not the Christ" (1:20). He also makes it clear that he is not to be identified as an eschatological figure of any sort: he is neither Elijah nor the eschatological prophet expected to appear just before the coming of the end. He is a witness, a *voice*.

The Array of Christological Titles

The transitional figure John the Baptist, some of his disciples that migrate to the group of Jesus's disciples, and the new disciples called by Jesus himself all immediately confess their faith in a variety of christological titles and images. The Fourth Gospel has no "messianic secret" in the Markan sense. From the first page on, John the Baptist, Jesus, and their disciples know the identity of Jesus and declare it openly. Authentic confession, however, is not simply ascription of the correct title to Jesus. New Testament Christology is built into the narrative; readers learn the true identity of Jesus in the course of the story, not merely from a list of titles. Yet in the story world of the Fourth Gospel, the evangelist finds it important to ring the chimes on the array of distinctive terms that sum up and convey Jesus's role and significance in the saving plan of God.

The Lamb of God, Who Takes Away the Sin of the World (1:29, 36)

The initial identification of Jesus is that he is "the lamb of God, who takes away the sin of the world." The evangelist considers this confession crucial and fundamental. It is the first confession of Jesus made by any human being after Jesus's appearance on the human scene (1:29). John the Baptist then proceeds to identify Jesus as the preexistent Son of God (1:30, 34), the one who is to be manifest to Israel by receiving the fullness of the Spirit with which he will baptize others (1:33), and then repeats and sums up his testimony by again pointing to Jesus as the Lamb of God (1:36). It is this preaching that leads John the Baptist's own disciples to join the community of Jesus's disciples. This terse confession includes four decisive points: world, sin, takes away, lamb.

World

From beginning to end, the Fourth Gospel is concerned with God's love and saving act for the world itself, the whole world, not, as in the proto-Gnosticism the evangelist opposes, the saving of individual souls out of the world.

Sin

This is the first reference to "sin." In the prologue's macrohistory of the cosmos, the world's problem was how the Light and Life of God could be communicated to a world of darkness and death. "Sin" was not mentioned. The world did not understand its dilemma to be how a guilty sinner could be acceptable before a righteous God. It was the coming of the Light into the world that revealed that the human problem was not only ignorance in need of instruction but also sin (singular), human self-willed rebellion, an enslaving power from which people needed not only forgiveness but also deliverance (1:29; 5:14; 8:21, 24, 34; 9:41; 15:22–24; 16:8–9).

Take Away

The verb *airō* is found twenty-six times in John, always translated as "take away," "remove," or the like. In the whole New Testament, it is never used for the forgiveness of sins, for which the primary word is *aphiēmi* and its cognates. The Johannine community is in fact concerned with the forgiveness of individual sins (1 John 1:9; 2:12; 5:16; John 20:23) and wants believers to know that they are delivered from the guilt of sins they have committed. But John 1:29 should not be understood in the modern individualistic sense of "Jesus the Lamb of God died so that those who believe in him might have their sins forgiven and go to heaven." The good news is that the creator is acting to *take away* the sin of the *world*. It is a matter not only of forgiving the world's trespasses but also of removing its injustice, its rebellion against the creator. God makes an end of sin's domination of the world and restores the world's status as God's good creation. John the seer of Revelation had pictured this in the imagery of the final battle. This is the Fourth Gospel's way of expressing the salvation of the world expressed by the more apocalyptic teachers in the Johannine community, with the same image and the same dialectic (see Rev 20–22).

Lamb

It is of utmost importance to recognize that the evangelist has prefaced the whole range of christological titles with the image of the Lamb of God. The Lamb is killed as a sacrifice but not as a sin offering. The Lamb is the Passover lamb, whose blood frees Israel from Egyptian domination. The image of Messiah as Passover lamb was current in the Christianity of the province of Asia when the Fourth Gospel was written. Already in the 50s, Paul had used this image without explanation, as though it were well known (1 Cor 5:7). The prophet John of Revelation made "lamb" a major christological category. Though the Fourth Evangelist uses a different word for "lamb" (*arnion* in Revelation; *amnos* in the Gospel), here, too, the evangelist shares the christological perspective of the author of Revelation (see the discussion of Rev 4–5). Like Revelation and traditional apocalypticism, the Fourth Evangelist can speak of the Messiah as "conquering" the world (Rev 5:5 and passim; John 16:33; cf. 1 John 2:13–14; 4:4; 5:4–5), but the means of his conquest are through the power of the sacrificial lamb who gives his life for others. In his part 1 (John 2–12), the evangelist will portray Jesus as the powerful one who defeats the world, but from beginning to end it must not be forgotten that John sees this conquest as effected through the power of God's love for the whole world, which will finally triumph. Just as John begins *Part 1: Triumphal Entry* with the revelation of God's power as Jesus the Lamb of God, so he will begin *Part 2: Triumphal Exit* with the picture of Jesus who divests himself of violent power and washes the disciples' feet.

Like the fundamental U-shaped descent-ascent pattern that provides the framework for all John's Christology, the image of Christ the Lamb becomes the root metaphor and orientation point for all John's other christological language and imagery. There is inadequate space to discuss each at length here. A number of christological terms and images have already appeared in the prologue: Logos, Light, Life, preexistent agent of creation, *monogenēs* (the Unique One), the one whose fullness (*plērōma*) consists of grace and truth, God-the-only-Son. Numerous other christological titles and images appear in the stories of Jesus's ministry, the Farewell Discourse, and passion (see Christology section of "For Further Reading"). We will only list and comment briefly on the array of christological titles that emerges in the opening scene of Jesus's earthly ministry. Though deceptively familiar, "Son of Man" is important and unfamiliar enough to require a separate section.

The One of Whom Moses and the Prophets Wrote (1:45)

Do the Jewish Scriptures play an important role in the life of the followers of Jesus? This was a disputed point in the churches of Roman Asia from 90 to 130 CE. Pauline and other Christian groups in Asia assumed that the church was incorporated into the ongoing history of Israel and had without question adopted the Jewish Scriptures as normative for Christian theology and practice. Revelation continues this assumption, constantly using biblical imagery and alluding to the Scripture *hundreds* of times. The Johannine letters, on the other hand, never make any explicit reference to the Bible. This hesitation would be in step with the emerging proto-gnostic theology popular among some Christians in the Johannine context who were suspicious of the God of Israel and the Jewish Scriptures. The Johannine teachers represented by the Gospel of John come down clearly on one side of this question: to believe in Jesus as the Christ means to understand him and the Christian community as in continuity with the Jewish Scriptures and the fulfillment of their hopes. The Fourth Gospel is not only replete with biblical imagery, but it often explicitly cites the Scripture—more often than any other of the Four Gospels, in fact—as a way of affirming the identity of Jesus and the meaning of Christian faith (cf., e.g., 1:17, 23, 45; 2:22; 3:14; 5:39, 46; 6:45; 7:19; 10:35; 12:38; 13:18; 15:25; 17:12; 19:24, 28, 36, 37; 20:9). This means, among other things, that John refuses to accept the alternative "Moses or Jesus" (9:24–28; see above on 1:17).

The One on Whom the Spirit Comes (1:32–33)

All believers, all members of the Johannine community, are born of the Spirit and experience the abiding presence of God's Spirit within the life of the church (3:5–8; 4:23; 7:39; 14:17, 26; 15:26; 16:23; 19:30; 20:22; 1 John 4:13). Jesus is the bearer of the Spirit in a unique way. He is designated and identified as Messiah by receiving the Spirit (John 1:32–34). He receives the Spirit without measure, in "fullness" (*plērōma*, 1:16), differing from Christian believers' experience of the Spirit not in degree but absolutely (3:34). With the Father, he sends the Spirit from heaven (14:26; 15:26). He is not only baptized, he himself baptizes in the Spirit (1:33).

Rabbi, Teacher (1:38)

"Rabbi" and "Teacher" are not secondary titles in Johannine Christianity, where it would be unthinkable to refer to Jesus as "just" a teacher. As manifest in Revelation and 1–3 John, the issues of who teaches, by what authority, and what is taught were important (and thus disputed) questions in the Johannine churches. "Teach," "teacher," and "rabbi" are found thirty-one times in the Johannine writings, almost all in reference to Jesus. As at Qumran, where the *Moreh Zedek* (conventionally "Teacher of Righteousness," better "the Right Teacher") was the founder, leader, and most significant figure, the issues of whom the community recognized as its Teacher and how this teaching was authorized and communicated were of supreme importance. The Johannine community was led by the group of teachers now often called the Johannine school, but the Johannine teachers themselves regarded the incarnate, crucified, and risen Lord as the one true Teacher of the church. Jesus himself claimed this role, on a par with "Lord": "You call me Teacher and Lord—and you are right, for that is what I am" (John 13:13). God himself is Jesus's teacher (8:26, 28). His teaching is from God (7:16–17). The disputed issue in the Johannine churches is not the teaching authority of Jesus but how the teaching of the risen Lord is mediated to believers. How are the church's pastor-teachers and preachers related to the church's one Teacher? This continues to be a crucial issue throughout John's Gospel, reflecting the ongoing tension in the Johannine community (see pp. 311–15 below).

The Messiah (1:41)

Along with "Son of God," the evangelist considers the confession of Jesus as the Christ to be the core confession of the community and intends his whole Gospel to lead to and nourish faith in this confession (20:30–31). *Messiah* (Hebrew)—*Christos* in Greek and "Anointed" in English—is a uniquely Hebrew-Jewish title for the promised savior figure of the end time. As he did with "Rabbi," John feels it necessary to remind his mostly gentile readers of the meaning of the word itself. Three types of mediators of divine power were anointed (their heads smeared with olive oil) as the legitimating sign that authorized them for their office: *prophets*, who spoke the word of God; *priests*, who interceded for the people, performed purifying rituals that removed sin, and maintained communication between God and the people; and *kings*, who ruled Israel on God's behalf. God is the actor in the ministry of prophets, priests, and kings. All are God's gifts to God's people. The passive (anoint*ed*) indicates that prophets, priests, and kings are not extraordinary functionaries in their own right but are authorized and empowered by God. To confess that Jesus is the Christ is not a claim about the specialness of the human being Jesus but is an affirmation that in him *God* speaks (prophet), reconciles (priest), and rules (king). In first-century Judaism, "Messiah" had become focused mainly on kingship—the Messiah was the promised king of the end time who would be the agent of God's rule of peace and justice.

King of Israel (1:49)

"Who is in charge of the world?" This was the issue in Jesus's own preaching and that of the early church, as it is throughout the New Testament. In Jewish expectation, "king" was virtually synonymous with "Messiah." The anointed king of Israel ruled in God's stead; the coming Messiah would establish God's kingdom. Such language was, of course, politically loaded and dangerous. The placard at the cross, the charge that led to Jesus's death, was "Jesus of Nazareth, king of the Jews," understood as a political rebel against Roman kingship ("king" and "emperor" are the same word in Greek, as are "kingdom" and "empire"). Throughout the Gospel, "Jew" is mostly a negative term that functions within the categories of this world but "Israel" designates the people of God. For John, Jesus is misunderstood as "king of the Jews" but is truly "king of Israel." John baptizes in order to reveal the Messiah to Israel (1:31). Jesus challenges Nicodemus's faulty understanding, because as the teacher of Israel, he should know that God's children are born from above (3:10; see pp. 188–200, 230, 264 above on 1:12–13). The crowds who herald the triumphal advent of the Messiah proclaim their blessing on "the one who comes in the name of the Lord—the King of Israel" (12:13). Thus Jesus can pronounce Nathanael to be "truly an Israelite" who confesses Jesus to be "Son of God" and "King of Israel" (1:47–49).

Son of God (1:34, 49)

Coupled with confession of Jesus as the "Christ," the Fourth Gospel presents "Son of God" as the summary and goal of Christian confession (20:30–31).

While Messiah/Christ was uniquely Jewish and required explanation to non-Jews, "Son of (a) God" was a common religious and political term in the Hellenistic world. The Caesar was often honored as Son of God, and a variety of semidivine beings could be designated by this term. John is primarily influenced by his biblical and Jewish tradition, but even here, "son of God" has a variety of meanings. In the Hebrew language, "son" has a distinctive use, which profoundly affected the terminology and imagery of the Hebrew Bible. Hebrew *ben* (Aramaic *bar*) not only means "male child" but is also used in a variety of ways that have no equivalent in English. Important for our purpose here is that *ben* is used often to indicate that something or someone belongs to a larger group or category. Although English speakers can occasionally use such metaphorical expressions as "son of a gun" (or stronger) or refer to a political candidate as a "native son" of their home state, Hebrew and Aramaic regularly use *ben/bar* as a way of indicating the identity of someone or something as inherently belonging to a larger reality. Thus a literal translation of the Hebrew text of Job 5:7 refers to sparks as "sons of the flame"; in Job 41:2 arrows are "sons of the bow"; in Leviticus 9:2 a calf is a "son of the herd." In 1 Kings 20:35 and elsewhere, "sons of the prophets" has nothing to do with biology but means belonging to the prophetic group. When Amos declares, "I am no prophet, nor a prophet's son," he means he does not belong to the prophetic guild (cf. NAB and other modern translations). Very important is the description of the Israelites as "sons of Israel" (637 times in Old Testament, often translated "children of Israel" [KJV and older translations]). "Sons" is generic, including male and female. It does not mean either "Israel's sons" or "Israel's children" in the biological sense, but "Israelite," "belonging to the category 'Israel.'"

The combination of "son" in its Hebrew sense and "God" generated a wide range of meaning for the expression "son(s) of God." In all the following examples, the Hebrew text reads *ben Elohim* (singular) or *bene Elohim* (plural), rendered in a variety of ways in English translations, sometimes in the interest of gender-inclusive language. A *ben Elohim* ("son of God") could be:

1. A divine being belonging to the heavenly world, such as an angel (Gen 6:2; Job 1:6 NRSV, "heavenly beings," footnote "sons of God").
2. Empirical Israel (Exod 4:22; Deut 14:1; Jer 31:9; Hos 11:1).
3. "True" Israelites, "eschatological" Israelites (Hos 1:10; 2:1). In Matt 5:9; Rom 8:14; 9:26, as in John 1:47, such believers are called "sons of God."
4. The Israelite king (2 Sam 7:14; Pss 2:7; 89:26–27).
5. An exceptionally righteous man or wise person (Wis 2:1–20) (first century BCE).

6. Human beings taken to heaven, after resurrection (Luke 20:36, i.e., same as "angels").
7. Adam, collective humanity, was "son of God" by creation. There is an authentic biblical sense in which every human being is a son/child of God the creator (Deut 32:6; Mal 2:10; Luke 3:38).

Such a list illuminates one of the semantic fields in which the church's language about Jesus functioned, but it also shows that there is little value in asking, "Is Jesus the Son of God?" as a yes/no question. The question is better posed by asking "What does it mean that John calls 'Jesus, son of Joseph, whose father and mother we know' (1:45; 6:42), the 'Son of God'?" For John, Jesus is the unique (*monogenēs*) Son of God, the preexistent Son who is one with the Father.

Israel's Vision: The Incarnate Christ as Jacob's Ladder

The climax and conclusion of this parade of christological images and claims is Jesus's own self-identifying kerygmatic statement, speaking of himself as the Son of Man. This is clearly an allusion to "Jacob's ladder" of Genesis 28:1–17. The biblical Jacob/Israel was a deceitful and clever manipulator who had seen a dream-vision in which a ladder was extended from earth to heaven, on which angels of God ascended and descended. In a strange and painful face-to-face encounter with God, wily Jacob became Israel, progenitor of the people of God through whom God's promised blessing would come to all nations (32:22–30; cf. 28:13–14). In the concluding scene of this section in which Jesus is gathering those who will become his witnesses, he addresses the new convert Nathanael as "truly an Israelite in whom there is no deceit" (John 1:47). This is not merely a one-time-only pronouncement addressed to Nathanael (the verbs of 1:51 are plural). All those who recognize Jesus as the one of whom Moses and the prophets wrote, the Son of God and king of Israel, are truly Israelites, the eschatological people of God. They will see the fulfillment of Israel's dream-vision of the eschatological purpose of God. The old biblical-Jewish Jacob/Israel *saw* the ladder in an apocalyptic dream-vision. Jesus *is* the ladder. This is analogous to Jesus's later statement, "I am the true vine" (15:1, also a symbol of Israel the people of God). True to form, the Johannine Jesus could have placed "I am the true ladder" among the series of christological "I am" sayings. He does not, but he anticipates the later statements that function this way.

Jesus is not one of the heavenly beings who go up and down the staircase connecting heaven and earth. He is himself the link, the bridge that encompasses all communication from earth to heaven. In the Genesis story, the ladder seems to be set on the earth and reaches to the heavenly world. (The Hebrew text of Genesis 28:13 can be understood as saying that the Lord stands "beside him" [Jacob] or "on it" [the ladder].) John does not elaborate his own metaphor, but in Johannine theology the ladder is let down from heaven, the initiative is with God, and the descent precedes the ascent (John 3:13). As the elect people of God, Israel was chosen and commissioned to be the priestly community mediating between God and the world (Exod 19:6). Here, Jesus identifies himself with Israel as the priestly mediator between heaven and earth (cf. also the "high priestly prayer" of John 17). "Nathanael" means "gift of God." In John's theology, Jesus is himself the true Israel(ite), the gift of God; those who believe in (God's act in) Jesus are united with him (John 14:20; 17:23), so that they too are "true Israelites" who share the priestly role and mission of Israel and Jesus. The Jesus of John's narrative thus affirms the same Johannine theology as in the prologue. The new disciples do not yet see it, but they *will* see Jesus's true identity expressed in all the christological titles and imagery.

In Israel's dream-vision, the Son of Man was promised to come soon, to come at the end of history and bring the kingdom of God to this world (e.g., Dan 2; 7). In the earliest gospel, it is not until the end of the narrative that Jesus identifies himself as the Christ, the Son of Man who will come at the end of history (Mark 14:62) in an event the first generation of Christians will see (Mark 13:30–31; 14:62). In Johannine theology, the Son of Man has come, the promised kingdom is already present, and after the resurrection the disciples will see that the vision and hope of Israel are already happening. John compresses this theology into the title "Son of Man." "Who is this Son of Man?" is a Johannine question posed not only by the characters in the story but also to the readers (John 12:34).

Son of Man as Key Johannine Christological Title

To understand the biblical phrase "Son of Man," we must keep in mind the ways "son" (*ben*) is used in Hebrew (see the previous section on "Son of God"). In the Old Testament, *ben adam*, "son of man," means "belonging to the category 'human,' a member of the human race," with the plural *bene adam* meaning "people," "human beings." "A man" (*adam, ish, enosh*) and "son of man" (*ben adam*) seem to mean exactly the same thing and can be used as parallel expressions in the same sentence (e.g., Num 23:19; Job 25:6; Ps 8:4; Isa 51:12). Here are a few of the numerous examples (from RSV; NRSV's gender-inclusive language blurs both the parallelism and the connections with the New Testament christological title):

Psalm 8:4:	What is man that thou art mindful of him, and the son of man that thou dost care for him?
Isaiah 51:12:	"I, I am he that comforts you; who are you that you are afraid of man who dies, of the son of man who is made like grass?"
Jeremiah 50:40:	"As when God overthrew Sodom and Gomorrah and their neighbor cities, says the LORD, so no man shall dwell there, and no son of man shall sojourn in her."
Ezekiel 2:1:	"And he said to me, 'Son of man, stand upon your feet, and I will speak with you.'" The phrase occurs ninety-three times in Ezekiel, in direct address to the prophet; twenty-three times the pronoun "you" is added, with the connotation "you human being, you," in contrast to the God who speaks.

The most important Old Testament text for understanding "Son of Man" as used by Jesus, the early church, and the Gospels is Daniel 7:13–14:

> I saw in the night visions,
> and behold, with the clouds of heaven there came one like a son of man,
> and he came to the Ancient of Days and was presented before him.
> And to him was given dominion and glory and kingdom,
> that all peoples, nations, and languages should serve him;
> his dominion is an everlasting dominion,
> which shall not pass away,
> and his kingdom one that shall not be destroyed. (RSV)

The scene is not in this world but in the transcendent world of God. Daniel sees a vision of the succession of future world empires in which the traditional four oppressive empires are represented in mythological form as wild animals, while the final kingdom of God is represented by a human figure—a "son of man." This vision became very significant for later apocalyptic writers such as Enoch who understood the human figure in the vision to be a real figure of the heavenly world, a divine being with the appearance of a human being: "I saw in the night visions, and behold, with the clouds of heaven there came one like a son of man, and he came to the Ancient of Days and was presented before him." In this interpretation, Daniel's "son of man" is no longer a symbolic human figure but is a heavenly being who comes with the clouds of heaven. In Jewish apocalyptic thought, this transcendent figure became a way of conceptualizing the future establishment of God's kingdom. At the end, God would send the Son of Man from heaven to be judge of the world and establish God's kingdom. So understood, the imagery and concept of the son of man were an important formative influence in the shaping of Jesus's message. After the resurrection, "Son of Man" became a christological title used in the earliest church and in the Gospels, where it occurs eighty-two times, all in reference to Jesus, by far the most frequent christological title for Jesus in the Gospels.

As Christianity became mainly a gentile religion, most streams of Christian tradition abandoned this strange term for confessing the faith, even when they preserved its apocalyptic framework. Paul and his followers make no use of the term. The Johannine community in Roman Asia (ca. 90–130 CE) had inherited "Son of Man" as part of what had become traditional Christian vocabulary, but, prior to the Gospel, it had made only limited use of it. Even the Johannine community had mostly abandoned this term strange to gentile ears, apparently considered a detriment in its attempts to communicate the Christian message to outsiders and nurture faith in insiders. It is absent from 1–3 John and found only twice in the thoroughly apocalyptic imagery of Revelation (1:13; 14:14). Late in its history, the teacher-authors of the Fourth Gospel considered it important to preserve and restore "Son of Man" to a central place in Christian confession and theology. Why they did so is of more than incidental significance for the broad streams of modern Christianity that have likewise virtually abandoned "Son of Man" as a way to confess faith in Jesus.

The Evangelist Appropriated the Gospel Form as the Principal Means of Expressing Christian Theology

The *epistolary* form gave instruction in the Christian faith to the post-Easter church by discursive teaching about Jesus. In the *gospel* form, the pre-Easter Jesus is portrayed as identifying himself in his words and actions. Modern

Christians tend to assume this had always been the case, but the gospel form did not become a genre of Christian confession until forty years after the crucifixion. The Gospels were all written after Paul's death. The gospel form was not available to him and his churches during his mission in Roman Asia, but by the time of the composition of the Johannine writings, it was an option for the Johannine school. When the Johannine teachers who composed the Fourth Gospel opted for the narrative gospel genre of Christian confession and instruction, they claimed a tradition in which Jesus had identified himself as the Son of Man, an identity not given him by his followers but given to the community in the words of the risen Christ himself, the one who spoke in the Gospels.

The Strangeness of the Term Is Not a Liability but an Advantage to Faithful Hearing

It is a plus, not a minus, that "Son of Man" requires some explanation, that hearers do not immediately suppose they know what it means, a signal that we have entered the strange new world of the Bible. John gives a clue to this when he provides translations of "Messiah" and "rabbi" (1:38, 41), words that had long since been part of the church's own tradition. Authentic listening requires that key theological terms should not be filled with meaning from the contemporary culture but should be heard with the overtones of their biblical context.

Son of Man

"Son of Man" preserves the biblical connotations of both Daniel (apocalyptic, divine being) and Ezekiel (the fragility of a human being who lives in this world, the Word become flesh). "Of all the titles assigned to Jesus in the New Testament, only 'Son of Man' is able to convey the simultaneous existence (we are talking haltingly about myth or mystery here!) of a being who, in his solemn reception of authority in heaven, symbolizes a scenario that is actually being played out on earth."[7]

John's Gospel contains thirteen instances of the phrase, eleven of them in Jesus's own speech, the other two in response to his use of this term (1:51; 3:13, 14; 5:27; 6:27, 53, 62; 8:28; 9:35; 12:23, 34 [twice]; 13:31). Here, as elsewhere, the Johannine Jesus speaks with the accent of a Johannine theologian—which John would express by saying that he and his colleagues in the Johannine school speak in accord with the revelation of the risen Christ. The synoptic Son of Man tradition is taken up, melted down, and recast to include distinctive elements of Johannine theology.

Jesus the Son of Man Is the Bridge between Heaven and Earth (1:51)

We have indicated above that the Johannine Jesus's first declaration about the Son of Man points to his being, not what he says or does. The designation "Son of Man" posits the cosmic, transcendent role of Jesus in revelation and salvation.

Jesus the Son of Man Is the Judge (5:27)

Of course, the Johannine theologians affirm that human beings are not finally the judge of their own actions but are accountable to their creator. Biblical and Jewish tradition were unanimous that God is the judge of the world and all people. But God has given Jesus Christ authority and power to execute God's own judgment, "because he is the Son of Man." This is existentially important for the Johannine community, whose members sometimes had been condemned before religious and Roman courts, just as Jesus of Nazareth had been. The Son of Man is not the defendant but the Judge. As Son of *Man*, Jesus does what *God* does.

Jesus the Son of Man, the One Who Raises the Dead (5:25–30)

A fundamental aspect of Israel's eschatological hope was that God would raise the dead. This was not only or mainly a way of expressing human hope for life after death, but represents a theodicy. Even after the coming of the Messiah, terrible injustice and suffering continue in the world, apparently with the permission of God the Almighty, the God of love. The imagery of resurrection and judgment is a way of holding on to faith in the ultimate justice of God when empirical observation seems to deny it. Resurrection faith is primarily a claim about God, but it is also a statement about God's people. Death is not the end for them. The story of raising Lazarus pictures God who not only will raise the dead at the last day but who already gives life to believers who are delivered from a world in which death seems to reign (11:1–44). As in Ephesians, written in the historical context of the Johannine theologians, those who "were dead through the trespasses and sins" have been made "alive together with Christ" (Eph 2:1–10).

Jesus the Son of Man Shares His Own Flesh (6:53)

That the transcendent, preexistent Logos became the flesh-and-blood human being Jesus of Nazareth is foundational for Johannine theology. Jesus shares with his disciples not only the revelation from the heavenly world but also his this-worldly being. In the Fourth Gospel, eucharistic theology that had become traditional by John's time is intensified by incorporating it in the Son of Man Christology.

Jesus the Son of Man Descends and Ascends (3:13–14; 6:62; 8:28; 12:23, 34; 13:31)

The synoptic Son of Man descends from heaven at the parousia (Matt 16:28; 19:28; 24:27, 30, 37, 39, 44; 25:31; 26:64; Mark 8:38; 13:26; 14:62; Luke 9:26; 12:40; 17:24, 30; 18:8; 21:27), but the Johannine Son of Man is the preexistent one who has already descended from heaven, the one encountered in the life and teaching of Jesus of Nazareth (John 3:13). The whole Christ event is thought of as a U-shaped event that began in the heavenly world and was enacted in the incarnation of the Son of Man in this world, who returns to his heavenly glory. This whole three-act drama of salvation is signaled by designating Jesus as Son of Man.

Jesus the Son of Man Heals Those Born Blind (9:1–41)

The Synoptics have stories of healing blind persons, but none of the persons in the stories were *born* blind, nor were those stories ever associated with the Son of Man. The Fourth Gospel's story of Jesus healing a man born blind, like each of the signs dramatized in the Johannine narrative, portrays the Christ event as a whole. J. Louis Martyn's brief but potent book focuses on the healing of the blind man in 9:1–41 and explicates how John's two-level drama encapsulates the message of the whole Gospel.[8] The evangelist makes clear that the narrative is not merely an account of an amazing happening in first-century Jerusalem, but he portrays God's saving action for the human malady as such. The victim had not *become* blind but had never seen, did not know and could not imagine what it would be to see. Jesus's scornful adversaries suppose they already see and thus bypass the saving opportunity given them. Even 20/20 natural vision at its best cannot see the reality of things as they are. On his own (God's) initiative, Jesus gives (not "restores") sight to the blind man. The Savior identifies himself as the Son of Man. This story gives even more potency to the repeated initial invitation to discipleship, "Come and *see*" (1:39, 46; cf. 4:29).

Christ Is the Question: "What Are You Looking For?"

Jesus's last words in this scene present his own confession of his transcendent cosmic role in God's saving plan for the world (1:51). But Jesus's first words in this scene, the tone-setting keynote address for the whole Gospel, are a *question*, two words in Greek (*ti zēteite*): "What are you looking for?"

(1:38)—words that address not only the characters in the narrative but also readers of every generation.[9]

All those who became disciples of Jesus in these opening scenes were already insiders, Jews, steeped in the Scripture, looking for the fulfillment of the hope of Israel. But most people, then and now, are not looking for a messiah. To those who are looking for the promised Messiah, the good news is that the Messiah has come, and he is Jesus of Nazareth. But the response of most of the world to the announcement "The Messiah has come!" is neither faith nor unbelief but a shrug. The followers of Jesus are charged to be witnesses to the good news of God's act in Christ. But how does one preach Christ where people are not waiting for a Christ and don't recognize anything of themselves or their own needs in the announcement?[10] The presupposition is that all human beings, just because they are human, long for the authentic, joyful life intended by the creator for all people. Jews express this as hope for the coming of God's kingdom, the Messiah, the Son of Man. Others express their deepest longings as hungering and thirsting for that which really satisfies, or the longing to know the way to live their one and only life. This human yearning for true happiness may not be consciously and conceptually expressed at all, but it is recognized when set forth in symbols that are universally human: bread, water, light, the way, the truth, life, my true self, God. To all these, the Johannine Jesus will say, "You may not recognize the question until you see the answer. *I am* what you are looking for."

The question of the Johannine Jesus is not merely adjusting his claim to the world's own questions, as though the world sets the agenda and Jesus responds in terms of good marketing strategy, "You tell me what you want, and I'll get it for you." "What are you looking for?" is not an informational question, just as God's first question in the Bible, "Adam, where are you?" was not asked in order to give God information but to give Adam a revelation of his status before God. For John, human beings as such are blind (John 9:1–41) and don't truly know how to name what they are searching for. The question first becomes clear in the light of the answer—"As you didn't know you were lost until you were found, so you don't know what you are looking for until you *see* it." Thus "Come and see," as Jesus says it (*erchesthe* [present imperative] *kai opsesthe* [future indicative]), is both command and promise, "Come, and you *will* see" (1:39). The promise has overtones of the eschatological future. Even believers both see and don't see. For John, as for Matthew (Matt 5:8) and Paul (1 Cor 13:12), there is always an eschatological reservation; in this world, even for the believer, the "already" is always conditioned by the "not yet." "Whoever has seen me has seen the Father" (John 14:9; cf. 3 John 11). But "No one has ever seen God" (1 John 4:12; John 1:18).

In all this, John does not abandon the traditional language of "Christ," "Son of God," and "Son of Man" but interprets it in universally human terms. Throughout the Gospel, the series of "I am" statements culminating in "I am the way, and the truth, and the life" (John 14:6) present Jesus as the fulfillment not only of biblical and Jewish hopes but also of the hopes and fears of all the years. The Gospel will conclude with the claim that this universal human longing for life that is eternal (not a matter of length, but of depth, joy, quality, authenticity) is met in the advent of the Christ, the Son of God (20:30–31).

Discipleship and Ecclesiology

Like every scene in the Gospel, the narrative in 1:19–51 points beyond itself to the reality of God's continuing mission in the world and in the life of the Christian community. The "you" of Jesus's final words addressing "Nathanael" shifts to the plural (*opsesthe*), speaking over the head of the character in the story to the later hearer-readers in the church. The overlapping and related scenes of 1:19–51 manifest six features important for hearing what John wants his readers to grasp in order to understand the Gospel narrative as a whole

"You" or "Y'all"?

English uses the same form for singular and plural second-person pronouns. Greek distinguishes singular from plural in both pronouns and verbs. The shift from singular to plural is not apparent in English but clear in Greek. This happens repeatedly, often affecting the theological meaning expressed. The nighttime visit of Nicodemus to Jesus begins as a one-on-one conversation, then the pronouns gradually shift to the plural. In John 3:7, the singular "you" addressed to Nicodemus becomes a plural "you" addressed to unbelievers in general, including the Gospel's readers (not apparent in English but clear in Greek). The singular "I" of 3:3 morphs into the plural "we" at verse 11, as Jesus's there-and-then address to Nicodemus becomes the here-and-now address of Jesus through the Johannine community to contemporary readers. John is influenced by the biblical style. For example, in Genesis 17:10–12 and 18:9–13, the pronouns alternate between singular and plural, as Abraham is addressed by the three "men" who become transparent to the God who speaks to Abraham. The Bible always tends to become contemporary. The conversation of characters in a story from the past seamlessly becomes the address of God to the readers' present.

Call Scenes, Not Conversion Scenes

Those here called to be followers of Jesus are all already members of God's people Israel, who have responded to the light of God that shines through the creation, Israel, and Scripture. As just described in the prologue, they are already born-from-above members of God's family. Becoming disciples of Jesus is neither conversion from irreligion to religion nor conversion from one religion to another, but it is responding to the full manifestation of the measure of light they have already perceived. Andrew, the anonymous disciple, Peter, Philip, and Nathanael are not told to "believe" or that they must be "born from above." The later scenes of chapters 2–12 tell about outsiders, but there, too, the stories themselves are addressed to insiders, the hearer-readers of John's Gospel. These opening scenes of the Gospel portray those who already belong to God's people as now called to follow Jesus and participate in the mission of God incarnate/embodied in him.

There Are Different Paths to Discipleship, but All Disciples Are Chosen and Called by Jesus

If we were to ask those church members who hear our preaching and teaching to describe how they became followers of Jesus, there would be a remarkable variety of responses. Some were born and nurtured in a Christian home and would never remember a time when they did not worship God and acknowledge Jesus as Lord. Others would tell of a dramatic conversion experience as adults, or a quest for meaning and relationship that finally brought them within hearing distance of the Christian gospel. Many would describe the words of a preacher or church school teacher, or the life and witness of a friend or neighbor, as the decisive influence in their becoming Christians. John, too, portrays the call to discipleship as coming to different people in different ways:

- Andrew and another disciple of John the Baptist hear his testimony that Jesus is the "Lamb of God." Though John the Baptist himself never becomes a disciple, they believe his testimony and become Jesus's disciples (1:35–39a).
- Andrew then finds his brother Simon Peter (who is pointedly *not* the first called by Jesus, and not directly), declares that they have found the Christ, and brings Simon to Jesus (1:39b–42).

- The Johannine Jesus calls Philip with the same words spoken by the synoptic Jesus, "Follow me," and without asking for any explanation, Philip immediately follows Jesus (1:43–44; cf. Mark 1:17; 2:14; 10:21; etc.). The invitation "Follow me" occurs fifteen times in the Synoptics, always with Jesus as the speaker. Disciple-evangelists never say "Follow him," even in the Acts sermons. Jesus is the one who calls.
- Philip then finds Nathanael, declaring that "we" have found the one of whom Moses and the prophets wrote, Jesus of Nazareth, the son of Joseph, and brings him to Jesus. Jesus declares that he already knows Nathanael and what he has been doing. Nathanael then confesses Jesus to be the Son of God and king of Israel (John 1:45–49).

Later in the narrative, the thoughtful reader may be stunned to hear Jesus himself say, in his private teaching to the Twelve, "You did not choose me but I chose you" (15:16, 19; cf. 6:70). From John's theological perspective, in and through a variety of human words and actions, all along it has been Christ himself (i.e., God through Christ) who calls people to discipleship. We make our own decisions, for which we are responsible, and must do so. We seek, for we know we are not complete in ourselves, but even in our seeking, God is the one seeking us (4:23). Philip may even say, "We have found . . ." (in 1:45), but the evangelist has already said that Jesus first found Philip (1:43). We are not finders but foundlings. John has many points of contact with Lukan tradition and would agree with the theology of Luke 15: The lost sheep does not seek but is found. The lost coin does not seek but is found. Even the lost son, who repents, makes his own decision, and returns to the father, is greeted by one who says, "This son of mine was dead, but now he is alive; he was lost, but now he has *been* found!" (Luke 15:24 TEV).

The Fourth Evangelist, like Paul and other New Testament writers, uses the language of election and predestination to express the sovereignty of God (see volume 2, *Hearing Paul's Voice*, on Rom 9–11). In this opening scene, the evangelist shows how this language should be understood throughout. People who become disciples make their own decisions, for which they assume responsibility, a matter taken with absolute seriousness. But at the end of the day, we realize we are not volunteers but draftees. We do not congratulate ourselves for choosing God but thank God for choosing us. This dynamic of call/response, divine initiative/human responsibility, is pictured as Jesus's instructions to his disciples at the end of his last day on earth with them, heard by John's readers as the instruction of the Holy Spirit that continues the teaching of the risen Christ to them. This is another way of saying that God's salvation is 100 percent gift, without decreasing the awareness that disciples are 100 percent responsible. This 100/100 (rather than, e.g., 50/50 or even 90/10) is the same theological paradox as the Christian confession that Christ is truly human and truly divine, and that Christology and ecclesiology are inseparably fused.

Finder and/or Findee?

We may or may not be aware that we are looking for something or Someone, or that Someone is looking for us. When we connect and realize what we have been looking for, we rarely say, "*I've* found *it*."

Francis Thompson's flight and depression finally asks,

> "Is my gloom, after all,
> Shade of His hand, outstretched caressingly?
> 'Ah, fondest, blindest, weakest,
> I am He Whom thou seekest!
> Thou dravest love from thee, who dravest Me.'"

—"Hound of Heaven"

Fanny Crosby's gospel song did not confess "I finally found love and mercy" but "Beneath the cross of Jesus, love and mercy found me."

"I once was lost, but now am found."

—John Newton, "Amazing Grace"

Augustine prayed, "We seek you because we were sought; we wish to find you because we have been found." (*Tractates on John* 7.21)

John 4:23: "The Father seeks such . . . to worship him."

Baptism Was Important

Jesus was baptized by John (John 1:32–34, though not narrated). Jesus will baptize others (3:26; 4:1–2). Jesus's first followers had (apparently) already been baptized by John (1:35–37, though not plotted any place in John's Gospel). The audience cannot come away from these opening scenes without being aware that baptism plays an important role in joining (= being joined to) the community of Jesus's disciples.

Community, Not Individuals

As the opening scenes of the Gospel identify the Messiah, they also portray the formation of a community of Jesus's followers, the church. The first words of those who have begun to follow Jesus include the "we" of the Christian community (1:41). The later church was true to John's intention in seeing its own experience in this gathering of the initial community of faith. After these call scenes, from 2:1 on, Jesus has a group known as his disciples. The dynamics of becoming a disciple includes a centripetal force. Christ himself is the center to which they are called. But believers find that their response to Jesus relates them not only to him but also to all those others called by him. John has in view not only the line between insiders and outsiders but also a borderline group that he urges to become public. For John, one can't be a private disciple but must take one's stand with the visible community of faith (12:42–43).

The Evangelistic Mission of the Church

Most interpreters now agree that the Fourth Gospel is not written as an evangelistic tract for outsiders but as a teaching document to nourish the faith of insiders and equip them for service. This service includes evangelism. The call to discipleship is not only gift and invitation; it is also an assignment (German: *Gabe/Aufgabe*). Finding/being found by Jesus brings one into a community that sends disciples out to others. Andrew seeks out Peter and shares the good news with him, Philip seeks out Nathanael to tell him, "We have found the one of whom Moses and the prophets wrote." Again, the ecclesiological "we"—the church, the community of faith—is spreading the good news. The centripetal force in Jesus's call that draws disciples together into a community is also a centrifugal force. Evangelism is inherent in believing the gospel, which is about God's saving act for all people. In these opening scenes, Jesus does not command his new believers to go and make other disciples. The good news they themselves have come to believe impels them to tell others. This is not because the gospel is theirs to share but because it already belongs to the whole world. Christians should not hesitate to encourage and participate in evangelism as though it were a matter of "imposing our religion on others." If the gospel is true, it is true for everyone, not as a particular religious theory but as an event that has happened (cf. discussion in the prologue section above). To use John's own metaphor, if in the Christ event God has given bread to a hungry world, evangelism is not attempting to sell our ideas in the religious marketplace as though our religion is better than theirs, but "one beggar telling another where to find bread."[11]

"Come and See"

To be a disciple is to have a message that must be shared with the world. The church's job is to attain substance and clarity of its message by *listening* to its living Lord witnessed in Scripture, tradition, and its own experience, then to *testify* to what it has heard, then to *invite* others to follow. The invitation is "Come and see," given first by Jesus (1:39) and then extended in his name by his disciples (1:46; cf. also the Samaritan woman in 4:29). Evangelistic preaching does not mean presenting evidence that God exists, that Jesus is the Son of God, that the church is the people of God, or that the Bible is the word of God. These opening scenes resist the idea that the Christian gospel can be presented in such a way that those addressed can have their own criteria, to which God, Christ, the church, and its Bible must be shown to measure up. When Philip announces, "We have found him about whom Moses . . . and . . . the prophets wrote" (1:45), this does not mean that he provided a list of texts his hearers could examine to see whether Jesus in fact measured up to their criteria. There is no approval, but a mild reproof, when Jesus asks whether Nathanael believes because he has revealed something of Nathanael's past by miraculous insight, but he will later *see* the unseeable: the angels of God ascending and descending on the Son of Man (1:47–51). No one can legitimately reject the call of Christ because Jesus fails to conform to our expectations of what the Christ "must" be, however reasonable, religious, or biblical they may be, just as no one can come to Jesus on the basis of personal criteria, coolly weighing the evidence and deciding that, after all, it does seem that Jesus does measure up and we could then say, "*We* chose *you*" (versus Jesus's own word in 15:16).

These hints in the opening scene are amplified with startling volume and clarity in the following stories of Jesus's encounters with the unbelieving world. John gives a cluster of examples in chapter 7:

- Some reject the possibility that Jesus is the Messiah, saying, "We know where this man is from; but when the Messiah comes, no one will know where he is from" (7:27). They suppose that Jesus is from Nazareth. Their data is correct. Their error is that they suppose they have in hand criteria by which to judge Jesus.

- Some "believe" in him because he has done enough signs to qualify as the Messiah (7:31), but the Fourth Gospel presents the Johannine Jesus, who rejects faith that trusts in signs and human ability to evaluate them (2:22–23; 3:2–13; 4:48). John has a positive view of the role of Jesus's signs in coming to faith, but he does not believe that even those who "believe" Jesus's signs, in the sense of merely accepting the miracles as events that really happened, have authentic faith. So also in 9:16, some are inclined to believe on the basis of Jesus's signs. Others disbelieve because Jesus breaks the Sabbath. But neither the one nor the other is the basis for belief or disbelief in Jesus. The signs point beyond themselves to God's act in Jesus. Would-be believers must "come and see" who Jesus is for themselves, not stop and admire the signs (5:1–40, with v. 40 being the key: "*Come to me* to have life").
- Some knew the Scripture text that they understood as a prediction that the Messiah was to come from Bethlehem (Mic 5:2). Since they knew Jesus came from Nazareth, he could not be the Messiah (John 7:40–42). The modern reader, who has the whole New Testament, should resist the temptation to say, "Aha! Jesus *was* born in Bethlehem, just as Matthew and Luke say." In John's eyes, this is doubly wrong. In the Fourth Gospel, Jesus comes from Nazareth, period (1:45, 46; 18:5, 7; 19:19). But the mistake is not a matter of biography or geography but of theology: they suppose they can validate or invalidate God's act in Jesus on their own terms.
- Some regard the common people as unqualified to make decisions of faith on their own, and pose the challenge, "Has any one of the authorities or of the Pharisees believed in him?" (7:48). For John, the truth of the gospel is self-authenticating. It is not validated by ecclesiastical, academic, or political authorities, nor by the appeal to common sense.
- Nicodemus, good and sincere teacher of Israel, accepts Jesus as a teacher who has come from God, "for no one can do these signs that you do apart from the presence of God" (3:2). Jesus's abrupt response bypasses Nicodemus's sincere opening gambit: "Very truly, I tell you, no one can see the kingdom of God without being born from above" (3:3). When Jesus heals a blind man on the Sabbath, some Pharisees decide that a Sabbath-breaker cannot be from God. Others, equally astute and sincere, in the same situation say, "How can a man who is a sinner perform such signs?" (9:16–17; 10:19–21). For the Johannine teachers, faith in Jesus is a gift from God, not a matter of inference based on our own evidences and judgment, however good and sincere they may be.

In all of this, John insists that while believing in Jesus is not blind faith and cannot mean celebrating ignorance or abandoning reason—Christ is the *logos* become flesh—even good, reasonable, biblical criteria cannot settle the issue of faith. The serious inquirer cannot objectively weigh the evidence and decide that, after all, it does seem that Jesus measures up to our criteria. One must make a commitment and lean into the truth. The existentialists have been right and in step with Johannine theology all along: the way out of the woods is never clear until one begins to march (7:17). No one can "see" first, then decide whether or not to follow Jesus. "Come and see."

Book One, the Triumphal Entry and Presence: The Incarnate Word Confronts the World (1:19–12:50)

In the prologue (1:1–18), John has narrated the incarnation of the Word and interpreted the comprehensive meaning of God's revelatory and saving act in the Christ event. In the testimony (1:19–51), the prefatory scenes to the ministry of the incarnate Word confronting the world lead the reader into the narrative of Jesus's ministry (1:19–51). In these programmatic opening scenes, Jesus neither preaches nor heals. His sole activity is to call disciples and form them into a community. The first part of the narrative proper begins at 2:1, with the Cana wine miracle as the first of Jesus's signs. These signs continue through chapter 12. There is no preaching of the kingdom of God, no explicit ethical teaching; there are no parables and no exorcisms. John configures the narrative of Jesus's ministry as a series of *signs* (see below).

Signs, Sign, and the *Sign*

All the Gospels use "sign" (*sēmeion*) as a component of their vocabulary for expressing extraordinary acts of God. John uses this term almost exclusively for God's saving acts in Jesus. "Wonder, miracle" (*teras*) is found only once (4:48), with a pejorative tone of voice.

	Matthew	Mark	Luke	John
Sign (*sēmeion*)	13	7	11	17
Wonder (*teras*)	1	1	0	1
Powerful Deed (*dynamis*)	12	10	15	0

As in English usage, so in secular Greek literature, the Hebrew Bible, the LXX, and the New Testament, "sign" can be used in the conventional sense as a marker that identifies or points to something else: a plus or minus sign, a street sign, the mark God placed on Cain to protect him from revenge (Gen 4:15), circumcision as the mark of the covenant (Gen 17:11; Rom 4:11). For the most part, however, biblical authors used the term in the sense common in the ancient world to refer to the extraordinary act of some divine being or power, as a synonym for "miracle" or "powerful deed." John, too, can use the word in this conventional sense, especially in the plural, to refer to Jesus's extraordinary deeds of healing. So understood, the word is used mostly by nondisciples, some of whom are said to "believe" on this basis (John 2:23; 3:2; 4:48 [with *terata*, "wonders"]; 6:2; 7:31; 9:16; 11:47). Understood in John's own sense, such faith is authentic. His final use of the word refers to the Gospel itself as presenting a collection of Jesus's signs that can lead to authentic faith in Jesus as the Christ, the Son of God (20:30–31).

The Johannine Teachers Developed a Distinctive Use of *Sēmeion* to Express a Particular Understanding of the Christ Event

The Johannine sign is more than a miracle, an extraordinary event that interrupts the normal course of events and evokes wonder and amazement. In Johannine usage, the sign *points*—points beyond itself to the revelation of God. Each sign is a pointer to the ultimate revelation of God in the Christ event. But characters in the story, including serious and sincere seekers, can see Jesus's signs as miraculous in the conventional sense, believe that they really happened, and draw their own conclusions about his identity, without ever grasping or being grasped by the truth of the reality to which the sign points. John himself makes this clear in the first sign-story, Jesus's transformation of water into wine. Jesus's act manifests the divine glory. The disciples see and believe. Others enjoyed the wine without knowing what had happened or becoming believers in Jesus (2:11). The cleansing of the temple immediately follows. Unbelieving opponents challenge him by asking for a sign that authorizes him to act with such authority (2:18). Jesus responds by speaking enigmatically of his death and resurrection as *the* sign. Outsiders do not perceive what is happening, and they cannot do so as long as they evaluate it in the framework of their this-worldly mind-set (2:19–21). Even those who have a tentative "faith" in Jesus on the basis of their own judgment about his signs cannot perceive the truth about Jesus, as illustrated in the dialogue between Nicodemus and Jesus that immediately follows (3:1–16).

Throughout the Gospel, the Johannine signs can be perceived at two levels.

2:13–22	Temple of stone in Jerusalem / *Body of Christ*
3:1–16	Gift of life by physical birth / *Life given by birth from above*
4:7–15	Water that quenches physical thirst / *Spring of water gushing up to eternal life*
4:8, 31–34; 6:25–59	Perishable bread for physical hunger / *Food that endures for eternal life*
6:31–40	Miraculous bread from the sky / *True bread from heaven, Jesus Christ*
8:31–36	Freeing those enslaved by society / *Freeing those enslaved by sin*
9:1–34	Giving sight to physically blind eyes / *Giving sight to those who suppose they see*
11:1–44	Giving life by restoring health / *Giving life by resurrection*

In all this, the Johannine Jesus does not merely teach ideals or principles, or act out object lessons illustrating ethics or the good life. He himself, that is, God's act in him, is God's gift of life. The one who says, "I am the living bread that came down from heaven" and "I am the resurrection and the life" (6:51; 11:25), *is* God's act that gives abundant life: God's temple, water, food, liberation, resurrection.

Each sign can thus be perceived on two levels. This does not mean, however, that the Fourth Gospel portrays Jesus as a "spirit-person" who lives in a spirit world unconcerned with the mundane realities of the material and social world that is the context of all human life. Throughout, the Johannine teachers have advocated exactly the opposite: the transcendent Word has entered this world of flesh and manifested the divine glory precisely in this world created and loved by God. The Johannine ethic for the followers of Jesus is not unconcern for the world or withdrawal from it, but loving ministry to it in God's name. The Johannine teachers urge Jesus's followers to give food and drink to those who literally hunger and thirst, to set free those that are literally enslaved in this-worldly bonds, to heal those sick with the ills this-worldly flesh is heir to. The Johannine ethic is not less than this but more, and provides the basis for such action, when those who see Jesus's acts as signs of God's transforming grace that are not ideals to be implemented but pointers to God's act in the Christ event. The Johannine Jesus does not teach sound theology to the hungry crowds *instead of* feeding them. He urges those he has fed to grasp the sign character of the event and seek the true bread that gives authentic life (6:26–29). Jesus's disciples believed the Scripture and the word of Jesus, the basis for understanding the meaning of the signs as revelatory acts of God, and others remain blind (9:1–41). The early dialogues about Jesus's first sign (chaps. 2–3) show that "sign," "see," and "believe" can be used in the double sense characteristic of John's theology. It is possible to "see" the "signs" without ever seeing *the* sign, to believe the miracle happened and still be clueless as to what is really going on. The Johannine teachers derive this theology from their Bible, expressed in God's charge to Isaiah:

> "Go and say to this people:
> 'Keep listening, but do not comprehend;
> keep looking, but do not understand.'
> Make the mind of this people dull,
> and stop their ears,
> and shut their eyes,
> so that they may not look with their eyes,
> and listen with their ears,
> and comprehend with their minds,
> and turn and be healed." (Isa 6:9–10)

By the time the Fourth Gospel was written, this text had been cited by numerous Christian teachers for over a generation (Matt 13:14–15; Mark 4:12; Luke 8:10; Acts 28:26–27; Rom 11:8). John himself would refer to this passage in the conclusion of his "book of signs" (John 12:36b–43). People saw the miracles, believed they happened, "believed" in Jesus, but were blind to what was really happening. Johannine theology offers a warning to "Bible believers" who "believe every miracle in the Bible just as it is written." This is not necessarily the same as Christian faith.

The other side of the coin, which can be good news to modern people who long to believe but don't know what to do with the Bible's miracle stories, is that people can hear and believe the Christian message communicated in reading and hearing the gospel without feeling they must accept a literal interpretation of every miracle story. One can come to faith in the God revealed in the Christ event without ever having seen a miracle. In his vicinity in Ephesus, John knew there were Pauline and other Christians who confessed and lived out a deep faith in God's saving act in Christ, without any reference to miracles worked by the pre-Easter Jesus. Such disciples of Christ, whatever they thought about the miracle stories, believed that in the life, death, and resurrection of Jesus, God had acted for the salvation of the world and shaped their lives by this conviction. The Johannine community itself was not altogether convinced that telling miracle stories about Jesus was an authentic way of communicating the faith—there is no reference to miracles in 1–3 John; Revelation points to miracles worked by false prophets but has nothing to say about miracles performed by Jesus or Christian believers (Rev 13:13–14; 16:14; 19:20). In John's time such believers were more numerous in the churches of Asia than those who had adopted the gospel genre, with its miracle stories, as a legitimate channel of Christian proclamation. On this important point, the Gospel of John has something crucial to say to all its readers, both those who suppose they believe in Christ because they believe the miracle stories about him and those who suppose they are barred from such faith because they cannot honestly believe such stories literally happened. The Gospel's narrative theology communicates an authentic way of seeing and hearing the signs as pointers to *the* sign, God's act in the death and resurrection of Christ. So understood, each miracle story calls for faith in God's saving act in the whole Christ event, regardless of one's view of particular miracle stories.

The Johannine Sign-Discourse Structure

We have seen that the Johannine authors, following the example of the Scripture and Jesus himself, chose narrative as the way to communicate theology, so that the structure of the story is important in communicating its theological message. We thus do well to delve more deeply into the Johannine narrative/discourse structure of the sign stories, of which John 6 is the parade example. The literary, historical, exegetical, and hermeneutical issues associated with the Johannine signs are all disputed points. The following seems to me to be closest to what the Johannine authors intended, and the most helpful for entering the circle of the Fourth Gospel's hearing distance.

Seven Signs?

The structure of the Gospel can best be seen as comprising seven signs. The explicit marking of the two Cana miracles as the "first sign" and "second sign" (John 2:11; 4:54) seems to indicate a specific total number of signs. For John, an important implication of designating the Cana wedding miracle as Jesus's first sign is that it excludes any interest in what Jesus was like prior to his baptism and the beginning of his public ministry, eliminating speculation about miracles of the superboy Jesus such as those narrated in the Infancy Gospel of Thomas and other gnosticizing interpretations. If the Cana miracle was Jesus's first sign, his boyhood and early adulthood prior to his baptism by John were truly human, lacking miraculous divine power. Designating the healing of the royal official's son in Cana (4:46b–54) as the "second sign" is more problematical. Interpreters have understood this enumeration in a variety of ways. Rudolf Bultmann popularized the view (not original with him) that the fragmentary enumeration is evidence of a "Signs Source" that was partially incorporated into the structure of John's Gospel. Most interpreters have now abandoned this view and regard the enumeration as from the evangelist himself.

Some interpreters have found the significance of the enumeration as pointing to a total of seven signs, since the Gospel appears to be permeated by series of sevens. These include not only seven miracles matched with seven discourses but also such details as seven periods of Jesus's life, seven christological titles in the first chapter, seven disciples, seven feasts, seven "I am" sayings, seven days delineated in chapters 1–2, and seven segments in the scene of Jesus's trial before Pilate. While this is probably more zealous about symbolic sevens than John himself intended, there does seem to be good reason to suppose that John constructs the whole Gospel as a series of seven sign/discourse units. Seven was considered the "perfect" number, the number of fullness and fulfillment, in many streams of Mediterranean culture. The key role that seven plays in the structure of Revelation is well known and undisputed.

The author of Revelation knows the literary device of beginning a list that is not explicitly completed, the open-ended enumeration pointing forward to an ultimate fulfillment. In Revelation, each of the first two series of announced sevens has no seventh scene that fulfills it, but each opens into a new series (Rev 8:1–2; 10:7; 11:15; 16:17). Only the first two of the announced three woes are actually plotted (9:1, 12). The author of the Gospel may also have used this literary strategy. Instead of providing a static, ready-made tidy arrangement, the incomplete enumeration "teases the mind into active thought" parable-like, into exploring more deeply what is being pointed to. John, of course, does not make his literary technique explicit, which would defeat its purpose![12] It could well be that John begins an enumeration with the first two signs, which also frame a literary Cana-to-Cana subdivision but function to point the reader ahead to other signs, all of which point to the ultimate sign, the self-giving love of God manifest in the Christ event as such.

The "Book of Signs" (John 2–12, the "Triumphal Entry") comprises six signs, followed by the seventh sign in the "Book of Glory" (chaps. 13–21, the "Triumphal Exit"). Each sign could be explored in depth and detail to better hear, grasp, and be grasped by the Word of God communicated in it; the following comments are the barest of descriptive handles.

Transforming Water into Wine, Temple into Community (2:1–22)

In the first sign, Jesus, on his own initiative, transforms the water used in the Jewish purification ritual into the wine of the messianic wedding feast. Coupled with this is the transformation of the Jewish temple (by its destruction/rebuilding, analogous to death/resurrection) into his own body, of which his disciples become members. The resurrection imagery is already signaled by the "on the third day" with which the sign narrative begins (2:1; cf. 2:19, 20). There is no extensive discourse to interpret the sign, as in the sign/discourse structure of chapters 5, 6, and 9, but Jesus's actions, misunderstood at the level of the ordinary material world, are interpreted in the dialogue/discourses with Nicodemus (3:1–36) and the Samaritan woman at the well (4:1–38).

Overcoming Distance and Death (4:46–54)

In the second sign, Jesus overcomes the threat of death without being physically present. Like all the signs, Jesus's act represents and mediates God's gift of life in the Christ event climaxed by his own death and resurrection. This happened at the "seventh hour" (4:52–53; some modern translations obscure the symbolism by adjusting to a modern pattern of timekeeping, but both "hour" and "seven" are important in Johannine theology). In the Johannine narrative, the first question addressed to Jesus by any human being is "Where are you staying?" (1:38). This is the question of those Johannine Christians who believed in the Christ who had come, had departed, and had promised to come back. Where is he now? Is his power to heal and save, once present in the world, still available? These questions will continue to be addressed, and answers will be given, in the signs and discourses to follow. In the second sign, some answers are already foreshadowed and symbolized: the "absent" Jesus is still Lord over life and death; faith is believing the word of Jesus, even without "signs and wonders" (4:48, 50). The discourses and dialogues between the first and second signs, "overheard" by the reader but unknown to the royal official, help the reader to see and hear what is *really* going on in the stories of Jesus's signs told by the Johannine preachers and teachers and communicated by the Gospel.

Healing, Christology, and Testimony (5:1–47)

In the third sign, Jesus again acts on his own initiative to heal the lame man. In accord with the standard pattern, the interpretative discourse follows. While in the Synoptics such stories centered on Jesus's violation of traditional Sabbath rules, in the Fourth Gospel this dimension is quickly transcended, and the issue becomes christological. Both Jesus and the narrator claim that Jesus does the work of God, including the eschatological acts of raising the dead and pronouncing the final judgment (5:19–30). Does this mean, as "the Jews" charge, that Jesus, or the Johannine church, really make Jesus "equal to God" (5:18)? In line with the courtroom drama, not only does Jesus testify for himself but a series of witnesses testify on Jesus's behalf: John the Baptist, Jesus's own works, the Father who sent him, and—elaborated most of all—the Scriptures (5:31–47).

True Bread, Enough for All (6:1–71)

The fourth sign is the clearest example of the Johannine theology as expressed in the sign/discourse pattern. We will go more deeply into this paradigmatic sign below, not only for its own meaning but as a model of how to interpret the other signs.

Congenital Blindness and the Gift of Seeing (9:1–41)

In the fifth sign, a man blind from birth is healed, once more at Jesus's initiative. It is another example of the two-level drama inherent in all the signs. The story narrated as a pre-Easter event in the life of Jesus is composed to be read/heard as post-Easter revelation to the Christian community, who recognize their own experience in the story and find it further illuminated. For those with ears to hear, whose own eyes have been opened by Christian faith, the symbolic, two-level nature of the narrative is *sign*aled by the blind man's obedience by washing in the pool of Siloam, which John pointedly translates as "Sent." Jesus himself is the Sent One in/by whom the blind are washed, given sight, and given new life. Unlike the similar synoptic stories, the blind man here does not have his sight "restored." He has never seen. The Johannine understanding of human existence as such is here represented. We human beings cannot help but see the world and life through our own distorted vision; that is, we do not see reality as it is—not ourselves, not the world, not God or the One God sent. We do not struggle and finally *regain* our sight, but for the first time, after being encountered by Jesus, obeying his command to wash in the pool of the Sent One, we can see—albeit still only "in part" (1 Cor 13:12; cf. Mark 8:14–25; 10:46–52). We do not find but are found (see pp. 226–27 above on John 1:43). Sincere and competent religious teachers who claim to see already, and to judge Jesus by what they see, cannot perceive their own blindness (9:39–41). Perceptive Johannine readers remember their former lives, their encounter with Jesus, their baptism.

> "Amazing grace! How sweet the sound,
> That saved a wretch like me!
> I once was lost, but now am found,
> Was blind, but now I see."
>
> —John Newton, "Amazing Grace"

The Last Enemy: Already Defeated, Still Active (11:1–53)

The sixth sign encapsulates all the preceding stories. Each sign has shown God-in-Christ as the one who overcomes the enemies of life, abundantly granting the gifts that make life what the creator intended it to be. As in the Pauline tradition, death itself is the ultimate enemy (1 Cor 15:26). For our purposes, two features of the story are to be noted.

Jesus does not respond immediately to his friends' call for help but intentionally delays his departure. When Jesus and his disciples finally arrive in Bethany, Lazarus has been dead four days. This delay is not to be interpreted at the *kata sarka* level ("according to the flesh," this-worldly empirical judgment, even if sound and sincere). The hearer-readers already know that the "absent" Jesus can heal from a distance (see the second sign, 4:46–54 above). Like the other signs, this story expresses the love of God in the Christ event as such, and pointedly does not fit into literalistic, reporter-mentality thinking about a particular event in a Bethany household. Like the wine-wedding miracle and the healing of the man born blind, the confessional-language story is transparent to the glory of God but can suggest misleading inferences if forced into the framework of conventional this-worldly stories.

The "standard" pattern is shifted so that the discourse comes before the event. The story is transparently not only about Jesus's compassion for a Judean family mourning the death of a relative; it is also about God's compassion for the world. Jesus's raising of Lazarus modulates into God's raising of Jesus. The structure is thus modified to conform to *the* sign that will be interpreted in the second half of John's Gospel, with the interpretation first, then the event itself (Farewell Discourse [chaps. 13–17] followed by Jesus's death and resurrection [chaps. 18–21]).

The Sent One Returns to the Father—by Being "Lifted Up" on the Cross (13:1–20:31)

The Sign is the Christ event itself, the personal, incarnate presence of God manifest in the life, death, resurrection, and exaltation of Jesus, who gives the Spirit that founds and guides the Christian community. The self-giving love of the creator *God* who gives life to the world through the incarnate Word is summed up in the self-giving of *Jesus,* who voluntarily goes to the cross. The unitary cross-resurrection-exaltation event is narrated in John's own way in chapters 18–21. The meaning of this event is not transparent, even to sincere and honest observers, but must be revealed. Jesus interprets this meaning in advance to his disciples in the Farewell Discourse in chapters 13–17. The cross-resurrection-exaltation event is not specifically called a sign, the term being reserved for Jesus's acts in chapters 1–12, for it is the transcendent meaning of all the signs and appears as the summary conclusion of the book as a whole in 20:30.

Bread for the World: The Messianic Banquet as Present Experience between Memory and Hope (6:1–71)

John knows that Jesus did many such signs and presents only an interpretive selection—the selection itself is already an interpretation of the meaning of the Christ event (20:30–31; 21:25). As a way of improving our hearing and refining our capabilities of interpreting all John's narrative signs, we will explore one key text, the narrative sign of feeding the five thousand and Jesus's hermeneutical discourse on the bread of life. This text is rightly regarded as a compendium of Johannine theology. First, we need to review the tradition in which John himself stands and interprets.

Tradition and Interpretation

The Gospels include six versions of the story, each communicating its own theological nuance in accord with the theology of each gospel (Matt 14:13–36; 15:32–39; Mark 6:32–56; 8:1–10; Luke 9:10b–17; John 6:1–71). Some distinctive elements of the Johannine narrative follow:

- Mark had included two versions of the story, the feeding of the five thousand on the west bank of the Sea of Galilee in Jewish territory, followed by the feeding of the four thousand on the east bank in gentile territory, suggesting the early Christian progress of the gospel. Matthew includes both Markan versions but has them both in Jewish territory, since he restricts the mission of Jesus and his disciples to Jews during Jesus's ministry, with the gentile mission beginning after the resurrection. John, like Luke, has only one account, the feeding of the five thousand, but on the east bank in gentile territory. In John, it is not unusual for Jesus to be in the gentile region east of the Jordan (1:28; 3:23; 10:40–41), just as he has Jesus and his disciples carry on a successful mission to the Samaritans (4:1–42). In John, as in Mark, the post-Easter mission to non-Jews is collapsed into the pre-Easter ministry of Jesus.
- In the Synoptics, the feeding(s) occur(s) during the ministry of Jesus in Galilee, which lasted less than a year, prior to the one trip to the Passover in Jerusalem that resulted in Jesus's death. John refers to three different Passovers (2:13; 6:4; 11:55), as well as an unspecified "festival of the Jews" in Jerusalem (5:1), which may also have been a Passover. In John, the feeding of the five thousand occurred after Jesus's second trip to Jerusalem, as the second or third Passover is approaching (6:4). Although Jesus and his disciples do not attend this Passover, John makes a point of connecting the feeding with the Passover festival.
- All the Synoptics stress compassion for the hungry crowds as the motive in Jesus's actions, whether this be the disciples' concern (Matt 14;

Mark 6; Luke 9) or Jesus's own compassion (Matt 15; Mark 8). His command to the disciples, "You give them something to eat," is found in all three (Matt 14:16; Mark 6:37; Luke 9:13). However other features of the story are understood, this focus on the responsibility of Jesus's followers to feed hungry people cannot be missed. Yet it is missing from John's account, though it is virtually certain that he knew one or more versions of the story that featured this challenge to the disciples. In John, Jesus does not *react* to the need of a hungry crowd (of which nothing is said) or to the disciples' concern (as in the other gospels). In John, Jesus is not reactive but proactive, the sovereign in every situation who acts with divine initiative (cf. this trait of the Johannine Jesus in 2:3–4; 5:1–8; 7:1–10). When Jesus asks Philip, "Where are we to buy bread for these people to eat?" this is not a matter of humanitarian compassion, for as the Son of God he already knew what he was going to do, before anyone asked (6:5–7). The omission of "You give them something to eat" does not mean that John's understanding of discipleship sacrifices social responsibility to individualistic interior spirituality. In John's own way, he too considers Jesus's call for his disciples to feed the hungry indispensable; this is considered self-evident in 13:29 (cf. 1 John 3:16–17). The Johannine Jesus has another, more radical, basis for the ethics of discipleship.

- The meal is extravagant. All ate "as much as they wanted" (John 6:11, added to the tradition as the concluding line). In John, this is an abundance that corresponds to the messianic extravagance of providing 180 gallons of wine for a village wedding reception (2:6), twelve ounces of perfume worth ten months' wages (12:3), a hundred pounds of burial spices for a royal funeral (19:38–39).
- As in Mark and Matthew, the feeding story is followed by the story of walking on the water, but in John this is not simply a matter of one miracle story followed by another, each with its own meaning in its respective context. The feeding story, located outdoors on the east bank of the sea in gentile territory, is not complete until the next day, when Jesus returns to Jewish territory on the west bank, where he delivers the synagogue discourse on the true manna and the bread of life. The disciples' boat trip back across the lake and Jesus's walking to them on the water serve as the narrative means of connecting sign and discourse, and are integrated into the complex of meanings communicated by the feeding miracle.
- By far the most significant change in the Johannine composition is the extensive discourse John adds to interpret the event (see the discussion

above on the revelatory gestalt as event + prophetic interpretation + reception by the community). In the Synoptics, the miracle stories are not merely sensational accounts of Jesus the itinerant wonder worker, but each story bears an implicit meaning, often a "gospel in miniature" pointing to the whole Christ event. John typically not only narrates the revelatory event but also appends a discourse and/or dialogue in which (the risen) Jesus himself interprets the miracle as a *sign*.

There are numerous other distinctive elements in the Johannine account, some of which will be explored in the discussions below, but we have done enough to illustrate the nature of the New Testament texts. The point of such analysis is neither a fascination with minutiae nor pickiness in regard to the historical accuracy of the Gospels' accounts, but to help modern interpreters gain a hands-on, firsthand impression of the nature of the gospel materials that can hardly be conveyed by reading secondary literature. Such direct engagement with the nitty-gritty of the biblical text is not a detriment to the interpreter's task but an illumination of what we are about. Like us, the author of the Gospel of John stood in the midst of a rich and varied tradition of interpretations of the meaning of the Christ event. He chose a few of these to interpret as *signs* pointing to the meaning of God's saving act (20:30–31).

Meanings: A Selective Theological Close Reading of John 6

The above discussions have prepared us for a close reading of the text, bringing us within hearing distance of some of the theological overtones built into the narrative. The Johannine teachers have not tried to say everything at once. Learning from *the* Teacher is incremental, a gradual perception of the one truth that can never be entirely grasped by any one narrative or discourse, nor, in this world, by all of them together. Objective knowledge of flesh-and-blood reality that we have heard, seen, and touched (1 John 1:1–3) is gradually broadened, deepened, and clarified by the post-Easter Spirit/Risen Christ/God, the church's true Teacher (1 John 2:20, 26–27; John 14:26; 15:26–27; 16:12–15). The narrative and discourse in John 6 are a model of the Johannine technique of instructing the *church* by retelling the story of *Jesus*, the risen Lord who is present and active in the life of the post-Easter community of faith. As we proceed through the text, we will trace some themes of this sign-story in a selection of notes.

6:2: Crowds, Seeing, and Signs. The crowd followed Jesus because they saw the signs. We have learned from the Johannine teachers that there is a "seeing" that is still blind to reality, a "believing" that is still superficial acceptance or rejection of miracles, making our own inferences in terms of our own commonsense, this-worldly logic. Or signs can be seen as pointing beyond themselves. Which will the crowds' "seeing" and "believing" turn out to be?

6:3: A Teacher Seated on a Mountain. Such details are neither the recollections of an eyewitness with a reporter's mentality nor incidental stage setting from the evangelist. These narrative features evoke images of both biblical and earlier Christian tradition. Throughout the Fourth Gospel, the Moses/Jesus comparison hovers in the background; it is here evoked by the introductory words to the feeding narrative. Matthew had already used similar imagery, with the same vocabulary as here, to set the scene for the Sermon on the Mount (Matt 5:1). In each instance, the role of Moses is affirmed, but Jesus is the definitive teacher for God's people. In the story that follows, Jesus does not teach the crowds until the next day, not on the eastern shore of the sea but back on the other side, in the synagogue in Capernaum (John 6:59). In this story, as in the Fourth Gospel as a whole, Jesus is the teacher of the post-Easter church.

6:4: Passover Imagery. The blood of the Passover lamb is the sign of God's liberation of Israel from slavery. The gospel that begins by introducing Jesus as the Lamb of God who takes away the sin of the world (1:29, 36) will conclude with the death of Jesus at the time the Passover lambs are being killed (see pp. 280–82 below on 19:28–42). No further direct reference to the Passover is made in the feeding story, but the whole event and discourse are set in the Passover framework. Jesus and his disciples do not go to Jerusalem for this festival. The real Passover is being celebrated in the presence of the true Lamb, the true Bread. The reference is not biographical or chronological; it evokes the Passover and exodus symbolism (manna!) as the context for hearing the story.

6:5: The One Who Knows Our Needs Before We Do. Hearer-readers first learn that the crowd is hungry (and thirsty) from Jesus (6:5; cf. 6:35). Jesus sees the approaching crowd. They do not speak. If they are hungry, they do not know what they are hungry for, but the Johannine Jesus sees them with the eyes of God, knows them better than they know themselves (2:24–25). Just as the lame man did not ask Jesus for healing (5:1–8), so too do the crowds that "follow" Jesus not know they are hungry and thirsty with a need that only Jesus could supply. The thirsty Samaritan woman does not ask

Jesus for a drink, for she doesn't know what she is thirsty for, but receives living water at Jesus's initiative (4:4–14; when she does ask, her question reveals her misunderstanding, 4:15). Lazarus doesn't know he is dead and cannot ask for life, but is raised and set free by Jesus's gracious act (11:1–19; cf. Eph 2:1–10, circulating in Ephesus when John was written, presumably known to both author and hearers). The Galilean crowd do not know their own need until they see it satisfied, do not know their own question until they hear the answer.

6:5–6: Jesus Tests the Disciples. Jesus knows the human problem. The disciples do not understand, and seem unconcerned about the hunger of the crowd. In contrast to the synoptic narrative, Jesus here initiates the action by asking, "Where are we to buy bread for these people to eat?" In the Fourth Gospel, Jesus does not ask informational questions, just as he does not act in response to the appeals of others. As the Son who represents God, Jesus already knows, and asks questions only to test others. Like God, he cannot be tested, but is himself the Tester. The Synoptic Gospels each have a scene in which Jesus is tested by Satan (*peirazō* here does not mean "tempt" in the moral sense; a test of power and will is what is involved). In Matthew and Luke (reflecting their common source Q), the scene involves changing stones to bread, which is not only to assuage Jesus's own hunger but is also a matter of becoming a king who has authority over the whole world (Matt 4:1–11; Luke 4:1–13). John too knows this story (whether from the Gospels or their common tradition) that involves testing, producing vast quantities of bread, and becoming king (cf. John 6:15). But Jesus's kingship is on another level (18:33–38), and he is not tested but is himself the one who tests others.

6:7–9: The Disciples Fail the Test. Even with commonsense realism, the disciples know that six months' salary would *not* suffice for everyone to have even a *little.* They locate a boy with five barley loaves, "but what are they among so many people?"

6:10–13: Jesus Feeds the Crowds an Extravagant Meal beyond Anyone's Expectation or Imagination. Jesus has taken the initiative throughout. Without the crowd ever asking, and without any participation from the disciples,

> Jesus said, "Make the people sit down." Now there was a great deal of grass in the place; so they sat down, about five thousand in all. Then Jesus took the loaves, and when he had given thanks, he distributed them to those who were seated; so also the fish, as much as they wanted. When they were satisfied, he told his disciples, "Gather up the fragments

> left over, so that nothing may be lost." So they gathered them up, and from the fragments of the five barley loaves, left by those who had eaten, they filled twelve baskets.

In contrast to the Synoptics, he doesn't say, "*You* give them something to eat." He doesn't ask them to go find out how much they have, so that he can multiply their resources. John seems to have intentionally blocked off the efforts of preachers and teachers to find moralizing "lessons" or "principles" we can "apply to today."

The brief story of Jesus feeding the hungry crowds overflows with layers of meaning extending from the 30 CE ministry of Jesus through the life of the church to the publication of the canonical form of the Fourth Gospel in the first part of the second century.

1. There can be no reasonable doubt that the historical Jesus of Nazareth had compassion on hungry people and encouraged his followers to help them (cf., e.g., Matt 25:31–46).
2. Jesus ate with "sinners," that is, he disregarded the rules that had developed restricting table fellowship to those who followed the regime advocated by the Pharisees (cf., e.g., Matt 9:10–13). Jesus did not reject sinners; indeed, they were guests at his table and he at theirs, where the note of joyous celebration permeated the whole, as in Luke 5:29–30 and 7:33–34. Especially in the ancient Near East and in Jewish tradition, eating together was a sacred bond of hospitality and sharing of life.
3. Eating with his own circle of disciples was a distinctive aspect of the community Jesus formed. Following Jesus meant not only devotion to him but also close relations with fellow disciples. A major dimension of Jesus's life was that he ate with people, freely welcoming them to his table and joining them in their dinner parties. Every Eucharist is a reliving of this table fellowship. Luke especially emphasizes the dimension of eating together as integral to discipleship (see 5:29–39; 7:36–50; 11:37–54; 14:1–24; 22:14–38; 24:30–32, 36–49; Acts 10–11; 15).
4. Not on a Galilean hillside but in a room in Jerusalem Jesus celebrated a last supper with the inner core of his band of disciples. Paul (1 Cor 11:23–34) and the Synoptics (Matt 26:26–29; Mark 14:22–25; Luke 22:15–20) place the institution of the Eucharist at this meal. The story of this meal implies five dimensions of Christian faith, but not all are actualized in each account.

a. The Eucharist points backward to the life and death of Jesus of Nazareth. Jesus did not live and die only in a story. The Eucharist points to the reality of tangible, touchable, tastable events that happened in this-worldly history (1 John 1:1–3). "Do this in memory of me" points to the death of Jesus and the forgiveness of sins, Jesus's self-giving for the life of the world. Jesus's death represented his life as a whole. Pouring out his blood means he gave himself, his very life, for us ("The life of the flesh is in the blood," Lev 17:11).
b. The Eucharist points forward to an event that will happen in the eschatological future. In the narrative frameworks in Paul and the Gospels, the meal points forward to the time of the church, when this meal will continue to be reenacted and celebrated. The primary future dimension, however, is eschatological, anticipating the joy of the messianic banquet. Israel's teachers had developed a broad range of imagery expressing the final triumph of God's kingdom. The image of the messianic banquet portrays eschatological salvation as a grand banquet in which everyone is present and there is food and drink aplenty (see Gen 49:10–12; Deut 12:9–14; Isa 25:6–8; 2 Bar 29:4–8). The fragments gathered by the disciples are not leftovers but signs of the unimaginable abundance of the eschatological banquet. Think of the best dinner party you have ever attended, and multiply it by infinity.
c. The Eucharist points inward as a call to reflection and self-examination. This was already explicit in the earliest extant account (1 Cor 11:28) but is implicit in all the accounts, which relate the eucharistic meal to Judas's betrayal and the startled response, "Surely not I?" (Mark 14:19).
d. The Eucharist points upward to the transcendent realm where the risen Christ is already enthroned as Lord. To eat the bread and drink the wine is to participate in the body of Christ, the body of Christian believers that—as John especially emphasizes—is united with the heavenly Lord. In the Johannine discourse that follows the feeding narrative, John portrays this dimension of the Eucharist in intensive, shocking images (John 6:52–59). Through a generations-long process of discussion and debate, sometimes acrimonious, Christian theology developed a variety of ways of explicating the "real presence" of Christ in the eucharistic celebration and the believer's communion in the body of Christ. All are efforts to follow the direction in which the sign points.

Did Jesus "Bless" the Bread or "Give Thanks" for It?

The tradition alternates between blessing (*eulogeō*) and giving thanks (*eucharisteō*). In English the two verbs are often understood as having separate meanings. "Give thanks" is understood as a human prayer directed to God, while "bless" is thought of as a pronouncement that affects a change in the person or thing blessed. In Greek, and the underlying biblical Hebrew tradition, the words function as synonyms in such contexts. To bless God is to thank God. A common Jewish table blessing is *Baruch atah Adonai Eloheinu Melech ha-olam hamotzi lechem min ha-aretz* (Blessed art Thou, Lord our God, King of the universe who brings forth bread from the earth). See John 6:11, 23; 11:41; 12:13. John uses "giving thanks" (6:11, 23; 11:41, *eucharisteō*, thanking/blessing God for the bread). A biblical understanding of "saying the blessing" before meals means thanking God for the food, not effecting a change in the food itself.

e. The Eucharist points outward to the whole church and the whole world. This is made explicit in the Pauline and long Lukan form, where the command to repeat is given and the meal is explicitly described as a testimony to others (1 Cor 11:26; Luke 22:14–20). Matthew too has this dimension of Christian faith elsewhere (e.g., Matt 5:16; 10:32–33) and specifically includes concern for others in the eucharistic overtones of the account of the feeding of the five thousand: "You [disciples] give them [the 'outsider' crowds] something to eat" (14:16). John is especially concerned with the unity of the church, with its visible unity a testimony "so that the world may believe that you have sent me" (John 17:21). There is no *breaking* of the bread in the Johannine account, just as the body of Christ is not broken in the passion story (19:31–33), the seamless robe is not divided (19:23–25), and the net full of 153 (different kinds of?) fish is not torn (21:9–11).

In his own way, John too includes all these theological overtones, but he does not locate them in his extensive account of the Last Supper (13:1–17:26). From the earliest extant texts, the story of the feeding of the multitudes was already replete with eucharistic echoes. John preserves and intensifies these reverberations, placing his explicit eucharistic teaching in this Galilean setting. When Jesus takes the bread, gives thanks, breaks it, and gives it to the disciples, the words in John are virtually identical with Jesus's words in the Pauline and synoptic eucharistic narratives. No one in the Johannine community could have heard this story without thinking of the eucharistic celebrations in their own congregations.

6:14–15: The Crowds See the Sign, Proclaim That Jesus Is the Expected Final Prophet, and Want Jesus to Be Their King. This is a positive response. But do they really see? And do they know what it would mean to have Jesus as prophet and king? The narrative raises these questions but does not deal with them here. They are planted in the reader's mind, and the scene will emerge again in 9:17 (John, the narrative theologian, works incrementally). There the man blind from birth, after the washing/baptism and reception of the gift of sight, recognizes that Jesus is a prophet. This preliminary form of faith is on the right track and is completed not by attempting to make Jesus king but by believing in Jesus and worshiping him as Son of Man (9:35–38). In later texts, it will become clear that this includes serving him as Lord.

6:16–21: The Disciples Cross the Sea by Boat, and Jesus Comes to Them on the Water. Only John adds to the traditional story that it was *dark* and that Jesus had *not yet* come to them (6:17). If one listens for what is being said beyond the narrative level, darkness is the situation of unbelievers or those of wavering faith. Nicodemus comes to Jesus at *night* (3:1–2). Judas, after he had received the piece of bread from Jesus, will leave the community of disciples and go out *into the night* to betray Jesus (13:30). Some of Jesus's followers in the Johannine churches had experienced this darkness. They had committed themselves to the God revealed in Jesus, but in the dark distress of their threatening situation they now wondered where Jesus is (cf. p. 237 above on 1:38). The Messiah had come, he had been killed, he had promised that he would come back, but "had *not yet* come to them" in their distress (6:17). In the story, he *could* not come. They were in the boat in the darkness, far from land. He had stayed behind on the distant shore. It was not possible that he could come to them. The impossible happens, and he is with them in the boat, and they are safely across. He speaks the words that reveal God's own identity and presence, "I am" (*egō eimi*). Jesus is not here claiming to be God, but John's readers who are encouraged to hear the Scriptures as testifying to Jesus (5:39) will remember the revelation to Moses in Exodus 3:13–15, in a context that includes "I have come down to deliver them" and "I will be with you." This absolute "I am" prepares the reader for the first of Jesus's explicit "I am" sayings in the Bread of Life Discourse that immediately follows.

6:22–71: The Bread of Life Discourse and Dialogue Weaves Together Key Johannine Themes. As Jesus speaks to the "crowds" who had seen the miracle and eaten the bread and fish (6:24; cf. 6:2, 5, 22), "the Jews" (6:4, 41, 52) and his own disciples—then and now—overhear key elements of his teaching (6:3, 8, 12, 16, 22, 24, 60–61, 66). We have repeatedly seen that John's narrative theology does not allow us to separate God, Christ, salvation, church, and eschatology as discrete, stand-alone topics. We can, however, distinguish threads and, without unweaving the rainbow, listen for key themes.

Christology, Soteriology, Eschatology

For John, the Christ event is not limited to the years 1–30, God's act in the life, death, and resurrection of Jesus. The reality and presence of Christ are identical with the presence of God: past, present, and future, transcending time, from precreation to posteschaton. The conviction that this Christ has come into human history is the basis for all realistic thought and life. The messianic work is not yet done, and the Christ is still to come in the future. The Christ is present, in the here and now, speaking and acting in the world and in the life of the Johannine community.

The discourse is replete with christological titles and imagery:

- In this discourse, *Son of Man* is the overarching christological title, which both frames the discourse (6:27, 62) and is the key term in the section of sacramental teaching (6:53). The Son of Man who was expected to come down from heaven at the end has already come down from heaven as the one sent by the Father who gives life to the world. Food is necessary for life. True, real food is given by God, who gives true, real life. Jesus's claim is not in competition with God as the source of true life, for the Father who sent him has set his seal on the Son of Man who gives life (6:27). The image of God the life-giver is present in all theistic religions. All people must have bread and water (food and drink) to live. Human existence is the search for life (see pp. 222–24 above on 1:38, "Christ Is the Question"). Jesus says, "I'm it."
- Jesus is the eschatological *Good Shepherd.* This motif will be amplified in John 10, but here it is already adumbrated by allusions to the "*wilderness*" (*erēmos*, 6:31, 49) and "*plenty of grass*" (6:10 REB).

Bultmann's Famous Footnote

In a footnote to his commentary on John 6:35, Bultmann distinguishes various forms of the *egō eimi* ("I am") formula:

1. The "presentation formula," which replies to the question, "Who are you?" In this form, the *egō* is the subject, "I am Plato."
2. The "qualificatory" formula," which answers the question, "What are you?" Here, too, *egō* is the subject, "I am a philosopher."
3. The "identification formula," in which the speaker identifies himself with another person or object. Once again, *egō* is the subject, "I am the one who taught Aristotle."
4. The "recognition formula" is to be distinguished from the others by the fact that here *egō* is the predicate. It answers the question, "Who is the one who is expected, asked about, spoken of?," to which the reply is "I am he," that is, "It is I and not someone else," more colloquially, "That's me." Thus the disputed identity of the healed blind man is resolved when he says "*egō eimi*" (John 9:9 NRSV, "I am the man"; NJB, "Yes, I am the one"; CEB, "Yes, it's me").

—Rudolf Bultmann, *The Gospel of John: A Commentary*, trans. G. R. Beasley-Murray (Louisville: Westminster John Knox, 1971), 225–26

Bultmann regards all the Johannine *egō eimi* sayings as "recognition formulae" except possibly 11:25 and 14:6, which may be qualificatory formulae.

- The crowds proclaim that Jesus is "*indeed the prophet who is to come into the world*" (6:14). Their understanding is true but inadequate. While in Johannine theology the identification of John the Baptist as the expected final prophet is not true (1:21), it is true that Jesus is God's eschatological prophet, God's ultimate Word to humanity (1:14; cf. 4:19, 44; 7:40; 9:17).
- When the crowds attempt to make Jesus *king* (6:15), the readers again know that they announce a profound truth (1:49). Like Caiaphas, they say more than they know (11:50). As the one who is always in union with the Father, Jesus is indeed king, but again, not in the way that either neutral observers or opponents can understand (12:13, 15; 18:33, 37, 39; 19:3, 12, 14, 15, 19, 21).

> "Only Thou art holy; there is none beside Thee,
> Perfect in pow'r, in love, and purity."
>
> —Reginald Heber (1783–1826), "Holy, Holy, Holy"

- Jesus declares himself to be the *Son* (6:40, identified with both the Son of God and the Son of Man).
- At the conclusion of this episode, Peter confesses Jesus to be "the Holy One of God" (6:69, the Greek genitive). This scene of "Peter's confession" corresponds to the key scene in the synoptic accounts in which Peter confesses Jesus to be "the Christ" (Mark 8:29), "the Messiah, the Son of the living God" (Matt 16:16), and "the Messiah of God" (Luke 9:20). John, too, regards confession of Jesus as the Messiah, the Son of God, as the fundamental Christian confession (John 11:27; 20:30–31, at the conclusion of each of the two major divisions of the Gospel). But "Holy One of God" is not secondary or of minor significance in identifying Jesus. In the John 6 context, it is the litmus test that distinguishes those who remain faithful to Jesus as he truly is and those within the community who are "offended" (*skandalizō* = "trip up, cause to stumble") and "go away" (6:61, 67). In the Fourth Gospel, it is not insignificant that *holiness* is ascribed only to God the Father (17:11), to Jesus the Son (6:69), and to the Holy Spirit (14:26; 20:22). Though common in the LXX and the New Testament for the people of God, "saints" (*hagioi*, "holy ones") is never found in this sense in the Gospel and letters of John (though cf. the cognate verb *hagiazō* in 17:17–19, and the adjective *hagios* in 1:33; 14:26; and 20:22, with reference to the Holy Spirit the disciples receive).
- Throughout, the story highlights understanding the Christ event as both in continuity with and in contrast to *Moses*. Reflecting the debates between followers of Jesus and synagogue leaders in John's own Ephesian context, John has the Jewish leaders who are cross-examining the healed blind man say, "We know that God has spoken to Moses, but as for this man, we do not know where he comes from" (9:29). For those in the synagogue who opposed the Johannine Christian community, faithful members of the people of God are disciples of Moses, who follow the biblical Torah, not disciples of Jesus, who "makes himself God" but has no legitimate authority. The Johannine Jesus will not accept this bifurcation and discourages the Johannine Christians from thinking along the lines

of "You can have Moses, we'll take Jesus," for Moses and the Scriptures belong to the Christian community too. God did give the people bread through Moses, but it was God who did it, not Moses, and the manna was this-worldly food, not the true nourishment that humanity needs that grants eternal life (6:32). John tells the Jesus story within the framework of the Moses story and with many of its features: in the wilderness at Passover time (6:4, 31), after bringing the Twelve (6:13; disciples, not tribes) miraculously across the threatening sea and to the safety of the promised land on the west bank (6:16–21), God's people are tested (6:6). The one who had gone up the mountain and come down teaches them (6:3, 15, 59). They murmur (6:41, 43, 61), and God gives them bread (6:10–13). But the true bread that gives true life is given through Jesus, the one who was with God from the beginning and has seen the Father (6:46).

Interstate Billboard: "All You Can Eat, $9.95"

"At mealtime Boaz said to her, 'Come here, and eat some of this bread, and dip your morsel in the sour wine.' So she sat beside the reapers, and he heaped up for her some parched grain. She ate until she was satisfied, and she had some left over. When she got up to glean, Boaz instructed his young men, 'Let her glean even among the standing sheaves, and do not reproach her. You must also pull out some handfuls for her from the bundles, and leave them for her to glean, and do not rebuke her.' So she gleaned in the field until evening. Then she beat out what she had gleaned, and it was about an ephah of barley. She picked it up and came into the town, and her mother-in-law saw how much she had gleaned. Then she took out and gave her what was left over after she herself had been satisfied."

—Ruth 2:14–18

"I am the bread of life" is the primal christological image. This is the first of Jesus's "I am" sayings and the only one that is repeated (four times in this section: 6:35, 41, 48, 51; for the others, see 8:12, light; 10:7, gate; 10:11, good shepherd; 11:25, resurrection and life; 14:6, way, truth, life; 15:1, true vine). In this story, the human problem is hunger. Historians of the Roman Empire are generally agreed that for most people in the Roman world of the first century, life was a perpetual struggle for survival. This is true not only in the Roman Empire: it may be difficult for many of us well-fed moderns of the Northern Hemisphere's Western world to grasp that for most of human history, most human beings have not taken "our daily bread" for granted. Many of us may still have difficulty realizing the depth and power of the equation *to be human = to be hungry*. For many of us, the daily problem is limiting our calorie intake, and eating all we want is nothing extraordinary. We might ponder the unsentimental paragraph from the biblical story of Ruth, typical of the biblical world in which hunger is a constant threat and "eating all you want" is the promised blessing for the faithful people of God, a symbol for salvation itself (Lev 26:5 [versus 26:26]; Deut 6:11; 11:15; Ezek 36:29–30; Joel 2:19, 26). In fact, "hunger" is one of the connotations of the Hebrew word for "self, soul, person." *Nephesh* does not refer to some immortal core nested inside a physical body but refers (like both *sōma* and *psychē* in Greek usage) to the whole person, the self. *Nephesh* often has the connotation of "throat, gullet, appetite" and is probably derived from the Hebrew word for throat. We are not self-made, not self-sufficient. Just as we had no part in the beginning of our life, which was given us without our decision, so we must be nourished from outside ourselves or we shrivel up and die. Physical hunger is fundamental to being human; hunger is a metaphor for the human situation itself. Having this human hungering finally satisfied is fulfillment, salvation.

The demonic evil of physical hunger is that it not only robs us of physical life but also robs us of our humanity, our true being as children of God created to love others. Elie Wiesel tells of the numbing indifference that hunger inflicted on him in the Nazi concentration camp. He felt no pity when other prisoners starved or were killed, no inclination to share his bit of bread with anyone. "I now took little interest in anything except my daily plate of soup and my crust of stale bread. Bread, soup—these were my whole life. I was a body. Perhaps less than that even: a starved stomach."[13] Such situations reveal the character of human life generally. Humans are not self-sufficient. Life requires constant nourishment. To be human is to be hungry, even for billionaires with lavish menus constantly at their disposal, and even if they don't know what they are hungry for.

Bread is salvation for the human dilemma. Bread satisfies hunger and gives life. Throughout the Bible, "bread" refers not only to the baked mixture of grain, yeast, and water but to food as such. For much of humanity through most of human history, bread has been the staple of every meal. The five loaves in the gospel feeding stories were not rolls on a side dish, and the two fish were not the main course; the loaves were substantial, pan-sized slabs of bread, for which the small dried fish were the condiment, not necessary for a nourishing meal and not always available (cf. the traditional English "bread and butter"). Many expressions, ancient and modern, express this deep-rooted image that identifies life-giving food as such with "bread," the "staff of life." "His day job puts bread on the table." "I hate doing this, but I need the bread." In German-speaking lands, *Abendbrot* (evening bread) refers to the evening meal as such. Marie Antoinette's callous "Let them eat cake" was the French queen's response to the plaintive announcement, "The people have no bread," that is, they are dying. Every culture understands "Give us this day our daily bread" as the *human* prayer, asking for the necessities of life. To be given bread is to be given life.

In the Boxcars En Route to Auschwitz

Elie Wiesel's novel, *Night*, tells of a line of boxcars stopped in a German village en route to Auschwitz. A few bypassers on the way to work threw pieces of bread to the hungry occupants. Their efforts at being merciful created a sad spectacle. Living skeletons fought each other for a few crumbs. People stomped each other, tore and bit each other, with animal hatred in their eyes. Fingernails became claws.

"A piece fell into our wagon. I decided that I would not move. Anyway, I knew that I would never have the strength to fight with a dozen savage men! Not far away I noticed an old man dragging himself along on all fours. He was trying to disengage himself from the struggle. He held one hand to his heart. I thought at first he had received a blow on the chest. Then I understood; he had a bit of bread under his shirt. With remarkable speed he drew it out and put it to his mouth. His eyes gleamed; a smile, like a grimace, lit up his dead face. And was immediately extinguished. A shadow had just loomed up near him. The shadow threw itself upon him. Felled to the ground, stunned with blows, the old man cried:

"'Meir. Meir, my boy! Don't you recognize me? I'm your father . . . you're hurting me . . . you're killing your father! I've got some bread . . . for you too . . . for you too.'

"He collapsed. His fist was still clenched around a small piece. He tried to carry it to his mouth. But the other one threw himself upon him and snatched it. The old man again whispered something, let out a rattle, and died amid the general indifference. His son searched him, took the bread, and began to devour it. He was not able to get very far. Two men had seen and hurled themselves upon him. Others joined in. When they withdrew, next to me were two corpses, side by side, the father and the son.

"I was fifteen years old."

—Elie Wiesel, *Night* (New York: Hill & Wang, 1960), 112–13

For centuries, Israel's Scriptures had declared that human beings must have bread to live, but "one does not live by bread alone, but by every word that comes from the mouth of the LORD" (Deut 8:3, quoted by Jesus in the temptation story in Matthew [4:4] and Luke [4:4]). In the first "I am" (*egō eimi*) declarations, Jesus proclaims himself, that is, God's act in him, the true "bread of life," the one who gives authentic, abundant life (John 10:10). The disciples are correct that two hundred denarii would *not* be enough for everyone to have even a *little.* The issue of "is there life after death?" is not a matter of survival but of true life. What God offers in the Christ event is not merely survival after death but the extravagance of the fulfilled life. Both the primacy and repetition of Jesus's claim to be the bread of life indicate that it is paradigmatic in John's proclamation of Jesus as the one who gives the true life sought by all human beings (6:27, 35, 41, 48–51, 53–58). This is the salvation for which all human beings hunger, God's act in Jesus Christ that overcomes all that opposes the life God created us to have, reconciling us to God, others, and ourselves, and allowing us to live joyfully and purposefully in this world and beyond. The New Testament nowhere gives a definition of either salvation or the kingdom of God. But both are used as synonyms for *life*, real life, as God intended it to be (see, e.g., Mark 10:17–31), which John calls "eternal life."

The work of the Messiah is not yet completed. Not only is the Christ still present with the church, the Christ will return at the consummation of history to bring the work of God to fulfillment. When the Gospel was written, apocalyptic ideas and images were vibrantly alive in other writings circulating in the Johannine community. Not only the letters of Paul, but Revelation and the Johannine letters proclaim a robust faith in the future return of Jesus (Revelation throughout, esp. chaps. 1–3; 20–22; 1 John 2:18, 22, 28; 3:2–3; 4:3, 17; 2 John 7). John does not adopt the specific apocalyptic imagery and timetable of Revelation's eschatological hope, but he neither rejects this traditional eschatological thinking that had been vigorously renewed at the end of the first century, nor does he merely fit Jesus into it. For John, as for Christian faith as such, the meaning of the Christ event is not forced into a prior understanding of eschatology, but the meaning of eschatology is redefined in light of the coming of Jesus. On the one hand, the Johannine Jesus proclaims that the central events that constitute the hopes of apocalyptic eschatology are not merely a future hope but are already fulfilled in the Christ event. With the coming of Christ, the hoped-for eschatological events are happening now, in the life of Jesus and the continuing life of the church: the resurrection, final judgment, and the defeat of Satan; the coming of the Spirit; and gift of eternal life are already real in the experience of the community of faith (John 3:18–19, 36; 6:27, 47; 11:21–27; 12:31; 17:3). Nonetheless, the Fourth Gospel resists any reduction of the eschatological hope to realized eschatology and clearly affirms the reality of future apocalyptic events. As Son of Man, Jesus is the one who will raise the dead on the last day (5:28–29; 6:39, 40, 44, 54;

11:24; 12:48). In the Fourth Gospel, eschatology continues to be an essential theme, and must be so wherever the fundamental confession is that Jesus is the Christ. The story of Christ's feeding the multitude, and every celebration of eucharistic worship, is a foretaste of the messianic banquet.

Bible Study as Plaster Removal

"In 1770 the enlightened cathedral chapter of Saint-Lazare in Burgundian Autun renovated its church and, in the process, had the Romanesque Tympanon with one of the most extraordinary portrayals of the Last Judgment plastered over, since this portrayal no longer suited the times. This procedure at the apex of the French Enlightenment is symptomatic of a paradigm shift in modernity. In contrast to an earlier period, this shift reversed the forensic relationship between God and humans. No longer must human beings, as sinners, give account before the throne of their God, but God must justify himself—in view of the suffering of the world, for example—before the forum of human reason. Even theologians sometimes perceive the concept of human responsibility before the divine judge as unreasonable heteronomy over autonomous humanity."

—Reinhard Feldmeier and Hermann Spieckermann, *God of the Living: A Biblical Theology*, trans. Mark E. Biddle (Waco, TX: Baylor University Press, 2011), 469

The plaster has now been removed from the Tympanon of Autun, and even casual visitors may find themselves addressed by it. My hope is that our study together in this book removes some plaster, allowing us to hear more clearly the Word of God that comes through Scripture.

The Son of Man sent by God to give life to the world is Christ the judge. In Scripture and Jewish tradition, God is the ultimate judge, but in Johannine theology, Jesus is in unity with God, who has given him authority to exercise God's judgment as the Son of Man (5:22, 27, 30; 8:16). As an eschatological event, judgment, too, is now/not yet. Believers not only look forward to the promise and threat of a last judgment but also experience life in the present as lived before God, responsible not merely to themselves but to God. In the theocentric Johannine theology, human beings always live before this God, who knows them, loves them, and wants them to acknowledge the God who speaks in the Bible and in the Christ event as their God. God is also their judge. The whole narrative of the Gospel of John is one continuous judgment scene, in which human beings suppose they can judge God by their own standards, when the reality is that God, the God revealed in Christ, is our Judge.

The Son of Man sent by God to give life to the world represents the saving love of God for the whole world. As with Paul, whose letters circulated among the Johannine congregations, this image of God the judge is held in dialectical tension with the image of God who loves and saves the whole world. The Johannine teachers have repeatedly declared that God does not merely love and save the individual souls of believers out of the world, but loves and saves the world (3:16–17; 4:42; 6:33; 9:5; 10:36; 12:32, 47; 17:15, 18, 21, 23; 1 John 2:2; 4:9–10, 14).

Ecclesiology: Life between the Times

As this story was heard in the worship and instruction of the Johannine house churches, the paradigmatic scene not only evoked christological images of God's saving act in Jesus. The hearers recognized themselves, the history and character of their own Christian experience as members of the Johannine churches. The story of feeding the five thousand is replete with churchly imagery: God's calling a large community into existence and nurturing its life by teaching, worship, Scripture, and sacraments. John's intended hearer-readers would likely resonate with the following aspects of their own Christian experience.

6:2, 9: "A large crowd . . . so many people." The traditional story had pictured the crowd that followed Jesus and was taught and fed by him as four or five thousand people (see above). The intention of Matthew's addition of "besides women and children" is to make the multitude even larger (Matt 14:21; 15:38). All the evangelists want to show that the community of believers to which the readers belong is a vast multitude. The Johannine community had suffered severe problems; many members had left; and they were tempted to bemoan the membership and attendance statistics in their shrinking congregations. They needed to be reassured that they belonged to something larger than the little house churches scattered about Roman Asia.

6:44: "Drawn by the Father." The church to which John's hearer-readers belong had been called into being by God. The story pictures Jesus, his band of twelve disciples, and the crowds that follow him (John 6:1–2). The crowds have seen his signs and, at Jesus's command, have been seated by the disciples, but they are fed personally by Jesus himself, have come to believe that he is the eschatological prophet sent from God, and want to make him king (6:14–15). They "seek" and "find" him (6:24–25; cf. 1:35–45!). Yet as the story unfolds, it becomes clear that the initiative in calling the church into being was not from them but from God. As in the call scenes of 1:19–51, there are those who "follow Jesus" who are not disciples. The church is not a voluntaristic association of good people seeking to become more spiritual or make the world a better place. It is God through Christ who calls the church into being. The Johannine teachers express this faith within their own version of the understanding of election and predestination developed by Paul and other early Christian teachers, whose writings were circulating among the churches of Roman Asia and would later be accepted as canonical by the whole church. Those who become followers of Jesus make their own decisions, but in retrospect, they come to see that God is the responsible actor in their conversion to Christ and inclusion in the Christian community. John's term for this is used for the first time in 6:44: "No one can come to me unless *drawn* by the Father who sent me." "Drawn" is a form of the verb *helkō*, defined in the standard Greek lexicon with the primary meaning "To move an object from one area to another in a pulling motion, *draw*, with implication that the object being moved is incapable of propelling itself or in the case of a person is unwilling to do so voluntarily, in either case with implication of exertion on the part of the mover."[14] The word was occasionally used metaphorically but always with the connotation of compelling force. Of the eight occurrences in the New Testament, only three are outside the Fourth Gospel: in Acts 16:19 and 21:30, of being physically dragged before the authorities or out of the temple, and in James 2:6, of poor people being dragged into court by their wealthy opponents. Three instances in John picture Peter drawing his sword (John 18:10), the disciples' inability to haul the net full of fish into the boat (21:6), and Peter hauling the net full of fish to shore (21:11). In John 12:32, Jesus declares, "And I, when I am lifted up (*hypsoō*) from the earth, will draw all people to myself." This has been (mis)understood to mean that the post-Easter preaching of the gospel "lifts up" Jesus, and that such preaching attracts people to become Christians; all who hear the message are invited, but the decision is theirs. In John's theology, however, "lifting up" is a double entendre; it is never used for what preachers and church members do but refers both to Jesus being lifted up on the cross by his human adversaries and to God's exalting him to heaven to be Lord of all (3:14; 8:28; 12:32, 34). The risen Christ calls all people to himself, that is, to God. The call is not just an invitation but an effective call. Jesus being "lifted up" on the cross does not make Jesus attractive. Crucifixions were horrible events. They might draw a crowd, but they did not generate disciples. In Johannine theology, human beings lifted up Jesus on the cross, but this was part of God's lifting up Jesus, exalting him to the transcendent realm as divine Lord. God's act in Christ relocates people, reconciling them to God and moving them into

God's kingdom. Through this event, the supreme manifestation of God's love, God reconciles the world and draws his children into renewed relationship with their Father. The feeding story of John 6 pictures large numbers of people who "follow" Jesus the prophet and wonder-worker, hoping for more miracles and wanting to make him king, but only a few who have been called by Jesus into the community of Christian faith. Again: what we have here is not a repudiation of human responsibility, nor is it an explanation that everyone is invited but only a few respond. This is the retrospective confessional language of the believing community, which affirms that they belong to the church called into being by God, not that they have formed a voluntary association of Jesus followers. God's drawing of people to himself is effective, will not finally be frustrated, will ultimately include all creation, and will do so without negating human freedom and responsibility.

Some members of the Johannine congregations addressed by the Gospel may have thought of themselves as having been persuaded by the miracles worked by traveling missionaries, by their powerful preaching, or by their example of unselfish love. Without denying their own decision and responsibility, the Johannine teachers want this story to communicate the word of the risen Christ, who teaches the church not to congratulate itself on its own insight, decision, and accomplishment but to give thanks to God who has *drawn* them into the community of faith (cf. Phil 2:12–13, probably known within Johannine circles).

Jesus/Disciples/the Twelve

The calling of the disciples generates a community. The Gospel narrative is about God's act in Jesus, but Jesus-and-his-disciples is an irreducible unit, like vine-and-branches: no vine, no branches, but also no branches, no vine (John 15:1–11). Until the passion story in chapters 18–19, the narrative is never about Jesus alone, but from the calling of the disciples in 1:19–51 onward, Jesus and the disciples are inseparable ("disciple," *mathētēs*, occurs seventy-three times in the Fourth Gospel). The abundant grass of the feeding scene (6:10) evokes the image of Jesus the Good Shepherd (10:1–30; cf. Ps 23). "Shepherd of the sheep" (John 10:2) seems redundant but emphasizes that shepherd-without-sheep is as unthinkable as sheep-without-shepherd. Jesus's call to decision implies an ecclesiology. Confession of Jesus as Messiah is at the same time confession of one's own self-understanding as a member of the flock. "The Lord is *my* shepherd" is not individualistic piety but means belonging to the community of disciples called into being by the voice of the shepherd/pastor who speaks in Christian preaching. To be a disciple of Jesus is to belong to this community. Though none of the Gospels uses the term *koinōnia* (fellowship, community), and *ekklēsia* (church) is found only in Matthew 16:18 and 18:17, both words were important expressions of the community's self-understanding (*koinōnia*, 1 John 1:3, 6, 7; *ekklēsia*, 3 John 6, 9, 10, and often in Revelation), just as they were in the neighboring churches in Roman Asia. For the Johannine teachers, to be a follower of Jesus is to belong to a large community nourished and taught by him.

The either/or dualism of the Fourth Gospel is both tempered and accentuated by John's repeated rejection of the attempt of some figures in the story to be in-between, to admire Jesus but not to identify with the church (John 12:42–43). This Johannine point is made by the hesitancy of the parents of the healed blind man, in contrast to the man himself, to name Jesus as the one who has given him sight (9:18–34), and the increasing courage of "believers" such as Nicodemus to publicly identify with Jesus (3:1–9; 7:50; 19:39). Willingness to be baptized, to participate in eucharistic worship, to be associated with the *name* of Jesus is the mark of a true disciple, for it can be dangerous to wear Jesus's name (1:12; 2:23; 3:18; 15:21; 20:31; see below on John's sacramental theology).

The Twelve emerge in this scene for the first time in the Fourth Gospel (6:67; cf. 6:70, 71; 20:24), introducing the issue of structured leadership among the followers of Jesus. The place of apostles and clerical leadership was a bone of contention in the Johannine community. Neither "twelve" nor "apostle" is found in 1–3 John, but Revelation is permeated by "twelve" (twenty-two times, including "the twelve apostles" at 21:14 as foundational for the new Jerusalem). Revelation describes the ecumenical church as constituted of "saints and apostles and prophets" (18:20), with the apostles playing an important role (2:2; 21:14). On the other hand, the Fourth Evangelist never uses the phrase "twelve disciples." "Apostle" is used only once, in the general sense of "messenger" (John 13:16). In the feeding story and discourse that begins in 6:1, Jesus and the disciples are distinguished from the crowd that follows Jesus (6:12), but as the story unfolds, "the disciples" seem to morph into "the Twelve." Only six are ever named: Andrew, Peter, Philip, Nathanael, Judas Iscariot, and Judas not Iscariot. In addition, there is the Beloved Disciple from 13:23 on, who may be identical with the anonymous disciple called along with Andrew in 1:35–42 as the first of Jesus's disciples. The teachers of the Johannine community offer incremental instruction to a group of congregations struggling with what it means to belong to the one, holy, catholic, apostolic church. Jesus's prayer in John 17:1–26 will encourage them along the way. In chapter 21, the teachers will offer their conclusive word, which they believe is instruction from the risen Christ.

Sacramental Worship of a Baptized Community.

The stories and discourses of the Fourth Gospel simply cannot be understood outside the context of Christian worship. A story that speaks of eating the flesh and drinking the blood of Jesus presupposes an audience of those who regularly meet together in eucharistic worship and hear Jesus Christ say, "This is my flesh, this is my blood," words that, if taken seriously at all, can only evoke consternation among outsiders. (The wording of the eucharistic liturgy had not been standardized when the Fourth Gospel was written. Like their contemporary Ignatius, the Johannine churches speak of "flesh" instead of "body," emphasizing the reality of the incarnation.)

Johannine worship and church life were sacramental. I here use "sacrament" in the rough-and-ready sense of "an outward sign of an inward grace, a human act in which God is present and active." In the Johannine congregations of the third Christian generation, believers were baptized, the Eucharist was celebrated, and the message of the Scripture and the teaching of Jesus were proclaimed, all by human beings. The Gospel narrative is so constructed that those who hear it read in worship and instruction are guided and encouraged to see the presence of and acts of God in these human acts.

Baptism: Water and Spirit

The feeding scene and related discourse make no direct reference to baptism. John's Gospel as a whole, however, makes it clear that baptism is presupposed throughout as integral to Christian discipleship. The following are tips of a Johannine theological iceberg:

- The narrative opens with John the Baptist, who preaches and baptizes converts, explaining that he is not the Messiah, and that the baptism he administers is inferior to the baptism to be given by the Messiah, Jesus the Son of God, who will baptize in the Holy Spirit (1:19–30).
- Jesus was baptized by John the Baptist, who testifies that he saw the Spirit descend on Jesus, that it was given to him "without measure," and that "it remained on him" (1:32–33; 3:34).
- With John the Baptist's encouragement, some of his disciples who had been baptized by him began to follow Jesus (1:35–37). According to Acts 19:1–7, "the" church in Ephesus had incorporated people baptized by

John the Baptist who knew nothing of the Spirit. This corresponds to the Fourth Gospel's account, in which John the Baptist's disciples became disciples of Jesus but did not and could not yet receive the Spirit (John 1:35–37; 7:37–39).

- The promised "baptism in the Holy Spirit" to be given by Jesus was not and could not be fulfilled during his earthly ministry. Though in the narrative of his pre-Easter ministry Jesus spoke of the necessity of being born of the Spirit (3:3–5) and of worship in the Spirit (4:23), and identified his word as Spirit and life (6:63), all this was spoken retrospectively, since in the evangelist's view the Spirit was not given until after the resurrection (7:37–39; 19:30; 20:22).
- Jesus himself began to baptize his own followers with water, and his converts became more numerous than John the Baptist's, evoking the complaint from John the Baptist's disciples, "Here he is baptizing, and all are going to him" (3:22–26). The narrator's clarification in 4:2 that "it was not Jesus himself but his disciples who baptized" is often explained as the evangelist's somewhat embarrassed attempt to reconcile conflicting traditions, but this hardly does justice to Johannine theology. John's narrative collapses the temporal horizons between the Jesus "back there" in history and the Jesus "up there" in the transcendent world who is also present and active in the life of the church. No one in the Johannine congregations of Roman Asia in 90–130 had been baptized by the flesh-and-blood Jesus of Nazareth of 30 CE; they had been baptized by Jesus's disciples, and their disciples. But the risen Christ was truly present in these acts. Christian believers of later generations were baptized by Christ. These pictures of Jesus who baptizes during his pre-Easter ministry but does not give the Spirit until after Easter are not to be logically or chronologically harmonized, but represent the Johannine narrative fusion of Jesus's life and the work of the risen Christ in the life of the church.
- John does not argue that those who become Jesus's disciples should be baptized, nor does he picture Jesus giving a command to be baptized. Like Paul (e.g., Rom 6), he assumes baptism as integral to the Christian life and argues from this presupposition, not for it. Thus the significance of baptism is implicit in some other stories and images. The man born blind is sent to "wash" (*niptō*) in the pool of Siloam. John goes out of his way to call attention to the translation of "Siloam" as "sent." Throughout the Gospel, Jesus is the Sent One; to be "washed" in Siloam/the Sent One seems to be the Johannine parallel to what the Christians in his neigh-

> borhood call being baptized into Christ (Gal 3:27; Rom 6:4; 1 Cor 12:13). Again, such sacramental language is incomprehensible to outsiders who do not share the experience. The invitation of the Johannine church is, "Come and see" (John 1:39, 46; 4:29). The story as a whole allows readers to see a reflection of their own experience: previously blind, then "washed," then growing through stages of their understanding of Jesus, from "prophet" to "Son of Man," then in conflict with the synagogue (9:1–41). At the Last Supper, Jesus washes the feet of the disciples. Among the meanings of this multilayered text, John's readers would be struck by Jesus's insistence that unless he "washes" them, they do not belong to him (13:8). These words at the beginning of Jesus's instructions to his disciples form a bracket with Jesus's declaration to Nicodemus at the beginning of his confrontation with the world, in which being born of water and Spirit is integral to being "born from above" (3:1–8).

The evangelist makes it unmistakably clear that the feeding scene is transparent to the eucharistic worship of the church. The word "Eucharist" was already present in the tradition, as evidenced by the synoptic accounts, but John repeats the word for emphasis, summing up the whole scene as "the place where the Lord said the eucharistic prayer" (6:11, 23 [my translation]).

The community of faith, "born from above" (1:12–13; 3:1–5), began as babes that must be nurtured. The story of feeding the thousands dramatically illustrated that what human beings hunger and thirst for has been provided by God in the Christ event. John's story has identified the gift given to the hungry people as Jesus's teaching, his own words, which are the spirit and life of the community (6:63). Jesus the teacher (6:69) is pictured as directly feeding the multitudes himself.

"How?"—Good Question or Unintended Arrogance?

In the Fourth Gospel, when Jesus makes assertions that transcend conventional human logic, his opponents regularly ask the logical question, "How?" (*pōs*). The first instance, from Nicodemus in 3:4, 9, sets the tone for the whole series. See 4:9; 6:42, 52; 7:15; 8:33; 9:10, 15, 16, 19; 12:34. On only one occasion do the believing disciples use this formula, giving Jesus the occasion to teach them better (14:8–12). For the Johannine school, posing the challenge "how" is the typical response of the unbeliever, who supposes that a satisfactory answer can be given within the this-worldly from-below framework of human reason, and that God must be accountable before the bar of human reason.

The main point, disputed among the Johannine Christians, concerned the presence of the Lord in the eucharistic celebration. In accord with the realism of the Johannine incarnational theology (see pp. 171–74, 200–204 above on 1:14), the eucharistic meal involves participation in the life given to the believer by the Lord, who became incarnate in flesh and blood. As the Messiah did not remain a purely spiritual heavenly being but shared our human life, the eucharistic meal unites believers with Jesus just as he is united with the Father. The evangelist's Jewish opponents reject this because they do not accept Jesus as the one sent by God from heaven (6:52). It is not always noticed that the story also pictures many of Jesus's own disciples leaving the community because they rejected his eucharistic teaching (6:60). John's readers recognize these as the "progressive" members and their teachers who advocate an early form of what came to be called docetism (see 2 John 9). The Johannine teachers insist that Christ himself is present in the Eucharist but not in some purely spiritual way that does not involve his flesh and blood. The factual reality of both the presence of the risen Christ and his incarnation in flesh and blood is affirmed, without presenting a theory of how this can be understood.

This corresponds to the view prevalent in the Johannine community and emphasized by the Johannine Jesus, who cites the prophetic word that "they shall all be taught by God" (Isa 54:13; Jer 31:34; John 6:45; cf. 1 John 2:20, 27, and Revelation's prophetic instruction with no reference to human teachers). Some in the Johannine community are advocating the necessity of authorized human teachers to keep the church on course amid the turbulence of church life at the end of the first century. Others claim to be nurtured directly by the risen Christ in the spiritual experiences of the whole congregation. In the story, *twelve* baskets of fragments are gathered, not by Jesus himself but by the Twelve. We might ask, "What happened to the twelve baskets of fragments?" Some of John's hearer-readers might see this picture as pointing to the Christian teaching, the bread of life that continues to nourish their own Christian faith. The fragments come from Jesus, are collected by the Twelve, and are handed on to the hearer-readers. Perhaps being taught by authorized human teachers is not an alternative to being taught by the risen Christ but a way the living Christ continues in the church as its Teacher. The Johannine teacher-authors cite both Scripture and Jesus to support a view already circulating in the Johannine community. They will not give up on the divine presence and teaching in the community, even though it is adopting human leadership, teachers, and structure. Jesus himself distributes, as Jesus himself baptizes. "Jesus himself" or "just his disciples" is a false choice, not an option for Johannine theology. How (not whether) Jesus's presence and authority are mediated by his disciples is the question in Johannine and Roman Asian Christianity in the transition from the first to the second Christian century. Jesus is not only handed on in the tradition but is directly present. Jesus is not only directly present but is mediated by the tradition. Just as not merely his disciples but Jesus himself baptizes (John 3:22, 26; 4:1–2), so he does not delegate the distribution of the bread and fish to the disciples but hands them out himself. Johannine theology affirms the "real presence" in both the Eucharist and baptism. This is also true of the church's preaching and teaching, which John sees from a sacramental perspective. The Johannine teachers would not have drawn a firm line between "word" and "sacraments."

Preaching and teaching function as the hearing and interpretation of Scripture. Both baptism and the Eucharist had a threefold orientation: significance for the individual believer, unity with the body of Christian believers, and evangelistic witness to outsiders. *Baptism* had always included taking a public stand that identified the believer with a group recognized and generally disdained by the public at large. John scorns those who claim to be followers of Jesus but are not willing to identify with the church (9:18–23; 12:42–43). Among the Pauline churches, one dimension of the *Eucharist* was that of testimony, the proclamation of the meaning of the Lord's death to outsiders (1 Cor 11:26). So also for John, eucharistic worship was not the private ritual of believers who wanted to keep a low profile but also make a testimony to the world. This may be one of the reasons John places his eucharistic scene and instruction not at the Last Supper, when Jesus is alone with a few disciples, but outdoors among the thousands of his public ministry.

So also the church's preaching and teaching were not only for nourishing the spiritual life of individual members and strengthening the corporate life and mission of the church, but were also directed to the world (see pp. 228–30 above on evangelistic mission). Here two distinctive Johannine perspectives are important. (1) The church's message from and about Jesus Christ is founded on the Scripture. (2) Jesus Christ is not only the content of the message but is himself the active Preacher and Teacher in proclaiming this message. The Johannine teachers have a sacramental view of the preaching and teaching ministry of the church.

The church's proclamation of Jesus Christ interprets the Scripture as the Word of God. Presumably the evangelist himself and a minority of members of the Johannine churches were ethnic Jews who had become Christian believers. They had grown up in the synagogue and had always assumed the people of God had Holy Scripture to guide them. They had internalized much of its content and imagery. They now heard the Scripture with new ears and saw its images with new eyes. The amazing thing to those of us who are gentile church members in the modern world is that the gentile majority of Johannine Christians, in a church now in its third generation, had also learned much of the Bible's content, so that only a phrase or two evoked images in their imaginations, images of the biblical world strangely different from their everyday world (cf. "Four score and seven years ago . . . ," "Mine eyes have seen the glory . . . ," "Remember Pearl Harbor . . . ," "One if by land . . . ," all of which are lost on outsiders not immersed in the stream of American history). The evangelist is a deft literary artist who knows how to evoke a whole scene with a phrase or image. The fleeting reference to "charcoal fire" of 21:9 recalls 18:18 and Peter's threefold denial, which is about to be redeemed by his threefold confession. The story of feeding the thousands, like the Gospel of John in general, not only includes explicit citations from Scripture by both his disputants and Jesus himself (John 6:31 = Ps 78:24; John 6:45 = Isa 54:13), but numerous allusions. The *barley* loaves, found only in John's version of the story, conjure up the whole biblical scene in which Elisha feeds a large group with a small number of barley loaves, with much food left over (John 6:9 = 2 Kings 4:42–43). The Gospel of John was written to be heard in a congregation that was familiar with, and nourished by, the reading and interpretation of Scripture.

Jesus Christ is both proclaimed and proclaimer. A key issue in the Johannine community was whether the risen Christ continued to act and speak directly in the life of the church, or whether only the emerging church leadership acts and speaks in his name, sometimes labeled "charismatic" and "institutional" leadership. When outsiders were converted by Christian preaching, was their call to Christian faith from Christ himself or only from his disciples, through a secondhand or thirdhand chain of tradition? When converts were baptized and received the Holy Spirit, were they baptized by Jesus or only by his (third-generation) disciples? When they received the eucharistic bread and wine, did they receive it from the risen Christ or only from their fellow Christians or congregational leaders? When they heard the Scriptures expounded in preaching and teaching, did human preachers and teachers speak to them or did Christ speak to them? When personal or church problems arose that required pastoral care, did the risen Christ, the Good Shepherd, continue to lead his people directly or did that leadership come only through authorized pastors? When new doctrines appeared, some of which could be an appropriate and necessary accommodation to changing circumstances and others of which could represent a dangerous betrayal of the faith, did the Good Shepherd himself protect them directly from wolves in sheep's clothing or should the Johannine members understand that the risen Christ acts and speaks through authorized agents? Or are these the wrong questions? The Johannine teachers affirm *both* that "Jesus baptized" (John 3:26; 4:1) and that "not Jesus himself" but his disciples baptized (4:2). This seems to be a sacramental understanding of the emerging Christian ministry. The church's pastors preach, teach, and serve the eucharistic meal. In and through their acts and speech, the living Christ continues to act and speak. This claim is made not by a discursive explanation of how this is so—note John's suspicion of this unbelieving "how" (*pōs*; see p. 264 above).

This was ministry in a shrinking church that was struggling between sectarianism and ecumenism. The Fourth Gospel's first audience had been encouraged to think of themselves as belonging to a large church, thousands of members consisting of both Jewish and gentile Christians (see pp. 90, 258 above on 4:21–24; 10:16; 12:20–26; 17:20–24). Their own experience of church life, however, threatened to be disappointing and depressing.

Exit Interview Overheard outside a First-Century Synagogue

"Heard you had quite a crowd at the outdoor service yesterday."

"Some say we had over five thousand. Miracles, food for everyone. A long sermon in the synagogue today, though."

"How many do you have today?"

"Twelve, and a couple of those are pretty shaky."

"And?"

"Some talk about getting a new preacher."

A major split had developed within the Johannine community itself. Conflicts not only were with unbelieving Jewish outsiders but also arose among insiders, many of whom left the Johannine authors' own community. There were presumably a complex of factors—social, political, personal, and theological—but the authors of the Gospel of John see this departure as triggered by the incarnational theology advocated by the Johannine school, in opposition to "progressive" proto-Gnosticism, especially as expressed in its understanding of the Eucharist. Those who departed were disciples of Jesus (6:60, 66), just as those who wanted to kill him were Jewish followers who *believed* in him, that is, they represented Jewish Christians of the evangelist's own time (8:30–31, 37). The majority departed. The canonical tradition we have in Revelation, 1–3 John, and the Gospel of John represents the minority viewpoint of the Christians of Roman Asia in 90–130. The Johannine teachers understand their adherence to the faith expressed in this tradition, its preservation and transmission to others, to be the gift of God and the answer to Jesus's own prayer. It was not theoretical, commonsense discussion but a question of how the faith that keeps one in the authentic people of God is generated and nourished. They understood this to be the Spirit of God, *pneuma*, not *sarx*, expressed in the *logos/logoi* communicated in the teaching of (the risen) Jesus. The issues were Eucharist, Christology, and baptism as public identification with the community and its confession. In the Gospel of John, "Peter's confession" comes in *this* context. Jesus is the "Holy One of God," whose words give eternal life. For the Johannine school, "holy" is reserved for God. Calling Jesus the "Holy One of God" both identifies him with and distinguishes him from God. His words communicate eternal life (6:66–70). The Johannine letters and the Gospel of John represent the minority remnant of a split in the Johannine community. The Pauline churches faithful to the apostle's tradition were also the minority (2 Tim 1:15; cf. 4:3, 10, 11, 16). We should not suppose that what became mainline Christian faith and the documents finally accepted as canonical were simply the popular majority.

In book one, the Triumphal Entry or Book of Signs (John 2–12), Jesus has been speaking to the world. When Jesus speaks to his disciples in the Farewell Discourse, one of the main issues will be "What is the way forward for this small community of believers in Jesus who understand their faith in a way that separates them not only from nonbelievers but also from the majority of others who identify themselves as followers of Jesus?"

Book Two, the Triumphal Departure and Return: Farewell Instruction for Those Left Behind (13:1–21:25)

In Book One, chapters 1–12, Jesus as the incarnate Word confronts and addresses the world. The world is his, belongs to him (*ta idia*), for it was made through him. He is no alien, no intruder from another world. Jesus speaks to the world. At the narrative level, his message and teaching are addressed to the world, not to his disciples. The people of the world (*hoi idioi*) are also his, the beloved creatures of God. But they reject him (1:11). This phrase is not used again until 13:1, where Jesus gathers those who have received him, *hoi idioi*, "his own," for direct, clear instruction on the meaning of the

Christ event. Book One portrays *hoi idioi* as rejecting their creator, though some receive him and become God's children. In Book Two, Jesus's "own," including the later believers who have never seen Jesus, acknowledge him as Teacher and Lord (13:13), climaxed by Thomas's confession, "My Lord and my God!" (20:28), and receive the blessing of the risen Christ (20:29).

Readers must attend to John's own narrative chronology. Book One comprises more than two years. Book Two recounts the last night of Jesus's life, his death, and his resurrection, Thursday evening through Sunday, with a climactic final appearance of the risen Jesus one week later. The Fourth Gospel narrates no "Holy Week." The narrative goes directly from Jesus's procession into Jerusalem, the announcement that Greeks are seeking Jesus, and Jesus's response (12:1–50), to the Last Supper. It is a meal, on Thursday evening, but not a Passover meal—the Passover will be celebrated the next day (18:28). Jesus's first and only action is to wash the feet of the disciples. There is no institution of the Eucharist—John's instruction has been given in the context of feeding the multitudes (6:1–53). Jesus is present and speaks, at great length, not to the world but to the disciples. All Jesus's teaching to his disciples is given on one evening, in the longest discourse in the New Testament, virtually unbroken for five chapters. The narrative does not focus on anything outside the room. The hearer-readers are in the presence of Jesus and his disciples, and only get one glimpse of the outside world, as they/we peer out into the darkness into which Judas departs (13:31).

The disciples, like the readers, have overheard Jesus's teaching in the previous chapters. Now they, and we the readers, are addressed directly and clearly. Previous instruction has been indirect, in figurative language. Now Jesus speaks to them "plainly, not in any figure of speech" (16:25–30). Jesus gives his own terse summary of the whole gospel: I came into the world; I am going back (16:28). In chapters 1–12, Jesus speaks objectively, about himself in symbolic figures such as the shepherd and the light of the world. The Farewell Discourse is dominated by the language of "you and I," as in "I am the vine, you are the branches" (15:5). Book One mostly uses the I-it objectifying language of "theology." The Farewell Discourse tends toward insider language, the I-thou language of personal address (classic distinction since Buber in 1958). The hearer-readers in the Johannine congregations, and we later "I" readers, still overhear what is said to someone else, but now we can identity directly with those addressed in the narrative.

The six signs in chapters 1–12 now find the fulfillment to which they have all pointed, the one sign in chapters 13–21, compressed into the narrative of Jesus's death and resurrection. The Farewell Discourse/Passion-

Resurrection Narrative is all one great sign, *the* sign of God's saving act in Christ that generates faith in the believing community.

The Christ Event Narrated and Interpreted: Collapsing of Temporal Horizons

The *contemporaneity* of the Gospel's narrative theology is sharply focused in the Farewell Discourse. The narrative level in which Jesus speaks to the there-and-then disciples on the night before he is killed is fused with the future perspective in which the risen Christ addresses Christian believers of later generations, from the beginnings of the church to the readers' own time and place, wherever the Gospel is read and proclaimed as Christian Scripture. Johannine theology proclaims that the Eternal One has come into time, the Absolute has lived among us in the relativities of human existence, the one true God (17:3) has entered into history and shared our finite existence. How is it possible to think and talk about this? John's answer, like that of New Testament authors generally, is to tell the story, to dissolve the irreducible affirmations of the good news into a narrative in such a way that they cannot be precipitated out into the consistent propositions of discursive language. Jesus's first words to his disciples in the Farewell Discourse are "You do not know now what I am doing, but later you will understand" (13:7). This "later" embraces not only the future insight of the disciples present at the Last Supper but that of all future believers who hear Jesus's words of the Gospel from the later perspective looking back on the cross and resurrection. We may ponder a few of these words that instruct us in how to understand them all, fusing past/present/future.

- The disciples, and the readers, have already been present in scenes that portray the divine glory revealed in the Christ event, beginning already in the prologue (1:14; 2:11; 11:4, 40). The narrator tells us readers that the disciples have already seen his glory, as in 2:11, but we readers are also told that Jesus was not yet glorified and that believers could not yet understand because they require the Holy Spirit, which was not yet given (7:39; 12:16). The "hour" of Jesus's glorification had not yet come prior to the crucifixion/resurrection (2:4; 4:21; 5:28; 7:30; 8:20; 17:1, 5). Yet the Johannine Jesus announces, during his ministry and on the evening prior to his crucifixion/glorification, that "the hour has come" (12:23; 13:1; 17:1) and that the Son of Man *has been glorified* (13:31). Occasionally the Johannine Jesus speaks of the hour as both "coming" and "now here"

(4:23; 5:25; 16:32). This already/not-yet is inherent in the confession that Jesus is the Christ, the one who has come and is to come.

- The Johannine Jesus speaks to people who have been washed, purified, and given the Spirit, though at the narrative level they (or some of them) have presumably been baptized by John the Baptist, just as Jesus was. All are washed and purified by Jesus at the Last Supper, and receive the Spirit from the crucified Jesus the next day (19:30, "he handed over the Spirit" [so NAB; cf. commentaries] to the disciples) or from the risen Christ on the first Easter (20:22). The speaker of the Farewell Discourse is the post-Easter, postconversion, risen Christ who speaks to the church, from within the same revelatory configuration as in the Apocalypse of John, which circulated in the churches of Roman Asia alongside the writings of the Johannine school. Revelation and gospel are, of course, different literary genres. Revelation represents the message of the risen Christ in the form of apocalyptic oracles. In the narrative form of John's Gospel, the pre-Easter Jesus speaks to pre-Spirit disciples. This revelatory gestalt is John's form of the messianic secret.

In 14:7–9 Jesus tells the disciples that the prospect of the eschatological vision of God is already realized in their present experience, collapsing the 30 CE experience of encountering the incarnate Word in the life and teaching of Jesus, Jesus's return to the Father at the death/resurrection, the disciples' insight into God's revelation mediated through the risen Christ/Holy Spirit in the life of the church, and the eschatological vision of God at the parousia (cf. 1 John 3:1–3; Matt 5:8, where present purity of heart and eschatological vision of God are combined, as in the Farewell Discourse).

In 16:33, Jesus declares, "In the world you face persecution. But take courage; I have conquered the world!" As in Revelation, "conquer" (*nikaō*) looks back on Jesus's life/death/resurrection/ascension as the saving act of God, who "conquers" by lamb-power.

In 17:12, "While I was with them . . ." looks back, from the church's stance, on the earthly life of Jesus.

John has repeatedly referred to the "lifting up" of Jesus in a way that collapses crucifixion, resurrection, and ascension into one event (3:14; 8:28; 12:32, 34). In the words of conventional narrative, everything cannot be said at once. The crucifixion and resurrection must necessarily be narrated diachronically—Jesus died on Friday and was raised on Sunday. But a picture can be synchronous, showing the crucified Christ as the glorified Christ (as do many artistic portrayals, e.g., by placing a halo on the head of the suffering Christ). The *word pictures* of the gospel narrative mode can do this too, allowing the glory of the risen Christ to shine through the crucifixion scene.

Narrative is necessarily diachronic: one word after another, one scene after another. Even flashbacks and flash-forwards remain diachronic skips along a chronological line. When John chose the gospel narrative genre, he opted for a rhetorical strategy of communication that necessarily calls for delineation of *the* sign as a series of separate signs. The crucifixion is a this-worldly event in history observable by spectators through this-worldly eyes, whether hostile or friendly. Vital to Johannine incarnational theology is the conviction that in God's saving act, the transcendent, transtemporal reality of God's act is grounded in the historical reality of the cross. Other events—the narrative of the meaning of Jesus's death, resurrection, ascension, sending the Spirit, and return in glory—are in a different ontological category than the observable events of this world. To be *narrated*, they must bend and collapse temporal categories. Giving narrative shape to a theological reality grounded in the cross produces some awkwardness in the traditional chronological story line. To make the point that the incarnate, human Jesus who had been known as a friend in 30 CE Palestine cannot be held on to, the risen Jesus forbids Mary Magdalene to touch him because he has "not yet ascended" (20:17). She is not to hold on to the "historical Jesus" of the past but to go and announce Jesus's resurrection/ascension (20:17). A week later, to make the point of the reality of Jesus's resurrection and the identity of the crucified and risen one, the risen Jesus invites Thomas to touch him (20:26–29; cf. 1 John 1:1–3). Each of these scenes communicates the reality and unity of Jesus's death and resurrection, but it would be a genre mistake to suppose that the narrative wants the reader to believe an ascension to heaven and return to Jerusalem had occurred between John 20:17 and 20:27, or to find a "contradiction" between "don't touch" to Mary and "touch" to Thomas.

Foot Washing as Paradigmatic Dramatization of the Christ Event

Jesus's only act in these five chapters is to wash the disciples' feet. The brief narrative dramatizes the whole Christ event. It parallels the celebration of God's saving act portrayed in a Christian hymn contemporary with the composition of the Fourth Gospel and probably known to both author and the Gospel's first audience (Phil 2:5b–11). The story of the foot washing has the same structure as the hymn, picturing the same U-shaped event of God's saving act in Christ:

I JOHN	I PHILIPPIANS	I
John 13:3: Jesus, knowing that the Father had given all things into his hands, and that he had come from God and was going to God,	Phil 2:5b–6: Christ Jesus, who, though he was in the form of God, did not regard equality with God as something to be exploited,	The drama begins with the preexistence of Christ in the heavenly world.
II	II	II
13:4–5: got up from the table, took off his outer robe, and tied a towel around himself. Then he poured water into a basin and began to wash the disciples' feet and to wipe them with the towel that was tied around him. . . .	2:7–8: but emptied himself, taking the form of a slave, being born in human likeness. And being found in human form, he humbled himself and became obedient to the point of death—even death on a cross.	Christ does not hold on to his heavenly glory but lays it aside and comes to this world as a truly human being. He lives out his life as a servant of others, giving his life for them in humble service and finally by dying.
III	III	III
13:12–13: After he had washed their feet, had put on his robe, and had returned to the table, he said to them, . . . "You call me Teacher and Lord—and you are right, for that is what I am."	2:9–12: Therefore God also highly exalted him and gave him the name that is above every name, so that at the name of Jesus every knee should bend, in heaven and on earth and under the earth, and every tongue should confess that Jesus Christ is Lord, to the glory of God the Father. Therefore, my beloved . . .	Christ returns to his heavenly glory. In the Philippians hymn, this is God's act in raising up Jesus. In John, the unity of Father and Son is pictured as Jesus himself putting his robe back on and returning to his previous status. In each text, instruction on the meaning of this event is given by the risen Christ or his apostle.

There are two important differences between the Philippians hymn and the Johannine narrative. First, the hymn portrays the content of act 2, the earthly life of the incarnate Son, as devoid of divine power. The incarnate Christ differs from other human beings not in his ability to perform miraculous deeds but in the one word that sums up his whole life: "obedience." The Fourth Gospel portrays the human life as paradoxically truly human and yet filled with the divine power that overcomes all the enemies of life. This is the consequence of John's adopting the gospel genre that paradoxically combines epiphany Christology and *kenosis* Christology. The epistolary mode of the hymn portrays the deity and humanity of Christ diachronically: deity in heaven → humanity on earth → deity in heaven, while the Johannine version of the gospel genre portrays the earthly life of Jesus synchronically as a simultaneous paradox: God → truly divine on earth / truly human on earth → God.

Second, in the Philippians hymn, the teaching that brings out the meaning and implications of the Christ event is given by Paul, the author of the letter. In the gospel form, the meaning and implications are given by the Johannine Jesus himself, a character in the narrative. Jesus returns to his place at the table and explicitly teaches the disciples the meaning of the event (John 13:12, followed by the exposition in the extensive discourse of chaps. 13–17). In Philippians, the risen Christ speaks through the apostle; the Fourth Evangelist understands the discourses of the Johannine Jesus to be the teaching of the risen Christ (see pp. 291–92 below on the Paraclete).

Following the foot washing, Jesus reclothes himself, returns to his former place, and instructs his disciples on the meaning of the comprehensive Christ event, from creation to eschaton. Jesus had already responded to Peter's objection by telling him that he could not understand its meaning now, but only later (13:6–7). The reader understands and sees the foot washing as a model of the complete Christ event. The Farewell Discourse makes contact with each of the acts of the saving drama: Incarnation → Life → Death → Resurrection → Ascension → Pentecost → Life and Mission of the Church → Parousia. These facets of Johannine theology have been woven into the narrative throughout.

Incarnation

The Jesus who speaks at the Last Supper is the one who knew he had come from God (13:1–3). In 16:27–28, Jesus presents the whole drama of salvation as the U-shaped Christ event, preexistence → incarnation → return to the Father. In 16:28, "that I have come from the Father" is the summary of the faith (cf. also 17:5, 8, 18, 24).

Life

We have seen that, in John's narrative, the "life of Jesus" is restricted to a limited number of "signs," each of which illustrates—John uses "testifies to," "witnesses to"—the meaning of the Christ event as a whole. Like the Philippians hymn, the Gospel portrays the life of the incarnate Word as summarized in obedience, in doing the will or works of the Father (4:34; 5:30, 36; 6:38–39; 9:4; 10:25, 37–38; 14:10, 12; 15:24; 17:4). This is the essence of a truly human life. Although the Fourth Gospel emphasizes *that* the divine Word became incarnate in Jesus, minimal attention is given to *what* the human being was like as a person. The life of Jesus is narrated as transparent to the character of God, who loves the world and acted in Christ for the world's salvation. The reader learns that Jesus lived a life of service to others and taught his disciples to do the same (13:1–10), and that he had friends whom he loved and for whom he wept (11:1–44), but for the most part the pictures of Jesus the compassionate human being give place to a somewhat austere, distant Jesus who represents the transcendent God.

Death as Being "Lifted Up"

God's self-giving love for the world is summed up in the story of Jesus's death. But how can the death of a divine being be *narrated*? The gnostic-docetic teachers also had their narratives, portraying a sham death that sacrificed Jesus's humanity in order to preserve the deity of Christ (see pp. 157–58 above). The Johannine teachers saw this as perverting the meaning of the gospel and retold the traditional passion story contained in the other gospels in a way that proclaimed both the deity and humanity of the Word-become-flesh.

The Johannine passion story testifies to the deity of Christ. The Book of Signs had developed the perspective on Jesus's person as the one who does not belong to this world but comes from above, from the Father. Jesus has a human mother and father, and human siblings, but places himself in a different category from them (2:4; 7:1–8). Even the story of the crucifixion testifies to the reality that Jesus is not victim but victor, and portrays him as the truly divine one: "No one takes it [my life] from me, but I lay it down of my own accord. I have power to lay it down, and I have power to take it up again" (10:18).

The Response of Jesus

Jesus's response to his mother in 2:4, *ti emoi kai soi*, is variously translated. The only other New Testament occurrence of this phrase is in Mark 5:7, paralleled in Luke 8:28, the challenge of the demons to Jesus. Literally, "what to you and to me?" that is, "what do we have in common, what is there that is both to you and to me?" meaning "we belong to two different worlds, two different orders of reality." So also in 7:1–8, his siblings belong to this world and are at home in it. Jesus comes from the transcendent world and does not fit into this world.

Jesus, "knowing all that was to happen to him" (18:4), identifies himself to his would-be captors, who are struck down by his "I am" (18:5). He is not passive but is in charge of his own arrest. He is the questioner, not the questioned (18:4, 7; cf. 18:34). In Mark 14:50, followed by Matthew 26:56, "all deserted him and fled," but the Johannine Jesus saves his disciples by commanding the Roman soldiers and Jewish temple police not to arrest them (John 18:7–9). The disciples do not flee, as in the Synoptics, but leave by Jesus's permission. He is in charge throughout.

The accusation is not merely that Jesus has violated Roman law but that he makes himself the Son of God (19:7).

As throughout the Gospel, Jesus is not from this world (19:9; cf. 3:13, 31; 6:62; 8:14, 23; 9:29–30; 13:3).

In obvious contrast to the synoptic Jesus who, after the beating, is too weak to carry the cross, the Johannine Jesus carries his own cross (John 19:16–17 versus Matt 27:31–32; Mark 15:20–21; Luke 23:26).

In Matthew 27:46–48, following Mark 15:34–36, Jesus was offered a drink in response to his despairing cry from the cross, "My God, my God, why have you forsaken me?" The Johannine Jesus could never have uttered such a cry, just as he did not shudder before death in Gethsemane (contrast Mark 14:32–42, absent from John, with John 12:27). When the Johannine Jesus says, "I thirst," it is not necessarily an expression of human thirst, but it is necessary to fulfill the Scripture (19:28). This is also an instance of the Johannine double entendre that functions at two levels. Not only do the executioners respond to Jesus's request but the whole event is the fulfillment of God's plan, in which Jesus's giving his life is in accord with the Scripture (cf. also 19:36–37).

Throughout the Gospel, Jesus himself decides when his hour has come (2:4; 7:30; 8:20; 12:23; 13:1; 17:1). He had already announced, "I lay down my life in order to take it up again. No one takes it from me, but I lay it down of my own accord. I have power to lay it down, and I have power to take it up again" (10:17–18). With sovereign authority, he decides when his work on earth is finished (5:36; 9:3–4; 10:38; 14:11; 17:4), and says, "*Tetelestai,*" "It is finished" (19:30). On his own accord, he then bowed his head and "gave up his spirit" (so NRSV and others) or "handed over the Spirit" (so NAB and others). This is yet another Johannine double entendre that can mean simply he expired (from Latin *exspirare*, "breathe out," "breathe one's last"), as clearly intended by the synoptic account (Matt 27:50; Mark 15:37; Luke 23:46). John uses a different phrase, *paredōken to pneuma*, literally "he handed over the spirit," which may refer to his own breath or to his giving the Spirit to his disciples. In the latter reading, which does not exclude the first, the "breath" is the divine breath, the creative Spirit of God that gives life to the world (Gen 1:2; 6:3, 17; Ps 104:30; etc.), the same *pneuma* given by the risen Jesus on Easter (John 20:22) and in the Lukan chronology on Pentecost (Acts 1:8; 2:1–21). It would be misguided to suppose that John intends to merge Good Friday, Easter, Ascension, and Pentecost into one event, but "the fundamental theological reality to which they point is the same," the act of God in the Christ event of Jesus's crucifixion, resurrection, exaltation, and post-Easter presence with his disciples.[15] The sending of the Spirit is analogous and parallel to the sending of the Son. The narration is necessarily diachronic but points to a synchronic reality, another example of the Johannine compression of time.

The Gospel is bracketed by the use of God language of Christ (1:1; 20:28), and throughout emphasizes the unity of the Son and the Father. To know and see Jesus is to know and see the Father (14:7). Jesus's prayer speaks of his unity with the Father as "You in me and I in you" (17:21). This unity is not explained but confessed in prayer. When the Johannine Jesus says, "The Father and I are one" (10:30), the word for "one" is here neuter (*hen*), one thing, one reality, not one person. John affirms the unity of Son and Father without erasing the distinction between Father and Son, which John also insists on maintaining (3:35; 5:19–26; 6:40; 14:13; 17:1). John makes it clear that the Father was not merely a spectator at the death of the Son, but that the one who dies represents the one true God who takes human death into his own divine experience. None of this is metaphysical speculation but is important for communicating the faith that *God* was present and active in the death of *Jesus*, the one who shares the frailty and vulnerability of our life.

The Johannine Passion Story Testifies to the Incarnation and True Humanity of Christ

The Jesus who lays aside his robe of divinity and stoops to wash the disciples' feet is the truly human one who shares the frailty of our life. The series of references in the passion story that portray him as weak like us, not powerful like God, does not just illustrate his "human side" but represents that in the death he shared the human experience in which death is not an option one may choose or reject but a power to which we are delivered over.

Those who arrest him take him, bind him, and hand him over to others (18:12, 35–36; 19:11, 16). As Jesus was active in the previous series of references noted above, he is passive in this series. The "passion" in the passion story is derived from Latin *passivus*, the opposite of "active." His captors slap, beat, and flog him (18:22; 19:1, 3).

The executioners crucify him. John uses "cross" or "crucify" fifteen times of Jesus, never metamorphically and never of the disciples. Only John refers to Jesus being *nailed* to the cross (20:25), just as only he refers to *blood* (19:34). Only in John is Jesus's death proven by the soldier's spear thrust (19:31–35; v. 33, they "saw that he was already dead . . .").

The Markan passion story reached its climax in the confession of the centurion, "Truly this man (*anthrōpos*, 'human being') was the God's Son" (Mark 15:39). Only John takes up this explicit paradox, emphasizing both sides of the confession. Not only, as noted above, does he emphasize the deity of the crucified one but he also explicitly takes up *anthrōpos* as essential to the confession. Caiaphas (John 11:50, repeated 18:14), the maid at the door (18:17), and Pilate (18:29) refer to Jesus as *anthrōpos*, and in the graphic double entendre of 19:5 Pilate presents the bloody and beaten Jesus with the words "Here is the man!" At the narrative level, this is further humiliation: "Just look at this miserable character. *He* is 'King of the Jews'?" Believers of the gospel hear the pronouncement that Jesus is indeed *the* human being, the model and realization of what God created humans to be (cf. Rom 5:12–21). Just as he is truly divine, so he is truly human.

The Gospel Portrays the Death of Jesus as the Liberating Act of God

New Testament authors interpret the salvific significance of Jesus's death in a limited variety of ways. No one interpretation can do justice to the mystery of God's saving act in Christ. To hear what the Johannine teachers want to say to us, it is important not to read the views of other canonical texts into the Gospel's theology. "God so loved the world that he gave his only Son . . ." is often read as though the meaning were ". . . who died to take the punishment for our sins," but there is nothing like this in John 3:16 or any other text in the Gospel.

We have seen that the Johannine community itself perceived the meaning of Jesus's death in a variety of ways. Jesus's death as a sacrifice that mediated God's forgiveness of sins was an image strongly present in some circles of the Johannine community, and integral to the theology of some fellow believers in other forms of Christianity in Roman Asia at the turn of the century (e.g., Rev 1:5; 5:9; 1 John 1:7, 9; 2:2, 12; 4:10; Paul in Rom 3:25; also 1 Pet 2:24; 3:18). The Gospel does not deny or polemicize against this view but makes minimal use of this imagery. John mentions forgiveness only once (20:23) and has only six texts that *may* refer to Jesus's death as a vicarious cultic sacrifice: 1:29; 6:51c; 10:11, 15; 11:51–53 (cf. 18:14); 15:13.[16] With less justification, a few others are also occasionally interpreted from this perspective (3:14, 16; 12:27; 17:19; 18:11). As in Luke-Acts, the atoning, sacrificial death of Jesus is almost absent. For John, as for Luke, the *death* of Jesus is not in itself a unique saving act but is seen as summing up his whole *life*.

Jesus's death as the Lamb of God does indeed represent God's saving act that takes away the sin of the world (1:29, 36), but this is interpreted primarily in terms of the Passover lamb of Exodus, not the sacrificial sin offerings of Leviticus. The Passover celebrated the deliverance of the people of God by overcoming the enslaving evil power of Egypt, not by making possible the forgiveness of the sins of believing, repentant Israelites. This annual freedom festival was feared by the Romans as a time of patriotic enthusiasm that could lead to riots. In Jesus's day, the Roman governor took the precautionary measure of reinforcing the military presence in Jerusalem during the Passover and temporarily moved his residence from Caesarea to Jerusalem. In John's time, the Jewish community looked back on the tragic rebellion of 66–70 CE that had resulted in the destruction of Jerusalem and the temple and the devastation of the Jewish homeland, and the fires that would be rekindled in the tragic revolt of 132–135 were already on the horizon. Jewish teachers were reconfiguring what obedience to the Torah means when the whole sacrificial system of the temple and its associated festivals no longer existed. In step with this tradition, the Johannine teachers too are vigorously engaged in reinterpreting the meaning of Torah, the temple and its sacrificial rituals, and the Jewish festivals. In ways analogous to the theology of the Pauline teachers in neighboring congregations, the Johannine teachers portray Jesus as representing the triumphant power of God, the Passover Lamb who does not deliver from Roman imperialism by military power but from the enslaving power of sin, whose kingdom is not of this world (1 Cor 5:6–8; Rom 6:12–23). This was a hotly disputed point in the Jewish Christianity with which the Johannine community was engaged. In John 8:31–38 it is "Jews who had believed in him" who resisted Jesus's teaching on the true meaning of freedom. Jesus is indeed the "king of Israel," but to call him "king of the Jews (= Judeans)" is a gross misunderstanding (cf. 1:49 [12:13–15]; 3:3–5; 6:15; 18:33–39; 19:3–15, 19–22). Jesus is the Messiah sent by God, who triumphs over the evil, enslaving power, but—as in Revelation!—he conquers as the Lamb of God who does not kill but is killed. Johannine Christians in Roman Asia are not encouraged to support the war movement in Judea, which would be a misunderstanding of the nature of the kingdom of God. It is thus important to see the Passover imagery woven into the narrative throughout.

The Synoptics, following Mark, refer to only one Passover, which Jesus and his disciples attend at the end of his ministry, during which he is arrested and executed. John refers to three Passovers, which frame the narrative and provide the context for many of Jesus's signs and discourses (2:13, 23; 4:45; 5:1; 6:4; 11:55–56; 12:1, 12, 20; 13:1, 29; 18:28; 19:14). Although in John Jesus's last meal with the disciples is not a Passover meal but occurs the night before Passover, the narrator begins the scene of the Farewell Discourse by setting the meal in the Passover context (13:1).

Historically, it is most likely that the date of the Roman execution of Jesus was during the Passover festival in 30 CE. All the Gospels interpret the crucifixion in reference to the Passover. Mark, followed by Matthew and Luke, portrays the Last Supper as a Passover meal (Mark 14:22–25; Matt 26:26–29; Luke 22:15–20). John has a different chronology that facilitates a more intensive use of Passover imagery to explicate the meaning of Jesus's death.

In John, Jesus dies on the day of preparation for the Passover (John 19:14, 31), at the time the Passover lambs are being killed. There is no preparation for a Passover meal, as in the Synoptics. The meal is neither called a Passover nor does it have any features of the Passover meal. During Jesus's trial the next day, the Jewish leaders ironically will not enter Pilate's courtroom lest they become ritually unclean and be unable to participate in the Passover, which will begin that evening (18:28).

During the crucifixion scene, the reference to Jesus being given a drink with a sponge soaked in sour wine *on a branch of hyssop* (19:29) is unique to John. It is a strange comment, difficult to imagine historically, since hyssop is a small flowering plant whose stems could hardly hold a sponge and would be too short for the purpose portrayed. The importance of hyssop in this scene is to link it to the Passover: on the night of the exodus, hyssop was used as a brush with which to smear the blood of the Passover lamb on the doorposts of Israel, to mark them as saved from destruction.

Also unique to John is the reference to breaking the legs of those being executed. This was done not as further punishment but as a way of hastening their death. The victims could no longer use their legs to straighten their bodies and breathe, and quickly died of suffocation. The purpose was to dispatch them without further ado, so they could be taken down and not remain exposed during the Passover that was to begin that evening (19:31–37; cf. Deut 21:23). But the Torah instructed that not a bone of the Passover lamb was to be broken (Exod 12:46 [+12:10 LXX]; Num 9:12; Ps 34:20). In all these ways, Jesus fulfills the Gospel's initial declaration, "Here is the Lamb of God who takes away the sin of the world!" (John 1:29).

Resurrection

Many readers of the New Testament have become conditioned by the portrayal of Jesus's death, resurrection, ascension, and conferral of the Spirit as configured in the liturgical calendar and the Luke-Acts narrative on which it is based, where each of these is a discrete event arranged diachronically. So understood, Jesus was not raised to the heavenly world but restored to life in this world, followed, after a period of some days, by an ascension to heaven. The climax of God's saving act in the Christ event is conceived to be five separate occurrences: crucifixion, resurrection, post-Easter ministry of Jesus, ascension, sending the Spirit. Of these, only the crucifixion is an empirical historical event observable by this-worldly human eyes. The Johannine teachers have vigorously argued for the tangible reality of the saving event, which occurred in the flesh-and-blood body of Jesus (1 John 1:1–3). Yet they saw the crucifixion of Jesus as the outcropping of a transcendent event, the visible surface sign of the incursion of the world of God into the human world of time and space. But to see more (not less, or other!) than the material reality requires both a healing of human blindness (John 9:1–41) and an apprehension of the truth of metaphorical language. The Johannine teachers knew that the transcendent reality of God's act in Christ cannot literally be parceled out chronologically in this-worldly space and time, and necessarily portrayed this reality in more than one way.

In one signification, the cross was the real death of the human being Jesus. In another signification, no less real, the cross was Jesus's being "lifted up" not by his executioners but by God to his transcendent status, and resurrection was not a separate event from crucifixion but identical with it. Jesus was raised from the cross. Paul's own encounter with the risen Christ was intensely real, but it was the Lord from heaven who appeared to him. Paul insists that his own experience was no different from the experiences of Peter and the other apostles, that it was explicitly not the case that Peter and the others saw the "real" resurrected Jesus prior to his ascension and Paul saw "only" the spiritual Christ who appeared to him in a vision (1 Cor 15:1–11; Gal 1:11–2:21). Paul has no concept of the later idea found in Luke-Acts that differentiates resurrection and ascension as two chronologically distinct events. The book of Revelation that circulated in the Johannine community passionately affirmed the real death and resurrection of Christ, who now reigns in the heavenly world and gives the Spirit to the church, without making Good Friday, Easter, Ascension, and Pentecost separate days in the Christian calendar. The author believes that the risen Jesus appeared to chosen followers, including himself, and continues to speak. This does not necessarily mean that he would reject such a chronological isolation of each event, but he never attempted to write a gospel, a narrative in which such chronological issues must be faced. Like the teachers in the Johannine school, other early Christian teachers in John's historical context also understood Jesus's resurrection to be from the cross to the heavenly world, without an intermediate period of earthly appearances followed by an ascension (Phil 2:5–11; Col 1:15–20; Eph 1:20; 4:10; 1 Tim 3:16; Heb 8–10).

John thus collapses life/death/resurrection/ascension/Pentecost/commissioning the disciples into one event. He portrays Jesus's exaltation and handing over the Spirit to the disciples as part of the crucifixion itself. Why then does he narrate separate resurrection appearances? This may be a minor concession to what had already become conventional tradition in his time, but he has his own theological reasons for doing so. His whole project has entailed *narrative* theology. Narrating the resurrection as a separate event allows him to explicate particular meanings of Christian faith he considers important. Faith in the resurrection is not just affirming that the tomb was empty or that Jesus is still alive. The way the event is pictured expresses a particular understanding of Christian faith and life. Space allows mentioning only a few of these meanings; each could be elaborated.

The role of women in the Johannine churches. The first appearance of the risen Lord was to a woman, Mary Magdalene, from whom the other disciples learn that Jesus's tomb is empty and that he has appeared to her (John 20:1–2, 18). During the extended period of the composition of the Fourth Gospel, the Christian congregations in Roman Asia were struggling with the issue of church leadership. The fresh experience of the Holy Spirit had propelled the first-generation Pauline churches into new formations of community life that broke through cultural conventions. The Pauline churches affirmed that "there is no longer male and female; for all of you are one in Christ Jesus" (Gal 3:28). Paul numbered several women among his coworkers (see, e.g., Phil 4:2–4; Rom 16 passim), and women played leading roles in founding and guiding the new congregations (e.g., Acts 18:2, 18, 26). The Johannine churches, too, lived in and by the immediate power and direction of the Spirit (John 3:3–8; 4:23; 6:63; 7:39; 14:17, 26; 15:26; 16:13; 20:22). Thus throughout the Gospel women are portrayed acting in significant roles, presumably reflecting the life of the Johannine congregations (2:1–12; 4:7–42; 11:1–44; 12:1–7; 19:25–27; 20:1–18). The story of Jesus, transparent to the story of the church, could not be told without portraying the various roles of the women who were his friends and disciples. Women are present at the meals Jesus shared with his friends; women serve as evangelists and missionaries; women are at the cross; women (note the "we" of 20:2) come to the tomb; the first appearance was to a woman, from whom the other disciples learn the good news of the resurrection.

The significant but secondary role of Peter. In some streams of early Christianity, Peter is portrayed as playing the leading role, both before and after Easter. He was the first to be called; he is always named first in the lists of the Twelve; he is charged by Jesus to gather the scattered disciples after Easter and reconstitute the apostolic group (Luke 22:32). One of the earliest Christian confessions documented this primacy of Peter by including the affirmation that the risen Jesus appeared first to Peter (1 Cor 15:3–5). It is not coincidental that the Fourth Gospel narrates the first appearance to Mary Magdalene, who tells Peter (John 20:1–2, 18), just as Andrew was the first disciple to be called—who then tells Peter (1:40–41). The emerging view of Petrine leadership of the whole church goes against the grain of the way the story of Jesus and his followers had been told in the Johannine community oriented to the Beloved Disciple. These Johannine perspectives on the story are retained in the final edition of the Gospel, which affirms both charismatic and structured leadership (cf. John 21).

Neither abandoning nor clinging to the past. In the Easter narrative, Mary Magdalene has insight the others do not yet have, yet her impulse to cling to the Jesus she had known in his pre-Easter history is gently but firmly countered by the risen Christ, who points her to the future, the ascended Lord who is still present and active in the life of the church, leading it in new directions. The Gospel retells the story the church has in common, the story of Jesus and his disciples, the church's own story, in such a way that each faction can claim as its own.

Faith and sight. At the dawn of the second Christian century, those who had seen and heard Jesus of Nazareth were virtually all gone, and the church was dependent on the living tradition, oral and written, that had been handed on. Does this mean that disciples of the second and following generation were second-class believers? Should the church cultivate and solidify links in the chain of tradition of those who had "really" seen? Already 1 John 1:1–3 had claimed that all members of the church belong to a community that had seen, heard, and touched the incarnate Word of life "from the beginning." In John's rendition of the Easter story, the risen Jesus himself pronounces the divine blessing on those who have not literally seen and touched but who believe (John 20:26–29). Thomas's confession, "My Lord and my God," is the climax of the Gospel, a bracket with the prologue's ". . . and the Word was God" (1:1). John does not berate "doubting Thomas," nor does he commend him for his hard-nosed insistence on empirical evidence before he will believe. As in 1 John 1:1–3, the Fourth Gospel presents Thomas as rightly insisting on the tangibility of the Christ event. It did not just happen "in our hearts" but in this fleshly world of space and time in which our own lives are embedded. In this regard, Thomas is the counterpart of the Beloved Disciple.

Gift of the Spirit as sharing the very life of Jesus and God. The Farewell Discourse has much to say about God's gift of the Spirit to guide and empower Jesus's disciples after his departure (John 14:17, 26; 15:26; 16:7, 13). The Easter narrative, like the crucifixion narrative (19:30), portrays the gift of the Spirit as imparted in the cross/resurrection event. Just as God the creator breathed life into the inert body of Adam, so that humanity and the world live by the very breath of God, the risen Jesus infuses the new creation of which the Christian community is the leading edge with his own life and breath.

Life and Mission of the Church

Transcendent Reality of the Church, Unity with God, Christ

The biblical-Jewish understanding of Israel had never been rendered in terms of voluntary membership in a human institution committed to practicing the ideals of Moses or continuing the causes advocated by the martyred prophets. Israel existed as part of the continuing act of God that called the covenant people into being for the sake of the world. In some streams of Jewish tradition current in the first century CE, the people of God already participate in the heavenly reality. When faithful Israelites gather for worship, they are joining the heavenly liturgy simultaneously celebrated by the angels in the heavenly temple. This is analogous to Paul's understanding of the nature of the church, incidentally documented in his instruction to women in the new Corinthian congregation to have a symbol of authority on their heads during worship, "because of the angels" (1 Cor 11:10; cf. 4:9; 13:1). No New Testament author regards the church as merely a human institution that attempted to continue Jesus's cause after his death. Though they have different ways of conceptualizing this, all regard the church as somehow participating in the transcendent reality of the Christ event. The first words of earliest extant Christian texts address new church members in Thessalonica as those who are "in God the Father and the Lord Jesus Christ" (1 Thess 1:1). Paul's understanding of Christian existence as participation in church life "in Christ" permeates the whole Pauline letter corpus.

The Johannine churches in Roman Asia are familiar with such language and imagery, which are not peculiar to Johannine "mysticism." In Johannine theology, the line between Christology and ecclesiology/discipleship is thin. The Johannine community was familiar with imagery in which the church already participates in the heavenly reality. The messages to the seven churches are transcendent communications "overheard" by the earthly church. The elders of Revelation are heavenly figures, not congregational leaders in provincial Asia (Rev 4:4, 10; 5:5, 6, 8, 11, 14; 7:11, 13; 11:16; 14:3; 19:4). The people of God are portrayed as the woman clothed with the sun, the moon under her feet, with a crown of twelve stars (12:1–17). In the Fourth Gospel, the church already shares in the reality of the Father, Son, and Holy Spirit. Just as the Father dwells in the Son and the Son in the Father, so Father and Son dwell in the believers (John 14:20). This is not individualistic "mystical" spirituality. It is belonging to a little congregation in Ephesus or Pergamon, the result of the historical act of God in Jesus Christ and the call of God's word through Christian preachers, which at the same time means belonging to a worldwide church that spans the generations and centuries and already participates in the life of God.

In worship and prayer, the church participates in the reality of God's world. In John 17, Jesus prays to God, and the prayer is "overheard" by disciples and by us, his later reader/hearers and worshipers. This climax of the revelatory Farewell Discourse does not take the form of teaching directed to the disciples but pictures the gathered community "overhearing" the prayer of Jesus, who already speaks as the exalted Lord. As in Paul's understanding, when the community prays, it is the Holy Spirit, the risen Christ as the glorified one, who speaks to God in and for the community that already partakes of his glory (Rom 8:12–30). In the Fourth Gospel, Jesus does not teach the disciples a prayer but prays for them, and for us later believers. As "friend of sinners," Jesus eats with them, prays with them (on "friend" as Johannine ecclesiological term, cf. 3 John 15; John 3:29; 11:11; 15:13–15). The Holy Spirit, the risen Christ, our mediator and intercessor, prays for us and in us. Jesus does not speak as a third party that tries to placate God; as in the Pauline gospel, God himself is for us (Rom 8:31). In Johannine theology, the meaning of prayer is coming to realize that you are prayed for, and not only by fellow church members. The church prays, and Father, Son, and Holy Spirit are present in this prayer not only as its hearers.

This participation is not a flight from the political and social reality of the empirical world. Here the church is nourished in eucharistic worship to be strong for service in the world. Here the church hears preaching and teaching in which the risen Christ instructs the church and sends it forth in mission.

Jesus's disciples are children of God. Without elaborating the point, the Farewell Discourse presupposes the self-understanding of the Christian community as "children of God." Like Jesus, the disciples have earthly parents and participate fully in the life and social conditions of this world, but they do not simply belong to this world and are not determined by it. In responding to God's word that has come through Christian preaching, they have been "born from above," "of water and Spirit" (John 3:3–5), and can be addressed by Jesus as *teknia*, "little children" (13:33). The self-evident way in which such language is used points to the transcendent reality of the church as understood in the Johannine community. This perspective is further indicated by the two "I am" sayings in the Farewell Discourse.

John 14:6: "I am the way, and the truth, and the life. No one comes to the Father except through me." This familiar text is often understood to refer exclusively to Christology and/or soteriology, as though it were addressing the question of whether those who do not confess faith in Christ have access to God. This question has already been dealt with. The Johannine teachers do affirm that God is universally available, and that the God revealed in nature and history is the one God definitively revealed in Jesus Christ. Those who come to God, of whatever time, place, and religion, come to the God who is universally revealed through the Word that became flesh in Jesus Christ. This is John's theology, yet that is not the point here. In the Johannine theological framework, "way," "truth," and "life" are all ecclesiological terms characterizing the people of God, as in Jewish tradition. "Way" (*hodos* = *halakah*) is resonant with the Hebrew understanding of Torah as the revealed will of God, the way that Israel must walk. "Truth" (*alētheia*) is not a matter of abstract, logical correctness but of reliability and faithfulness (*emet, emunah*). God is faithful and requires faithfulness of his covenant people. "Life" (*zōē*) is the gift of God to those who walk faithfully in God's revealed way of life, the Torah (*chai, chayyim*; Deut 30:15, 20; Jer 21:8; Mal 2:5; Ps 56:13; Job 33:30).

John 15:5: "I am the vine, you are the branches. Those who abide in me and I in them bear much fruit." Likewise, the vine image is not only christological ("who is Jesus?") but also ecclesiological ("what is the church?"). The Johannine Christ does not teach his disciples "I am the trunk, you are the branches," as though he were one part and they another. Christ is the whole vine, into which the branches are incorporated. This is analogous to Paul's understanding of the church as the body of Christ, not the post-Pauline view in which Christ is the head and Christians are the body (1 Cor 12:4–13; Rom 12:3–8; cf. Acts 9:1–6; to persecute Christians is to persecute Christ; contrast, e.g., Col 2:19; Eph 1:22–23; 4:5). Both views circulated in the Johannine churches. For the Johannine teachers, it is important to see that Christ claims to be the real (*alēthinos*) vine. "True" is not in contrast to "false" but in contrast to "unreal, inauthentic." The imagery is biblical and Jewish. The people of God are a vine, planted by God, expected to bear fruit (Ps 80:8, 14; Isa 5:1–7; 27:2–6; Jer 2:21; 6:9; 8:13; Ezek 19:10–14; Hos 14:7; cf. Deut 32:32; Ezek 17). Just as Daniel's apocalyptic image of the transcendent Son of Man is identified as Israel (Dan 7:1–27), so the prophets' apocalyptic image of the vine that will fill the whole earth (Isa 27:6) is Israel, and both are identified by the Johannine teachers with Jesus Christ. Just as some of Israel's teachers identified the people of God as the true temple, the dwelling place of God in this world—especially after the destruction of the Jerusalem temple—so the Johannine teachers identified the true temple as Jesus Christ. This imagery would be evoked in the Johannine community by Jesus's claim to be the "true vine." God does not plant a new vine. There is one vine, one people of God, represented by Jesus Christ in person. To believe in Christ is to be incorporated in this transcendent reality. Every Eucharist in which believers drink the "fruit of the vine" symbolizes and makes real this identity.

Paraclete, Spirit-Filled Community

The Fourth Gospel's numerous declarations about the Holy Spirit are to be seen in the ecclesiological context that embraces God, Christ, Spirit, and believers (John 1:32–33; 3:5–8, 34; 4:23–24; 6:63; 7:39; 14:16–17, 26; 15:26; 16:7, 13; 19:30; 20:22). The Johannine teachers share much of the vocabulary and understanding of the Spirit with other Christians in Roman Asia, where the Pauline heritage was very much alive. In Paul's image of the body of Christ, the Spirit is the breath that animates the body (see 1 Cor 12; Rom 12; *pneuma* means both "breath" and "spirit"). The body is alive because the breath animates the whole, with breath breathed into it by God (cf. Gen 2:7). Those who respond to the gospel in faith are baptized into this body energized by the breath/Spirit (1 Cor 12:13) and participate in the life of the Spirit that breathes through the Christian community. The Spirit is given to the community, to the people of God. For Paul, the way to have a "Spirit-filled church" is not to assemble a group of individuals who have been filled with the Spirit. The thrust of the metaphor moves in the opposite direction: the way to have a Spirit-filled life is to participate in the life of the church. John shares this perspective that is already prevalent in the congregations of Roman Asia. In Johannine theology, the Spirit is at work in the community in the following ways.

Revealing New Truth from the Risen Lord

The Revelation of John of Patmos circulated among the Johannine churches of Roman Asia, with the claim that the risen Jesus continues to speak, especially through Christian prophets. Jesus of Nazareth had not given specific instructions about how his followers should respond to the political threats and claims involved in the propagation of the emperor cult. Nor could his later disciples simply "apply" the "principles" once taught by the rabbi Jesus. Jesus's followers in the 90s in Roman Asia needed a clear word from the Lord for decisions they had to make in the present. The Johannine teachers who adopted the narrative gospel genre as their mode of presenting the message of Jesus for their own time do not deny the claim of apocalyptic Christian prophecy that Jesus continues to speak, but they express it in a different literary mode. The gospel genre does not merely point back in history to an admirable figure who once lived but narrates stories and sayings set in the pre-Easter framework of his life that mediate his message to the present. The Johannine teachers believed that the Holy Spirit at work in their community was not giving new revelations independent of the man of Nazareth who had lived, died, and been raised, but was continuing, expanding, and interpreting the message of Jesus Christ (John 14:25–26; 15:26; 16:12–15; 1 John 1:5). In contrast to their contemporary author who wrote the two-volume Luke-Acts, the Johannine teachers do not compose a narrative that distinguishes a pre-Easter "time of Jesus" from a post-Easter "time of the Spirit," but emphasize that the whole public life of Jesus was actuated in the power of the Spirit (John 1:32–33). The Fourth Gospel has repeatedly made clear that adequate, authentic knowledge of Jesus's identity and God's presence and acts in and through him can only be perceived after his resurrection (2:22), glorification, and sending of the Spirit (7:39). Though he utilized a different literary form and had a theology with different emphases, John of Patmos would have agreed.

Recalling and Enlivening the Tradition

The revelatory work of the Spirit is not an alternative to affirming the church's tradition. The Spirit enlivens the community's memory (14:25–26). The church's ministry is a continuation of the ministry of Christ. The Holy Spirit at work in the whole church energizes and guides the church's ministry of preachers and teachers to remember, understand, and proclaim the faith preserved (but not ossified) in tradition. The Johannine churches to which the Gospel is directed are in the third generation of church life. In every generation, for both individuals and community, memory is not an optional accessory but is constitutive of identity. Learning my tradition is not carrying around baggage; it constitutes who I am, both for individual and church. No memory, no me; no tradition, no church. Neither the individual believer nor the community begins at square one with every decision. Whether I am a 3rd- or 103rd-generation believer, I belong to a church that has members who have been with Jesus "from the beginning"—of my congregation, denomination, and the one church around the world and through the generations that embraces them all (15:27; 1 John 1:1–3). Tradition and the new life of the Spirit are not alternatives or opponents but corollaries. To claim to be without tradition is to be a leaf that doesn't know it is part of a tree—in Johannine imagery, a branch that doesn't know it is part of the vine.

The Continuing Ministry of Jesus Is Represented by the Image of the Paraclete

All New Testament authors presumably affirm the presence and power of the Holy Spirit in the life of the church. Most speak of this explicitly, but only the Johannine community expresses this with the term "Paraclete," with a single reference in 1 John 2:1 and five "Paraclete sayings" in the Farewell Discourse of the Gospel (John 14:15–17, 25–26; 15:26–27; 16:7–11, 12–15). Revelation and Book One of the Gospel, in which Jesus confronts the world (chaps. 2–12), have much to say about the Spirit but say nothing of the Paraclete. The word is rare in nonbiblical Greek and absent from the LXX, though a variant form occurs in Job 16:2, usually translated "comforter." "Paraclete" is thus not general Jewish or Christian theological vocabulary but part of the insider language of the Johannine community. The word is derived from *para* ("beside"; cf. "parallel") and *klētos* ("called," as in Matt 22:14; Rom 1:1; 1 Cor 1:1). Thus "one called alongside" is the etymological meaning. The term has been variously understood, as reflected in the translations:

- "Comforter" (KJV). Understood in the biblical sense, this is a proper translation, but it has rightly been mostly abandoned by modern English translations, since it has come to connote subjective feel-good sentimentality, which is far from its biblical meaning (see the second volume, *Hearing Paul's Voice*, on 1 Thess 4:13–18).
- "Helper" (NAS, TEV, ESV, NKJV). The Holy Spirit is understood generically as one sent by God/the risen Christ to help the church and individual Christians to fulfill their calling.
- "Companion" (CEB) and "Friend" (Message). These images suggest that the Spirit is sent by God as the one who shares the individual's experience and helps him or her through difficulties.
- "Counselor" (RSV, NIV). This translation is not intended to portray the Holy Spirit as a giver of advice but is to be understood in the forensic sense: the lawyer in the courtroom called alongside the accused as counsel for the defense, or prosecuting attorney who presses the state's case against the defendant.
- "Advocate" (NRSV, REB, NAB, NIVI). This translation also assumes the forensic world of meaning but specifies that the Holy Spirit is the one who aids the accused, speaking for them before the court.
- "Paraclete" (NJB). This rendering regards the term as better transliterated than translated, lest biblical meaning be lost in another language

(cf. "baptism," "Eucharist," "presbyter," and other terms kept in Greek as an effort to preserve their biblical meaning).

In Johannine theology, the figures of the risen Christ and the Holy Spirit/Paraclete are fused. The sole reference to the Paraclete in the Johannine letters refers to Jesus Christ, the believers' advocate with the Father (1 John 2:1). As in Romans 8:26–34, Christ/the Spirit intercedes for the believer in the divine courtroom, and God acquits those who are charged. So also in the Fourth Gospel, the Paraclete performs the same function as the risen Lord (John 14:16, "another Advocate") and has a forensic role, but the scene is the world, and the Paraclete is not the believer's defense attorney but the divine prosecuting attorney who presses God's case against the world (16:7–11). The whole Gospel narrative is cast as a trial, but it is the world, not Jesus or believers, who are on trial.

Beloved Disciple

The narrator has waited until the Farewell Discourse to introduce the figure of the Beloved Disciple. He is probably hinted at by the reference to the unnamed disciple of 1:35–42 who, along with Andrew, was one of the first two called by Jesus, pointedly called before Simon Peter. The Book of Signs (Triumphal Entry, chapters 2–12) has no reference to him. He first becomes prominent at the Last Supper, where he reclines in the place of honor next to Jesus, and Peter must ask him to explain what Jesus had said (13:21–30). He then appears in key scenes in the trial, crucifixion, and resurrection. At Jesus's hearing before the high priest, the Beloved Disciple intercedes with the doorkeeper so that Peter can enter the courtyard of the high priest's house (18:15–18). He is the only male disciple present at the crucifixion, where the dying Jesus commits the care of his mother to him (19:25–27), and is thus among the small group of disciples at the foot of the cross to whom Jesus hands over the Spirit (19:30). The Beloved Disciple witnesses the spear thrust that certifies Jesus's death (19:31–37). On the first Easter morning, the Beloved Disciple outruns Peter to become the first disciple to respond to Mary Magdalene's announcement that the tomb was empty, and, though Peter was the first to enter the tomb, the Beloved Disciple is the first to believe (20:1–9). He is among the group on the first Easter evening that receives the Spirit and is commissioned by Jesus to convey God's forgiveness to the world (20:20–23). On the next Sunday, he is the first to recognize the risen Jesus, and again is the one who tells Peter (21:7).

The Beloved Disciple "on Jesus's Bosom"

En tō kolpō, literally "on his chest." This idiom, reflecting the ancient banqueting practice (cf. Luke 16:23), has been variously translated ("on Jesus' bosom," KJV, NAS, NKJV; "close to the breast of Jesus," RSV; "reclining next to him," NIV, NRSV; "his head on his shoulder," Message). It is significant for John, since it is the same expression used of the transcendent relation of the Son to the Father (John 1:18). The Beloved Disciple has the same relation to Christ that Christ has to God, further suggesting that the Beloved Disciple is closely associated with imagery used of the Holy Spirit: Father → Son → Spirit is analogous to God → Jesus → Beloved Disciple. Cf. the "hierarchical chain of command" familiar to the Johannine community from Revelation 1:1–3 and John 20:21–22, in each case related to the Holy Spirit.

All these vignettes are unique to the Fourth Gospel. Interpreters are largely agreed that they point to three theological foci of the Johannine school:

1. There was a historical figure, an early Judean (not Galilean) disciple of Jesus, not one of the Twelve, who was the founder and initial leader of a group of Jesus's followers. Like some of the other members of the early Johannine community, he had been baptized by John the Baptist, then left the group of John the Baptist's followers to become a disciple of Jesus.
2. He was regarded as the guarantor of the reality of the central kerygmatic events, the death and resurrection of Jesus, the fountainhead of the tradition represented in 1 John 1:1–3, what had been received "from the beginning." This tradition was a mainstay of the community's resistance to the "progressive" gnosticizing tendencies threatening to undermine or erode the Christian gospel's grounding in flesh-and-blood historical events.
3. The Beloved Disciple was idealized in the community as the figure who represented authentic discipleship and the true nature of the church. "Beloved Disciple" did not mean "teacher's pet." The Farewell Discourse begins by declaring that Jesus loved all the disciples fully, to the very end (13:1). This has an important bearing on the dispute concerning church structure and leadership among the Christian congregations of Roman Asia in 90–130 CE. The Beloved Disciple was repeatedly "first," ahead of Peter, but this primacy is not chronological or hierarchical. The ideal

disciple represented the leadership of the Spirit and the power of love in guiding the community.

Johannine Ethics: The Unity of Mission and Ethics

Jesus's call to discipleship includes instruction on living an ethically responsible life, but the Fourth Gospel expresses this differently from the other gospels. John's Gospel urges faith and love but manifests a disconcerting lack of specific directions. The only specific command is to wash one another's feet (13:14), which is not intended as a literal example but as a Johannine sign. There is nothing in the Gospel like the Sermon on the Mount (Matt 5–7) or Jesus's parable of the last judgment (Matt 25:31–46), no instructions on particular ethical issues such as Paul gives in, for example, Romans 12 or 1 Thessalonians 4–5. The love command is general. We have noted above that the command to feed hungry people is omitted from the Johannine version of feeding the multitudes. In the Gospel of Mark, Jesus instructs his disciples that, after he has departed, feeding the poor is part of their mission. This instruction is missing from the parallel in John 14:8. When Judas objects to Mary of Bethany's anointing Jesus's feet with perfume costing almost a year's wages (John 12:1–8), we might have expected that Jesus would have responded with something like, "Don't squander all this money on perfume when there are hungry people in the world!" Yet, in the way the story is told, the only person to explicitly express concern for the poor is Judas (12:5), though the narrator immediately informs us that he actually cared nothing for the poor—in obvious contrast to authentic disciples—but used money intended for them to enrich himself. Yet it is clear that helping the poor is self-evidently what Jesus and his disciples do (13:29). Once again, we must attend to the Johannine perspective. John's way of ethics does not reject explicit, pragmatic concern for needy people but puts it in a larger and deeper context.

The lack of explicit ethical directions is in part due to the polemical slant of the Johannine narrative, which concentrates on the twin, inseparable aspects of Christology and ecclesiology. The debate with "the Jews" is about issues on which they disagree, not on common ground. Nowhere in the Gospel do Jesus's opponents accuse either him or his disciples of sin (cf. 8:46), of practicing or teaching false ethics. Even the controversy about the Sabbath quickly becomes a dispute about the christological claim of the

Johannine Jesus (5:1–18). Here and elsewhere, all concerned assume that Jesus and his followers respect and abide by the basic ethical instructions given by Moses. It is further simply assumed that, as an aspect of their religious faith, Jesus's disciples engage in compassionate and socially constructive acts such as helping the poor. The love that Jesus's disciples receive from God and pass on to others is not restricted to insiders but, like the love of God, is directed outward to the world (13:29; cf. 3:16; 1 John 4:19). It is indeed true that John offers no essay on the nature of Christian ethics, but the value system and way of life to which Jesus calls his disciples are integrated into the narrative and are everywhere implicit. John's readers are challenged to perceive the ethical dimensions, personal and social, inherent in the call to discipleship and to respond in the particular ways appropriate to their own situations.

As a guide to deeper exploration, an initial survey might include the following four overlapping handgrips for grasping Johannine ethics: (1) incorporation into the people of God, (2) being sent, (3) abiding in love, and (4) doing God's work.

Incorporation into the People of God

The Johannine ethic does indeed have a personal, individual aspect. The Johannine Jesus teaches his followers that they, like all human beings, live their lives before God-the-judge, who holds each person accountable for his or her decisions and actions (John 5:22–28). Unfortunately, however, the root metaphors of new birth into the family of God, the Good Shepherd who guides and cares for the sheep, and the vine and branches have sometimes been understood too narrowly in an individualistic sense, with a corresponding distortion of the Johannine understanding of ethics, as though right and wrong were entirely a personal matter between the believer and God, just "letting my conscience be my guide."

In the Fourth Gospel, however, this individualistic understanding of ethics is integrated into the encompassing imagery of the covenant people of God. Jesus's followers belong to Israel. We have seen that "family of God," "sheep in the flock of the Good Shepherd," and "true vine" are in each case metaphors for Israel, God's covenant people called to live a separate life among the nations of the world as the means of God's blessing for the whole. "Family of God" is ultimately to include all. The Good Shepherd looks beyond the little flock to which John's hearers belong and encourages them to do the same. Even the vine does not exist for itself but exists to bear fruit—for others (15:1–7, 16). "Bearing fruit" as an image for *ethical* action is common in the whole tradition of Israel and the church (2 Kings 19:30; Prov 12:12; Isa 37:31; Jer 17:8; Ezek 17:8, 23; Matt 3:8–10; 7:17–19; 13:23; Luke 13:9; Col 1:6, 10). As biblical Israel was called and chosen, so Jesus insists that his followers are not volunteers but have been called and chosen (John 13:18; 15:16). For John, as for Jesus and his Bible, the moral life for such believers is responsible ethical living within the covenant people of God, the life of a "true Israelite" (1:47).

Just as John asserts the continuity of Jesus's followers with biblical Israel, so he presupposes the biblical ethic, the ethic of the Jewish Scriptures, as normative for the Christian life, as reinterpreted by Jesus as the "new" love command (see below). This ethic involves the individual believer in the Christian community and its social context, and concerns one's relation to other people, to society, and to the world at large as God's creation (ecology, environmental concerns). Such an ethic is inherent in the believer's incorporation into Christ, one's belonging to the church. From within this Johannine mind-set, believers are left to their own insights on ethical decisions in particular situations, with every individual always remembering the wider implications of his or her personal decisions. This means that within the Christian community, different people may sometimes have differing convictions on individual ethical issues without being compelled to exclude the others as "not really Christian."

Being Sent

The call to be a disciple means being incorporated in God's mission to the world. The christological encompassing image of the Johannine narrative is that Jesus is the Sent One. Disciples are also sent, not only *like* Jesus but *as* Jesus, extending God's mission to the world. As Jesus was the incarnation of God's love for the world, there is a sense in which this once-for-all event is continued in the lives of those who have been incorporated into the body that is Christ, who are branches of the vine that is Christ (see pp. 288–89 above on 15:1–10). When Jesus returns to God, leaving the disciples behind, they are explicitly *not* taken out of the world (17:11). Johannine Christians cannot turn inward merely to cultivate their own spirituality, nor share the new life in Christ only in the coziness of the spiritual community of insiders. The doors of the Johannine church open outward.

"In the World but Not of It?"

This common phrase is not found in the Gospel of John but comes from William Hazlitt, a nineteenth-century advocate of the good life understood as individualistic hedonism. In "On Living to Oneself" he wrote, "What I mean by living to oneself is living in the world as in it but not of it. It is to be a silent spectator of the mighty scene of things, to take a thoughtful eager interest or curiosity in what is passing in the world, but not to feel the slightest inclination to bother with it" (cf. Gospel of Thomas 42). Like the Gospel of John, Hazlitt understands authentic human life as a life of freedom, but in contrast to John, he understands the meaning of this freedom as adopting a tourist mentality. In an essay called "On Going on a Journey," he writes, "The soul of a journey is liberty, perfect liberty. To think, feel, to do just as one pleases." Being in the world is for him like being in a foreign country where one is not a citizen and has no responsibilities. It's a very interesting experience, and a very liberating one, to be a guest in somebody else's country. One is free to criticize, to observe the interesting things that happen there, to talk about what "they" do, without the slightest weight of responsibility. It's their world, I don't belong to it, and I can, gnostic-like, observe from my detached spectator stance what fools these mortals be.

The images of Israel as born-from-above family of God, sheep in the flock of the Good Shepherd, and branches of the true vine are not static, passive images. As Israel was called into being as God's agent for blessing the whole world (Gen 12:1–3), as Christ, the Sent One, represents God's mission to the world (John 3:16–17), so Jesus's disciples are called not only to live their personal, family, and social lives in a way that manifests ethical responsibility but also to participate in the mission of God's people. This would have been a new idea of the meaning of religious faith to many of John's readers, just as it is to many church people in our own time. Imagine Andronicus, a businessman in Ephesus who made a decent living but whose life revolved around making money, exploiting his employees, taking advantage of his competitors, taking pride in his sexual and business conquests. He was not a criminal but sometimes came home drunk, mistreated his wife and children, measured himself by his neighborhood standards, admired himself and was admired for his "success." He comes in contact with the new local Christian community, is converted by its message, and his personal, social, and business life is transformed. He and his family experience a new life, a new happiness. Variations of this story have actually happened millions of times through the centuries and around the world, rightly celebrated as testimony to the truth and power of the Christian faith. After a few weeks or months of participation in the church, it might still be a strange new idea to Andronicus that when he was baptized he was incorporated into the worldwide and centuries-old people of God, with a mission to the world. This, however, is the Johannine perspective on the new life that is given to every believer, just as it is the perspective of the New Testament in general. This mission involves both words and deeds. Loving care for the needy of this world involves not only helping particular people but also attending to the systemic social and political structures that afflict the weak and disenfranchised.

Such deeds are a testimony in themselves, but they also need to be accompanied by words of witness, the testimony of the Christian gospel that is the basis for all Christian ethical action. "Witness" is an important *ethical* term in Johannine theology.[17] Identifying oneself publicly with the Christian community by being baptized and participating regularly in eucharistic worship is not merely for the spiritual benefit of the believer but also for taking one's place on the witness stand (12:42–43!). One of the most insightful interpreters of New Testament ethics of our generation contends that "To abide in Jesus's logos entails abiding in the community [not leaving it, as the heretics had done], and 'to abide' carries the strong connotation of resistance to the dark and hostile world."[18] The Johannine ethic almost boils down to abiding in the community as witnesses to God's act in Christ. For the Johannine teachers, this means "abiding in love."

Abiding in Love

As the narrative shifts from Jesus's encounter with the world in chapters 1–12 to his instruction to his disciples in the Farewell Discourse in chapters 13–17, there is a decided shift in vocabulary as well. In the first part of the Gospel the focus is on the universal values of "life" and "light" in the revelation of the Son, and a call for faith (eighty-two references to life, light, darkness; only six references to love). When Jesus begins to speak directly to his disciples in 13:1, the predominant word is "love" (of forty-four references to love in the Fourth Gospel, thirty-seven are found in the latter half, the highest density by far being in the Farewell Discourse). Churchgoers and Bible readers have become accustomed to this kind of talk and may not notice its radical dimension, but it was strangely new in Roman Asia of 90–130.

In the Farewell Discourse, Jesus commanded his disciples to "love one another," repeated three times (13:34; 15:12, 17), and already found seven times in the Johannine letters, as "the message you have heard from the beginning" (1 John 3:11, 14, 23; 4:7, 11, 12; 2 John 5). The biblical command to love the neighbor, included by the Jesus of the Synoptics in the supreme commandment, is not found in John, who presents the love command as a new commandment directed only to insiders of the believing community (John 13:34; cf. 1 John 2:7–8; 2 John 5). Is this love limited to insiders? Such a love that began with Jesus's command and includes only fellow believers seems contrary to what Jesus taught and lived, and is rightly regarded with suspicion, or at least is in need of clarification. This was already a matter of discussion in the Johannine community. The dialectic of 1 John 2:7–8 explains that the love command is both new and not new. The Jesus of the Fourth Gospel typically declines to provide a systematic, consistent "explanation"; the words are more evocative and thought-provoking than definitive. We have seen that Johannine narrative theology embeds its truth in the story itself, from which we may glean at least the following:

Not Narrow or Sectarian. It is, unfortunately, possible to interpret "Love one another" in a narrow and sectarian perspective. Some members of the Johannine congregations seem to have understood it this way, being not only uninterested in mission to the world but also unenthusiastic about *koinōnia* with other Christian groups in Roman Asia. Such an attitude was an impediment to the mission in which they had been called to participate. "See how they love one another" was sometimes said not with admiration but with disdain, first of the Jews, the "haters of humanity," those who seemed to have withdrawn from society and who "take care of their own but don't care about the community as a whole." The epithet pointed to the clannishness and lack of social responsibility of those who seemed unpatriotic and refrained from participation in community life and celebrations. This was a misunderstanding that Judaism had learned to live with. Now the church, understanding itself as incorporated into the ongoing people of God, faces the same misunderstanding. The Johannine narrative itself excludes such a misunderstanding (John 10:16; 17:20–23; 20:21), but some of John's hearer-readers needed to be reminded that they did not belong to an ingrown sect. This misperception of Christian discipleship is not neutralized or diluted by Jesus's harsh-sounding prayer, "I am asking on their [the disciples'] behalf; I am not asking on behalf of the world." Since the world is God's beloved creation, prayer for the disciples is indirectly prayer for the world. If the incarnation happened, it is the most important event in the history of the *world.* "World" (*kosmos*) is used in more than one way in the Johannine tradition. Cosmos can mean the beloved creation, or it can refer to human society structured in rebellion against God. The different sets of statements about "the world" that can be abstracted from the Gospel should not be harmonized; each has its own witness to make. The tension created by this variety points to the broader narrative context in which they should be understood.[19]

Security in Belonging. John's community had suffered persecution and had insiders in prison and in need of economic and physical help provided by a loving, supporting community. Andronicus's business may have declined as a result of his membership in the new Christian group. Others, day laborers, may have lost their jobs and needed help just to put food on the table. If Andronicus still has adequate means, he now learns that he belongs to a loving community; if he is not in need, others, who are now sisters and brothers in God's family, need his help. Church members who had lost their jobs because of their Christian identity need the support—financial, not just "thoughts and prayers"—of those still employed or with savings accounts. All believers should make their ethical decisions in the confidence that if it costs them their job, they belong to a church that offers loving support, including financial help offered without condescension. Thus "love one another" need not be sectarian or exclusive. Christian love realized in practice within the community is an identifying mark, a testimony. Jesus's command does not limit love to the community. "Love one another" is also a radical, new command directed outward to the world.

The Difficulty of Loving One's Fellow Church Member. It is often easier to love the outsider, whom I do not know and may tend to romanticize, which can be done in a condescending way, than to love the insider, the cranky churchpeople I have to live and work with. The Johannine dictum in 1 John 4:20 boldly declares, "Those who say, 'I love God,' and hate their brothers or sisters, are liars; for those who do not love a brother or sister whom they have seen, cannot love God whom they have not seen." This could be appropriately extended and paraphrased, "If you do not love the insider, whom you have seen, how can you love the outsider, whom you have not seen?"

Doing God's Work

For the Johannine teachers, as for the Bible generally, doing good means doing the will of God. "Good" is not an ideal or principle but what God wills. The good God not only wills, God acts. Doing what is right means entering into God's own work. This is what human life is *for.* Human morality and decency are not a matter of *humanitarian* ideals but of doing the will of *God*. John's ethic is not based on any humanitarian abstraction, whether cynical selfishness, "enlightened self-interest," or philosophical idealism, but on the being and will of God, disclosed generally in nature and history but definitively in the once-for-all incarnation of the Word. This concern for the welfare of all human beings is in fact an element in the universal revelation of God, the light that enlightens all human beings (see pp. 185–200 above on the prologue). But other powers active in the world claim a different basis for deciding how to live one's life, different standards for deciding what constitutes decent, moral human conduct. These alternative standards include not only active criminal hostility against others but also commonsense priorities such as tolerant "live-and-let-live," narrow "me first," "me and my family," "my country first," and impersonal survival-of-the-fittest perspectives that include a necessary thinning of the herd that leaves the weak behind or actively eliminates them.

God's Work Must Truly Be Our Own

The Johannine Jesus would approve these concluding words of John F. Kennedy's inaugural address, made in a secular political setting, with three crucial qualifications: (1) Christian believers receive as their sure reward not only a good conscience but the gift of salvation, now and in the world to come. (2) History will judge our deeds, but the final judge is God. (3) "The land we love" is not only our own nation but God's world.

> "With a good conscience our only sure reward, with history the final judge of deeds, let us go forth to lead the land we love, asking His blessing and His help, but knowing that here on earth God's work must truly be our own."
>
> —John F. Kennedy, "Inaugural Address" (January 20, 1961)

Doing God's Work Is Not an Alternative to "Believing"

Earlier in the Gospel, the crowds had asked, "What must we do to perform the works of God?" Jesus responded, "This is the work of God, that you believe in him whom he has sent" (John 6:28–29). In the Johannine understanding, Jesus's declaration has a double meaning, functioning on two different planes.

First, it points to the nature of faith as the gift of God—to believe in Jesus as the Sent One is itself the work of the God who generates faith. Faith is the gift of God. Does this mean that God gives faith to some and not to others? Or does the decision of each individual determine faith or unbelief? This theological discussion was under way in the neighboring Pauline churches with which the Johannine community had some interchange. The narrative theology of the Johannine teachers affirms the same understanding as the more discursive epistolary form of the Pauline school: the gospel calls for decision, but those who believe it give thanks for their faith as God's gift (see Eph 2:1–10).

Second, Jesus's declaration also points to the nature of ethics, the life of the believer. To do God's work is to believe in Jesus. This must not be understood within the Pauline framework as it is popularly understood, as though the question were, "How can a person be saved?," to which the answer is, "Not by any of your own works, but by faith in Christ." Already in this interchange with the crowds present at the feeding of the five thousand, the nature of Christian ethics is revealed. This includes social responsibility, portrayed in the traditional story as feeding hungry people ("You give them something to eat"). To be sure, human beings cannot live by material bread alone, the perspective assumed by the crowds in the Fourth Gospel (and by Satan in the Q version of the temptation story; cf. Matt 4:4; Luke 4:4). Nonetheless, Jesus does literally feed literally hungry people, just as he heals those who are weak and sick. In the Farewell Discourse, he promises that his disciples will do even greater works than those done by the pre-Easter Jesus (John 14:12). Jesus's disciples will not only preach and teach the message of salvation, they will give people material bread to satisfy the gnawing of hungry stomachs, and work in political and institutional settings to minimize the systemic problems that allow people to be hungry in a world in which there is enough for everyone. For the Johannine Jesus, nothing can take this away—no symbolism, no theology. God's work is believing in the one God sent, believing in the God who sent Jesus. Such faith means living in the community of faith that sees all of life and the world as different, living the compassionate life of caring for others, because this is the reality of the world and life disclosed in God's sending of Jesus.

"I Will Come Again"

In each of the Synoptic Gospels, Jesus's farewell discourse shortly before his death was a prediction of the troubles the disciples would suffer after his death; a prediction of the intensification of these tribulations just before the end; a discussion of the cosmic signs that would signal the parousia of the Son of Man, who would appear on the clouds of heaven to execute God's judgment on the world; and warnings about the shortness of the time (Mark 13:1–37; Matt 24:1–25, 46; Luke 21:5–36). In Mark 13:30–32, which Matthew and Luke adopted, each in his own way, Jesus had assured his disciples that the end would come in their own generation. This expectation had been slightly moderated in Mark 9:1 (with minor adjustments in Matt 16:28 and Luke 9:27) by Jesus's declaration that "some" of those then living would see the kingdom of God come in power. The Johannine Farewell Discourse, though much longer than any of its synoptic parallels, has only a minimum of apocalyptic imagery and expectation. Yet the discourse has the same structural location and plays the same theological role as in the Synoptics. The eschatological expectation does not disappear and retains some apocalyptic features. The Johannine Jesus explicitly promises that after his death "I will come again" (John 14:3), "I am going away, and I am coming to you" (14:28), and "I will see you again" (16:22). We may draw more closely within hearing distance of Johannine eschatological teaching if we take a brief glance at the historical trajectory of the formation of early Christian eschatological views and the options within which the churches of Roman Asia, in 90–130 CE, were working out their theology.

- Biblical-Jewish hope for the consummation of God's purpose often, but not always, included the expectation of the Messiah, who would be the agent of establishing God's universal peace and justice. Faith in the coming of a Messiah was by definition eschatological. The Messiah brings the end, after which there can be no further development and no reversion to the previous troubled state of the world. Nothing can come after. "They lived happily ever after."
- At least from the time of Daniel on (ca. 165 BCE), this eschatological hope was expressed apocalyptically, as the coming of the Son of Man, the resurrection, and the last judgment, preceded by a time of terror, tribulation, and cosmic upheaval.
- John the Baptist was one of several Jewish apocalyptic prophets in the first century CE whose message focused on the soon coming of a mighty deliverer sent by God.
- Jesus and his message are best understood within this stream of apocalyptic tradition. When Jesus was baptized by John, and then began his own preaching of the presence and near consummation of the kingdom

of God, his message of the kingdom of God was his own distinctive adaptation of Jewish apocalyptic.

- Jesus's resurrection was proclaimed by his earliest followers not merely as a sensational event that happened to Jesus but as the beginning of the promised resurrection of all the dead at the end of history. However Jesus's own message is understood, virtually all interpreters agree that earliest Christianity began as an apocalyptic group within Judaism, identifying Jesus himself as the Messiah and Son of Man.
- This was the situation when our earliest Christian document appeared about twenty years after the death of Jesus. First Thessalonians expects Jesus to return soon, within the lifetime of Paul himself (4:13–18). All Paul's letters, earliest to latest, were written in the expectation of the near parousia, though in his later letters, as he faced sickness, imprisonment, and death, he was no longer confident that he himself would still be alive at the parousia (Phil 1:23; 2 Cor 5:1–10). For the first Christian generation to which Paul belonged, the first and second coming of Christ could be seen as a unit. When it was objected, "If the Messiah has come, why does the evil world continue in its perverted state?" Christians could respond, "The Messiah was killed, raised from the dead, and will return soon to complete the messianic salvation."

The passing of the first generation without the return of Jesus having occurred does not seem to have generated a general crisis for Christian believers. Nor is there evidence that the Johannine community was engaged in a debate, with some still proclaiming, "Jesus is coming soon," others explaining, "The Christ has already come," and some talking about the Jesus who has come to the church in the Holy Spirit, who comes into our hearts, or who comes to receive us into heaven at our death. Although there was no theological crisis, in the second or third generation there was a need for the church to make sense of its eschatological traditions, just as there is in our own time. This need not be done polemically, and John does not engage in eschatological polemics (as he does with Christology and ecclesiology, which were burning existential issues). The Messiah was to come at the end of history. The Messiah had come, but history moved on as before, in some ways worse. How should they understand Jesus's promise, "I will come again"? Three options were available to Christian believers in Roman Asia, in 90–130, which can be summarized as (1) rejection, (2) reaffirmation, and (3) reinterpretation.

Rejection: "We Were Wrong"

This approach simply abandons previous convictions and the theology in which they were expressed.

"We Were Wrong about Jesus"

Some rejected the Christian faith and returned to their previous Judaism or Greco-Roman religion. Some in the Johannine community may have abandoned the faith, but the Fourth Gospel addresses those who had continued within the community, not lapsed believers.

"Jewish Apocalyptic Thinking about Jesus Was Wrong"

The predominately gentile church in Roman Asia had accepted much of the Jewish theological framework for thinking about the identity of Jesus and the meaning of the Christ event. Apocalyptic thinking in particular was alien to the everyday thought world of typical gentiles. Thinking about Christian faith conceived and expressed in these terms seems to have been proven wrong: the Son of Man had not appeared on the clouds of heaven to judge the world and complete the saving act of God. Faith in Jesus could be retained, but apocalypticism must be rejected. A favorite alternative was presented by emerging Gnosticism, which seemed more in step with traditional Greek thought. Jesus was a great teacher sent from God who taught true knowledge. There was no incarnation. There will be no "second coming." There will be no transformation of the world, no new creation. Salvation comes by knowledge that enables individual souls to live in this evil world with good conscience in detached serenity, and finally to escape and return to the soul's heavenly home.

Reaffirmation: "Now the End Is Near"

Chronology is recalibrated. The earlier Christian generations had understood apocalyptic prophecies of the near end to refer to their own time, which turned out to be a misunderstanding. But some Christians in Roman Asia, guided by the preaching of Christian prophets and teachers interpreting biblical and early Christian traditions, see the events of their own time as signs that now the end is indeed very near. The increased pressure to conform to the emperor cult and threats of persecution to those who resisted could be understood as the tribulation of apocalyptic thought scheduled to occur just before the final end.

John the prophet of Revelation proclaimed the soon coming of the Lord at the end of the first century. His prophetic letter circulated among the Johannine churches, retaining and reasserting the vivid apocalyptic imagery to express the urgency of holding on to the faith.

In 1–2 John, the elder dispenses with the details of the apocalyptic drama—"what we will be has not yet been revealed" (1 John 3:2). Nonetheless, the elder still affirms that the end is coming soon ("it is the last hour," 1 John 2:18), that the antichrist is real and already present in the false teachers (1 John 2:18; 4:3; 2 John 7), and that "when [Christ] is revealed, we will be like him, for we will see him as he is." This hope is the foundation and motivation for the life of discipleship (1 John 3:1–3).

Reinterpretation: "We Need to Rethink 'Jesus Is Coming Soon'"

The "second coming" is an authentic part of Christian faith that must not be abandoned, but what it means needs to be rethought in the light of our new situation. Such reinterpretations tended to assume two main forms, focusing on either "soon" or "end."

"Soon"

This language need not be taken with chronological literalness. Jesus was remembered as having promised, "A little while, and you will no longer see me, and again a little while, and you will see me" (John 16:17). A generation or two later in Roman Asia, the Johannine churches are echoing the question of the disciples at the Last Supper: "What does he mean by this 'a little while'?" The intensity of the discussion is indicated by the repetition of the phrase eight times in the Farewell Discourse (14:19; 16:16–19). Since Jesus did not return in "a little while" as promised, "soon" must not have its conventional meaning. As the first generation began to pass away, a saying (probably the oracle of a Christian prophet speaking in Jesus's name) reassured the church that at least "some standing here" would not die until "the kingdom of God has come in power" (Mark 9:1). A Christian teacher writing in Peter's name about the same time as the publication of the final edition of the Fourth Gospel explained that God's time does not correspond to our time and was glad to find a text in his Bible that declared a thousand years in God's sight to be only a day. This helped him to understand "soon" in a different way than had the first generation of Christians; "soon" for God may be a very long time for humans (2 Pet 3:3–13; Ps 90:4). About the same time, the author of the

Gospel of Luke was rewriting the story of Jesus and the early church to show that the Christ comes not at the end of history but "in the midst of time," allowing for many generations of church history between the first and second comings of Jesus.[20]

In the Johannine community, the problem posed by the delay of the parousia was intensified by the expectation that the Beloved Disciple, presumably the founder and original leader of the community, and the guarantor of its traditions, would be among the few that *would* live to see the parousia. Both Peter and Paul had been regarded by some as the principal leaders and teachers of the whole church, but they were both gone, both martyred in Rome in the 60s. The Beloved Disciple lived on in Asia, fueling the hope of the Johannine community that he was the church's principal teacher and would live until the parousia (John 21:20–24). When the Beloved Disciple died, this generated some disappointment and consternation in the community, but the final form of the Gospel explained that this had been a misunderstanding all along: Jesus had never promised that he would not die before the parousia, but that neither Peter nor anyone else should be concerned about when the end would come (cf. the Synoptic Gospels' dealing with the question in Mark 13:30–32; Matt 24:34–36). The Johannine Jesus "knows everything," including the future, including the date of the parousia (John 16:30). Again, the Johannine teachers correct what they perceive as a misunderstanding of the earlier tradition. In Mark 13:30–33, Jesus doesn't know and the revelatory angels that communicate God's message through Christian prophets don't know (Rev 1:1; 10:1–3; 22:6), but the disciples in the Johannine narrative finally come to see what had previously been obscured by Jesus's figurative language, that the definitive summary of Christian faith is "Jesus *has* come from God" (not "will come *back* . . ."; cf. John 16:28–30). The first coming is now decisive and is not preliminary to the Messiah's work at the second coming (though that is not necessarily denied). The language of *nikē* (victory) is used of the past and present: "I *have* overcome the world" (cf. 16:33). The eschatological victory of God does not await the parousia. The definitive victory is already won, realized and shared by the faithful community, and will achieve its consummation at the parousia (1 John 2:13–14; 4:4; 5:4–5). This is Revelation's own message, already centered in the slain lamb. The Gospel of John is not a replacement of Revelation but an interpretation that allows this book that had circulated in the Johannine community for a generation to be retained and proclaimed among the normative documents of the faith (Rev 2:7, 11, 17, 26; 3:5, 12, 21; 5:5; 15:2; 17:14; 21:7).

"End of the World"

This idea need not be taken with cosmological literalness. The "antichrist" who was to appear at the end refers not to an evil mythological figure, as in Revelation 13, but to the false teachers who are already present (1 John 2:18–22; 4:3; 2 John 7). The destruction of the power of evil that was to happen at the end did indeed occur in the event of Jesus's death/resurrection/ascension, God's victory over the cosmic power of evil (John 12:31; 14:30; 16:11). The resurrection promised for the end of history did indeed happen in the resurrection of Jesus and continues to happen in the new life received by those who believe in him (11:17–27). The meaning of "Jesus is coming soon" is redefined in terms of what actually happened and is happening. Jesus's promise to come again, and soon, was indeed fulfilled and is still being fulfilled. Jesus came back at the resurrection (20:1–23), and/or with the coming of the Spirit (14:15–17, 25–26; 15:26–27; 16:7–11, 12–15), and/or at the believer's death to take the believer to heaven (14:1–3; cf. Rev 6:9–11; Phil 1:23; 2 Cor 5:1–8).

Eschatology in the Johannine Community

Each of these eschatological views was circulating in the Johannine community as the teachers in the Johannine school formulated their definitive retelling of the Jesus Christ story. Their narrative theology allowed them to incorporate more than one view as authentic Christian understanding—but not just any view. *That* Jesus is the Messiah, the eschatological fulfillment of God's promise, is indispensable. The eschatology inherent in confession that Jesus is the Messiah is not limited to one theology, and cannot be. Multiple, overlapping points of view and frames of reference are not a problem to be resolved or an embarrassment to be avoided, but they testify to the mystery of God's ultimate purpose that cannot be captured in any one view. There is thus no comprehensive, systematic discussion of "Johannine eschatology," in the Bible or out. The message is in the story itself. Insights into how Johannine Christians should understand the promised "second coming" are shared incrementally and worked into the narrative. The following channel markers may help the preacher and teacher to negotiate the deep waters of John's narrative.

The Center of Gravity of the Christian Life Is Shifted, without Abandoning the Future Hope

The earliest extant Christian text, already circulating in Roman Asia in the first century CE, on its first page addressed new converts as those who had "turned to God from idols, to serve a living and true God, and to wait for his Son from heaven, whom he raised from the dead—Jesus, who rescues us from the wrath that is coming" (1 Thess 1:9–10). On the one hand, the Johannine Jesus proclaims that the central events that constitute the hopes of apocalyptic eschatology are not limited to the future hope but are already fulfilled in the Christ event. With the coming of Christ, the hoped-for eschatological events are happening now, in the life of Jesus and the continuing life of the church: the resurrection, final judgment, defeat of Satan, coming of the Spirit, and gift of eternal life are already real in the believer's present experience (John 3:18–19, 36; 6:27, 47; 11:21–27; 12:31; 17:3). Nonetheless, the Fourth Gospel resists any reduction of the eschatological hope to realized eschatology and clearly affirms the reality of future apocalyptic events. As Son of Man, Jesus is the one who will raise the dead on the last day (5:28–29; 6:39, 40, 44, 54; 11:24; 12:48). In the Fourth Gospel, eschatology continues to be an essential theme and must do so wherever the fundamental confession is that Jesus is the Christ. The story of Christ's feeding the multitude, and every celebration of eucharistic worship, is a foretaste of the messianic banquet.

The Work of the Messiah Is Not Yet Completed

Not only is the Christ already present with the church but the Christ will return at the consummation of history to bring the work of God to fulfillment. John declares that after Jesus's departure, his disciples will do even greater works than Jesus had done during his earthly ministry (John 14:12), but the Johannine Jesus says nothing like, "I've started the work and shown you the way; now it is up to you." Neither is it the faithful disciple's task to simply sit back and wait for the second coming, when God will make everything right. God is faithful and will complete the work he has begun, and disciples are not only called to enter into that work but are already placed in it by their baptism. In Johannine theology, ethics and eschatology are inseparable.

Conventional Apocalyptic Imagery Is Minimized without Abandoning Its Underlying Convictions

Apocalyptic ideas and images were vibrantly alive in other writings circulating in the Johannine community. Not only the letters of Paul but also Revelation and the Johannine letters proclaim a robust faith in the future return of Jesus, portraying it in vivid and dramatic mythological imagery (Revelation throughout, esp. chaps. 1–3; 20–22; 1 John 2:18, 22, 28; 3:2–3; 4:3, 17; 2 John 7). The "wrath of God" is not only proclaimed but also portrayed in graphic, violent images. The Fourth Gospel adopts neither the specific apocalyptic imagery nor the timetable of Revelation's eschatological hope, but it does not reject this traditional eschatological thinking that had been vigorously renewed in Roman Asia at the end of the first century (Revelation, 1 Peter, 1 John, 2 Thessalonians). John's minimizing of the imagery of apocalyptic is not a matter of squeamishness or theological sophistication; he does so partly because he has adopted the narrative form rather than the genre of apocalyptic vision, and partly because he assumes and affirms the language of Scripture that is regularly read in the Johannine congregations. Not only Daniel but also Isaiah, the Psalms, and other biblical texts are packed with dramatic eschatological images of the final victory of God. The Fourth Gospel retains the fundamental apocalyptic images of the coming wrath (3:36), resurrection (5:25–29; 11:17–27), and judgment (5:22–27; 8:50; 12:48) without explicating them in lurid detail. Those in the Johannine congregations who backed away from the violent imagery of Revelation could not avoid apocalyptic by reading the Gospel of John, but this retelling the Jesus Christ story did offer a way of appropriating the Christian message more in tune with their own cultural sensitivities.

All Apocalyptic Imagery Is Defined by the Christ Event

For John, as for Christian faith as such, the meaning of the Christ event is not forced into a prior understanding of eschatology. Rather, the meaning of eschatology is redefined in light of the coming of Jesus. As in Revelation, the Jesus who appears at the end of history (and the end of our life) is the Jesus we have already known as the incarnate Word. The fulfillment of God's purpose at the consummation of history offers no surprises, not a different God or Jesus from the one we know in the Gospels. Love and judgment are not parceled out between the first and second comings, but the God whose love and judgment are both beyond all our understanding is the God who was present at creation, in the covenant history of Israel, supremely and definitely in the Christ event, and who continues with the church and world until the end. The life of the believer is lived in the framework of the divine plan for history.

Johannine Ecumenism: Joining the Mainstream, Swimming Upstream (21:1–25)

Unity and Diversity

The Farewell Discourse, like John's Gospel as a whole, concludes with a concern for the unity of the church. Jesus had prayed for the visible unity of the church, a unity that could be seen in the world and would be integral to the church's evangelistic message, a united witness that would encourage the world to believe (17:11–23). A divided church was a hindrance to the church's mission through which the love of God flows to the world. The Johannine community became increasingly aware of others in Roman Asia and the wider Mediterranean world who confessed Jesus to be the Christ. The Johannine congregations were a distinctive group with their own particular history and character, with tendencies toward a dualistic sectarianism. They had become aware that they were members of the one church, incorporated into Israel, the one people of God, the one vine (15:1–11), sheep of the one Shepherd—but there were other sheep, other flocks, that needed to be, and would be, brought into the one fold (10:1–16). Jesus's self-giving love manifest on the cross is to unite the scattered people of God (11:45–52). For the Johannine community, Christian unity was not a memory to be restored but a hope to be realized. The people of God are essentially one. The unity of Jesus's followers was not merely a human ideal; it is already a divine reality. This unity begins with Christology. Jesus Christ is not merely an *agent*, not even the supreme or primary agent, but is *one with the Father.* As always in the Fourth Gospel, Christology morphs into ecclesiology. The mission begins with God and is directed to the world. The Johannine church understands itself to be caught up in this divine mission. As was being said in other churches in Roman Asia, there is (not "ought to be") "one Lord, one faith, one baptism, one God and Father of all, who is above all and through all and in all" (Eph 4:5–6). There is the unity God gives, but there is also a unity to be attained. The fragmented churches of Roman Asia discussed and debated what role the apostles play in the realization of this hope.

Apostolic Authority Becomes Important for the Johannine Christians

In some other branches of the Christian community present in Roman Asia, *apostolic leadership* was becoming a focus of church identity, a means of sorting out authentic from questionable or false understandings of the faith and direction for Christian mission. The Pauline churches were gathering around the Pauline tradition as their guide. A broader tradition, stretching from Antioch to Rome, was beginning to congeal around the Petrine tradition, sometimes combining the figures of Peter and Paul as the church's apostolic leadership designated by Jesus.[21]

The Johannine community had been hesitant, and somewhat skeptical, about this development. Their congregations had not been founded by an apostle. The apostolic status of the Beloved Disciple was vague or unimportant to Johannine Christians. The Johannine community had not countered the emerging movement toward accepting Peter or Paul as symbolic leader for the whole church by proposing its own founder and "patron saint," the Beloved Disciple. Nor had the concept "apostle" ("one sent," in the sense of "authorized representative") become a focal point in considerations of the nature of the church and its unity. *Apostolos* is found only once in the Gospel and letters of John (John 13:16; *apostolos*, translated "messenger[s]" in many English translations). Even here, "apostle" is not used in the "official" sense it was assuming in other churches, but as an incidental illustration of the identity of Jesus, *the* Sent One. Johannine Christianity had focused on the democratic perspective of the Spirit, given to the whole church, not bound to the apostles, and illustrated in the charismatic leadership of Christian prophets and the Beloved Disciple. The Fourth Gospel refers to the "twelve" disciples but never gives a list and mentions only six by name (Andrew, Simon Peter, Philip, Nathanael, Thomas, Judas Iscariot). The Beloved Disciple is assumed to be among the Twelve, and "the sons of Zebedee" are mentioned in 21:2. None are ever called apostles.

Throughout Book Two of the Gospel, the reader has been made aware of the ways in which the emerging prominence of Peter in other streams of Christian tradition is juxtaposed to the figure of the Beloved Disciple, who always comes off better. During its first generation, the Johannine community seems to have resisted the rising prominence of Peter as a symbol figure under whose banner the fragmented and dispersed church could gather. Earlier edition(s) of the Gospel had favored this primacy of informal and charismatic leadership over structure and the growing "centralization of authority" in Rome. Without discarding this earlier perspective and its values, the concluding scene of the final edition of the Gospel—which is its only canonical form—finds a way to affirm the growing commitment to Petrine leadership and to encourage the Johannine community to join the emerging mainstream. This was not a decline from the spontaneity and Spirit-filled enthusiasm that characterized the earliest church into the "institutionalized religion" of "early catholicism," but the dynamic and necessary structuring of the church for its long-term mission in the world. The following facets may be highlighted:

21:3: "I am going fishing." Though the Johannine teachers obviously are aware of the synoptic tradition in which Peter was one of the four fishermen first called to be disciples (Mark 1:16–20 pars.), the Fourth Gospel has not previously mentioned that Peter was a fisherman. In the Gospel's narrative world, this is not a "return to the old life" before Jesus had called them to be his disciples, a decline into the mundane world after the excitement of Easter, sometimes taken as the theme of the sermon on the Sunday after Easter. In this Gospel, Peter begins his work as fisherman after the resurrection. All the disciples—likewise not previously fishermen—say, "We'll go with you," not "We'll follow you." In Johannine perspective, Peter is not yet their leader. That night they catch nothing. The perceptive reader may remember the Gospel's pervasive symbolism of night and darkness (John 1:5; 3:2, 19; 6:17; 8:12; 9:4; 11:10; 12:35, 46; 13:30; 19:39; 20:1). Without "abiding" in Jesus, they are "in the dark" and can do nothing on their own (15:5).

21:6–7: "They were not able to haul it in . . ." "Haul in" is *helkō*, as in 6:44 discussed above: "No one can come to me unless drawn by the Father who sent me." The disciples can't bring the fish into the boat on their own (on a boat as a common early Christian symbol for the church, cf. p. 249 above on 6:16–21, and Matt 8:23–27; 14:22–33, and commentaries thereon). Reminiscent of the story in Matthew 14 where Peter gets out of the boat—and promptly sinks—here he eagerly jumps into the sea and comes to Jesus. The version of the story that had circulated in Matthew 14 is here redeemed.

21:11: "Peter went aboard and hauled the net ashore, full of large fish." After Peter's meeting with the risen Jesus, and at his command, Peter does what the other disciples could not do. Despite the large number of fish, the net is not broken. Through Peter's ministry, the large "catch" remains united. Church imagery shimmers in the background of the readers' imagination.

21:15–17: "Do you love me? . . . Feed my lambs. . . . Tend my sheep. . . . Feed my sheep." The fleeting mention of the charcoal fire is enough to conjure up the only previous reference, when Peter stood around the fire and three times denied Jesus. His failure is here redeemed, and he is three times commissioned to be the shepherd of Christ's sheep. Members of the flock remain "my lambs," "my sheep," "my sheep." The risen Christ remains the one Good Shepherd, but he no longer pastors the church directly, as in the view of those in the Johannine community who resisted the developing ecclesiastical structures. Some among the Johannine congregations continue to advocate the kind of charismatic leadership of the previous generation represented by the Beloved Disciple and by the imagery of Revelation (7:17), which likewise had advocated charismatic ministry over against structured church leadership (see the contrast between the true Good Shepherd and the paid-ministry "hirelings" opposed in John 10:12). Here, as in 1 Peter 5:4 (1 Peter was circulating in the churches of Roman Asia), Christ exercises his shepherding ministry through human pastors but remains the Chief Shepherd (cf. Heb 13:17, 20, 24). Simon Peter is here commissioned to be this pastor of the whole church. The Johannine community is encouraged to join the mainstream that is adopting Peter as its symbolic leader under whose shepherding care the church is to be united. The church needs pastors ("pastor," of course, means simply "shepherd") not only to guide and nourish the flock but also to protect it from wolves, the purveyors of false teaching that erodes Christian faith (John 10:12; cf. Matt 7:15; 10:16; Luke 10:3).

21:19: "(He said this to indicate the kind of death by which he would glorify God.) . . . 'Follow me.'" When the Fourth Gospel was written, it was known throughout the churches of the Mediterranean world that Peter, like Paul, had died as a martyr in Rome. His martyr's death authenticated his testimony (*martys* means "witness"). After the resurrection, he is called and commissioned directly by the risen Christ. "Follow me" is now said to Peter for the first time in the Fourth Gospel (21:19, repeated 21:22; cf. Mark 1:17 par.; 2:14 par.; 8:34 par.; 10:21 par.).

21:20–25: "Lord, what about him?" Some in the Johannine community respond to the encouragement to accept Peter as the church's symbolic leader by asking about the role of the Beloved Disciple, their founder and "patron saint." He had not died a martyr's death but had apparently lived to an advanced age, a living witness to Jesus's promise that at least some of the first generation would continue until the parousia. This is corrected; it had been a misunderstanding (see above). The Beloved Disciple had not become a martyr, as had Peter and Paul, but he is now considered the author of the church's normative witness (John 21:24) and continues to be the guarantor of the church's tradition "from the beginning" (see pp. 155–56, 162 above on 1 John 1:1–3). Accepting Petrine leadership does not mean abandoning the

Beloved Disciple and the tradition he had founded. Accepting the emerging church leadership structures does not mean rejecting the guidance and power of the Holy Spirit, who continues to work not only through officially authorized leaders but also in the congregation as a whole. This same pattern of growth and development was happening in the neighbor churches of the Pauline tradition, to which we will turn in the second volume.

Epilogue

Two travelers walk along the road together, engaged in serious and friendly conversation. It turns out they had both been wrong. They are disappointed. Shattered. They had met a young man, a life-changer and world-changer. They had believed in him and his cause, had believed that the world could be different. He had given them hope. The road they were on was going someplace. Now he was dead, done in by the world he had tried to make a better place. They still had his teaching, his example, but now his vision of what he had called the "kingdom of God" would have to join the many other shattered dreams along the road. "We had hoped," they said, but now he is dead. "Of all sad words of tongue or pen, the saddest are these: 'it might have been.'" Would it have been better never to have hoped, never even to have asked where the road is going? Now, it's too late.

As they approach a village where they would share the evening meal, a third traveler joins their conversation. A pleasant chap, though not very up to date, not even aware of recent events in the capital. During the meal, he speaks directly to them, as though he had always known them. Then he disappeared. They returned to the city, and in their efforts to tell their fellow disciples what had happened, said things like "Were not our hearts burning within us while he was talking to us on the road, while he was opening the Scriptures to us?" and "He was made known to us in the breaking of bread." While they were trying to tell this good news, Jesus himself stood among them and said to them, "Peace be with you. . . . You will be my witnesses in Jerusalem . . . to the ends of the earth." Even when it's too late, it's not too late.

It turns out, there is only one road. It is going someplace, and there is One who has been there and back. We didn't figure this out—it has been revealed to us, by One who once walked with us on the road, and still does. We are all on the same road, all children of the same Father, the creator, who stands at the beginning and end of the road, who is with us on the road, and will bring us and the whole creation to the Holy City.

In the meantime, a job to do . . .

Notes

FOREWORD

1. William Sloane Coffin, "White Harvest, Few Reapers," in *The Collected Sermons of William Sloane Coffin*, vol. 2 (Louisville: Westminster John Knox, 2008), 166.

PROLOGUE

1. This is my elaboration of the brief parable in John Hick, *Faith and Knowledge*, 2nd ed. (Ithaca, NY: Cornell University Press, 1966), 177–78 and 195.

CHAPTER 1

1. Unless otherwise noted, translations are quoted or adapted from the NRSV.

2. Karl Barth, *The Word of God and the Word of Man* (Gloucester, MA: Peter Smith, 1978), 12–25.

3. Barth, *The Word of God*, 104.

4. Claude Lévi-Strauss, *Structural Anthropology*, trans. Claire Jacobson and Brooke Grundfest Schoepf (London: Penguin Books, 1968), 1:221.

5. Richard B. Hays, *The Conversion of the Imagination: Paul as Interpreter of Israel's Scripture* (Grand Rapids: Eerdmans, 2005), 99.

6. George Orwell, *1984* (New York: New American Library, 1949).

7. Stephen W. Hawking, *A Briefer History of Time* (New York: Random House, 2005), 17 and 134.

8. M. Eugene Boring, "Matthew: Introduction, Commentary, and Reflections," in *The New Interpreter's Bible*, ed. Leander Keck (Nashville: Abingdon, 1995), 148.

9. John J. Collins, *The Apocalyptic Imagination: An Introduction to Jewish Apocalyptic Literature*, 3rd ed. (Grand Rapids: Eerdmans, 2016).

10. Peter L. Berger and Thomas Luckmann, *The Social Construction of Reality: A Treatise in the Sociology of Knowledge* (New York: Doubleday, 1966); Udo Schnelle, *Theology of the New Testament*, trans. M. Eugene Boring (Grand Rapids: Baker Academic, 2009), chaps. 1–2.

11. The following content borrows from and adapts the content in M. Eugene Boring, *Revelation*, Interpretation: A Bible Commentary for Teaching and Preaching (Louisville: Westminster John Knox, 1989), 35–45.

12. This list is adapted from Boring, *Revelation*, 68–70, and M. Eugene Boring, *Introduction to the New Testament: History, Literature, Theology* (Louisville: Westminster John Knox, 2012), 639–41.

13. Some material in this paragraph is adapted from Boring, *Revelation*, 41–42.

14. Karl Barth, *Evangelical Theology: An Introduction*, trans. Grover Foley (New York: Holt, Rinehart & Winston, 1963), 160.

15. Rudolf Bultmann, *Jesus Christ and Mythology* (London: SCM, 1958), 21.

16. Reinhard Feldmeier, *The First Letter of Peter*, trans. Peter H. Davids (Waco, TX: Baylor University Press, 2008), 4–5.

CHAPTER 2

1. Leander Keck, *Why Christ Matters: Toward a New Testament Christology* (Waco, TX: Baylor University Press, 2015), 32.

2. The following paragraphs borrow from and adapt the content of "Jesus' Call to Decision Implies an Ecclesiology—the Church in the Theology of the Apocalypse," *Perspectives in Religious Studies* 45, no. 2 (Summer 2018).

3. Cf. M. Eugene Boring, *Revelation*, Interpretation: A Bible Commentary for Teaching and Preaching (Louisville: Westminster John Knox, 1989), 81.

4. Luke Timothy Johnson, "The New Testament's Anti-Jewish Slander and the Conventions of Ancient Polemic," *Journal of Biblical Literature* 108, no. 3 (1989): 419–41.

5. Craig R. Koester, *Revelation: A New Translation with Introduction and Commentary*, Anchor Yale Bible 38A (New Haven: Yale University Press, 2014), 367.

6. Koester, *Revelation*, 341.

7. Some material in the following paragraphs is adapted from Boring, *Revelation*, 112–19, and M. Eugene Boring, *Introduction to the New Testament: History, Literature, Theology* (Louisville: Westminster John Knox, 2012), 653–54.

8. Paul S. Minear, *The Kingdom and the Power: An Exposition of the New Testament Gospel* (Louisville: Westminster John Knox, 1950).

9. Frederick W. Danker, Walter Bauer, William F. Arndt, and F. Wilbur Gingrich, *Greek-English Lexicon of the New Testament and Other Early Christian Literature*, 3rd ed. (Chicago: University of Chicago Press, 2000), 300.

10. Richard Bauckham, *The Theology of the Book of Revelation*, New Testament Theology (Cambridge: Cambridge University Press, 1993).

11. Elisabeth Schüssler Fiorenza, *Invitation to the Book of Revelation* (Garden City, NY: Doubleday, 1981), 119.

12. Walter J. Harrelson, *Interpreting the Old Testament* (New York: Holt, Rinehart & Winston, 1964), 486.

CHAPTER 3

1. Rudolf Bultmann, *The Gospel of John: A Commentary*, trans. G. R. Beasley-Murray, R. W. N. Hoare, and John Kenneth Riches (Philadelphia: Westminster, 1971), 323.

2. J. K. Elliott, *The Apocryphal New Testament: A Collection of Apocryphal Christian Literature in an English Translation Based on M. R. James* (Oxford: Oxford University Press, 1993), 317.

3. Elliott, *The Apocryphal New Testament*, 320.

4. Elliott, *The Apocryphal New Testament*, 320–21.
5. Elliott, *The Apocryphal New Testament*, 141.

CHAPTER 4

1. Gerhard Ebeling, *Evangelische Evangelienauslegung: Eine Untersuchung zu Luthers Hermeneutik* (Darmstadt: Wissenschaftliche Buchgesellschaft, 1962), 108.

2. Ernst Käsemann, *The Testament of Jesus: A Study of the Gospel of John in the Light of Chapter 17*, New Testament Library (London: SCM, 1968), 8–9, 26–27, 66, 73, 75.

3. William Loader, *Jesus in John's Gospel: Structure and Issues in Johannine Christology* (Grand Rapids: Eerdmans, 2017), 412. The list: 2:1–11; 3:1–21; 4:4–42; 6:1–71; 9:1–41; 18:1–19:42.

4. Some material in the following list is adapted from M. Eugene Boring, *Introduction to the New Testament: History, Literature, Theology* (Louisville: Westminster John Knox, 2012), 667–68.

5. Gustaf Aulén, *Christus Victor: An Historical Study of the Three Main Types of the Idea of the Atonement*, trans. A. G. Herbert (London: SPCK, 1970).

6. On entry/exit terminology, see Loader, *Jesus in John's Gospel*, 41–71.

7. John Ashton, *Understanding the Fourth Gospel* (New York: Oxford University Press, 1991), 362.

8. J. Louis Martyn, *History and Theology in the Fourth Gospel*, rev. and exp. ed. (Nashville: Abingdon, 1979).

9. Wayne A. Meeks, *Christ Is the Question* (Louisville: Westminster John Knox, 2006).

10. Reinhold Niebuhr, *The Nature and Destiny of Man*, 2 vols., Gifford Lectures (New York: Scribner's Sons, 1964), 2:1–35.

11. D. T. Niles, "Evangelism Is Just One Beggar Telling Another Beggar Where to Find Bread," in *They That May Have Life* (New York: Harper & Brothers, 1951).

12. C. H. Dodd, *The Parables of the Kingdom* (New York: Scribner's Sons, 1961), 5.

13. Elie Wiesel, *Night*, trans. Stella Rodway (New York: Avon Books, 1960).

14. Frederick W. Danker, Walter Bauer, William F. Arndt, and F. Wilbur Gingrich, *Greek-English Lexicon of the New Testament and Other Early Christian Literature*, 3rd ed. (Chicago: University of Chicago Press, 2000), 318.

15. D. Moody Smith, *The Theology of the Gospel of John* (Cambridge: Cambridge University Press, 1995), 141.

16. See full discussion in Loader, *Jesus in John's Gospel*, 126, 194–203.

17. Thomas G. Long, *Testimony: Talking Ourselves into Being Christian* (San Francisco: Jossey-Bass, 2004).

18. Wayne A. Meeks, "The Ethics of the Gospel of John," in *Exploring the Gospel of John: In Honor of D. Moody Smith*, ed. R. Alan Culpepper and C. Clifton Black (Louisville: Westminster John Knox, 1996), 323.

19. Russell Pregeant, *Knowing Truth, Doing Good: Engaging New Testament Ethics* (Minneapolis: Fortress, 2008), 199–207.

20. Hans Conzelmann, *The Theology of St. Luke*, trans. Geoffrey Buswell (New York: Harper & Row, 1961).

21. M. Eugene Boring, *An Introduction to the New Testament: History, Literature, Theology* (Louisville: Westminster John Knox, 2012), 141–42, 184–85, 312–14, 320–27, 357–58, 372–95, 400–433, 581–83, 590–621.

Bibliography

General Studies of the New Testament

Boring, M. Eugene. *Introduction to the New Testament: History, Literature, Theology*. Louisville: Westminster John Knox, 2012.

Boring, M. Eugene, and Fred B. Craddock. *The People's New Testament Commentary*. Louisville: Westminster John Knox, 2004.

Brown, Raymond E. *An Introduction to the New Testament*. New York: Doubleday, 1997.

Holladay, Carl R. *A Critical Introduction to the New Testament*. Nashville: Abingdon, 2005.

Schnelle, Udo. *The History and Theology of the New Testament Writings*. Translated by M. Eugene Boring. London: SCM; Minneapolis: Fortress, 1998.

Biblical and New Testament Theology

Bultmann, Rudolf. *Theology of the New Testament*. With a new introduction by Robert Morgan. Translated by Kendrick Grobel. 2 vols. New York: Scribner's Sons, 1951, 2007.

Childs, Brevard S. *Biblical Theology of the Old and New Testaments: Theological Reflection on the Christian Bible*. Minneapolis: Fortress, 1992.

Feldmeier, Reinhard, and Hermann Spieckermann. *God of the Living: A Biblical Theology*. Waco, TX: Baylor University Press, 2011.

Hurtado, Larry W. *God in New Testament Theology*. Library of Biblical Theology. Nashville: Abingdon, 2010.

Minear, Paul S. *The Kingdom and the Power: An Exposition of the New Testament Gospel*. Louisville: Westminster John Knox, 1950.

Schnelle, Udo. *Theology of the New Testament*. Translated by M. Eugene Boring. Grand Rapids: Baker Academic, 2009.

Stuhlmacher, Peter. *Biblical Theology of the New Testament*. Translated and edited by Daniel P. Bailey, with the collaboration of Jostein Ådna. Grand Rapids: Eerdmans, 2018.

Eschatology and Apocalyptic

Boring, M. Eugene. *Revelation*. Interpretation: A Bible Commentary for Teaching and Preaching. Louisville: Westminster John Knox, 1989.

Charlesworth, James H., ed. *The Old Testament Pseudepigrapha*. 2 vols. Garden City, NY: Doubleday, 1983, 1985.

Collins, John J. *The Apocalyptic Imagination: An Introduction to Jewish Apocalyptic Literature*. 3rd ed. Grand Rapids: Eerdmans, 2016.

Jones, Larry Paul, and Jerry L. Sumney. *Preaching Apocalyptic Texts*. Saint Louis: Chalice, 1999.

Käsemann, Ernst. "The Beginnings of Christian Theology." In *New Testament Questions of Today*, 82–107. New Testament Library. London: SCM, 1969.

Moltmann, Jürgen. *The Coming of God: Christian Eschatology*. Translated by Margaret Kohl. Minneapolis: Fortress, 1996.

Russell, D. S. *The Method & Message of Jewish Apocalyptic, 200 BC–AD 100*. Old Testament Library. Philadelphia: Westminster, 1964.

Christology

Aulén, Gustaf. *Christus Victor: An Historical Study of the Three Main Types of the Idea of the Atonement*. Translated by A. G. Hebert. London: SPCK, 1970.

Boring, M. Eugene. *Truly Human/Truly Divine: Christological Language and the Gospel Form*. Saint Louis: CBP, 1984.

Brown, Raymond E. *An Introduction to New Testament Christology*. New York: Paulist, 1994.

———. *Jesus: God and Man*. Modern Biblical Reflections. Impact Books Series. New York: Macmillan, 1967.

Fuller, Reginald H. *The Foundations of New Testament Christology*. New York: Scribner's Sons, 1965.

Hurtado, Larry W. *Lord Jesus Christ: Devotion to Jesus in Earliest Christianity*. Grand Rapids: Eerdmans, 2003.

Keck, Leander. *Who Is Jesus? History in the Perfect Tense*. Columbia: University of South Carolina Press, 2000.

———. *Why Christ Matters: Toward a New Testament Christology*. Waco, TX: Baylor University Press, 2015.

Meeks, Wayne A. *Christ Is the Question*. Louisville: Westminster John Knox, 2006.

Interpretation

Barth, Karl. *Evangelical Theology: An Introduction*. Translated by Grover Foley. New York: Holt, Rinehart & Winston, 1963.

———. "The Strange New World within the Bible." In *The Word of God and the Word of Man*, 28–50. New York: Harper & Brothers, 1957.

Bryan, Christopher. *Listening to the Bible: The Art of Faithful Biblical Interpretation*. Oxford: Oxford University Press, 2014.

Bultmann, Rudolf. *Jesus Christ and Mythology*. London: SCM, 1958.

Feldmeier, Reinhard. *The First Letter of Peter: A Commentary on the Greek Text*. Translated by Peter H. Davids. Waco, TX: Baylor University Press, 2008.

Gilkey, Langdon. *Naming the Whirlwind: The Renewal of God-Language*. Indianapolis: Bobbs-Merrill, 1969.

Hays, Richard B. *The Conversion of the Imagination: Paul as Interpreter of Israel's Scripture*. Grand Rapids: Eerdmans, 2005.

Language

Boring, M. Eugene. *Truly Human/Truly Divine: Christological Language and the Gospel Form*. Saint Louis: CBP, 1984.

Buber, Martin. *I and Thou*. 2nd ed. Edinburgh: T&T Clark, 1958.

Frye, Northrop. *The Great Code: The Bible and Literature*. New York: Harcourt, Brace & World, 1982.

Lévi-Strauss, Claude. *Structural Anthropology*. Translated by Claire Jacobson and Brooke Grundfest. 2 vols. New York: Basic Books, 1963.

Silva, Moisés. "Biblical Perspectives on Language." In *God, Language, and Scripture: Reading the Bible in the Light of General Linguistics*. Grand Rapids: Zondervan, 1990.

Revelation

Bauckham, Richard. *The Theology of the Book of Revelation.* New Testament Theology. Cambridge: Cambridge University Press, 1993.

Blount, Brian K. *Revelation.* New Testament Library. Louisville: Westminster John Knox, 2009.

Boring, M. Eugene. *Revelation.* Interpretation: A Bible Commentary for Teaching and Preaching. Louisville: Westminster John Knox, 1989.

———. "Revelation 19–21: End without Closure." *Princeton Theological Seminary Bulletin* (1994).

Koester, Craig R. *Revelation: A New Translation with Introduction and Commentary.* Anchor Yale Bible, vol. 38A. New Haven: Yale University Press, 2014.

Rowland, Christopher C. "The Book of Revelation: Introduction, Commentary, Reflections." In *The New Interpreter's Bible*, edited by Leander Keck, 12:501–743. Nashville: Abingdon, 1998.

1–3 John

Black, C. Clifton. "The First, Second, and Third Letters of John." In *The New Interpreter's Bible*, edited by Leander Keck, David L. Petersen, and Marion L. Soards, 11:363–470. Nashville: Abingdon, 1998.

Brown, Raymond E. *The Epistles of John.* Anchor Bible. Garden City, NY: Doubleday, 1982.

Smith, D. Moody. *First, Second, and Third John.* Interpretation: A Bible Commentary for Teaching and Preaching. Louisville: Westminster John Knox, 1990.

Strecker, Georg. *The Johannine Letters: A Commentary on 1, 2, and 3 John.* Minneapolis: Fortress, 1996.

Trebilco, Paul R. *The Early Christians in Ephesus from Paul to Ignatius.* Wissenschaftliche Untersuchungen zum Neuen Testament 166. Tübingen: Mohr Siebeck, 2004.

The Gospel of John

For an anthology of comprehensive articles on the current state of Johannine studies, with extensive bibliographies, see Judith M. Lieu and Martinus C. De Boer, *The Oxford Handbook of Johannine Studies* (Oxford: Oxford University Press, 2018).

Anderson, Paul N. *The Christology of the Fourth Gospel: Its Unity and Disunity in the Light of John 6*. Valley Forge, PA: Trinity Press International, 1996.

Ashton, John. *Understanding the Fourth Gospel*. New York: Oxford University Press, 1991.

Barrett, C. K. *The Gospel according to St. John*. 2nd ed. Philadelphia: Westminster, 1978.

Brown, Raymond E. *The Community of the Beloved Disciple: The Life, Loves, and Hates of an Individual Church in New Testament Times*. New York: Paulist, 1979.

———. *The Gospel according to John*. Anchor Bible, vols. 29–30. New York: Doubleday, 1966, 1970.

Bultmann, Rudolf. *The Gospel of John: A Commentary*. Translated by G. R. Beasley-Murray, R. W. N. Hoare, and John Kenneth Riches. Philadelphia: Westminster, 1971.

Culpepper, Alan. *The Gospel and Letters of John*. Interpreting Biblical Texts. Nashville: Abingdon, 1998.

———. *The Johannine School: An Evaluation of the Johannine-School Hypothesis Based on an Investigation of the Nature of Ancient Schools*. Society of Biblical Literature Dissertation Series 26. Missoula, MT: Scholars Press, 1975.

Dodd, C. H. *The Interpretation of the Fourth Gospel*. Cambridge: Cambridge University Press, 1953.

Käsemann, Ernst. *The Testament of Jesus: A Study of the Gospel of John in the Light of Chapter 17*. New Testament Library. London: SCM, 1968.

Koester, Craig R. *Symbolism in the Fourth Gospel: Meaning, Mystery, Community*. Minneapolis: Fortress, 2003.

———. *The Word of Life: A Theology of John's Gospel*. Grand Rapids: Eerdmans, 2008.

Kysar, Robert. *John the Maverick Gospel*. 2nd ed. Louisville: Westminster John Knox, 1993.

Loader, William. *Jesus in John's Gospel: Structure and Issues in Johannine Christology*. Grand Rapids: Eerdmans, 2017.

Martyn, J. Louis. *History and Theology in the Fourth Gospel*. Revised and expanded ed. Nashville: Abingdon, 1979.

Meeks, Wayne A. "The Ethics of the Gospel of John." In *Exploring the Gospel of John: In Honor of D. Moody Smith*, edited by R. Alan Culpepper and C. Clifton Black, 317–26. Louisville: Westminster John Knox, 1996.

Moloney, Francis J. *The Gospel of John*. Sacra Pagina, vol. 4. Collegeville, MN: Liturgical Press, 1998.

O'Day, Gail R. "The Gospel of John." In *New Interpreter's Bible*, edited by Leander Keck. Nashville: Abingdon, 1995.

Schnelle, Udo. *Antidocetic Christology in the Gospel of John*. Translated by Linda M. Maloney. Minneapolis: Fortress, 1992.

Smith, D. Moody. *John*. Abingdon New Testament Commentary. Nashville: Abingdon, 1999.

———. "The Presentation of Jesus in the Fourth Gospel." In *Johannine Christianity: Essays on Its Setting, Sources, and Theology*, 175–89. Columbia: University of South Carolina Press, 1984.

———. *The Theology of the Gospel of John*. Cambridge: Cambridge University Press, 1995.

Thompson, Marianne Meye. *The God of the Gospel of John*. Grand Rapids: Eerdmans, 2001.

———. *John: A Commentary*. New Testament Library. Louisville: Westminster John Knox, 2015.

Other Sources Cited in the Text

Boring, M. Eugene. *1 Peter*. Abingdon New Testament Commentaries. Nashville: Abingdon, 1999.

———. "Matthew: Introduction, Commentary, and Reflections." In *The New Interpreter's Bible*, edited by Leander Keck. Nashville: Abingdon, 1995.

Conzelmann, Hans. *The Theology of St. Luke*. Translated by Geoffrey Buswell. New York: Harper & Row, 1961.

Dodd, C. H. *The Parables of the Kingdom*. New York: Scribner's Sons, 1961.

Ebeling, Gerhard. *Evangelische Evangelienauslegung: Eine Untersuchung zu Luthers Hermeneutik*. Darmstadt: Wissenschaftliche Buchgesellschaft, 1962.

Harrelson, Walter J. *Interpreting the Old Testament*. New York: Holt, Rinehart & Winston, 1964.

Hawking, Stephen W. *A Briefer History of Time*. New York: Random House, 2005.

Hick, John. *Faith and Knowledge*. 2nd ed. Ithaca, NY: Cornell University Press, 1966.

Johnson, Luke Timothy. "The New Testament's Anti-Jewish Slander and the Conventions of Ancient Polemic." *Journal of Biblical Literature* 108, no. 3 (1989): 419–41.

Long, Thomas G. *Testimony: Talking Ourselves into Being Christian*. San Francisco: Jossey-Bass, 2004.

Niebuhr, Reinhold. *The Nature and Destiny of Man*. 2 vols. Gifford Lectures. New York: Scribner's Sons, 1964.

Orwell, George. *1984*. New York: New American Library, 1949.

Overton, Patrick. *Rebuilding the Front Porch of America: Essays on the Art of Community Making*. Hayden, ID: Bitterroot Mountain Publishing, 1997, 2017.

Pregeant, Russell. *Knowing Truth, Doing Good: Engaging New Testament Ethics*. Minneapolis: Fortress, 2008.

Wiesel, Elie. *Night*. Translated by Stella Rodway. New York: Avon Books, 1960.

Index of Names and Subjects

Index of Scripture and Other Ancient Sources

Apocrypha / Deuterocanonical Works

Tobit

Wisdom of Solomon

Ben Sira / Sirach

Baruch